Fourth Edition

Home and School Relations

Teachers and Parents Working Together

Glenn Olsen
University of North Dakota

Mary Lou Fuller
University of North Dakota, Emeritus

Boston   Columbus   Indianapolis   New York   San Francisco   Upper Saddle River
Amsterdam   Cape Town   Dubai   London   Madrid   Milan   Munich   Paris   Montreal   Toronto
Delhi   Mexico City   São Paulo   Sydney   Hong Kong   Seoul   Singapore   Taipei   Tokyo

Vice President and Editor in Chief:
Jeffery W. Johnston
Senior Acquisitions Editor: *Julie Peters*
Editorial Assistant: *Andrea D. Hall*
Vice President, Director of Marketing:
Margaret Waples
Senior Marketing Manager:
Christopher D. Barry
Senior Managing Editor:
Pamela D. Bennett
Senior Project Manager:
Linda Hillis Bayma

Senior Operations Supervisor:
Matthew Ottenweller
Senior Art Director: *Diane C. Lorenzo*
Text Designer: *Element LLC*
Cover Designer: *Kristina Holmes*
Cover Image: *istock*
Full-Service Project Management:
Element LLC
Composition: *Element LLC*
Printer/Binder: *Courier Stoughton*
Cover Printer: *Courier Stoughton*
Text Font: *Sabon*

Credits and acknowledgments for materials borrowed from other sources and reproduced, with permission, in this textbook appear on appropriate page within text.

Every effort has been made to provide accurate and current Internet information in this book. However, the Internet and information posted on it are constantly changing, so it is inevitable that some of the Internet addresses listed in this textbook will change.

Library of Congress Cataloging-in-Publication Data
Home and school relations : teachers and parents working together / Glenn Olsen,
    Mary Lou Fuller. – 4th ed. p. cm.
 Includes bibliographical references and index.
 ISBN 978-0-13-237338-8
 1. Home and school—United States—Case studies. 2. Parent-teacher relationships—United States—Case studies. 3. Early childhood education—Parent participation—United States—Case studies. 4. Special education—Parent participation—United States—Case studies. I. Olsen, Glenn W. (Glenn William) II. Fuller, Mary Lou. III. Title.

LC225.3.H65 2012
371.19'20973—dc22

2011002144

10 9 8 7 6 5 4 3 2 1

www.pearsonhighered.com

ISBN-10: 0-13-237338-6
ISBN-13: 978-0-13-237338-8

To my wife, Barbara Hager-Olsen;
our three daughters, Sarah, Ann, and Becca;
and my parents, Helen May and Kermit Olsen.
My parents provided the early inspiration to continue learning
and to pursue teaching and writing.
Barbara and my daughters continue to motivate me to take
risks and meet challenges.

—Glenn Olsen

Grandchildren are to grandparents like sunshine to a day (anonymous)
and to my rays of sunshine I dedicate the joy I have had
working on this book and hope that they too will find the same joy
in whatever they do:
Amy Broome, Amanda Broome, Amber Fuller, Quinn Slotnick,
Sophie Slotnick, Natasha Slotnick, and Kacie Fuller.

—Mary Lou Fuller

About the Authors

About the Editors

Glenn Olsen is currently a professor and department chair in the Teaching and Learning Department at the University of North Dakota in Grand Forks. He has a bachelor's degree from Macalester College, St. Paul, Minnesota, a M.Ed. in Curriculum and Instruction from the University of Oregon, a M.S. degree in Child Development from the University of Wisconsin–Madison and a Ph.D. in Educational Leadership from the University of Wisconsin–Madison. He has taught American History and Urban Studies in Jefferson School and South High School in Minneapolis, Minnesota. He has also directed child care centers in rural communities and in technical colleges in Minnesota and Wisconsin. He has over 25 articles on different education issues published and another book co-authored with John Hoover called *Teasing and Harassment: The Frames and Scripts Approach for Teachers and Parents*. Glenn can be reached by e-mail at glenn.olsen@mail.und.edu.

Mary Lou Fuller has been an elementary school teacher, a school psychologist, and a university faculty member. At the time she retired from the University of North Dakota, she was a Chester Fritz Distinguished Professor and held the Rose Isabelle Kelly Fischer Chair of Education. She received three Master's Degrees from Arizona State University and her Ph.D. from the University of New Mexico. Her studies dealt with diversity in the classroom and in families, and diversity is central to most of her research and publications. Among her publications are two other college textbooks, *Teaching Hispanic Children* and *Adult Learners on Campus*, co-authored with colleagues. Mary Lou now lives on a ranch in the high desert of Arizona and teaches off-campus classes for Northern Arizona University. She enjoys communicating with other educators and welcomes e-mail at mary.fuller@und.edu.

About the Contributors

Barbara Arnold-Tengesdal is an assistant professor in the School of Education and early childhood program director at the University of Mary in Bismarck, North Dakota. She has been advocating for children's issues on a local, state, and national level for more than 25 years. Awards received include the inspiration award for advocacy from the North Dakota Commission on the Status of Women, the NDAEYC meritorious award for outstanding service in the field of early childhood, and a public policy fellowship with the national Children's Defense Fund. She enjoys traveling with her family, and believes parenting is the most challenging classroom she will ever have in which one is both teacher and student.

Pamela Beck is currently an assistant professor in the Teaching and Learning Department at the University of North Dakota. She teaches reading courses at both undergraduate and graduate levels. Prior to UND, Dr. Beck's professional experiences included 25 years in the public schools. During that time, she served as a classroom teacher in the primary grades, a reading specialist, and a full-time mentor teacher assigned to first-year teachers participating in the Elementary Education Resident Teacher Program—a collaborative partnership between the University of North Dakota and the Grand Forks Public Schools. She has presented both locally and nationally on topics related to strategic reading behaviors, process writing, and mentoring beginning teachers. Her research interests focus on literacy learning and assessment and effective instructional methods in the elementary school.

Dennis Campbell is an associate professor of special education at the University of South Alabama. He received his Ph.D. from Auburn University. Dr. Campbell is a parent of a young lady with an intellectual disability. Currently, he is principal investigator of Project Choices, a Secondary Transition Project for families of children with disabilities funded by the Institute for Educational Sciences, U.S. Department of Education.

Kari Chiasson is an associate professor in special education at the University of North Dakota. She teaches in the areas of early childhood special education, autism, and visual impairments. She has worked in the field of special education for more than 25 years and continues to consult with families of children who have disabilities.

Sara Fritzell Hanhan is an associate professor emeritus of early childhood education and associate provost emeritus at the University of North Dakota for Undergraduate Education. Since retirement she has served as a consultant for a number of early childhood programs and volunteered regularly at her local preschool. She presently teaches part-time for Bemidji State University and is a Master Coach with the Minnesota Reading Corps Program. She lives on Lake Garfield in northern Minnesota.

Charles B. Hennon is a professor, Department of Family Studies and Social Work, and associate director, Center for Human Development, Learning, and Technology at Miami University. Educated at Geneva College and Case-Western Reserve University, he is the founding Editor of the *Journal of Family and Economic Issues*. He has been a visiting scholar at the John E. Dolibois European Center, Grand Duchy de Luxembourg, as well as at several universities in Brazil and Europe. His scholarly interests include family life education and other family supports and interventions, family stress, rural families worldwide, and families in cultural context. Dr. Hennon is a certified family life educator and is the author of numerous articles, book chapters, and books including the co-edited *Families in a Global Context*.

John Hoover is a professor of special education and the associate dean at St. Cloud State University, St. Cloud, Minnesota. His academic interests are in developmental and cognitive disabilities, child-on-child aggression, and secondary education for students with disabilities. His Ph.D. is from Southern Illinois University at Carbondale. He is married to Elizabeth Weber Hoover and has three children, Amelia, Ray and Donny.

Kathryn E. Johnson is an associate professor in the Department of Special Education at St. Cloud State University. She has more than 16 years of teaching experience as a deaf/hard of hearing teacher in public schools and 5 years of experience in higher education. Dr. Johnson's area of research and development is in international education and intercultural competencies for students in teacher preparation programs. Her Ph.D. is from the University of Minnesota.

Yuliya Kartoshkina holds one B.A. in education from Lviv Pedagogical College, Ukraine, and two B.A. degrees in international studies and German from the University of North Dakota. She earned her M.A. in communication from the University of North Dakota. Currently, Yuliya is completing her Ph.D. in education. She works as a graduate research assistant in the Teaching and Learning Department and as an instructor of public speaking in the Communication Program at the University of North Dakota. She has several presentations and publications in the fields of communication and international education. Dr. Kartoshkina has experience in teaching elementary and middle school students in Ukraine and college students at the University of North Dakota. She is married and has an 8-year-old daughter.

Douglas D. Knowlton presently serves as the president of Dakota State University. His B.A. degree is from the University of Denver, his M.A. and Ph.D. in clinical psychology from the University of North Dakota; and he did postdoctoral studies at Baylor College of Medicine in Texas. He started his career as director of a Pediatric Rehabilitation and Evaluation Center at the Medical Center Rehabilitation Hospital in affiliation with the University of North Dakota and was on the faculty in the Special Education Department at UND. For 11 years, he was a licensed (ND and MN) clinical psychologist in private practice with the Family Institute in Grand Forks, North Dakota.

Soo-Yin Lim has been with the University of Minnesota, Crookston, for more than 25 years. She is an associate professor in the Early Childhood Education Department, where she teaches undergraduate courses including a course in home, school, and community relations. In her earlier career, she was a classroom teacher, parent coordinator, and administrator in early childhood programs. She has conducted family involvement research for the last 15 years and has made numerous presentations at local, state, national, and international conferences. Her research interests are in the areas of family involvement in early childhood and elementary schools, and technology (photography) with young children.

Judith B. MacDonald is a retired professor who most recently taught in the Department of Curriculum and Instruction at Montclair State University in New Jersey. Her research interests have focused on the reciprocal effects of being a teacher and a parent.

Carol Marxen is a professor of education at the University of Minnesota, Morris, where she teaches courses in preprimary theory and pedagogy, elementary science, and place-based education. Her research interests include the education of young children and their families, and how curriculum and general teacher development relate to multicultural education in urban and rural school districts. She served on the Multicultural Committee for the American Association of Teacher Education, and has written numerous articles and book chapters including "Highly Qualified Kindergarten Teachers: Have They Been Left Behind?" published in the *Journal of Early Childhood Teacher Education* (2008).

Tara Lea Muhlhauser is the director of the Children and Family Services (CFS) Division of the ND Department of Human Services and a former administrator for Child Protective Services in CFS. She was previously a special assistant to the assistant secretary in the Children's Administration in Washington state working on best practice initiatives involving Safety, Permanency, and Well-Being of Children in conjunction with the Kids Come First: Phase II Comprehensive Reform Plan and other foundation-supported projects. In 2003, she completed a year-long Child and Family Leadership Fellowship with the Annie E. Casey Foundation in Baltimore. Prior to that Tara worked in North Dakota where she led the Child Welfare Training Center, was a faculty member in the Social Work Department at the University of North Dakota, directed the ND Guardian ad Litem Project, and held the position of Assistant Dean in the UND School of Law.

Glen Palm is a professor of child and family studies at St. Cloud State University where he joined the faculty in 1983. He currently is serving as interim dean of the College of Education at St. Cloud State. From 1995–2008, he coordinated The Dad's Project, a local initiative of the Early Childhood Family Education program in St. Cloud that focuses on supporting father/male involvement in the lives of young children. He continues to teach a parenting class for inmates at the Minnesota Correctional Facility–St. Cloud. As a researcher/practitioner he has studied ethics in parent and family education, fathers' perceptions of attachment, the parent education needs of incarcerated fathers, and the role of fatherhood in influencing men's values and moral/religious beliefs, fathers and their influence on social emotional development in young children, and fathers' role in early literacy development. He has worked as a program evaluator for Early Head Start, Even Start Family Literacy, and Child Abuse Prevention Programs. Dr. Palm served as a board member of the National Practitioners Network for Fathers and Families (NPNFF) from 1998–2004, the Minnesota Fathers and Families Network (MFFN) from 2005–2009, and is currently a board member of the National Council for Family Relations (NCFR). Dr. Palm has written extensively about fathers and parent education including co-authoring two books: *Fathers and Early Childhood Programs* (2004) with Jay Fagan and *Group Parent Education: Promoting Parent Learning and Support* (2004) with Deborah Campbell.

AmySue Reilly is an associate professor at Auburn University. She received her Ph.D. from the University of New Mexico. Dr. Reilly is co-director of Project AIM (Auburn Intervention Model), an early intervention program for very young children and their families. Currently, she is the project director of a U.S. Department of Education project that helps prepare professionals to work in the field of early childhood special education.

Margaret (Peggy) Shaeffer is the associate dean of Education at James Madison University in Harrisonburg, Virginia. She has worked in the field of early childhood/early childhood special education for more than 30 years, focusing on curriculum development and collaboration with parents in education.

Gloria Jean Thomas is an associate professor in the Graduate Department of Educational Leadership and Instructional Design at Idaho State University. She received her Ph.D. from Brigham Young University, specializing in school law. She taught school law at the University of North Dakota for 9 years before returning to her home state of Idaho. Her major teaching and research interests are school law and finance at the K–12 and higher education levels.

Sandra Winn Tutwiler is a professor in the Education Department at Washburn University in Topeka, Kansas. She previously taught at Hamline University in St. Paul, Minnesota, and had been a teacher or counselor at the elementary, junior high, high school, and community college levels prior to becoming a teacher educator. Her research and writing focuses primarily on school–family relations and the educational experiences of students of color. She has written journal articles and book chapters on this subject. Dr. Tutwiler is the author of *Teachers as Collaborative Partners: Working with Diverse Families and Communities*.

Karen W. Zimmerman is professor emeritus of the School of Education at the University of Wisconsin-Stout. She received her Ph.D. in family environment and family and consumer sciences education from Iowa State University. She taught courses in child development, parent education, family life issues, and family and consumer sciences education. Dr. Zimmerman has recently revised her text for teen parents entitled *Helping Your Child Grow and Develop*. Currently she supervises graduate student research, supervises student teachers, writes tests that are given to early childhood professionals so that they may earn continuing education credits, and gives presentations at professional conferences.

Brief Contents

Contents

Chapter Six

Parent–Teacher Communication: Who's Talking?   101

Sara Fritzell Hanhan and Yuliya Kartoshkina

Chapter Seven

Family Involvement in Education   130

Soo-Yin Lim

Chapter Ten

Education Law and Parental Rights   203

Gloria Jean Thomas

Chapter Eleven

Family Violence: The Effect on Teachers, Parents, and Children   239

Tara Lea Muhlhauser and Douglas D. Knowlton

Foreword

Home and School Relations: Teachers and Parents Working Together is a thoughtful guide to more productive relationships between parents and teachers, homes and schools. It begins with the premise that parents are their children's first and most important teachers, and further, that the dispositions, language, values, and cultural understandings that help guide children and young people are learned most fully within families (and, importantly, this book makes the conception of families inclusive of the many child-nurturing arrangements that exist).

While those in schools often say that they value active parent participation, parents are not always treated as full partners. They typically don't learn enough about what their children will be learning in school, how their children's growth as learners will be assured, what special efforts will be made to support their children if they begin to struggle academically or socially, or how they, as parents, can be most helpful to their children's academic learning beyond school. They need all of this information if they are to be the full partners they want to be.

Sometimes, the messages that come to parents about the foregoing are not in their languages. At other times, those in schools suggest times for meetings that are in conflict with other family-related commitments. Moreover, when parent conferences occur, they are scheduled most often for a short time period, the teachers do most of the talking, and the child is most often absent. It is an exchange teachers in most schools don't look forward to with great enthusiasm. And parents don't often come expecting to learn very much. Such conditions need to change. If the schools do not actively acknowledge and encourage a strong partnership role for parents, children's education will be limited—not as intense, as full, as it needs to be.

How does a productive partnership get constructed? What do teachers need to know to be a part of the construction? This book provides a useful map—an inspiring guide—that grows out of a set of solid commitments to parents as well as to the preparation of teachers able to extend themselves on behalf of parents. I suggest "able to" because I understand that the desire to involve parents is insufficient. Knowledge of how to proceed, the realities of family life across cultures, and skills are also needed. This book provides that kind of assistance.

The editors and contributors to *Home and School Relations* are people with experience as classroom teachers, parents, and teacher educators. They use that experience well, providing numerous examples of productive home–school interchange. It is important to note that little attention has been placed on home–school relations in teacher education programs, in part because there hasn't been much credible literature. This book fills a large share of that void. It helps change the landscape, placing before us a vision of what is possible when teachers and parents work closely together. I am pleased the editors and contributors are sharing their work with the educational community and with parents.

Vito Perrone
Harvard Graduate School of Education

In order to be effective as educators, we must understand the families from which our students come and the opportunity and encouragement they receive to develop the skills necessary in creating positive working relationships. This book examines the nature of the contemporary family—what it looks like, how it functions, and its relationship to the schools. This includes the important related topics of diversity (cultural, racial, religious, sexual orientation) and the effects of income on families. To understand a family you must understand diversity. This book also includes topics that have been neglected by other work in the field, such as fathers' roles, poverty, and parents' perspectives of schools, in order to help educators better understand the complexities of home–school relations.

In addition to providing the reader with an understanding of what families look like and how they function, this book is highly practical. It includes descriptions of successful parent-involvement programs, contains an excellent chapter dealing with communication skills and activities (newsletters, conferences, etc.), and provides the reader with much-needed information about family violence. Also, with the incorporation of students with special needs into the classroom, many teachers find they have not been prepared to work with parents of these students. This text will be very useful to these teachers. Other chapters help educators understand the important and neglected areas of the legal and policy aspects of home–school relations, school violence and bullying, and educational choices.

New to This Edition

In this fourth edition, you will find:

- ▶ The latest information on bullying and school violence
- ▶ Updated information on domestic violence and its impact on children
- ▶ New information about poverty and homelessness
- ▶ Additional information, including current use of technology, to communicate more with parents and families
- ▶ The most recent information about children with special needs and the services provided by schools
- ▶ Information about diversity including the role teachers play in refugee families' lives
- ▶ Three new coauthors for Chapters 6, 8, and 9

For Students

The organization of this book is based on the principles of good learning. First and foremost, you must become actively involved in your own learning. Objectives are presented at the beginning of each chapter, as an overview of the material. There are also exercises throughout each chapter to help the reader reflect on the material they have read. Finally, there are lists of resources at the end of each chapter that allow students to further pursue any of the topics that were addressed in the chapter.

For Instructors

College instructors have many demands on their time; this text has been designed to be as helpful to the instructor as possible, by providing suggested activities designed to help make the class interactive, reflective, and stimulating.

This text employs the Internet as a teaching tool and provides World Wide Web addresses to help students get started. There are also lists of resources, including children's books, articles, and videos that may be assigned by you or referenced by students for their own professional development.

New to this edition are instructor support materials. Go to www.pearsonhighered.com, click on Educators, register for access, and download instructor ancillaries for use in planning.

Key Features

Diversity

Chapter 3 is devoted to diversity (cultural/racial, economic, religious, as well as family structure). Diversity is woven throughout the book as well. This topic is of particular importance since most pre-service teachers come from white, middle-class backgrounds. Most have had few meaningful interactions with families that differ from their own. Immigration issues are also discussed here and in Chapter 12.

Poverty

Chapter 12 discusses the effects of poverty on the family. No other book that we reviewed looks at this important topic, even though the statistics are surprising: 16 percent of all children live below the poverty line, and of those, 21 percent are children 6 and under. Economic status has a tremendous effect on the academic performance of children, yet this subject is often ignored. An important part of this chapter now includes information on homelessness and its impact on children, families, and teachers.

Voice of the Parent

Generally the voices of parents are missing from books of this nature. This book not only includes parents' perspectives on parenting but also their feelings about their relationships with schools and educators.

Families of Children with Special Needs

Students with special needs were at one time the exclusive domain of special education programs. However, with the widespread move to classroom inclusion, teachers must understand how to work well with the parents of children with special needs.

Fathers' Roles

Fathers are generally only footnotes in educational literature. It is important to understand the father and his role if we are to understand the family in its totality.

Bullying and School Violence

Teasing and bullying are discussed in greater depth, emphasizing the connection with school violence. Since these topics have become important issues within the school environment, in this edition we offer suggestions for ways to stem bullying and school violence.

Advocacy

There is more and more discussion of advocacy for all children—prenatal to age 18. Since children cannot vote, they rely on adults to act as their voting advocates. Advocates look at public policy at the local, state, and national level to encourage an agenda supportive of children.

We hope that you will find this book to be thorough, thought-provoking, current, and practical. We designed this book out of frustration with the limited available material, particularly on some topics, and are very happy with the results. We hope that you will be, too. Please feel free to contact us if you have questions or comments about the book. We would love to hear about your successes so we can pass them on to other teachers.

New! CourseSmart eTextbook Available

CourseSmart is an exciting new choice for students looking to save money. As an alternative to purchasing the printed textbook, students can purchase en electronic version of the same content. With a CourseSmart eTextbook, students can search the text, make notes online, print out reading assignments that incorporate lecture notes, and bookmark important passages for later review. For more information, or to purchase access to the CourseSmart eTextbook, visit www.coursesmart.com.

Acknowledgments

We would like to thank a number of people who helped us complete this book. A special thanks to Yuliya Kartoshkina for providing references and resources for most of our authors. Jolene Marsh was a great help in turning the rough draft into the final product for our editors. The 15 youth artists who did the drawings on the first page of every chapter made the book more personal. We would also like to thank the reviewers: Donna Keller Bush, Eastern Kentucky University; Marilyn L. Cavazos, Laredo Community College; Hengameh Kermani, University of North Carolina, Wilmington; Tara Newman, Stephen F. Austin State University; Jennifer Prior, Northern Arizona University; and Susan Skinner Wyatt, Eastfield Community College.

Chapter One

An Introduction to Families

Mary Lou Fuller
University of North Dakota

Glenn Olsen
University of North Dakota

This chapter provides the background information you'll need to understand families—an understanding that will benefit your students and their families by making you a more effective educator. More specifically, this chapter helps you consider:

▶ The purpose and behaviors of families.

▶ The need for families to protect their children.

▶ The need to socialize children into the familial culture.

▶ The teacher's role in interacting with families.

▶ Home–school relations of the past.

▶ The changing family.

The job of an educator is much more complicated today than it was in the past. Educators must not only understand the issues traditionally embodied in home–school relations but also view families in a sociological and educational framework to understand how they function. Only by doing so can teachers work with students' families in the most effective manner.

As always, teachers must conduct parent–teacher conferences and understand various parent involvement models—preschool, elementary, middle school—as well as models for parents of students with special needs. Now, however, teachers also must know about changes in contemporary families and their effects on how families function. They must understand how families are influenced by cultural backgrounds, financial resources (or lack thereof), and the changing roles of parents. Students may be from homes headed by single parents, foster parents, grandparents, or gay/lesbian parents; the family may practice a nontraditional religion or speak a language other than English; the family may be intact or blended—the variation in family types seems innumerable. The greater responsibilities that come with more diverse families require teachers to go beyond classroom walls to understand the relationships between families and schools.

Teachers must also be aware of ways education can be influential in supporting families. This involves understanding and using public policy, advocacy, and the laws that pertain to issues involving families and schools. Without this knowledge, teachers can react only to the needs of individual students and their families when their efforts could benefit families more generally.

Defining "Family" and Determining Family Responsibilities

The U.S. Census Bureau (2010) defines a family as "two or more persons related by birth, marriage, or adoption who reside in the same household." Notice that this is a legal definition relying solely on relationships determined by blood or contract that contrasts with the sociological definition of families that considers the ways families function. Though not a sociologist, a second grader offered a sociological definition when he observed, "A family is people who live together and who help and love each other."

The second grader's definition was insightful because it focused on what families *do* as opposed to how they *look*. Families, for example, do two important things for children: protect them from harmful influences and prepare them to function within their cultures (that is, society). Whether we look at pre-Colombian Mayan families in Central America, Chinese families of the Ming Dynasty, contemporary Buddhist families of Thailand, or middle-class families in Houston, the primary purpose of these families was and is the same—to protect and prepare their children. These families differ, of course, in terms of the everyday conditions they face and the manners in which they protect and prepare their children.

Protecting Children from Danger

The nature of danger differs over time and with location. While prehistoric Aleutian parents feared wild animals, and parents of Charles Dickens's industrialized England were concerned about their children working long hours in unhealthy environments, contemporary U.S. parents worry about their children's exposure to sex and violence in the media and on the Internet. The attribute shared by parents in all times and places was, and remains, concern about their children's health, nutrition, and safety. Again, what has changed is not the function of the family, but the nature of the dangers against which parents protect children and the character of the society in which parents prepare their children to live.

Although families in the past worked hard to ensure their children's health and physical survival, contemporary parents can generally (sadly, there are exceptions) expect their children to survive and grow to maturity. Parents today also include in their concerns their children's emotional health.

Preparing Children for Society

How did you learn the proper way to act in a place of worship, in a museum, at a party, or at a family reunion? Although there usually is no formal instruction in these areas, most people know what is expected of them and behave accordingly. As children, we learned these skills through a combination of parental guidance and observation of others as they interacted in various social settings. Anthropologists refer to this process as *enculturation* or *socialization*—the process by which a family and/or society prepares children to behave appropriately and appreciate their cultural values and traditions. Enculturation ensures that people in a given society understand and can interact appropriately with others in their society.

Families, Their Children, and Teachers

Stated simply, families strive to provide safe, nurturing environments in which children can enculturate. When most families lived in isolated rural areas, this socialization occurred predominantly under parental supervision. As the family was much more an isolated unit, parents also played the roles of teachers, doctors, psychologists, and spiritual leaders for their children. Families continued to protect and nurture children as society became more industrialized, urbanized, and complex, with this complexity meaning that parents found it more difficult to be totally responsible for their children's needs. People (such as teachers, physicians, ministers, and social workers) and institutions (such as schools, public health services, churches, synagogues, community social services, and others) began to play greater roles in the upbringing of children. For example, schools assumed more educational responsibilities, though families continued to be the first and most important teachers of children because it is through families that children learn how to live in their worlds.

Schools' increased responsibilities now include teachers taking on some tasks that have historically been within the parents' domain. Teachers assumed these tasks because they require skill and knowledge beyond what can be expected of laypeople in contemporary society. Even if parents have the skill and knowledge needed to handle these responsibilities, they may not have the time to provide a formal education for their children. The result is that educators' skills and knowledge allow them to complement and overlap things done in the family. Both parents and teacher, in short, are needed to enculturate children.

This being the case, if teachers' professional efforts are to complement those of parents, teachers need to have an understanding of families and how they function. First, to be maximally effective, educators need to know about their students' families. Second, by understanding those responsible for children at home, educators can work with parents to help children be safe and move comfortably into society. And third, this understanding will help teachers to be better educators.

Changing World, Changing Families

As noted, families are changing because society as a whole is changing. It hasn't been that long since you and the others in your family started communicating by sending text messages on cell phones instead of using a land-based telephone, using a computer rather than a typewriter, purchasing products online, cooking in a microwave instead of on a stove, watching movies via a DVD player or downloading them onto your television or laptop rather than in a theater, transferring money electronically via the Internet rather than through a bank teller, and using a debit card instead of writing checks.

Schools have also changed. There are computers in the classroom that allow students to go online, and teachers' filmstrips and films have been replaced by CDs and DVDs. Similarly, students use their cell phones and iPods as well as the Internet and interactive television for communication and entertainment, and they can choose from salad bars and specialty foods in the school cafeteria. Yet, in spite of these changes, schools are still often viewed as unchanging institutions represented by the red, one-room schoolhouse with a bell tower that is often found on classroom bulletin boards in September—this despite the fact that such school buildings are as much like today's schools as a No. 2 pencil is like a word processor.

Schools reflect the changes in the demographics of our society, changes including, but not limited to, family structures, available economic resources, and what those resources will (and will not) purchase. All of these changes—technological, societal, and demographic—are reflected in the demands placed on families. Although families have always been under pressure, the nature of this stress has changed and, in the process, increased significantly. Evidence of the changes include increased incidences of divorce, single parenting, remarriage, blended families, adoption of children of other races, gay/lesbian families, mothers who never marry, the new sets of grandparents, interracial marriages, and other extended family members created by remarriage. The list could go on for pages.

Reflection...

Consider your immediate and extended family. How many different types of families are represented? Make a list and ask your parents (or someone from your parents' generation) how many of those family styles were present when they raised their children and when they were kids.

Home–School Relations in the Past

As educators, our relationships with parents have an interesting history that parallels the economic history of this country. Although public schools were initially legislated in Massachusetts in the 17th century, it was many years before most parents saw public schools as a realistic opportunity for their children. At that time the economy was agrarian and the population rural; parents in these rural areas had a tremendous influence on the schools, the teachers, the curriculum, and even on how teachers could and could not behave outside of the classroom.

Initially rural schools outnumbered urban schools and were governed by a school board made up of men from the community. As the United States become more industrialized in the mid-1880s, a mass migration from rural to urban areas resulted in fewer and larger communities, and the influence of the individual parent on the school decreased. School board members, generally prominent businessmen, were not people most parents knew or could easily access. At the same time, school districts increased in size and their boards came to rely more heavily on school administrators for the day-to-day operation of the schools. Put simply, the power shifted from the parents (generally fathers) to male administrators and board members.

The role of parents shifted from being actively involved in running the school to being guests of the school. Parents were invited to school for specific events and to confer about problems. Furthermore, whereas earlier it had been primarily fathers who dealt with schools and educational issues, the relationship between home and school gradually changed until the responsibility of dealing with schools rested with mothers. Dealings with the school became "women's work," and because the status of women was low at this time, mothers had little input and even less power in the education of their children.

Between the 1950s and 1970s, the parental role remained that of little influence, and mothers continued to be the parent most likely to interact with the school. Parent Teacher Association (PTA) meetings, parent–teacher conferences, and other parent activities were generally held in the afternoon, thus making it difficult for working fathers to attend. In fact, fathers were seen as not needing to be actively involved with the day-to-day care and education of their children.

There were serious problems with this arrangement. Contrary to popular belief, a large number of mothers were part of the workforce. These mothers were most often from ethnically/racially diverse groups and/or low-income families. Because these women were not able to attend afternoon meetings, parent involvement in the schools became primarily an activity of white, middle-class women. This made a loud and clear statement about how minorities and the poor were valued by the schools during this time period.

The U.S. economy has changed dramatically since the 1970s. Presently, two salaries are needed to provide an equivalent spendable income that one salary made in 1970 (Pew Research Center, 2010). Consequently, to maintain a middle-class standard of living today, most mothers of schoolchildren are a part of the workforce. As a result, even middle-class mothers are generally not available during school hours. The unavailability of parents from all economic and ethnic/racial segments of society during the school day demands a rethinking of both how to involve parents in the schools and what the nature of that involvement might be.

At the same time, many parents want to be more actively involved in their children's education, as opposed to being merely recipients of test scores and grades. This desire is complicated by the amount of time (or lack of time) parents can devote to the schools. These and related issues will be discussed in detail in the following chapters.

Looking at Families

Because children bring their family experiences with them to school, educators must understand families so they can best understand children. Most books on home–school relations focus on skills (parent–teacher conferences, parent involvement programs, etc.), which are certainly important issues; indeed, they are covered in depth in this book. However, a knowledge and understanding of families are prerequisites to truly meaningful relationships between the school and the home.

To assist you in acquiring the knowledge and skills to meet this goal, we examine four factors influencing families and focus on their impacts (see Figure 1.1).

1. The spendable income available to a family
2. The ethnic, racial, and cultural background of the family
3. The structure of the family
4. Individual familial differences

Changing Income Levels of Families

Income, more than any other single factor, determines the quality of life for most families, with an alarming 21% of the children in the United States living in poverty. As Fuller points out in Chapter 12, poverty can be devastating to families generally and can make learning more difficult for children in particular.

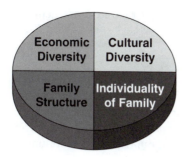

Figure 1.1 Factors to Consider When Examining Home–School Relations

Largely for economic reasons, the experiences low-income families share with those from middle-class families are minimal. This is important because educators tend to come from middle-class homes (Shaughnessy, 2005) and so have sensibilities and experiences that are very different from those of the impoverished students they teach. The result is that although educators are caring, intelligent people who want what's best for students, the disparity between their middle-class life experiences and those of their students coming from poor families is often unrecognized even though it often means that teachers hold inappropriate expectations for their students. The outcome is that educators often hold stereotypes of poor people that impede their working effectively with students from low-income families.

Changing Demographics of Ethnicity/Culture/Race

The families of children in the public schools exhibit greater diversity than ever before, whereas teachers and preservice teachers are still largely white, middle class, and female.

Approximately 31% of public school students are children of color and, in fact, children of color make up the majority of schoolchildren in some states. Currently, 58% of schoolchildren in California are members of underrepresented groups, and by 2020, these groups are expected to exceed the white mainstream population in schools (Gollnick & Chinn, 2008). These children live in a range of ethnic, cultural, racial, familial, and economic milieus that are frequently different from those in which educators lived as children.

The ethnic/racial diversity of families has changed for a variety of reasons: Higher birthrates for people of color and changes in immigration patterns are two of the primary reasons for change. Although early immigrants were generally from northern Europe or Canada (between 1951 and 1960, 67% of U.S. immigrants came from Europe or Canada, 25% from Mexico or Latin America, and only 6% from Asia), in 1998, 34% of immigrants came from Asia, 44% were from Mexico and Latin America, and only 15% were from Europe and Canada (U.S. Census Bureau, 2001). This trend results in a change in the traditionally northern European appearance of many of our students and their families. But more important, it also means that in addition to cultural diversity, non-Judeo-Christian religions, such as Islam, Buddhism, and Hinduism, are also adding to the richness and variety of our classrooms. Winn Tutwiler discusses ethnicity, culture, and race in more depth in Chapter 3.

Understanding Diversity in Families

First, educators must understand their own cultural behaviors, values, traditions, and family backgrounds, because it is difficult to see how our backgrounds differ from others if we can't identify the characteristics of our own experiences. Without this conscious awareness of our own cultural and familial backgrounds, our perceptions of students' families may be limited by our individual histories and so cause us to make ethnocentric judgments about other families. At best, these judgments will hinder communication; at worst, they will cause irreparable harm to the working relationships we attempt to establish with our students and their families. It is only through understanding the needs and expectations of diverse groups that we are able to tailor our efforts in a manner appropriate to our students' (and their families') needs.

It is important to remember that there is great diversity within all cultures (as well as within socioeconomic groups, family structures, etc.) and that this diversity is as great within a given culture as it is among groups. This means that multiple factors must be considered to appreciate families from any given culture.

Tradition and Assimilation.   One of these factors is the *degree of assimilation* exhibited by children and their families. Assimilation indicates the degree to which a family moved from one or more cultures to another—usually from the birth culture into the mainstream culture. For example, the more assimilated American Indian children are, the less likely they are to be like kids from their traditional culture and the more likely they are to be like kids in the dominant culture. Even if families are closer to being members of the mainstream society than their traditional culture, knowledge about their traditional culture is important because it will help educators better understand the background influences on the student and their families' behaviors and attitudes.

Because there is great diversity within cultures (socioeconomic groups, family structures, etc.), it is impossible to describe families in their entirety; it is similarly impossible to produce a single generalization describing all the people in a culture. Thus any such descriptions that exist about cultures and the people who participate in them are overgeneralizations and constitute *stereotypes*. Stereotypes are harmful because they deny that variability exists within a culture and its people and, in so doing, limit what the observer can see and expect of the people observed.

One way stereotyping causes problems for both teachers and their students' families is that a single description is forced to apply to all circumstances. In other words, simple explanations are offered for what are complex cultural phenomena. When teachers use stereotypes, they overlook the complexity of factors that influence behavior and thus cannot recognize patterns in their students' actions. This means that behaviors not fitting the stereotype will appear haphazard and uninterpretable when, if properly interpreted, those behaviors make sense. When this happens, teachers find it difficult to understand families of cultures that differ from their own.

Changing Family Structure

Throughout history there has been a multiplicity of family styles: married, single parents (widow/widower), polygamous, polyandrous, stepfamilies, and so on. In contemporary Western society, it is not new configurations of the family that society is experiencing, but simply changes in the number of certain configurations. For example, single-parent households are not new though the number of such families has increased significantly, with 58% of children currently living in single-parent homes. In other words, more children live in single-parent homes than in two-parent homes. These figures are of particular importance because they help teachers better appreciate and so meet the needs of their students' families (Wolf, 2007). Another change in the family is the increasing age of first-time parents. In 2007, men were approximately 28 years old and women were 26 years old when they married for the first time—an increase of more than 5 years for both men and women over the 1950 data (Infoplease, 2009). This means that, among many other changes, schools will be dealing with an older parent population than in the past.

Among the many familial changes is the role of fathers, who are now more actively involved in parenting than at any other time since the industrialization of Western society. Divorce has also created different roles for fathers because of the growing number of custodial fathers. In addition, noncustodial fathers may well want to continue to be involved in their children's education. The large number of fathers in the schools suggests generally new relationships for most educators. Hennon, Palm, and Olsen discuss fathers in more detail in Chapter 13.

Individuality of Families

Every family is different. Each brings a unique history and attributes that affect their family experiences. All families have their successes and failures; some families are more functional and some more dysfunctional. Marxen and Fuller discuss families in more detail in Chapter 2.

Some families have children with special needs, which Reilly, Campbell, and Chiasson discuss in Chapter 8, and all educators—whether they are teaching children with special needs or not—need to understand the families of these children because there is an inclusion of children with special needs all around us. In classrooms today, we have students who not long ago would have been segregated into "special" classes, but who are now mainstreamed into the traditional classroom. School buildings and transportation have been modified to allow students with disabilities to become a more integral part of the schools. This means that we must also rethink our relationships with the parents of students with special needs to ensure that they are a more integral part of the educational system.

Families are constantly changing to meet the influences of society, and consequently, we as educators must make adjustments to meet the needs of the children from these families. For example, due to the opportunities and responsibilities that civil rights laws have afforded women, they have become an active part of the military and now find themselves in military conflicts. Many of these women (and men)

Case Study

Jordan is a 10-year-old fifth grader who plays third base in little league and is active in his church youth group. He makes average to above-average grades and spends time with several friends he has known since first grade. He is generally a "good kid" who gets in trouble occasionally, usually for fighting with his brother and sister.

In fact, this description applies to Jordan's father when he was Jordan's age. However, their childhoods differ in some significant ways. Whereas Jordan's father's family was intact and headed by a father who worked and a stay-at-home mother, Jordan's parents divorced when he was 5 years old. He lives with his mother and his brother and sister and visits his father, stepmother, and two stepbrothers every other weekend. His mother works and his father pays child support, but family finances are nevertheless limited.

Jordan initially had difficulty adjusting to his stepmother and stepbrothers, but things have improved somewhat and there is much less tension when he visits. Also, his stepfamily is Hispanic, and he had to work through the stereotypes he had inadvertently acquired. Although his mother, father, and stepmother want what is best for Jordan, his life is much more complicated than his father's life as a child.

Questions and Considerations

1. How does Jordan's life differ from that of his father when he was a child?
2. What are the strengths in Jordan's family structure?
3. What are some potentially problematic areas?

have children, and of this group, 90,000 women (and a limited number of men) are single. This presents problems as to who will be responsible for a child's care when a parent is deployed to places where children are not allowed. To make this situation even more difficult, the pay for enlisted personnel is exceptionally low (a supply specialist makes about $2,000 a month), making arrangements for long-term child care problematic (Piore, 2003).

Educators must also be informed about the nightmare of violence experienced by numerous children and their families. Knowledge and skills for dealing with the aftermath of violence are imperative before we can be effective advocates for the abused. Muhlhauser and Knowlton discuss the issues relating to violence in Chapter 11.

Parent Involvement

Hanhan and Kartoshkina, in Chapter 6, discuss the history of home–school relations to help give us a historical perspective. Currently, parent involvement seeks to return parents to the school to become team members in the education of their children. This is because educators are experts in children generally, whereas parents are experts on their children specifically. However, because past experiences have given either parents or teachers disproportionate power in their relationship, both now have to learn to work as a team. For teachers, this starts with a basic understanding of families and families' views of parental responsibilities, as well as educators' views of these same responsibilities. Zimmerman (Chapter 4), MacDonald (Chapter 5), and Soo-Yin Lim (Chapter 7) discuss parents, schools, and teachers and their interrelationships.

Understanding families is the initial step in working with the families of students; the next step must be to involve parents in their children's education. There are a variety of good parent involvement models to consider: early childhood, elementary, middle school, and special education (Chapter 9). In addition, it is helpful to understand the experiences of parents who have decided to remove their family and children from the traditional school experience. Thomas, in Chapter 10, analyzes the laws and responsibilities surrounding parents and their rights. We as educators are sometimes ill informed about advocacy and public policy, and this makes it difficult to make systemic changes in home–school relations.

Because violence is a reality in contemporary America, Hoover, Johnson, and Olsen (Chapter 14) discuss school violence and bullying as a major education issue.

On Understanding Families

This book evolved out of a desire to better prepare teachers to work with families and to better serve students. We (Olsen and Fuller) teach in the area of home–school relations, as well as write and conduct research in this important discipline. We have used a variety of different books with our classes and were impressed by the quality of most, but we had a different vision—a vision that teachers would develop an in-depth understanding of families and consequently better meet the needs of their students. With this goal in mind, we spent considerable time deciding what to include in this book. We then invited people with special expertise in these areas to contribute. We wrote this book for our students, you, your students, and their families.

Recommended Activities

1. Looking back at elementary school, what things had changed about education by the time you were a junior or senior in high school?
2. Describe what you thought about school when you were growing up compared with what

your parents or grandparents thought about school.
3. Identify five positive things that happened in your K–12 education experience.

Children's Books

The following children's books are suggested as a way of helping your students consider issues in this chapter.

Families

ABC: A Family Alphabet Book
Bobbie Combs, Desiree Keane (Illustrator), Brian Rappa (Illustrator)
Reading Level: For infants or children in preschool
Two Lives Publishing (2000)

My Family's Changing: A First Look at Family Break Up
Pat Thomas, Lesley Harker (Illustrator)
Reading Level: Ages 4–8
Barron's Educational Series (1999)

All Families Are Special
Norma Simon, Teresa Flavin (Illustrator)
Reading Level: Ages 4–8
Albert Whitman & Company (2003)

The Family Book
Todd Parr
Reading Level: Ages 3–6
Little, Brown & Company (2003)

Who's in a Family?
Robert Skutch, Laura Nienhaus (Illustrator)
Reading Level: Ages 4–8
Ten Speed Press (1998)

All-of-a-Kind Family Uptown
Sydney Taylor, Mary Stevens (Illustrator)
Reading Level: Young Adult
Taylor Productions (2001)

References

Gollnick, D. M., & Chinn, C. (2008). *Multicultural education in a pluralistic society* (6th ed.). Upper Saddle River, NJ: Pearson.

Infoplease. (2009). Median Age at First Marriage, 1890–2007. Retrieved from www.infoplease.com/ipa/A0005061.html

Pew Research Center. (2010). *All social & demographic trends reports*. Retrieved from http://pewsocialtrends.org/pubs/

Piore, A. (2003, March). Home alone. *Newsweek*, 53–54.

Shaughnessy, M. F. (2005). An interview with Ruby Payne: About teaching children in poverty. *Education News*. Retrieved from http://educationnews.org

U.S. Census Bureau. (2001). *Statistical abstract of the United States 2001: The national data book*. Washington, DC: U.S. Government Printing Office.

U.S. Census Bureau. (2010). Poverty in the United States (*Current Population Series P60–185*). Washington, DC: U.S. Government Printing Office.

Wolf, J. (2007). Retrieved from http://singleparents.about.com/od/legalissues/p/portrait.htm

Chapter Two

Families and Their Functions—Past and Present

Carol Marxen
The University of Minnesota–Morris

Mary Lou Fuller
University of North Dakota

For educators to provide the best learning environment for students, they must understand the families from which the students come. The majority of families do not fit the stereotype of the "all-American family." This chapter introduces you to contemporary families and helps you:

▶ Trace the history of the family.

▶ Identify the structures and needs of the contemporary family.

▶ Compare historical and contemporary families.

▶ Describe a functional and a dysfunctional family.

Happy

I'm happy when my family's together.

Love

I love my brothers even when we fight.

This chapter provides the background information needed to help you understand families and consequently become a more effective teacher. More specifically, the chapter will help you (1) take a historical perspective in viewing families of the past and the issues affecting them, (2) develop a perspective on how families look today, and (3) examine the characteristics of functional and dysfunctional families. In other words, reading and understanding the material in this chapter provides you with a basic understanding of families and how and why they operate as they do. Because we are all fascinated by learning about ourselves and others, this chapter should be personally enlightening as well as informative.

The Evolution of the Family

Why Take a Historical Perspective?

Although the structure of families is changing, our stereotype of families is not. Our perception of the all-American family is still an intact family with children, father employed outside the home, and mother staying at home, even though our observations tell us differently. In reality this family currently accounts for less than 4% of U.S. families, and this percentage is declining. Is this decline (which some perceive as a breakdown in family values) the cause of societal ills such as poverty, crime, drug abuse, and school failure? Or are the societal ills the cause of family problems? In other words, does a stronger family unit create a more stable economic, social, and political environment? Or does a growing, supportive, and prosperous economic, social, and political environment increase family stability? Looking at families from earlier times can help us consider these questions.

Skolnick and Skolnick (2009) encourage us to view families from other eras the way we would view families from different cultures. The comparison is appropriate because families at each point in history have their own sets of family values and family functions, which developed in response to the social, political, and economic environments of the time. They used those values and functions to do the same things contemporary families do: to protect their children and to prepare those children to take their places in society. Families have always struggled (as contemporary families do) with problems resulting from political, economic, and societal forces, so it is quite reasonable to look at earlier families in the same way as we look at present-day families. Indeed, doing so offers insights into how families develop their practices and values. Adopting a historical perspective may do more than document changes in families; it may offer insights concerning future trends. In particular, we look at a range of historical families, seeking to discover how they protected their children from threats to their well-being and how they prepared their children to be members of the societies in which they lived.

Early History

Prehistoric Families.   Conditions faced by primitive societies dictated that families work together for survival; constant effort was needed to protect everyone—especially children—from starvation, exposure to the elements, and disease. Practicality dictated that families sharing specific customs and beliefs band together for mutual security; these groups were called *clans*. *Tribes* were multiple clans living in the same vicinity and sharing the same culture. Tribes were better able than clans to protect their members against enemy tribes and to ensure that everyone had sufficient food to eat. Individuals who were disabled were cared for according to tribal custom. Children observed their parents, other adults, and members of their tribe and emulated what they saw. They learned from those responsible for them and, in so doing, became acculturated (socialized) into their culture. Because the continuation of the tribe was dependent on children carrying traditions from one generation to the next, a measure of how much children were valued is found in the fact that they were taught traditions, rules, and customs (Berger & Riojas-Cortez, 2012).

As cultures learned to meet basic survival needs more effectively (e.g., as food supplies became more reliable through domestication of animals and the cultivation of crops), the threats to the family changed. In particular, new problems of social organization emerged both within and among populations. Internally, individuals became more dependent on others outside their families, and externally, groups of people needed to learn how to deal with other groups. In a word, society became more complex, and children needed to learn much more if they were to become productive adults.

Greek and Roman Period Families.   We may speculate that this was the time when the task of educating children first became sufficiently complex. Moving education out of the realm of parental responsibility might allow parents to better protect their children while ensuring that their children learned what they needed to take their places in society as they reached adulthood. More specifically, Plato (427–347 B.C.), Aristotle (384–323 B.C.), Cicero (106–43 B.C.), and Polybius (204–122 B.C.) were Greek and Roman philosophers who believed that educating parents and children was important for the benefit of the state. However, their interest was reserved only for boys born to wealthy families. Boys needed to learn about governing, military strategy, managing commerce, and so forth—all activities expected of those who would lead their cultures.

Such a view represented little departure from earlier times. Families were still responsible for protecting their children, and because formal education was reserved for boys from families of nobility, girls still learned domestic skills at home. Boys from less prosperous families continued to learn within the family environment the skills and knowledge they needed to assume their roles in society. Although there were laws and customs allowing infanticide and the sale of children, Greek and Roman civilizations were generally supportive of families and children (Berger & Riojas-Cortez, 2012).

Family life and the role of children as members of family units changed considerably after the decline of the Roman Empire. Deterioration of the fabric of society meant that some threats that had been dealt with by large groups of people (e.g., defense of the community) again became the responsibility of families and family groups during the Middle Ages (400–1400). Simple survival reemerged as the primary goal for many individuals, and so children came to be viewed as property. In addition, the harshness and brevity of life meant that children were expected to become adults at a very young age and there was no time for education. Indeed, family life for the children of peasants was a constant struggle to simply satisfy the basic needs of food, clothing, and shelter.

Only those few children born to noble families were educated. In addition, they were also prepared to be responsible for the property and the traditions they would inherit.

European Medieval Families.   Life was difficult for children during the Middle Ages, and harshness became a predominant focus of parenting behaviors. Families from both noble and peasant classes treated their children as miniature adults. Families had no appreciation of the developmental processes of childhood. The church of the time had an extraordinary influence on governmental matters, family life in general, and child-rearing practices.

The church taught that children were naturally evil, had to be told what to do, needed to be corrected constantly, and had to be punished harshly so that they could function well in society as adults. The phrase "beat the devil out of the child" came into existence because of this belief. It was very common for parents of all classes to emotionally neglect their young children or abandon them to a wet nurse, monastery, or nunnery. In other words, economic difficulties of the time and the church's view of children during medieval times meant harsh treatment of children and little support for family life. Children generally were not well protected, and even though the boys of the wealthy were educated (as proposed by the Greeks and Romans), this experience was often a perversion of a healthy educational experience. We can be certain, however, that children learned how to behave as adults by watching and emulating the society surrounding them.

Renaissance and Reformation Families.   The Renaissance (1300–1400) and Reformation (1500–1600) periods that followed saw increased concern about freedom for common people. This concern, accompanied by increased social organization that relieved some of the threats to families, and the important idea that a person is an individual rather than only a part of a group, made social classes less significant than during the Middle Ages. Individuality and freedom were extended to children and their schooling and better ensured that children were educated. The belief that children were pure and good was promoted in contradiction to the idea of original sin that the church had advocated during the Middle Ages.

Martin Luther (1482–1546), the father of the Reformation, proposed revolutionary child-rearing practices. He advocated that parents educate their children and teach them morals and the catechism. He maintained that families were the most important educators for children, that education was appropriate for both girls and boys, and that both genders would become better adults if they were educated.

Luther's ideas, followed by Johannes Gutenberg's invention of the printing press in 1439, meant that a few families would have access to books and could educate their children. In Europe, there were also more schools for the families who could afford them. However, school was still reserved for the sons of nobility, and education for the common person was not to come until much later.

The Age of Reason

The Age of Reason (1600–1700), also called the Enlightenment, was an era of notable intellectual activity. Numerous religious leaders, philosophers, and educators introduced ideas about the way children learn and how families could best educate them. Comenius (1592–1670), a bishop, teacher, and writer, believed that all children were basically good; and Locke (1632–1704), an English philosopher, promoted the idea that children's minds are like "clean slates" on which parents and teachers could write what students were to learn.

Although Comenius and Locke promoted education for maintaining a democracy, the philosopher Rousseau (1712–1778) took a social view of children. In his book *Emile,* he advocated a child's world that would be free from society's arrogant and unnatural ways. He introduced the concept of the whole child and promoted the idea that children needed a flexible, free atmosphere in which to mature according to their own natural timetables. Pestalozzi (1746–1827), a Swiss educator, was influenced by Rousseau. He expanded on Rousseau's belief of allowing a child's development to occur naturally by encouraging the child to learn basic skills. In addition, he believed that mothers from all socioeconomic classes should teach practical skills to their children at home, stressing the development of the whole child. Thus, the notion that families need to prepare their children for adulthood grew and included the important precept that children are individuals who need to develop in a broad range of areas. Notice, though, that the family was still the central feature in the child's education.

Froebel (1782–1852) was a German educator who became known as the "father of kindergarten." He studied with Pestalozzi and eventually started a school for young children that promoted learning through play. Children's play, however, was guided by a trained teacher who planned activities that encouraged learning. Once again, a specially trained teacher relieved the family of some responsibilities for their children gaining the skills and knowledge they needed as adults.

Thinkers during the Age of Reason emphasized the worth and the dignity of humans and agreed with Francis Bacon's belief that "knowledge is power." In spite of the progress that was made toward valuing all individuals (including children), the Industrial Revolution changed how children were treated—in undesirable ways.

The Industrial Revolution

From the Age of Reason to the Age of Darkness—the Industrial Revolution was a period of child exploitation. The advent of the Industrial Revolution in the 1700s and 1800s brought social and political crises in France and England. During the Industrial Revolution, the economic condition was so desperate that families could no longer protect their children adequately; indeed, children became a liability to their families. Children from poor families, many as young as 10 years of age, commonly worked 10- to 14-hour days in factories as cheap laborers.

This was not true for all children. Wealthy families hired others to raise their children and were not interested in them. The new middle class wanted to guide their children to meet their own mold, and the poor did not have much of a family life (Berger & Riojas-Cortez, 2012). Despite social class differences, children were still expected to act like adults from a very young age.

The political and economic structure of Europe during the Industrial Revolution changed how society viewed children and families. Concomitantly, colonies in the new world were developing their own political, economic, and social environment.

Colonial North American Family

While many city children were slaving in factories and living on the streets in the 1700s and 1800s, other children were helping on family-owned farms and businesses. Though economic life was a struggle, many colonial families were self-sufficient and so able to protect their children. In addition, they socialized them through secular and religious education—including opportunities for recreation.

It is important to realize that these families did not do this all on their own. Coontz (2000) reminds us that the government provided resources not available to families in Europe. Prairie farmers and other pioneer families owed their existence to massive federal land grants, government-funded military mobilization that disposed of hundreds of Indian societies and confiscated large portions of Mexico, and state-sponsored economic investment in new lands, many of which were sold to settlers or speculators at prices far below the cost to the public treasury of acquiring them. During the 1700s, political and religious conflict, a growing economy, and free land allowed young families and individuals to move out on their own. The result was the emergence of an independent family structure (Skolnick & Skolnick, 2009). But what about the children? Although children were viewed as important and necessary for the family economy in the new world, child rearing in Puritan families remained as it was in Europe, strict and humiliating. Children were perceived as corrupt, and it was the parent's responsibility to break their wills to rid them of their basic evil natures. Physical punishment was common and legitimate in this patriarchal society for wives as well as children (Skolnick & Skolnick, 2009), and obedience to the father was strictly observed.

Despite the romantic image of the family during this period, many children died in early childhood, and a person's life expectancy was less than 50 years. The average length of one third of all marriages lasted only 10 years due to the number of women who died in childbirth (Skolnick & Skolnick, 2009). Widowers remarried quickly because of necessity, and, consequently, there were few single-parent homes and numerous blended families (stepfamilies) during colonial times. Black families were brought from Africa and did not have the advantages that were enjoyed by the new colonists. Because members were frequently separated from one another, the structure of black families varied significantly from the rest of society. We continue to feel the effects of the devastation of the black family today (Berger & Riojas-Cortez, 2012).

American Industrialization and the Family

From the 1850s to the 1920s, there was a dramatic shift away from the Puritan ideas of colonial America. The country became more industrialized, urbanized, and prosperous. There was growth in manufacturing, with immigrants providing cheap labor for factories; gold was found in California; western lands were opened; and prosperous agricultural crops provided a surplus of food.

By 1920, the workweek was shortened from 6 days to 5, and the middle class had become larger. The working class profited, too; the strong economy and political climate allowed them many luxuries previously available only to the wealthy. Because of the country's affluence, society altered its beliefs about the duties of the family, the role of its members, and the image of the child.

A change in the function of the family appeared in rural areas. Increased agricultural productivity meant farm families began to raise cash crops rather than provide solely for their immediate needs, and families began to rely on the money they received to buy goods produced by others. At the same time, larger and more prosperous farms were possible because mechanization reduced the number of laborers needed. The need for fewer farm workers, in turn, began a migration from rural to urban areas.

An increase in income is usually accompanied by more time for one's own life and a focus on family and children (Skolnick & Skolnick, 2009). Thus, economic growth was accompanied by an increase in the popularity of the writings of Locke, Rousseau, Pestalozzi, and Froebel, and childhood came to be viewed as a stage of development, with children being recognized as inherently good. Freud's psychoanalytic theory became popular, and John Watson's behaviorist theory strongly influenced child rearing (Skolnick & Skolnick, 2009). In 1912, the government created the Children's Bureau to address concerns about undernourished, neglected, and abused children.

These changing attitudes toward children prompted further changes in the family unit. Relationships became more loving between husband and wife and between parent and child. Family members' roles were specific: fathers worked for financial security and mothers took care of the home and children. Middle- and upper-class mothers had servants to help take care of their children.

There was, however, a new middle-class working woman who challenged traditional gender roles, brought about the suffrage movement, and eventually, in 1920, earned women the right to vote. More women went to college as well.

The emergence of mandatory, free public schools was another major social change during the mid-1800s. Although schools assisted families with the education of their children in the past (that is, families still maintained the major responsibility for children's education), the government now took over primary responsibility for formal education with the advent of public schools. The government believed that females were not able to properly teach their children to become effective citizens for a democratic society, especially women of immigrant families. Thus Horace Mann's Common School was created for the purpose of Americanizing all citizens. Families were still responsible for protecting children and educating them for adulthood, but much responsibility for the latter was now formally in the hands of the government.

World War I and the Great Depression brought many new ideas to a halt as mere survival became a daily struggle. As in the past, the functioning of the family and the roles of its members changed in response to economic and societal exigencies of the time.

The Great Depression and World War II

The political and economic impact of the Great Depression and World War II dramatically affected the functioning of the family. When men lost their jobs because of the Depression, they also lost their roles as family providers. They were further devastated as women joined the workforce and families moved in together to share resources and reduce expenses. The pattern of women working and families sharing housing continued through World War II as husbands and fathers became part of the military. In extreme cases, families were simply torn apart and children were often taken care of by their grandparents.

Educators saw the importance of education for young children, and child-care centers were created because of a need for them. The government, through the Works Progress Administration (WPA), came to the aid of families by funding nursery schools using unemployed teachers. From 1941 to 1946, the Lanham Act War Nurseries were supported by the government to provide child care for children whose parents were part of the war effort. The most famous of these nurseries were the Kaiser Child Care Centers, which provided 24-hour day care for working mothers during the war. The centers were closed when the war ended and the mothers gave up their jobs and returned to their homes (Gordon & Browne, 2011). Indeed, women working outside the home were viewed as wartime sacrifices, with men assuming the breadwinner role when they returned home from military service. It appeared that traditional gender-specific roles had been reestablished.

Reflection...

Imagine yourself living during the time of the Depression. What would your life be like? How would the Depression affect your family? Compare a family of the Depression era with a contemporary family.

1950s to 1970s

Americans experienced the greatest economic boom in history from the 1950s through the 1970s. Many sociologists believe that, because of the strong economic and political climate during the 1950s, societies in general and families more specifically were secure and solid (Coontz, 2000). The nuclear family of the 1950s was thought to be the main source of childhood socialization and center of all personal happiness (Coontz, 2000) and completely independent from all outside sources.

Like the farm family of the 1920s, the idea of a completely self-reliant family is a myth. Government assistance programs of the 1950s helped veterans (primarily middle-class white men) obtain college educations and buy homes. In other words, it gave them a head start. Unfortunately, these programs did not assist people of color; ethnic groups; or single, divorced, and working mothers. The fact is that 30% of families lived in poverty during this supposedly "golden" period (Coontz, 2000). Moreover, women lost much of the independence they had gained before and during World War II.

At the same time, middle-class women were having more children and were tied to their suburban homes. Child-rearing practices of the 1950s were influenced by child development experts such as Erik Erikson, Arnold Gesell, and Benjamin Spock, whose messages were that children have individual differences that need to be nurtured and that each child proceeds through developmental stages at a rate that cannot be rushed. What each child needs, they argued, is not the stress that comes with being rushed through development, but the love that comes with being recognized as a unique and valued member of the family.

The 1960s and 1970s were times of social and political revolt. The children of the 1950s were raised to be independent, critical, and creative rather than obedient (Skolnick & Skolnick, 2009), and when they entered colleges and universities (which they did in record numbers), they questioned and criticized all institutions—family, education, religion, economics, and government (Berger & Riojas-Cortez, 2012). They witnessed a society that ignored poverty and sanctioned racial injustice, and they accepted neither (Skolnick & Skolnick, 2009). The Vietnam War also served to tear the country apart with protests against U.S. involvement—protests that frequently caused strife and strained family relationships. The lack of a unified effort in favor of the war meant family conflicts were magnified.

Economic and political upheaval again caused the family's structure and function to change. More women went back to work, either as single mothers or to supplement the family income, making child care an important issue. Jean Piaget, a Swiss psychologist, gained in popularity at this time. He proposed a theory of cognitive development in children and expressed concern for their intellectual development, in particular the intellectual development of young children. On reading Piaget and his followers, parents were eager to help their children develop cognitively rather than simply letting nature take its course.

At the same time, the government began its War on Poverty with hopes of providing children from families of low socioeconomic status educational, medical, and mental health services. Head Start, a preschool program that included parent involvement, provided disadvantaged children the opportunity to get a head start before entering school. Because of Head Start's success, other programs for young children expanded rapidly. An important feature of Head Start is that in addition to having trained teachers work with children, parents are also involved and taught to work with their children.

In summary, families have had and will continue to have two responsibilities toward their children: They need to protect children from threats to their well-being, and they need to educate them so they can be productive members of the societies within which they live when they reach adulthood. What has changed has been the cultural matrix within which families function, a matrix to which families are bound by particular circumstances and events, and to which they react. In other words, families react to society's current dilemmas, and their reactions create new dilemmas (Skolnick & Skolnick, 2009).

Changes have been both positive and negative. When they were positive, society grew in ways that made it easier for families to both protect and educate their children. This was the case, for example, in Greece and Rome, where social organization reduced the effort parents had to make to protect their children. It was also true of the Renaissance and Reformation periods when societal threats were reduced and the first recognition was made that children were individuals to be valued as such. And finally, after the Civil War and during the post–World War II period, the combination of economic prosperity and support from the government allowed families to expend more energy educating their children for adulthood.

Periods when families were most frustrated in addressing their responsibilities toward children were the Middle Ages and the Industrial Revolution, when economic deprivation threatened adults so severely that they were unable to look after their children. These were also times when society failed to recognize that being a child was different than being an adult, and that the proper maturation experiences for children did not include being treated like miniature adults.

Contemporary U.S. Families

We turn now to families in the United States at the close of the 20th century and the ways in which they address the two tasks of protecting children and preparing them for adulthood. In doing so, we must consider the varieties of families commonly found in our contemporary society.

Most people think of children when they think of families. Yet only 25% of all families have minor children in their homes. Moreover, there is considerable diversity within that 25% (Dobbins, 2010). In addition to intact families (both biological parents and minor children), there are households headed by single parents, cohabitating couples, and gay parents; there are blended families and families headed by grandparents rearing minor children, in addition to numerous other structures. To make matters even more complex, there is great diversity within each of these family structures.

The family has changed not only in its structure but also in its cultural makeup. The number of interracial marriages in the United States has risen 20% since 2000 to about 4.5 million, according to the census figures. The figures for interracial marriages still represent a small population; however, interracial marriages have grown from 1% in 1970 to 5% in 2000 to 8% in 2010. These figures demonstrate a growing a population of culturally diverse families, and as teachers it is important to be knowledgeable about the culture(s) of your students (Harlem World, 2010).

It is true that the structure of families has changed since the end of World War II and continues to change. Nonfamilies (single men and women) have become more prevalent than in the past, perhaps because society has become more accepting of individuals who choose not to marry or who postpone marriage. Another area of change involves the increase in the number of other types of families (single-parent families, grandparent-headed families, foster homes, gay/lesbian families, etc.)—structures that in the past would not have been seen as "real" families.

Although the number of married couples without children does not appear to have appreciably changed, the reason for their status has. Currently, couples may delay parenting for a variety of reasons (careers, etc.) or they may choose not to have children. At one time it was assumed that all married couples would have children if they could—infertility was a greater medical problem in the past than it is today. Although there are reasons for remaining childless that are shared by both groups, couples may plan to have children in the future and are only temporarily childless or they may have already reared their children and they are no longer part of the immediate household.

The big difference between families in the 1970s and families currently is the number of married couples with children. The advent of reliable, inexpensive birth control means that women can put off childbirth until they have established themselves professionally; consequently, families are smaller and women are older than their mothers were when they had children. The number of single-parent families has also increased; indeed, it has doubled since 1970, due to the increase of divorces and the number of children born to unmarried mothers. In addition, the remarriage rate following divorce has grown, increasing significantly the number of blended families. Finally, baby boomers are moving out of the child-rearing years, and there has been a decrease in the number of married couples with children (Lehman, 2004).

As an educator who shares responsibilities with families for educating children, you must be well informed about the range and nature of family structures in your classroom. Though there are many different familial structures and they are all equally important, we focus primarily on three groups: single unmarried mothers, single divorced mothers, and blended families. These three were selected because they are more apt to be misunderstood than the intact (traditional) family.

Single-Parent Families

In 2007, a record 40% of births in the United States were to unmarried women (National Center for Health Statistics, 2007). Currently, half of all children will spend at least part of their lives in single-parent homes, and the mother will most likely be the custodial parent. These children will be in your classroom, and you must be knowledgeable about them so you can effectively meet their needs. The two largest groups of children of single-parent families are families headed by unmarried mothers and single-parent homes created by divorce. Single-parent homes account for a large number of families and, unfortunately, single-parent households are perhaps the most stereotyped of all family structures.

Unmarried Mothers

Twenty and Over.   The twenty and over category (29%) is divided into two types: (1) those who chose to become pregnant and (2) those for whom the pregnancy was not planned. The first group is older, more affluent, better educated, and not in a position to marry. They are generally 30 or older and have decided that if they are going to have a baby they must, for biological reasons, have one soon. This is normally a well-thought-out decision with issues ranging from options for impregnation (in vitro, artificial insemination, a male partner, etc.) to adoption. Also, financial security generally is considered well in advance for this population and these women generally report satisfaction with their decisions.

The second group tends to be in their early 20s and less well off financially and educationally. They do not plan the pregnancy and frequently have neither the maturity nor the resources available to properly rear a child. It is important to recognize that even though the pregnancy was not planned, this does not mean that the baby was not wanted or loved at the time of birth.

Reflection...

Think about the structure of students' families when you were in elementary school. How do they differ from what you would see in a present-day classroom?

Teen Mothers.   Unmarried teenagers give birth to approximately 11% of the children born in this country each year. Very few teens who become mothers plan on doing so. Out of all teen pregnancies, 82% are unintended. Although 11% is still a considerable amount, it is a significant decrease in the number of births to unmarried teens in the past. But what has increased is the number of young women between the ages of 15 and 17 who are having babies. These births are particularly problematic because they bring many serious complications to motherhood, including a lack of maturity and limited financial resources. These mothers are apt to live in poverty, be unemployed, have low-level employment skills, possess narrow educational backgrounds, and have limited parenting skills, to name a few (Lehman, 2004).

Due to the increase in the numbers of very young unmarried teenage mothers, there has been an increase in another kind of family structure—households headed by maternal grandmothers who are rearing the children of these young mothers. Sociologists call this phenomenon *skip generation parenting*. As a teacher, you may well be working with your student's grandparents. To complicate matters even more, you also may be working with both the grandparents and the child's young mother.

You will be a teacher for children of unmarried mothers and, as with all families, you will find great diversity amongst these families. A student from a home headed by an unmarried mother may be the child of a mature, well-educated, financially secure woman who is interested and involved in her child's education. Or the student may be the child of a mother who was 15 years old at his or her birth, and this could be problematic. The young mother may be unable to attend school functions because she cannot take time away from her job, either because her employer won't let her or because she cannot sacrifice the income. The variances in these families are as innumerable as they are within all family structures.

Case Study

Sherrie, Age 12

Sherrie's mother was 15 when she gave birth and although her mother tried to finish high school, she eventually dropped out. Sherrie and her mother lived with her grandparents for her first 2 years but since then have lived in public housing. Her mother's lack of education has decreased her vocational opportunities and her employment has generally been in fast-food restaurants that provide few benefits.

Nancy, Age 12

Nancy's mother was 35 when she gave birth. She had a college degree and a well-paying position providing excellent benefits. Nancy's mother had always assumed that she would, at some point, get married and have children. Since she hadn't married she decided that if she were to have children she needed to act. Nancy attends an excellent school and lives in a nice neighborhood. She plays soccer, plays the flute, takes gym lessons, and goes on trips with her mother—they both enjoy skiing.

Questions and Considerations

1. Compare and contrast the lives of Nancy and Sherrie.
2. How do you explain these differences in their lives?

Patterns of Divorce and Remarriage

The following two family configurations to be explored are single-parent families due to divorce and blended families. These two families share a common attribute: In both types parents are married or have been married at least once.

Single-Parent Families: Divorce

Time Period.   Children who have recently experienced a divorce are children in a crisis that generally lasts about 18 months. During this period, children can be expected to display grieving-cycle behaviors: denial, anger, depression, and finally acceptance (or in the case of divorce, adjustment). All children don't necessarily go through each of these stages, and the intensity and duration will vary according to the individual child. However, the majority of children will go through these stages. Grief is a response to loss and even if a child's home situation has been undesirable, they will still feel a loss. The loss in those cases is the loss of a dream—the dream that they will become a happy family.

It is common for children to feel guilt and fear during this period—guilt that they are in some way responsible for the divorce and fear that they might also lose the custodial parent. During this crisis period, children need understanding, sensitivity, and emotional support so their lives can continue as normally as possible. Too often, people focus solely on the crisis period of divorce because it is a high-profile, dramatic time marked by increased stress, heightened needs, and new or intensified behaviors. It is easy to think that the crisis will continue forever, but children are resilient and the majority of them will work through their grief.

Finances.   Income must be taken into consideration when trying to understand children from single-parent homes. A startling 57% of all female-headed households have annual incomes below the national poverty line. Ninety percent of all custodial parents are women (Field & Casper, 2001).

Living in poverty has major negative implications for single-parent families, from inadequate nutrition (which may appear in the classroom as lethargy) and medical concerns (inadequate immunization, etc.) to lesser quality of both the physical and emotional environment than children from families with adequate resources. In other words, fiscal matters must be considered when trying to understand the lives of your students from single-parent families. Often, problems that children of divorce experience are blamed on the structure of the family as opposed to the stresses and restrictions of poverty. An important question to ask would be "Are the problems your student brings to class due to the absence of a second parent or to the absence of adequate financial resources or both?"

Stigmatization.   We have all heard people explaining a child's behavior by saying, "She's from a broken home." If the divorce is recent, a better statement would be, "That child is going through a crisis," because that more correctly describes the situation. After your student has worked through his or her crisis, blaming the divorce for a child's behavior is both inadequate as an explanation and inappropriate as a justification. Divorce (after the crisis period) no more produces juvenile misbehavior than an intact home guarantees acceptable behavior. Moreover, the language that is used to describe these children and their families is often negative (for example, "broken home"). Broken means defective and surely no one would purposely purchase something that is defective. Yet the term is used frequently to describe divorced families. There was a break in the family at the time of divorce but then a new family evolved. Single-parent homes may be exemplary, undesirable, or, like most homes, somewhere in the middle—doing the best they can. Describing children of divorce as being from a broken home stigmatizes them and their families.

To complicate things even further, most of the research describing children from single-parent homes is about children of divorce and generally does not include the children of never-married women. Consequently, when looking at the research on single-parent families you need to ask, "Which single-parent families?"

As educators, we are particularly interested in the academic implications of children of divorce. The general assumption is that children of divorce make lower grades than they did prior to the divorce. However, a number of recent studies have reported that there is little or no difference in the academic achievement between children of divorce and children from intact homes (Painter & Levine, 2000; Shim, Felner, & Shim, 2000). Unfortunately, the media hasn't reported this research, which finds that the children of divorce, following the grieving period, are pretty much like other children. The media's omission results in the support of faulty perceptions of children of divorce.

There are a few differences between the children of traditional (intact) homes and children from single-parent homes. After all, children of these two families live in different structures and environments. The following paragraph cites some of these differences.

The parents in single-parent homes talk more to their children than parents in two-parent homes (there are no other adults around to talk with), and consequently children from single-parent homes tend to be more comfortable talking with adults. Also, children in single-parent homes are apt to be more independent and have greater feelings of efficacy than children from two-parent families; because there are fewer adults in the home, everyone must assume more responsibility. Also, parents in single-parent homes are less likely to pressure their children into social conformity and more likely to praise good grades than parents in a two-parent household. On the other hand, single parents on a whole spend less time supervising homework or interacting with the school than do parents from two-parent homes. In addition two-parent homes can provide a more solid financial base, are less apt to be in poverty, and can provide greater security.

The statistics about divorced single-parent homes are often confusing. When you hear that half of all children will live in a single-parent home due to divorce, it doesn't mean at a given time. Those figures mean at some time before they are 18 years of age.

Blended Families

Blended families (stepfamilies) are growing in number. This is not surprising because there has been an increase in the number of single-parent families (unmarried and divorced) and most of them will remarry. Although the term *stepfamily* is commonly used, the term *blended* better describes this family unit and is used in this chapter. The latest sociological term for a stepfamily, however, is *recoupled*.

The term *step,* as in stepparent, has an interesting history. It is derived from the Old English word *steop*, which meant "bereaved." The man who stepped into a family after the death of the father was seen as a committing a heroic act that often saved a woman and her children from economic ruin. Death was the most common cause of blended families; currently, however, the marriage of divorced and unmarried mothers is the most frequent reason. Death of either parent was problematic, but the death of the father was the most disastrous. Women generally were not part of the workforce and, furthermore, for much of history they were not allowed to own property or have wealth. In other words, remarriage could save a widow and her children from financial disaster.

Although children of single-parent homes are most apt to get the attention of the media, blended families may eventually become the largest family structure. The blended family is the most misunderstood of all family structures. In fact, the single-parent home is more like the intact home than like the blended family. Educators are often uncomfortable with the single-parent family and tend to breathe a collective sigh of relief when the single-parent family becomes a blended family. After all, it looks like the family we are most comfortable with—the traditional (intact) family.

However, the only thing that the intact family and the blended family have in common is their appearance. The blended family functions differently from other family structures. The members of a blended family bring with them to their new family a complex history as well as different traditions. Whereas there is diversity within any given family structure, none approach the complexity of the blended family. As an example of this complexity, the Institute for Clinical Social Work in Northbrook, Illinois, has defined 32 categories of blended families. As an educator, it is imperative that you have an understanding of these family structures if you are to serve students well.

Research on blended families is limited, and the findings are anything but conclusive. Some researchers view members of blended families as having more problems than the traditional family, whereas others view their problems as simply being different. These latter researchers also see children from blended families as equally well adjusted as children from intact homes (Coontz, 2000).

Facts About Blended Families.   What is the truth about blended families? The following is a list of facts on which most researchers agree:

- Younger children tend to make the best adjustment to blended families.
- Adolescents, particularly those of the same sex as the stepparent, are apt to feel resentful of the stepparent.
- Children generally adjust better to a stepparent after the death of a natural parent than after a divorce.
- Following divorce, the attitudes of the adults involved (custodial, noncustodial, and stepparents) will contribute significantly to the child's adjustment to a blended family. Not surprisingly, positive attitudes are more apt to result in a healthier adjustment than negative attitudes.
- Most blended families report being happy.

Reflection...

Consider the stereotype of the fairy tale stepmother. How many negative portrayals can you remember? How many positive? How might you explain this disparity?

Myths About Blended Families.   Unfortunately, too often the expectations for blended families are based on myths rather than facts. The following are four particularly dangerous myths.

Myth 1.   Family roles in blended families are similar to those of intact families. Although other adults can replace a spouse, they cannot replace a parent. The role of the stepparent is ill defined and, as children often remind them, "You are not my parent!" Though stepparents may nurture and support the children, they seldom play the role assigned to the natural parent.

Myth 2.   Members instantly love each other. It took the adults in the blended family time to build their relationship and yet there is an unrealistic expectation that the stepparent and stepchildren will automatically love one another. They need time to build a relationship, but even with given time there are complicating factors. Mixed loyalties present problems for many blended families: "If I love my stepparent, am I being disloyal to my natural parent?" Also, jealousy of stepsiblings and stepparents is often a problem that must be addressed prior to the development of a functional family.

Myth 3.   Blended families function just like "traditional" families. Although traditional families share common histories, traditions, and relatives, blended families do not. In contrast, blended families share the richness that goes with diversity—although that diversity may require change. Family traditions (birthdays, Christmas, Hanukkah, family trips, etc.) provide opportunities for enjoyable and enriching new experiences, but they also may result in conflict. In addition, relationships between stepsiblings (custodial and noncustodial, etc.) must be negotiated. In many families stepsiblings add to the richness of the family as well as the friction.

Myth 4.   Life is just a family sitcom. Perhaps the most detrimental myth of all comes to us from television. Although the stepfamily myths of the past (e.g., Cinderella, Hansel and Gretel, Snow White) have been examined and found wanting, we have replaced them with a new set of myths about the blended family, such as in the *Brady Bunch* (an old television show that lives on in reruns) and more recent shows about blended families. The *Brady Bunch* may technically be a blended family, but the scriptwriters have them acting just like an intact family. It is important that you as an educator be aware of the realities of blended families. The Utopian adjustment made on television programs is more dangerous than the myth of Cinderella. In Cinderella, the wicked stepmother is accepted as a storybook character, but blended families may see the Bradys as a real possibility and feel guilty when they don't live up to this contemporary fairy tale.

When examining any family that differs from the traditional family, there is a temptation to dwell on the differences between the two. Often the behaviors that are unlike those of traditional families are seen as undesirable.

The strengths of the nontraditional family are apt to be ignored. The characteristics listed below help us examine the strengths of blended families (Ganong & Coleman, 2008).

- **Flexibility.** Stepchildren often learn to adjust to different value systems. Thus they may adapt more easily and flexibly to new traditions and situations. These children generally know how to negotiate new situations and compromise when necessary. Consequently, when situations require new behaviors (new schools, teachers, etc.), the child from a blended family may have already developed some important coping skills that can be generalized to these other situations.

- **Multiple Role Models.** There are generally more adults in the lives of children of blended families than those of other family structures, and these adults provide a variety of models from which a child can choose. Aunt Susan is a good businessperson, Cousin Jim is very creative, and Grandma Mae is a scholar, and they are all role models for the child from the blended family.

- **Experience with Conflict Resolution.** It has been said that children from blended families should be excellent in politics or business management because they know how to negotiate. Their negotiation skills are generally well developed because they may have positive relationships with people who may otherwise be hostile to each other (i.e., their divorced parents).

- **An Extended Kin Network.** The child of a blended family has more parents, grandparents, aunts, uncles, and cousins than children from other family structures. There are not only more people to learn from, but also more people to love and support them.

- **Higher Standard of Living.** Most children from blended homes previously lived in female-headed, single-parent homes with limited economic resources. With marriage, the total family income is generally increased. With the increase in resources, there is also a rise in the standard of living, as well as added opportunities available for the children. In addition, there is a decrease in the stress caused by worrying about financial instability.

- **Happy Parents.** Remarriage may provide children with a more supportive emotional environment because their parents are happier. Children who have experienced hostility in a previous family may benefit greatly from a more caring, loving environment. Happier remarriages may also provide exposure to a good model of marital interaction.

Stepfamilies are not traditional families warmed over. They are families with their own unique strengths and needs. By understanding the realities of the blended family and dispelling the myths, you can work with these children and their families more effectively. Knowledge allows us to look past the differences and appreciate the strengths of the blended family.

With all the positive possibilities for the blended family there is a big negative aspect to be considered—60% of second marriages end in divorce. This divorce rate demonstrates the difficulty of building working relationships with a new family, immediate and extended. It takes time and hard work to develop the necessary familial relationships (U.S. Census Bureau, 2007).

In summary, it is necessary that educators know about, and appreciate, the families of their students. It is also necessary that they know how changing family structures play out in the lives of children. Families have become a fluid concept, and the following scenario could easily be one of your students. Angie was born into an intact family, her parents divorced, she then lived in a single-parent family, her mother then remarried, and she then lived in a blended family. Angie's father also remarried and she was part of his blended family, but he has since divorced and is planning to remarry. Angie will have been a member of a number of family configurations during her childhood, not only with her custodial parent but also with her noncustodial parent. Angie's experience is representative of a large number of children.

In addition, as families change, so do their needs. For example, as the number of single-parent families increases so does the need for child care. There is continual change in all families, even within traditional (intact) families. There may be changes in the parents' employment, child-care arrangements, or the economic status of the family. Furthermore, families are more mobile and move more frequently than they have in the past. Families are in a continual state of change.

Reflection...

Think of a family that you feel is a functional (good) family. What would be the adjectives that describe this family?

Functional Families

What are the characteristics of a functional family? What do good families look like and what do they do? What are the effects of a dysfunctional family on the lives of children?

It is important to be careful in making judgments about families. Contrary to popular belief you cannot determine the effectiveness of a family by its structure. The intact family with two children, in an upper-income neighborhood, may or may not be more functional than the single-parent family with two children living in a working-class neighborhood. It is not the way a family looks, but rather the way it acts. For many years the body of literature on families was on the dysfunctional family—they were more obvious and easier to study. Presently, there is a considerable body of literature on the functional family, and some identifiable characteristics have emerged. We have a sense of what healthy families are and what they are not.

Functional families are not perfect. If a family seems too good to be true, they probably are. All families have problems; only the nature, severity, and ability of the family to solve problems differ. Because a family seeks professional help does not mean they are dysfunctional. In fact, it may be a good example of their ability to address problems (problem solving).

Characteristics of Functional Families

Communication. The presence of effective *communication patterns* is one of the most frequently mentioned characteristics of strong families. Researchers characterize the communication patterns of strong families as clear, open, and frequent. Family members talk with each other often, and when they do, they are honest and open with each other. The *encouragement of individual members* encompasses a range of affective dimensions related to mutual support.

Recognition and Respect.   Strong families cultivate a sense of belonging to a family unit, but also nurture the development of individual strengths and interests. Members enjoy the family framework, which provides structure but does not confine them.

Appreciation.   Appreciation is an important characteristic of strong families. It includes delivering a high level of positive reinforcement to family members, day in and day out, and doing things that are positive from the other person's perspective, just for their sake, not merely as a strategy for "buying their love." It is important to emphasize the delight, liking, warmth, and humor that family members share, which are all aspects of this construct and which distinguish some families from others.

Religious or Spiritual Orientation.   A religious or spiritual orientation is identified by many researchers as an important component of strong families. All studies have found some aspect of religiosity or spirituality as a component of strong families. However, there is disagreement over which aspects of religion are most critical to family functioning.

Ability to Adapt.   A family's ability to adapt to stressful and potentially damaging events, as well as to predictable life cycle changes, has also been identified as an important characteristic of strong families. Strong families are those with an ability to absorb stress and cope. The more rigid a family system, the more disturbed. Some researchers equate adaptability with flexibility, which they describe as the capacity of a family system to change the power structure, roles, and rules within the family.

Connectedness.   Successful families are not isolated; they are connected to the wider society. One effect of *social connectedness* is the availability of external resources, identified by researchers as important to effective coping by families. A family's social connectedness can be measured in terms of the availability of external resources in the form of friends, family, and neighbors, as well as participation in community organizations.

Clear Role Definition.   Many researchers identify clear role definition as an important characteristic of family functioning, and as essential for a family's ability to adapt to changing situations. With a clear, yet flexible structure in place, family members are aware of their responsibilities in and to the family.

Time Together.   Successful families spend time together, and the shared time is high in both quality and quantity. The number of activities done as a family and the extent to which family members enjoy spending time together tell a lot about successful families. They like to spend their free time with each other (Krysan, Moore, & Zill, 2006).

Note that none of these characteristics describes the appearance of a family. A good family may be a single man and his adopted child, a young couple with children, a couple over the age of 30 who have just had their first baby, or an infinite number of other family configurations. What is important is not the appearance but how well a family functions.

Dysfunctional Families

Whereas functional families allow children to grow to independence in a safe and supportive environment, dysfunctional homes do not. They may or may not provide for basic physical needs, but they do not provide for the development of an emotionally healthy individual.

Dysfunctional families are often unpredictable, with little or no structure, leaving the children anxious and unsure of themselves; or they may be too structured, resulting in a lack of sense of self. It is difficult to identify an exhaustive list of characteristics for dysfunctional families. Consequently, it is more productive to examine some of the effects of the dysfunctional family.

Dysfunctional Family Characteristics

Addiction.   A major characteristic of a dysfunctional family is addiction. This addiction need not be to drugs or alcohol, but it typically manifests itself by making it difficult for family members to communicate, and may affect the family financially.

Control.   Control means that one member of the family exerts his or her will on some or all of the other family members. For example, a parent may not allow his or her child to go to reasonable school events, such as football games and dances.

Unpredictability and Fear.   Unpredictability and fear are two common signs of a dysfunctional family. This may be unpredictability with regard to financial matters or emotional states. This affects a family by making its members fearful of the actions.

Conflict.   A more obvious indicator of a dysfunctional family is conflict. Although a certain amount of conflict is expected in a normal family, constant, heated conflict is not.

Abuse.   Abuse, whether physical or emotional, is another characteristic of a dysfunctional family. The way in which abuse affects a family is obvious, as it punishes and diminishes a single or multiple family members.

Perfectionism.   Although it may not seem to be a characteristic of a dysfunctional family, perfectionism very much is one. Perfectionism can be a reflection of unrealistic expectations and may also be an indicator of the areas in which the perfectionist family member feels that he or she is inadequate.

Poor Communication.   Communication may be strained, ineffective, or nonexistent. Family members may have difficulty communicating their wants and needs to other members, which can result in misunderstandings and little self-expression. Poor communication often occurs throughout the entire dysfunctional family.

Lack of Diversity.   A lack of diversity in a family is a sign that a family may be dysfunctional. Diversity, in this instance, refers primarily to differences in interests and beliefs between family members. An example of this would be several children from a family who all have the same interests and aspirations as one of their parents.

Reflection...

It is one thing to memorize lists of the desirable and undesirable characteristics of families and quite another to be able to identify them in action. For novices in this field, movies and TV can be a good way to practice identifying these characteristics. Remember that all families display behaviors from both lists of behaviors. However, the frequency and nature of the behaviors is an important element when trying to understand the dynamics of a family. The following movie and TV programs provide good practice activities.

▶ *Parenthood* (1989) PG-13
  A comedy about life's most rewarding occupation: parenthood. Gil and Karen Buckman are facing the age-old dilemma of trying to raise their children the "right" way. But as Gil and the rest of his clan soon discover, being the "perfect" parent often means just letting children be themselves. Although this film is old, it is still timely.

▶ *Parenthood* (TV)
  Parenthood is an American comedy-drama television series based on the film of the same title. It is like the movie in that it is amusing and interesting and it provides a number of families each with their own idiosyncrasies to lend to the mixture. Last (Spring 2010) season's programs are available for purchase. The program is scheduled for the 2010–2011 season. You may need to watch two or three programs to understand the dynamics.

What makes the effects of a dysfunctional family particularly disturbing is that often these feelings do not cease or even decrease when children leave their dysfunctional homes. Unless there is some sort of positive intervention, they will become adults that are handicapped by the messages they received from their dysfunctional families and are often doomed to repeat them. Their legacy is a lifetime of trying to prove that they are worthwhile people. In addition, they may become parents who perpetuate the pain of the dysfunctional family.

Summary

The family is a wonderful institution. It prepares children to fit into the larger world while teaching them that they have a responsibility to family, community, country, and others. It is a place where children are loved and nurtured and experiment with new behaviors in this secure social laboratory.

The idea of what constitutes a family has changed dramatically in the last 50 years. We know that it is the way a family functions, as opposed to its configuration, that tells us how successful a family is. No family is perfect. All families have problems and challenges, but in a functional family those become part of the learning experience.

We as educators handicap ourselves if we do not understand the nature of families. And, as part of this understanding, we are obliged to be generous with our appreciation of the efforts that parents make. We must also remember that the great majority of parents love their children and want the very best for them.

Recommended Activities

1. Write a description of your family of origin. Include a description of family roles, rituals, relationships, and so forth. You may wish to include pictures and mementos to support your description.
2. Select a period of history and describe family life, then compare it to your family unit.
3. Interview a parent of a single-parent home, a blended family, and an intact family. You might want to ask about family rituals, roles, decision making, and so forth.
4. Examine popular magazines, cut out pictures of 50 families, and make observations.
5. Invite a family therapist to discuss with the class functional and dysfunctional families and therapeutic interventions for the latter.

Children's Books

The following children's books are suggested as a way of helping your students consider issues in this chapter.

Children and Divorce

It's Not Your Fault, Koko Bear: A Book for Parents and Young Children During Divorce
Vicki Lansky, Jane Prince (Illustrator)
Reading Level: Ages 4–8
Book Peddlers (1998)

Don't Fall Apart on Saturdays! The Children's Divorce-Survival Book
Adolph Moser, David Melton (Illustrator)
Reading Level: Ages 9–12
Landmark Editions Inc. (2000)

What Can I Do? A Book for Children of Divorce
Danielle Lowry, Bonnie J. Matthews (Illustrator)
Reading Level: Ages 9–12
Imagination Press (2001)

*Help! A Girl's Absolutely Indispensable Guide
    to Divorce and Stepfamilies (American Girl
    Library)*
Nancy Holyoke
Reading Level: Ages: 9–12
Sagebrush (1999)

Unmarried Parents

*The Red Blanket: Children's Adoption by Single
    Parent*
Eliza Thomas, Joe Cepeda (Illustrator)
Reading Level: For infants or children in preschool
Scholastic, Inc. (2004)

*Everything You Need to Know About Living
    with a Single Parent*
Richard E. Mancini
Reading Level: Young Adult
Rosen Publishing Group (1999)

*Best Single Mom in the World: How I Was
    Adopted*
Mary Zisk
Reading Level: Ages 5–8
Albert Whitman (2001)

Stepfamilies

*Chelsea's Tree: A Story for Step Children and
    Stepkids*
March McCann (Author)
Reading Level: Ages 9–10
Inspiration Publisher (2001)

Two Homes
Claire Masurel, Kady McDonald Denton
    (Illustrator)
Reading Level: For infants or children in
    preschool
Candlewick (2003)

My Stepfamily
Julie Johnson
Reading Level: Ages 4–8
Stargazer Books (2004)

The Steps
Rachel Cohn
Reading Level: Ages 8–12
Simon & Schuster (2004)

*I Only See My Dad on Weekends: Kids Tell
    Their Stories About Divorce and Blended
    Families (Kids Helping Kids)*
Beth Matthews, Andrew Adams, Karen
    Dockrey
Reading Level: Young Adult
Chariot Family (1994)

*Stepliving for Teens: Getting Along with
    Stepparents and Siblings*
Joel D. Block, Susan S. Bartell
Reading Level: Young Adult
Penguin Putnam Books for Young Readers
    (2001)

Additional Resources

Family Organizations

National Council on Family Relations
Phone: 888-781-9331
www.ncfr.com

National Congress of Parents and Teachers
Phone: 312-670-6782
www.NCFR.org

Single-Parent Families
Books

Teyber, E. (2001). *Helping children cope with divorce*
    (Rev. ed.). San Francisco: Jossey-Bass.

Child psychologist Teyber, who teaches psychology
at California State University at San Bernardino,
says parents can ameliorate the harsh impact by

addressing their children's concerns with sensitivity and compassion. Among the difficulties he covers are children's separation anxiety at a parent's departure; guilt feelings ("If I was good . . ."); and fantasies of reuniting Mom and Dad. Teyber also discusses custody disputes and arrangements, post-divorce parenting concerns, and stepparenting. Urging parents to watch for and respect their children's responses to the alterations of divorce, he offers an understanding guide to negotiating this disturbing process.

Single Parenting

Organizations

Parents Without Partners, Inc.
Email: pwp@jti.net
www.parentswithoutpartners.org/index.htm

Single Parents Association Online
Phone: 623-581-7445
Email: spa@singleparents.org
www.singleparents.org

Stepparents

Books

Shimberg, E. F. (1999). *Blending Families: A Guide for Parents, Stepparents, and Everyone Building a Successful New Family.* Berkley: Berkley Publishing Group.

Today more Americans are part of a second-marriage family than a first. Inevitably, these newly blended stepfamilies will be confronted by their own special problems and needs. This insightful problem-solving guide offers solid solutions and includes real-life stories from families that have been through the adjustment process. ISBN: 0-425-16677-5.

Videos
An American Step Family

This video examines some of the problems faced by blended families. (26 minutes, color). Purchase and rental.

> Films for the Humanities & Sciences
> Phone: 800-257-5126

Divorce and the Family: When Parents Divorce

A clearheaded, unemotional look at the reality of a divorce. It takes viewers inside the minds of parents and teenage children to learn their fears and hopes as their world changes. A Learning Seed video. (24 minutes)

> Magna System, Inc.
> www.magnasystemsvideos.com/index.html

Organizations

Stepfamily Association of America
Phone: 402-477-7837
www.saafamilies.org/index.htm

References

Berger, E. H. & Riojas-Cortez, Mari. (2012). *Parents as partners in education: Families and schools working together* (8th ed.). Upper Saddle River, NJ: Pearson.

Coontz, S. (2000). *The way we never were: American families and the nostalgia trap* (2nd ed.). New York: Basic Books.

Dobbins, A. (2010). *Number of married families with children.* Retrieved March 4, 2007 from www.huffingtonpost.com/2007/03/04/number-of-married-familie_n_42568.html

Field, J., & Casper, L. M. (2001). *America's families and living arrangements: Population characteristics (Current Population Reports P20–537).* Washington, DC: U.S. Census Bureau.

Ganong, L. H., & Coleman, M. (2008). *Stepfamily relationships: Development, dynamics, and interventions.* New York: Plenum.

Gordon, A., & Browne, K. (2011). *Beginning and beyond* (8th ed.). Albany, NY: Delmar.

Harlem World. (2010, May 26). Census: Interracial marriage rising [Web log post]. Retrieved from http://harlemworldblog.wordpress.com/2010/05/26/census-interracial-marriage-rising/

Krysan, M., Moore, K. A., & Zill, N. (2006). *Research on successful families.* Retrieved from http://aspe.hhs.gov/daltcp/Reports/ressucfa.htm

Lehman, J. (2004). *The Total Transformation Program.* Westbrook, ME: Legacy Publishing.

National Center for Health Statistics. (2007). *First births by unmarried women.* Retrieved from www.unmarried.org/statistics.html

Painter, G., & Levine, D. I. (2000). Family structure and youth outcomes. *Journal of Human Resources, 35*(3), 524–549.

Shim, M. K., Felner, R. D., & Shim, E. (2000, April 24–28). *The effects of family structures on academic achievement.* Paper presented at the annual meeting of the American Educational Research Association, New Orleans, LA.

Skolnick, A. S., & Skolnick, J. H. (2009). *Family in transition* (16th ed.). Boston: Pearson.

U.S. Census Bureau. (2007). *America's families and living arrangements.* Retrieved from http://mbhs.bergtraum.K12.ny.us/cybereng/nyt/unwed-mo.htm

Chapter Three

Family Diversity

Sandra Winn Tutwiler
Washburn University

Diversity comes in many forms when discussing families. Even "mainstream" families (generally white, middle class, etc.) are different from one another. Still, there are some family characteristics that bind families together into various groups. This chapter examines some of those characteristics: structural, ethnic/cultural, and religious. This chapter helps you:

▶ Become better informed about nontraditional families, such as gay and lesbian families and grandparent-headed families.

▶ Consider the degree of assimilation of ethnic/cultural families and recognize the importance of this information.

▶ Consider some of the familial characteristics of African American, Asian American, Hispanic, and American Indian families.

▶ Consider how religious diversity affects families.

The Changing Family

Families in the United States have historically varied in structure, social and economic status, ethnic/cultural background, and religious tradition. These characteristics contribute to diversity among families. They underpin differences in language, customs, attitudes, behaviors, values, and everyday living circumstances existing among family units.

This chapter focuses on three attributes that contribute to family diversity: family structure, ethnic/cultural background, and religious traditions. Although each of these family characteristics is discussed separately, it is the particular combination of attributes that comprises a family's distinctiveness and influences the manner in which a family conducts its day-to-day functioning. Understanding differences among families allows school personnel to structure a variety of strategies for working with families. School and home connections are likely to be enhanced when teachers and other school personnel are respectful of a family's living circumstances, as well as the unique ways a family might support the education of their children.

As noted in the previous chapter, conventional notions of a traditional or typical family are influenced by a family structure that gained prominence in the late 18th and early 19th centuries and again in the 1950s. However, the family as a social institution has experienced many transformations that profoundly influence not only the ways in which we understand what constitutes "family," but also the function of the family unit. A discussion of diversity among families promotes more awareness and acceptance of differences among family units as they exist in contemporary life.

The relationship between parents and schools may be affected by faulty perceptions schools hold of given groups. Typically, school expectations of families reflect behaviors, value orientations, and capabilities of middle-class nuclear families. In this way, uniform standards for measuring familial competency exist that often ignore the diversity of contributions families may bring to the educational setting. Stephanie Coontz, author of *The Way We Never Were* (2000), points out that unrealistic expectations about what families can and should do detract from the confidence families from diverse families may feel as they attempt to solve problems based on circumstances in which they live. Given the increase in diversity among school populations today, it is very important for school personnel to recognize the variety of ways families may conceive of and carry out their roles in the educational lives of their children.

Family Structure

There are perhaps as many family types as there are individual families, but broad configurations of these families allow us to consider and understand families more easily. The previous chapter carefully examined single-parent families and blended families. This chapter will briefly examine the functioning of two-parent families, grandparents as parents, and gay and lesbian families, but it is primarily dedicated to the ethnic/cultural diversity of families.

We all know the stereotype of the family—a mother, a father, and two children. In actuality, only 35% of families fit this picture of the stereotypical U.S. family, with twice as many families fitting into some other family model (Frey, 2003).

Married-Couple Families

One form of married-couple family includes a husband, wife, and their biological and/or adopted children. Sociologists often call this family form an *intact family*. It is important to note that this is not a value judgment but merely a descriptive term. Another configuration of the married couple with children is the blended family. Although these two families function very differently, they have a similar appearance. Slightly more than one-third of all family households consist of married couples with children. This family structure is represented at all economic levels, as well as among all ethnic/cultural groups in the United States.

Families are not static and throughout history have changed, often due to social forces outside of the family unit itself. For example, economic changes, job opportunities, and changes in social perceptions of who can be in charge of children's care have resulted in an increased number of women working outside the home. The increase in dual-earner families, where both mother and father work outside the home, and the concomitant decrease in the number of stay-at-home moms present families with the issue of ensuring that children are cared for while they are working. Affordable and quality child care, flexible work schedules, and more flexible maternal and paternal leave policies from employers are major concerns, not only for married-couple families but also for other families who have children home alone while adults are working. Just as employers have incorporated ways to accommodate the needs of working couples, many schools have also made changes to facilitate involvement of these parents in their children's education. A modification such as scheduling parent–teacher conferences for evening hours acknowledges the need for change in some school practices to adapt to the living circumstances of working couples.

Some working married couples prefer that a family member care for children while they are working. In some instances they reach out to an extended family member. This is the child-care solution for many ethnic minority couples who have maintained culturally valued extended family ties. Other dual-earner families may seek creative work schedules so that they may alternate being home to care for children.

Increased numbers of women in the workforce do not always result in dual-earner families. In some cases the mother is the primary wage earner, and fathers take over children's care and primary responsibility for the home. There was an 18% increase in the number of stay-at-home dads between 1994 and 2001, and in 2006, children were cared for by 143,000 men who had been out of the workforce for more than a year (Rochlen, McKelley, Suizzo, & Scaringi, 2008). Although men being primary caretakers in the home may be viewed as unique, it is simply a return to earlier practices where men were at the center of family life prior to early 19th century changes in the family. According to a study conducted by Rochen and colleagues (2008), stay-at-home dads in contemporary families tend to be satisfied with their roles in their families.

Another type of married-couple family on the rise is the biracial/multiracial family. This family structure may consist of a husband and wife from different races with biracial/multiracial children, or parents of the same racial background who adopt a child from a different racial background. In 2008, 14.6% of new marriages were made up of spouses from different race or ethnic backgrounds, with 9% of whites, 16% of blacks, 26% of Hispanics, and 31% of Asians engaged in this type of union (Passel, Wang, & Taylor, 2010). Married couples from different racial or ethnic backgrounds experience the same issues as other married couples. However, they may also be confronted with lingering oppositions to interracial marriage and the impact this may have on their children both within and outside of school. As a result, some aspects of family dynamics may be influenced by the reactions of those outside of the family to the unique makeup of these families.

Alternative Family Structures

The U.S. family is diverse in a variety of ways (culture/ethnicity, economic status, etc.). We tend to see this as a recent phenomenon when in fact there always has been diversity within and between family groups. However, the numbers and the nature of them are certainly changing: father-headed homes, foster homes, children living with a variety of relatives, and so forth. This section examines two nontraditional families: grandparent-headed homes and gay/lesbian families.

Grandparents as Parents

The number of homes in which grandparents are rearing the children of their children is increasing. Grandparents rarely become responsible for their grandchildren under pleasant circumstances. Parental neglect, illness, substance abuse, and incarceration are among the reasons grandparents become responsible for raising grandchildren. Most grandparents are unprepared for the social, emotional, and financial toll that accompanies taking on responsibility for raising children. Social time with peers becomes more limited, and it is not uncommon for grandparents to experience depression, health problems, and fatigue as a result of their new responsibilities. Although grandparents may feel totally committed to their grandchildren, they may hold resentment toward their children for placing them in an unanticipated position. Further, many grandparents experience financial pressures brought about by the need to support their grandchildren (Gladstone, Brown, & Fitzgerald, 2009).

Custodial grandparents are often in positions where they can work with social welfare agencies, given the circumstances that led to them becoming responsible for their grandchildren. In some instances, issues such as a lack of trust of the agency or a social worker, feelings that their challenges will not be understood, and obstructive agency policies may interfere with grandparents taking full advantage of services and supports social welfare agencies may be able to offer. Viewing grandparents as consumers as opposed to clients may alleviate some of the tension that interferes with grandparents and agencies working together (Gladstone, Brown, & Fitzgerald, 2009).

Teachers can also play a role in support of custodial grandparents by making them aware of available supports, such as after-school care or programs, support groups, or additional agencies that may offer support (Winn Tutwiler, 2005).

Although the number of grandparents as primary caregivers has increased due to a variety of societal problems, there are other more positive reasons for this family configuration. It is common for grandmothers in some cultures (many American Indian groups, for example) to assume parental responsibilities.

Gay- and Lesbian-Headed Families

Gay and lesbian families are more conspicuous and more numerous than in the past. Whereas this family structure may be controversial in some sections of society, an increasing number of children are being raised in gay and lesbian households. Although there are societal hesitations to label these households "families," their numbers are underestimated by as much as 60% (Smith & Gates, 2001). The reluctance of many gay and lesbian parents to let their sexual orientation be known accounts for much of the difficulty in gathering exact numbers for this family type.

For many gay and lesbian parents, children were the result of a previous heterosexual bond. However, artificial insemination and adoption are increasingly used as means for becoming parents. Gay and lesbian families may take a number of forms and span the socioeconomic continuum. Many families are headed by two women or two men in a partner relationship; some are blended families in which both parents bring a child or children to the family unit; some are single-parent families; and in some instances, a gay man may father a child with a lesbian and parenting is shared.

Reflection...

Explore your thoughts and feelings about gay and lesbian parents. How will your attitude affect the children of gay and lesbian parents?

Gay and lesbian parents differ in the extent to which they prepare their children for possible negative experiences in reaction to the parents' lifestyle. Some children are accepting of their parents' lifestyle, whereas others may feel they have a secret that must be kept. School personnel must reflect on their views of families headed by homosexuals. Behaviors that inhibit or support school–home relations will not go unnoticed by these parents. Attitudes that allow parents to interact on school- or family-related issues based on their chosen level of openness about their sexual orientation are more likely to enhance school–home relations.

Ethnic and Cultural Diversity

A position of dominance for European American culture occurred in the 17th century. The English language, customs, laws, and religion were transported to the colonies by English immigrants, who made up the majority of early settlers. Although cultural shifts have evolved over the centuries, Euro-American cultural dominance has been maintained and is now known as mainstream America—white and middle class. Perceptions of suitability for and/or acceptance into the Anglo-American way of life has differed for various groups. For example, blacks who inhabited the colonies in the 17th century were viewed as unsuitable for assimilation into the Anglo-American way of life. Immigrants from Germany, Ireland, and Scandinavia were more readily accepted than were Italians, Jews, Croatians, Poles, and other southern and eastern Europeans who immigrated to the United States.

Assimilation-Acculturation-Enculturation Continuum

The assimilation-acculturation-enculturation continuum describes the range of ways ethnic/minority families today may choose to interact with the dominant culture (Winn Tutwiler, 2005). In the past, immigrant groups were expected to conform to the established way of life in the United States. Families and schools were pivotal institutions in the process of conformity, with the latter positioned to play a major role in the process of assimilation. Assimilation is the process by which one group adopts the cultural norms of a more dominant group—and incorporates the behaviors, beliefs, language patterns, and values of that group into their everyday lives. In the United States, assimilated individuals conform to cultural norms set by European Americans and abdicate cultural characteristics of their ethnic group. However, assimilation into a mainstream culture represents but one possible outcome of interaction between a dominant culture and various ethnic groups.

Some individuals from ethnic/cultural minority backgrounds engage in a process of acculturation. Acculturated individuals are fully aware of dominant culture norms, behaviors, values, and language, and use these to interact with dominant culture social institutions. However, unlike fully assimilated individuals, acculturated individuals maintain aspects of family life that are closely tied to ethnic cultural traditions. They are often equally knowledgeable and comfortable in two cultures and may be described as being *bicultural*.

A third possibility is enculturation. *Enculturation* or *ethnic socialization* is a process by which developing individuals acquire cultural teaching from family, peers, and the ethnic community that allows for development of qualities necessary to function as a member of the ethnic group. The individual develops an ethnic identity. Ethnic group members, to varying degrees, may engage in enculturation.

The distinctions between assimilation, acculturation, and enculturation should be viewed more in terms of degrees rather than rigid categories of family behavior. For example, the fluidity between acculturation and enculturation may be difficult to discern to someone outside of a family unit. However, acculturated families are more like assimilated families than are enculturated families. As a result, there may be less pressure for children of acculturated families to engage in culturally based traditions than there would be for children in enculturated families. Still, it is important for school personnel to understand how families identify themselves with respect to their ethnic/cultural backgrounds. Differences among various ethnic/cultural groups in language, customs, child-rearing practices, and values existing in the home could be explained in part by a family's position along the assimilation-acculturation-enculturation continuum (Winn Tutwiler, 2005).

A focus on culturally relevant education recognizes that children from diverse ethnic/cultural backgrounds may have a range of needs in terms of ensuring a connection between learning experiences and the background experiences children bring to school from the home. Hence, it is important to view ethnic/cultural distinctions routinely associated with a particular group, not so much as prescriptions for the functioning of particular families, but rather as descriptions of possible characteristics, behaviors, or attitudes a family may incorporate into day-to-day existence.

Reflection...

Consider the cultural behaviors of your family. Do your family traditions include special foods, activities, celebrations, and so on? How do these tie into your cultural background?

Mainstream Families

As mentioned early in this chapter, a "typical" U.S. family does not exist. Still, values, customs, and behaviors exist within certain families that are more reflective of values and attitudes accepted as mainstream cultural norms. For example, when compared with the norms of some minority ethnic group families, mainstream culture families tend to be more democratically oriented, with children having the opportunity to express their views and wishes. It would not be disrespectful for the child to question or challenge authority figures, including parents themselves.

Children are encouraged to be individuals and to make decisions for themselves early on, with parents in the role of providing support and guidance. Parents have high expectations that children will develop a sense of responsibility for their actions, learn to rely on themselves, and, over time, develop a level of independence believed necessary to function as adults.

This focus on individualism envelops the family unit as well, because the nuclear or immediate family is valued over an extended one in the day-to-day functioning of the family. In fact, mainstream culture families generally confer less respect to the elderly when compared with some minority ethnic group cultures.

Another characteristic generally attributed to mainstream culture families is the focus on the importance of punctuality and attention to schedules. An adherence to both is seen as a sign of politeness and responsible behavior. The maxim "getting the job done" is an expression of an orientation toward completing tasks in a timely manner.

A competitive spirit underlines a drive for personal accomplishment in education, work, and play. A mainstream culture belief that the individual has some control over his or her destiny supports the notion that adversity can be overcome through hard work.

Although formal education is highly valued, children are given the opportunity and expected to achieve in other learning and performing situations as well. Activities such as athletics and vocal or instrumental music, whether an extension of school activities or privately arranged, are examples of areas in which hard work leads to personal accomplishment and contributes to the development of a well-rounded individual.

Although these family characteristics may be observable in any number of family situations, they are more likely observable in European American middle-class families, as well as in more assimilated middle-class ethnic minority families.

African American Families

The history of African Americans in the United States, including 200 years of enslavement, followed by years of segregation, discrimination, racial oppression, and both overt and institutionalized racism, plays a large role in characteristics exhibited in varying degrees among these families. Today, African Americans are approximately 12% of the population nationally (U.S. Census Bureau, 2004), with substantial numbers living in urban cities where crime, poor housing, high unemployment, underemployment, and the lack of adequate services persist. Despite an increase in the number of African Americans acquiring post–high school education and attaining middle-class status, substantial numbers continue to live in poverty. Inequities continue in health care, employment, and quality of life between African Americans and European Americans.

Even with differences in social and economic class, survival and protection of one's family remains a predominant theme among African Americans. Concern over racism and biased treatment from both individuals and institutions influences many behaviors and attitudes among African American families. Valuing an extended family, for example, represents a belief that a larger, interdependent group stands a better chance of moving through barriers to survival. As part of the value of an extended family, the elderly are held in a position of respect, and African American children learn early to value and obey the elderly, even those to whom they are not related. Indeed, a sense of kinship often extends beyond blood relations to other members of the community.

Kinship ties also play a role in ensuring that children are cared for. When parents and children were sold away from each other during slavery, children were taken care of by other adults on the plantation. Today informal adoptions by an aunt, uncle, grandmother, or even a cousin are common. Additionally, single parents (mother or father) faced with raising children without a spouse may turn to their kinship network for help and support.

The nurturance and protection of children is highly valued among African Americans. A strong belief that children need to be disciplined is complemented by the belief that children need time to be children. Hence, in many African American families, there is less focus on pushing the child toward independence and/or detachment from the family. When compared with peers in other ethnic groups, it is common to find African American young adults remaining with the family of origin for longer periods before establishing a home as an independent adult.

African American families have flexible family roles, a characteristic borne out of the social and economic circumstances faced by many African American families. Traditional gender roles for males and females may be reversed based on the needs of the family. Children may also assume some roles normally taken by parents. Historically, because both African American parents had to work, it was expected that older siblings would look after and often discipline their younger siblings. Generally, family members adapt to whatever role is needed for the family to function (Ladson-Billings, 1997).

Education is viewed as the way to a better life and thus has traditionally been held in high esteem by African Americans. This characteristic was supported by a study conducted by Ritter, Mont-Reynaud, and Dornbusch (1993), which focused on minority parent attitudes toward the education of their children. The study included students and parents from various ethnic minority groups, at various social and economic levels. Based on survey responses, African American parents emphasized hard work in academic areas (e.g., math, English, social studies) and more frequently reacted both positively and negatively to grades of their high school students. Although these parents also appeared to have more working knowledge of "school ways," including awareness of homework, school schedules, and the importance of course selection, they also tended to have higher levels of mistrust toward schools than some of the other ethnic minority parents included in the study.

Many African American families believe that it is necessary for children to understand racism, as well as the history and the contribution of African Americans in the United States, as a means for the child's self-protection and survival. African Americans are particularly sensitive to acts perceived as racist. They want children to be able to discern negative actions directed toward them that are based on the color of their skin and have little to do with their character. This distinction is seen as important in helping the child develop a positive self-esteem. The movement by some African American parents to seek alternative educational experiences (e.g., Afrocentric schools, charter schools, homeschooling) highlights, in part, the importance of the development of this self-protective capacity.

Reflection...

Do you have African American or other ethnic minority friends? If not, why not? Describe ways we can develop friendships with people of different ethnic backgrounds and how we can model this for the children we teach.

Like many other ethnic minority families, African American families are challenged by the assimilation-acculturation-enculturation dilemma. Historically, African Americans have come together as an interdependent group to address issues that might improve the life circumstances (e.g., education, employment, and housing) of the group. In fact, it is common to hear African Americans speak of "the community" as an entity that embraces all African Americans. There is an underlying expectation that the community should receive benefits from the successes of the individual. However, being successful in academic and work settings is often tantamount to leaving the community, an action believed to be an integral part of upward social mobility. This circumstance presents a dilemma for some African American families. Broadway (1987), for example, found that African American middle-class families were specifically concerned that their children learn to function in Euro-American middle-class contexts, while at the same time maintaining close cultural ties with the African American community.

Implied is a recognition among some African American families of the bicultural nature of African Americans. For example, many African Americans, particularly middle-class African Americans, are well versed in both Standard and Black English and can switch into using either, depending on the situation. W. E. B. Dubois referred to this talent as having a double consciousness. This consciousness basically allowed African Americans to exist in two different worlds, one black and one white (Lewis, 2003). African Americans have a prized oral tradition in which the use of language is highly valued. Indeed, some African Americans describe themselves as bilingual as well as bicultural, believing that some expressions lose richness of meaning when translated into Standard English.

As is the case with other ethnic minority groups, African Americans are a very diverse group. The extent to which they embrace the characteristics cited above will vary. School personnel are thus challenged to get to know individual families in order to understand more clearly how they identify themselves with respect to ethnic group characteristics.

Asian American Families

Asian Americans originate from countries including China, Japan, Korea, Cambodia, Laos, Vietnam, and India. They are clearly a very diverse people. The experiences of Asian American families will depend to some extent on the circumstances surrounding their immigration to the United States. Some Asian Americans arrived in the United States as highly educated professionals, having marketable skills, and/or as bilingual and familiar with the mainstream culture in the United States. Still others arrived with low levels of education, languages other than English, and experiencing high levels of culture shock due to a lack of familiarity with this country. For example, Korean Americans have one of the highest levels of education among all ethnic groups, as well as high rates of self-employment. Like the first wave of Vietnamese, they were well educated in their homeland. More recent refugees from Vietnam,

Cambodia, and Laos tend to have lower levels of education and experience higher levels of unemployment in the United States (Chan, 1992).

The assimilation-acculturation-enculturation balance also influences the experience of Asian Americans. Throughout their history in the United States, Asian Americans have experienced varying levels of acceptance and rejection. For example, Chinese Americans, a culturally diverse group among themselves, were the first Asians to immigrate to the United States. Forty-two years later, they were banned from immigration as a result of the Chinese Exclusion Act of 1882. Anti-Chinese sentiment, fueled by racism and economic tension, led to this federal law, which was not repealed until 1943. We might also remember the imprisonment of people of Japanese ancestry, the vast majority of whom were U.S. citizens, in relocation centers during World War II. Today, however, Asian Americans are stereotypically looked upon as a "model minority" (Lee, 1996).

Like other racial/ethnic minority groups, Asian American families are subjected to additional stereotypes that function to minimize the diverse cultural and historical backgrounds existing in this group. As Yao (1993) points out, it is impossible to describe a "typical" Asian American family. Although there is great diversity in the backgrounds, languages, religions, and customs among Asian Americans, there are some generalizations that can be stated about Asian American families.

The family is the primary social unit among Asians; hence its preservation is important to the maintenance of the social, political, religious, and economic order. The strongest familial bonds are between parent and child, rather than between parents themselves. The male is perceived as the head of the family. Unlike the democratic model existing in many mainstream culture families, parents are clearly the authority figures in Asian American families. Unquestioning obedience to parental control is expected from the child. In fact, the close supervision children receive from their parents is perceived as a sign of parental love. It is considered disrespectful for a child to question parental love and authority.

Asian Americans have high expectations for their children academically and also value upward mobility. Achievement is considered part of the child's obligation to the family, rather than a personal accomplishment. The child's success, or lack thereof, is a source of pride or embarrassment to parents. Asian American parents believe that children should not be rewarded for what they are expected to do. In fact acknowledgment of accomplishments comes in the form of encouragement to do better, whereas failure to meet parental expectations results in punishment. The child may be chastised verbally and excluded from family social life (Espiritu, 1992).

At the same time, parents make many personal sacrifices for their children in order to facilitate their success. Family goals of achievement and upward mobility result in a high number of families in which both parents work outside the home. For recent immigrants who may have education and job skill limitations, it is not uncommon for parents to work long hours and/or have more than one job.

Asian American families tend to have distinct boundaries between educational responsibilities of the home and school. Teachers are highly respected and parents are not likely to contradict what is said by the teacher in his or her presence. Concurrently, matters more directly connected to the process of schooling (e.g., curriculum, discipline) are believed to be the province of the school. Within the home, parents closely watch the progress of the child, while encouraging the child to increase his or her performance.

Despite striking differences between behaviors, attitudes, and values of Asian American and mainstream culture families, it is often suggested that other ethnic minorities adopt Asian American child-rearing practices. Indeed, some Asian Americans view the label of "model minority" as a burden. The concomitant label of "superior students" assigned to Asian American children adds to the pressure these students already feel from high expectations emanating from the home. Additionally, the academic difficulty experienced by some Asian American students is often overlooked because of a perception that Asian American children are "smart students" (Shen & Mo, 1990). Academic pressures and other difficulties felt by Asian American students may go unnoticed, owing to some extent to the lessons taught in the home regarding social and emotional restraint. Discussing problems may be difficult for students, as well as for their parents.

Tradition passed through the ages continues to have a valued position within some Asian American families. The differences between Eastern and Western beliefs, customs, and values are often the basis of conflict between Asian American children and their parents. In fact, some families attempt to protect their children from outside influences by controlling those with whom the child comes in contact (e.g., peers, playmates). Nonetheless, influences of Western customs and values inadvertently cause tension in many Asian American families, especially families of more recent immigrants who may be less familiar with customs in this country. Schools and other social service institutions working to assist and support the transition of these families into their new home in the United States must take care not to undermine parental authority in the process.

Hispanic Families

Hispanics are not only the fastest growing minority group, but also the fastest growing segment of the population. They include Mexican Americans, Cuban Americans, Puerto Ricans, and other Central and South Americans. Each of these groups has a different historical background that continues to influence their experience in contemporary U.S. society. Many Mexican Americans, or Chicanos, as many prefer, trace their ancestry to those who lived on the land that is today California, Texas, New Mexico, and Colorado. This land was ceded to the United States at the conclusion of the Mexican War in 1848. Others trace their ancestry to immigrants who fled Mexico in search of work during the Mexican Revolution of 1910.

Like many Mexican Americans, Puerto Ricans are U.S. citizens as a result of land ceded to the United States following a war. The United States obtained Puerto Rico at the end of the Spanish-American War and later made the inhabitants of the island citizens of the United States. Today, Puerto Ricans live on both the island and mainland United States.

Cuban Americans immigrated to the United States as refugees beginning in 1959, with the reign of Castro. Early Cuban immigrants were wealthy professionals. However, the last wave of Cuban immigrants, those who were a part of the Mariel exodus of 1980, consisted of what Cuba referred to as its "social undesirables" (Suarez, 1993). The experience of the earlier Cuban Americans differs from that of the general population of Puerto Ricans and Mexican Americans, who tend to experience more discrimination, poverty, and higher school dropout rates. Approximately 26% of Hispanics live in poverty (Jones & Fuller, 2003), and, as noted earlier, this number increases when the family is headed by a single parent. In addition, Hispanics have a disproportionately high dropout rate (National Center for Educational Statistics, 2001).

Even with these differences, there are commonalities shared by Hispanic families that provide insight into the dynamics operating within these families. Regardless of class, religion, and length of time in the United States, Hispanics traditionally value the family as an important resource for coping with life's stresses. Family is defined as a closely bonded group that may extend beyond bloodlines. It is common for family members to prefer living close to each other, in order to more easily accommodate the financial and emotional support extended to family members.

Children hold an exalted position in the family. In fact, the birth of a child validates a marriage (Jones & Fuller, 2003). Hispanic families are generally less concerned about children reaching developmental benchmarks and tend to be more permissive and indulgent with young children when compared with mainstream culture families. Still, children have family-related responsibilities, such as helping with household chores or caring for siblings. Children are taught to respect elders and are expected to interact with others in a respectful and polite manner. Child-rearing practices among Hispanics are traditionally geared to prepare children for their role in sustaining the function of the family in Hispanic culture.

There is concern, however, among some Hispanics over what appears to be an erosion of traditional supports expected of the family. More-assimilated, younger Hispanics who are focused on upward mobility are leaving the more traditional customs behind, including the traditional values of sharing and support among family members. The concern over the rift between old ways and new, more-assimilated ways also extends to the implications these divisions have for the Spanish language as essential to maintaining a Hispanic culture. Younger Hispanics may not speak Spanish, whereas the elderly may not speak English. This lack of communication contributes to the erosion of traditional ways.

Parents of children in public schools may have limited English as well. When combined with poverty, this lack of English proficiency often results in barriers between schools and Hispanic families, as well as for other language minority parents (e.g., Asian American parents). Language proficiency is to not be confused with parental competency. Hence, a number of schools seek ways to minimize language barriers (e.g., through translators) in order to maintain communication between the school and the home.

Case Study

Jimmy Yazzie, age 5, lives in Los Angeles where he attends kindergarten. He loves to go on picnics at any of a number of ocean beaches. He enjoys playing in the sand, picking up shells, and running along the ocean edge, but most of all he likes surfing. His big brothers are accomplished surfers and often help Jimmy pretend that he is surfing. He can hardly wait until he is old enough to have his own surfboard to surf in the deep water with his brother.

Jimmy Yazzie is Navajo and lives in Los Angeles with his family. Both of his parents were also born in Los Angeles, as were his brothers. Although both sets of his grandparents were born on the Navajo reservation, they moved to Los Angeles with their families while they were in high school. Jimmy has never been on a reservation and knows very little of his Indian heritage. He and his family are generally assimilated into the mainstream society.

His kindergarten teacher is a well-meaning woman who cares very much for her students and works hard to meet their needs. However, she sees Jimmy as an "Indian" boy and tries to modify her teaching style to meet his perceived needs. This would be highly appropriate if he were a traditional Indian; however, although Jimmy is proud of being Navajo, his family is generally part of the mainstream population.

Questions and Considerations

1. How might Jimmy's teacher determine his degree of assimilation into the mainstream population?
2. How might his teacher celebrate his background? Or should she?
3. If a teacher has a number of children of a given culture other than mainstream in his or her class (e.g., Hispanic), how might the teacher determine levels of assimilation?

American Indian Families

At the time of the arrival of Columbus in 1492, an estimated 5 million American Indians (labeled Indians based on European explorers' mistaken belief that they had traveled to the Far East) lived in North America. Nearly 400 years later, the American Indian population had decreased to approximately 600,000. Warfare and death due to new contagious diseases introduced by Europeans decimated tribes who inhabited the land before the Europeans' arrival. The remaining American Indians were left without benefit of their warriors and their elders. The continuous loss of warriors left tribes unable to defend themselves in battle, and among some tribes the loss of elders equaled the loss of historical and cultural knowledge that sustained the social order and way of life for tribal members.

The American Indian way of life was further assaulted by continuous attempts at assimilation by European Americans. The English initially viewed American Indians as unworthy of the land they lived on because they were not Christian and later as unworthy of being included in an evolving European American way of life. By the late 1800s, however, concerted efforts were initiated to assimilate the now conquered indigenous peoples of North America. History is replete with descriptions of methods aimed at purging American Indians of their culture. The young have been the major target of these efforts. For example, the Bureau of Indian Affairs made an intensive effort to assimilate American Indians into the larger U.S. culture. This was accomplished by establishing industrial schools off the reservation. These schools were designed to eradicate American Indian culture and customs and replace them with European American culture (Trennert, 1990). Perhaps the most widely known effort of assimilation is the removal of American Indian children from their families on the reservation. These children were sent to boarding schools in which they were discouraged from using traditional ways and inculcated with European American culture and values. Today, there is an effort among American Indians to reestablish traditional values.

As we have observed with other ethnic minorities in this chapter, American Indians are also culturally diverse. As noted with other families, the discussion of family characteristics of American Indians is generally applicable to the group as a whole. The issue of assimilation and enculturation exists for American Indians as for other groups, with families fitting at various points along a continuum of traditional and more European ways of life.

Not surprisingly, children are prized in American Indian families. The family has traditionally played an intimate role in the education of children. In American Indian families, the term *family* is broadened to include the immediate and the extended family, and all adults in the family are responsible for teaching children. In fact, biological parents may not have primary responsibility for the child's care. There is traditionally a strong bond between grandparent and grandchild in American Indian cultures. The elderly are highly revered for their wisdom and experience in all areas and are thus consulted on issues of child rearing as well. Aunts and uncles are also involved with child rearing; in fact, the same kinship terms are used for mother-aunt and uncle-father (Cleary & Peacock, 1998).

Children are accorded respect in American Indian families and are not scolded or admonished. Rather, they are taught through explanation and example and provided with the reason a behavior is expected. The lessons of an expected behavior may be embedded in stories, which are also commonly used to provide children with knowledge of American Indian traditions, rituals, and beliefs.

The structure and functioning of American Indian families, like those of African American and Latino families, are consistent with a value in collectivism over individualism. Actions that support the needs of the community are more positively regarded than accomplishments and achievements motivated solely by self-aggrandizement. One's personal well-being is enhanced by giving to and sharing with others. As a result of this focus on the group rather than the individual, some American Indian children may exhibit behavior that could be labeled as shyness. They would rather not draw too much attention to themselves as individuals.

American Indian families currently have the lowest income and employment rates in the United States, and their children have the highest dropout rates of any group of students. In keeping with their cultural tradition, American Indian parents are calling for a larger role in making decisions about their children's education. They are especially interested in a culturally relevant curriculum and an increase in the number of American Indian teachers (Cleary & Peacock, 1998). Assimilationist educational practices historically disparage American Indian culture. Thus, parents are also interested in cross-cultural training for teachers in order to reduce the discontinuity between home and school (Szasz, 1991).

Reflection...

Too often we focus on the negative stereotypes and characteristics of ethnic groups. What are some common strengths of African American, Hispanic, Asian American, and American Indian families?

Religious Diversity

A majority of European immigrants during the colonial period were members of Protestant denominations. Not surprisingly, public education was founded on Protestant beliefs and values. Protestant denominations, including Lutheran, Methodist, Presbyterian, and Baptist, collectively make up the majority of religious affiliations in the United States today.

Students live in homes ranging from those in which religion is of little or no consequence to those in which religion is integral to the everyday functioning of the family. In some cases, religious tradition is intimately tied to ethnic/cultural traditions. For example, among some American Indian tribes spirituality is manifested through a belief that every living thing on earth is interconnected. Respect for all living things leads to harmony, an important attribute of American Indian culture. Among Asian Americans, life values, social norms, and beliefs are supported by the religious-philosophical teachings inherent in Confucianism, Taoism, and Buddhism (Chan, 1992). And although Judaism provides a link among many Jewish Americans, some Jews view themselves as a cultural minority as well.

The previously mentioned assimilation-acculturation-enculturation dilemma becomes an issue for ethnic/cultural groups for whom particular religious teaching is part of an ethnic/cultural group identity, because mainstream assimilation may lead to changes in religious beliefs and practices as well. In a similar manner, members of ethnic groups may follow nonmainstream religious practices and beliefs, albeit those that are not traditionally associated with their ethnic/cultural group. African Americans, for example, traditionally belong to Protestant denominations, although they may also follow the teachings of Catholicism or Judaism, and growing numbers are becoming Muslims. Hispanics in the United States are traditionally associated with the Roman Catholic church; however, this number has decreased approximately 20% over the last 25 years because immigrant Hispanics as well as those living in poverty are shifting to denominations believed to better serve their needs (Deck, 1994).

Even though schools have improved in their efforts to be more sensitive to the impact of school activities and practices on diverse religious traditions, instances continue to occur in which families perceive their religious values and beliefs to be in conflict with school practices. Moreover, the possibility of misunderstanding increases as religious beliefs and practices veer further away from traditional Protestantism. For example, the doctrine of Jehovah Witnesses forbids the celebration of holidays and birthdays. The children of these families will be in conflict if you expect them to join in the celebration. In addition, the rights of the family would be violated. Lunch menus with ham as the only entree overlook the Muslim and Jewish practice of not eating pork.

The freedom to worship at the church, synagogue, or mosque of one's choice contributes to the religious diversity of the United States. As educators, we must guard against making assumptions about the religion of our students. School personnel need only be prepared to listen to the family to accommodate the family's wishes, while taking care not to infringe on the rights of other families.

Reflection...

Consider your attitudes toward various religions. Do you have biases concerning other religions? Are there stereotypes that have affected your thinking? How could you investigate the accuracy of your perceptions?

Summary

Any general discussion of diversity among U.S. families is necessarily hindered by the richness and extent of that diversity. Additional family customs and values could be discussed within each of the broader ethnic/cultural groups mentioned. Characteristics of mainstream culture families discussed previously, for example, do not include the diversity of customs inherent in European American families. Additional families of African descent (e.g., Haitian, Ethiopian), Asian/Pacific Island families (e.g., Hawaiian, Samoan, Filipino), and American Indian Eskimo families could be discussed within the context of their respective ethnic groups. At the same time, the needs and challenges facing the growing number of transracial families could be addressed as well. Extension of a discussion on family structure might include the growing numbers of grandparents now raising their children's children, as well as families with adopted children.

Addressing family diversity is central to building constructive home–school relations. The combination of family characteristics (e.g., middle class, African American, single parent, United Methodist) provides important information for understanding how to work with a particular family. It is even more important, however, to learn from families how they define themselves within the context of observable characteristics in order to understand more clearly the attitudes and values operating within the family.

Teachers must be prepared to work with families who challenge their personal notions and experiences of what constitutes family. For this reason, it is important to read about and become familiar with cultures that are different from one's own. We may well be facing the eradication of the assimilating role historically assigned to schools. An understanding of diversity among families is not meant to provide information for development of strategies to change families so that they fit the needs of the school. Rather, it provides information that allows schools to change, so that they are inviting to the variety of families represented in contemporary school settings.

Recommended Activities

1. Interview (or videotape) families of two different ethnic/cultural groups and identify unique familial behaviors and those that are generally universal to all families.
2. Invite gay and lesbian parents to visit your class and share with you their family experiences.
3. Volunteer to work in a day-care center with children and families that are different from yours.
4. Visit churches different from your own and speculate how the doctrine of these churches would affect family life.
5. If families of particular ethnic or cultural backgrounds are not present in your community,

identify such families in other communities and have a telephone conference call. It would be helpful to the family for you to send pictures of the class members so that they can visualize the people to whom they are speaking. Also, ask them to send you some family pictures.

6. Identify the cultural characteristics of your family and how those characteristics have affected your family life. Describe a family you have known with a different cultural background and compare and contrast the two families.

Children's Books

The following children's books are suggested as a way of helping your students consider issues in this chapter.

The Family Book
Todd Parr
Reading Level: Ages 3–6
Little, Brown & Company (2003)

Who's in Family?
Robert Skutch, Laura Nienhaus (Illustrator)
Reading Level: Ages 4–8
Ten Speed Press (1998)

Socioeconomic Diversity

Going Home
Eve Bunting, David Diaz
Reading Level: Ages 4–8
HarperTrophy (1998)

Cultural Diversity

The Mexican American Family Album (The American Family Albums)
Dorothy Hoobler, Thomas Hoobler

Reading Level: Ages 9–12
Oxford University Press (1998)

The Chinese American Family Album (The American Family Albums)
Dorothy Hoobler
Reading Level: Ages 9–12
Oxford University Press (1998)

In My Family/En mi familia
Carmen Lomas Garza, Harriet Rohmer, David Schecter (Eds.)

Reading Level: Ages 4–8
Children's Books Press/Libros Para Niños (1996)

The Watsons Go to Birmingham—1963
Christopher Paul Curtis
Reading Level: Middle School and High School
Yearling (1997)

Less Than Half, More Than Whole
Kathleen Lacapa, Michael Lacapa
Reading Level: Ages 4–8
Rising Moon (1994)

Additional Resources

Cultural Diversity

Books

Erera, Pauline Irit. (2001). *Family diversity: Continuity and change in the contemporary family.* Thousand Oaks, CA: Sage Publications.

This nonjudgmental, inclusive, and far-reaching text focuses on the diverse patterns of family structure prevalent in our society today. *Family Diversity* presents empirical research on the internal dynamics, social environments, support factors, prevalence of discrimination, and common stereotypes that account for the issues surrounding current family relations. By examining the history and nature of foster and adoptive, single-parent, lesbian/gay, step- and grandparent family units, Pauline Irit Erera is able to challenge both the idealized family prototype and the hegemony of the traditional structure.

Hildebrand, V., Phenice, L. A., Gray, M. M., & Hines, R. P. (2008). *Knowing and serving diverse families* (3rd ed.). Upper Saddle River, NJ: Pearson.

This book, divided into four parts, offers suggestions on how to serve individual families and explores ethnic diversity and lifestyle variations among contemporary American families. It contains chapters that focus on African American, Hispanic American, Asian American, Arab American, Native American, and Amish families.

Kendall, F. E. (1996). *Diversity in the classroom: New approaches to the education of young children* (2nd ed.). New York: Teacher's College Press.

This is a book of contributions by some of the leading proponents of multicultural education. This book has a number of selections that will be helpful to a classroom teacher (talking with parents, preparing for a multicultural classroom, affirming diversity, etc.).

Organizations

Intercultural Development Research Association
Phone: 512-684-8180
www.idra.org

National Association of Multicultural Education (NAME)
Phone: 301-951-0022
www.name.org

African American Families

Books

Connor, M. E., & White, J. L. (2006). *Black fathers: An invisible presence in America.* Mahwah, NJ: Lawrence Erlbaum.

In the parlance of social psychology, social work, and urban social scientists, African American fathers have often been described as "absent," "missing," "nonresidential," "noncustodial," "unavailable," "nonmarried," "irresponsible," and "immature." It is wondered why it is so difficult to find literature, research, and comments regarding positive attributes of African American families in general and African American fathers in particular. This book fills a void in attempting to offer a broader picture of African American males as fathers.

Hutchinson, E. O. (1992). *Black fatherhood: A guide to male parenting.* Fort Atkinson, WI: Highsmith.

Black men of different generations tell what it means to be a father in America. The book features interviews with fathers of different occupations, incomes, and family circumstances.

Johnson, A. E., & Cooper, A. M. (1996). *A student's guide to African American genealogy: Oryx American family tree series.* Phoenix, AZ: Oryx Press.

This book is an excellent way to help African American students learn about their family history as well as informing non–African American teachers about native families. This book provides cultural background, an annotated bibliography, and interesting historical facts. In addition, it comes with color and black-and-white photographs and features a glossary and an index.

McLoyd, V. C., Hill, N. E., & Dodge, K. A. (2005). *African American family life: Ecological and cultural diversity* (Duke Series in Child Development). New York: Guilford Press.

This volume offers new perspectives on the cultural, economic, and community contexts of African American family life. Recognizing the diversity of contemporary African American families, leading experts from different disciplines present the latest knowledge on such topics as family formation, gender roles, child rearing, care of the elderly, and religious practices. Particular attention is given to how families draw on cultural resources to adapt to racial disparities in wealth, housing, education, and employment, and how culture in turn is shaped by these circumstances. Factors that promote or hinder healthy development are explored, as are research-based practices and policies for supporting families' strengths.

Taylor, R. J., Jackson, J. S., & Chatters, L. M. (1997). *Family life in black America.* Thousand Oaks, CA: Sage Publications.

Over the past 20 years, African American families have undergone tremendous changes, both demographically and socially. During this time, most of the studies of black families have focused on problems, such as out-of-wedlock births, single-parent families, and childhood poverty. Although an accurate appreciation of the challenges confronting black families is important and needed, a "problem focus" tends to offer a narrow, negative view and restricts the consideration of other important issues affecting families. *Family Life in Black America* moves away from this deficit perspective, and the result is enlightening both in its comprehensive reach and systematic scholarship. Readers of this volume will be pleased with the wide range of issues dealt with in this volume, including maturation, mate selection, sexuality, procreation, infancy, adulthood, adolescence, gender issues, young adulthood, cohabitation, parenting, grandparenting, and aging.

Chapter

Hildebrand, V., Phenice, L. A., Gray, M. M., & Hines, R. P. (2008). African American families. In *Knowing and serving diverse families* (3rd ed.), (pp. 63–83). Upper Saddle River, NJ: Pearson.

Article

Jones, E. (1993). An interview on the topic, "Changing church confronts the changing Black family." *Ebony, 18*(10), 94–100.

Massaquoi, H. (1993). The Black family nobody knows. *Ebony, 18*(10), 28–31.

Videos

Black History: Lost, Stolen, or Strayed

Although this film is old, starring a very young Bill Cosby, it is not dated. It is still the best video available that provides an in-depth examination of some of the influences that affect African Americans. 1965. (60 minutes, color)

Insights Media
Phone: 212-721-6316
www.fmgondemand.com/id/4502/

I'll Fly Away

This is a PBS video series that helps the viewer understand a white and a black family in the 1960s. This series is not only very well done and entertaining but also allows the viewer to better understand the functioning and stresses of black families of that period, consequently better understanding today's families. (60 minutes)

PBS Television Series
Phone: 703-998-2600

Organizations

National Black Child Development Institute
Phone: 202-387-1281
www.nbcdi.org

American Indian Families

Books

There are a limited number of books pertaining to American Indian families, and although Cleary and Peacock's book covers a wider area than just the family, it does provide a lot of valuable information that will help the reader better understand the American Indian family specifically and the culture generally.

Cleary, L. M., & Peacock, T. D. (1998). *Collected wisdom: American Indian education.* Boston: Allyn & Bacon.

How do cultural differences and real-world issues affect the education of students, in this case, American Indian students? What approaches have real teachers found that work well with American Indian students? This book answers these and other thoughtful questions about teaching in today's diverse school communities. This book captures the collected wisdom of nearly 60 teachers of American Indian students, their frustrations, joys, and challenges. It provides, in a very real way, a portrait of the issues that challenge these students, as well as the successes some teachers have in working with American Indian students.

Hispanic Families

Books

Gaitan, C. D. (2004). *Involving Latino families in schools: Raising student achievement through home-school partnerships.* Thousand Oaks, CA: Corwin Press.

Anyone involved in preservice training for future and present classroom teachers should read this book. Both the content and context of the book are practical, timely, and necessary as our country and classrooms become more diverse.

Jones, T. G., & Fuller, M. L. (2003). *Teaching Hispanic children* (pp. 99–112). Boston: Allyn & Bacon.

Jones and Fuller present information about the role of national origins and cultural backgrounds in teaching and learning and why it is important for teachers to know about culture in general and about Hispanic culture groups in particular.

Ryskamp, G., & Ryskamp, P. (1996). *A student's guide to Mexican American genealogy.* Phoenix, AZ: Oryx Press.

This book is an excellent way to help Mexican American students learn about their family history as well as informing non–Mexican American teachers about native families. This book provides cultural background, an annotated bibliography, and interesting historical facts. In addition, it comes with color and black-and-white photographs and features a glossary and index.

Valdes, G. (1996). *Con respeto: Bridging the distance between culturally diverse families and the schools—An ethnographic portrait.* Williston, VT: Teachers College Press.

This is a study of 10 Mexican immigrant families, describing how such families go about the business of surviving and learning to succeed in a new world. Valdes examines what *appears* to be a disinterest in education by Mexican parents. This book examines a number of important issues and helps the teacher have a better understanding of these families. This is a well-written and informative book.

Zambrana, R. E., Carter-Poras, O., & Nunez, N. P. (2004). *Drawing from the data: Working effectively with Latino families.* Elk Grove Village, IL: American Academy of Pediatrics.

This book provides the information needed to foster healthy growth and development for Latino children. It addresses demographic and socioeconomic characteristics, health insurance, health behaviors, nutrition, infectious diseases, oral health, mental health, guidelines for pediatricians, and more.

Chapters

Hildebrand, V., Phenice, L. A., Gray, M. M., & Hines, R. P. (2008). Hispanic American families. In *Knowing and serving diverse families* (3rd ed.), (pp. 84–110). Upper Saddle River, NJ: Pearson.

Jones, T. G., & Fuller, M. L. (2003). Hispanic families. In *Teaching Hispanic children* (pp. 99–112). Boston: Allyn & Bacon.

Videos

The Latino Family

This video shows both the changes in and the endurance of traditional Latino families. In following three generations of one Mexican American family, it traces the pattern of migration and cultural change. It shows how the traditional roles of the Latino elderly are being altered by their families' needs and also how the traditional pleasures can still be celebrated.

Films for the Humanities and Sciences
Phone: 800-257-5126
www.films.com

The Status of the Latina Women

This video compares the Latina of the United States with those of Latin America. It also examines how Latino men perceive Latina women—the myth and reality, as well as the Latina woman's role in the family and in the community. 1993. (26 minutes, color)

Films for the Humanities and Science
Phone: 800-257-5126
www.films.com

Organizations

Mexican American Legal Defense and
   Education Fund
Phone: 213-629-2512
www.discoverthenetworks.org/groupprofile
   .asp?grpid=6156

Asian American Families

Books

Detzner, D. F. (2004). *Elder tales: Southeast Asian families in the United States*. Lantiam, MD: Altamira Press.

Forty life histories of Southeast Asian elders are gathered in this volume. Collectively they reveal insider personal perspectives on new immigrant family adaptation to American life at the end of the 20th century.

Fadiman, A. (1998). *The spirit catches you and you fall down*. New York: Farrar, Straus and Giroux.

Lia Lee was the 13th child in a family coping with their plunge into a modern and mechanized way of life. The child suffered an initial seizure at the age of 3 months. Her family attributed it to the slamming of the front door by an older sister. They felt the fright had caused the baby's soul to flee her body and become lost to a malignant spirit. The report of the family's attempts to cure Lia through shamanistic intervention and the home sacrifice of pigs and chickens is balanced by the intervention of the medical community that insisted on the removal of the child from deeply loving parents with disastrous results. This compassionate and understanding account fairly represents the positions of all the parties involved.

Pyong, G. M. (2005). *Asian Americans: Contemporary trends and issues* (2nd ed.). Thousand Oaks, CA: Pine Forge Press.

Offering a broad overview of the Asian American experience, *Asian Americans* provides an accessible resource for all students interested in the expanding and important Asian American population. Although historical information is provided for each group, the main focus is on the variables and issues that impact Asian American life today. The scholars who author the chapters look at topics such as labor force participation and economic status, educational achievements, intermarriage, intergroup relations, and settlement patterns. Photo essays help to enhance the presentations.

Gay and Lesbian Families

Books

Drucker, J. (2001). *Lesbian and gay families speak out: Understanding the joys and challenges of diverse family life*. New York: Perseus Publishing.

With an estimated 6 to 14 million children living with a gay or lesbian parent, there is a real need for accurate information for and about the realities of these families. With honesty and compassion, *Lesbian and*

Gay Families Speak Out explores the variety of issues they face—interpersonal relationships, sexual and psychological development, coming out, dealing with prejudice, and finding a spiritual foundation. Using the compelling stories of over two dozen families in which gay fathers and lesbian mothers are raising children in a wide variety of settings and style, Drucker proves that children thrive in an environment of love, regardless of the number, gender, or sexual orientation of the adults who provide that love.

Sherman, S. (Ed.). (1993). *Lesbian and gay marriages: Private commitments, public ceremonies.* Philadelphia, PA: Temple University Press.

The bulk of this book consists of interviews with long-term couples, some who had public ceremonies, some who did not. Appendices include directory of organizations.

Video

We Are Family: Parenting and Foster Parenting in Gay Families

We Are Family won four major film awards. This video deals with what life is really like in three homosexual families. First, two gay fathers tell of their efforts to create a secure environment for their 16-year-old foster son. In another family, two lesbian mothers have helped their adopted 11-year-old boy overcome early neglect. In the third family we hear how two adolescent daughters have accepted their father's homosexuality. 1988. (57 minutes)

Filmaker Library
Phone: 212-808-4980

Organization

American Civil Liberties Union (ACLU)
Phone: 212-944-9800, ext. 545
www.aclu.org/lgbt-rights

Miscellaneous

Video

Teenage Pregnancy

This video follows several teenagers through the births of their children and subsequent changes in their lives. It is a sobering look at the problems these girls face. (26 minutes, color)

Films for the Humanities and Sciences
Phone: 800-257-5126
www.films.com

Websites

African American

African American Resources
www.strategenius.org/african_american
  _resources.htm

NAACP
www.naacp.org

National Urban League
www.nul.org

Asian American

Asian American Resources
www.strategenius.org/asian_american
  _resources.htm

Hmong Home Page
www.hmongnet.org

Hispanic/Latino

Azteca Web Page
www.mexica.net

American Indian

American Indian Movement
www.aimovement.org

Native American Nations
www.nativeculture.com

Native Web
www.nativeweb.org/resources

Resources for Native American Families
www.familyvillage.wisc.edu/frc_natv.htm

Smithsonian Institution: Native American
  Resources
www.si.edu/resource/faq/nmai/start.htm

Other Diversity Sites

National Center for Research on Cultural
  Diversity and Second Language Learning
www.diversitybookmarks.net/bilingual_ed.html

Pathways to Diversity on the World Wide Web
  www.diversityweb.org/about.htm

References

Banks, C. M. (1993). Restructuring schools for equity: What have we learned in two decades? *Phi Delta Kappan, 75*, 42–44, 46–48.

Broadway, D. (1987). *A study of middle class black children and their families: Aspirations for children, perceptions of success, and the role of culture.* Doctoral dissertation, Ohio State University.

Chan, S. (1992). Families with Asian roots. In E. W. Lynch & M. J. Hanson (Eds.), *Developing cross-cultural competence* (pp. 181–257). Baltimore: Paul H. Brookes.

Cleary, L. M., & Peacock, T. D. (1998). *Collected wisdom: American Indian education.* Boston: Allyn & Bacon.

Coontz, S. (2000). *The way we never were: American families and the nostalgia trap* (2nd ed.). New York: Basic Books.

Deck, A. F. (1994, April 6). Latinos shift loyalties. *The Christian Century*, p. 344.

Espiritu, Y. L. (1992). *Asian American panethnicity: Bridging institutions and identities.* Philadelphia: Temple University Press.

Frey, W. H. (2003). Married with children—Decline in traditional-family households. *American Demographics.* Retrieved September 22, 2005, from www.findarticles.com/p/article

Gladstone, J., Brown, R., & Fitzgerald, K. (2009). Grandparents raising their grandchildren: Tensions, service needs and involvement with child welfare agencies. *International Journal of Aging and Human Development, 69*(1), 55–78.

Jones, T. G., & Fuller, M. L. (2003). *Teaching Hispanic children.* Boston: Allyn & Bacon.

Ladson-Billings, G. (1997). *The dreamkeepers: Successful teachers of African American children.* San Francisco: Jossey-Bass.

Lasch, C. (1977). *Haven in a heartless world.* New York: Basic Books.

Lee, S. J. (1996). *Unraveling the "model minority" stereotype: Listening to Asian American youth.* New York: Teachers College Press.

Lewis, D. (2003). *W. E. B. Dubois: Biography of a race, 1868–1919.* New York: Henry Holt.

Mintz, S., & Kellogg, S. (1988). *Domestic revolutions: A social history of American family life.* New York: Free Press.

National Center for Educational Statistics. (2001). Dropout rates in the United States: 2000 (NCES 2002-114). Washington, DC: U.S. Department of Education. (ED 460 174)

Passel, J., Wang, W., & Taylor, P. (2010) *Marrying out: One-in-seven new U.S. marriages is interracial or interethnic.* Washington DC: Pew Research Center.

Ritter, P., Mont-Reynaud, R., & Dornbusch, S. (1993). Minority parents and their youth: Concern, encouragement, and support for school achievement. In N. Chavkin (Ed.), *Families and schools in a pluralistic society* (pp. 107–119). Albany: State University of New York Press.

Rochlen, A., McKelley, R., Suizzo, M., & Scaringi, V. (2008). Predictors of relationship satisfaction, psychological well-being, and life satisfactions among stay-at-home fathers. *Psychology of Men & Masculinity, 19*(1), 17–28.

Shen, W., & Mo, W. (1990). Reaching out to their cultures: Building communication with Asian-American families. (ERIC Document Reproduction Service No. ED 351 435)

Smith, D. M., & Gates, G. (2001). *Same-sex unmarried partner households.* Retrieved from www.urban.org/url.cfm?ID=1000491

Suarez, A. (1993). Cuban Americans: From golden exiles to social undesirables. In H. McAdoo (Ed.), *Family ethnicity: Strength in diversity.* Newbury Park, CA: Sage Publications.

Szasz, M. C. (1991). Current conditions in American Indian and Alaska Native communities. Indian Nations At Risk Task Force. (ERIC Document Reproduction Service No. ED 343 756)

Trennert, R. (1990). Educating Indian girls in non-reservation boarding schools, 1878–1920. In E. C. Dubois and V. L. Ruiz (Eds.), *Unequal sisters: A multicultural reader in U.S. women's history.* New York: Routledge.

U.S. Census Bureau. (2004). *Fact sheet.* Retrieved September 6, 2005, from www.urban.org/publications/1000491.html

Winn Tutwiler, S. (2005). *Teachers as collaborative partners: Working with diverse families and communities.* Mahwah, NJ: Lawrence Erlbaum.

Yao, E. L. (1993). Strategies for working with Asian immigrant parents. In N. Chavkin (Ed.), *Families and schools in a pluralistic society* (pp. 149–156). Albany: State University of New York Press.

Chapter Four

Parents' Perspectives on Parenting

Karen W. Zimmerman
The University of Wisconsin–Stout

Too often the study of the relationship between home and school fails to address the component of parenting. Schools will be able to form better working relationships with the home if they understand parenting practices and problems. This chapter uses the parent's voice to investigate parenting. The first two sections examine families from the perspective of demographics and structure. This chapter takes a different perspective—that of the parenting present in these families—and introduces you to:

▶ How parenting affects the lives of parents.

▶ The nature and complexities of dual-employed parents.

▶ The views of single-parent families.

▶ The parenting concerns of noncustodial fathers and mothers.

▶ The complexities of parenting in a stepfamily.

▶ How parenting adults and children differ.

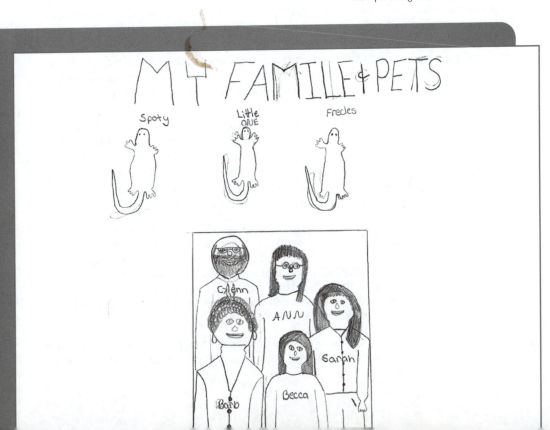

Kenneth and Grace, a dual-employed couple, have two children. Joyce is raising her child as a single parent. Robbie and Kathy, along with their children from previous marriages, form a stepparent family. In this chapter, we look at each of these family situations and the perspectives these mothers and fathers have on parenting.

This chapter focuses on parents and how they see themselves. It begins by examining how becoming a parent changes one's life and affects the marital relationship. Parenting styles and the parents' perspectives are explored. In addition, this chapter explores several familial structures from a parenting perspective. Dual-employed parents identify the coping patterns they use in dealing with role overload and role conflict between work and family. Viewpoints of single parents, divorced parents, and stepparents are shared. Finally, this chapter concludes with a discussion of what parents perceive as the rewards and satisfactions of parenting.

Becoming a Parent

New Parents

New parents are generally very concerned with how to raise their children. They want to incorporate their personal beliefs about child rearing and develop healthy parent–child relationships. These parents seek to understand and explore their feelings as they assume the parental role for the first time.

The changes in becoming a parent for the first time are abrupt. Newlyweds usually interact with each other as personally as possible, trying to mesh as a couple. But when the first child arrives, the couple will likely begin to respond to each other as mommy and daddy instead of as marriage partners. The responsibilities of parenthood take priority over personal gratification. New mothers feel tired, lose sleep, and worry that their personal appearance and the appearance of the home are not up to par. In addition, they feel frustrated about having less time for friends and not having a social life.

New fathers also have many of the same complaints, but men and women differ in how they adjust to the new circumstances. Women tend to think of themselves in a *new* role, whereas men are more inclined to see themselves in an *additional* role. This can be especially frustrating for the husband, as the wife becomes more of a mother and less of a wife. Women are quicker to identify the change in the couple's relationship. One young mother describes this change as follows:

> We aren't able to pay much attention to each other, because Amy needs so much. She's great, don't get me wrong. But Daniel comes home from work cranky, I'm cranky because I haven't talked to anyone who says anything back to me, Amy's cranky because she wants to eat right now, and we don't have time to find out how each other's day went. So I'm making dinner for three cranky people. And as a consequence, we have not been as close as before she came. (Cowan & Cowan, 2000, p. 77)

Marital satisfaction declines somewhat in the early stages of the family life cycle when children are added to the family. Infants and young children demand much time, energy, and attention, and parents have less time for each other. Both mothers and fathers miss the attention of their partner. Having children reorganizes the marriage along traditional sex-role lines (Cowan, Cowan, Heming, & Miller, 1991). The decrease in marital satisfaction is greater for women than for men. This is often attributed to women's feelings that their partners are not as involved as they are in dealing with child care and household tasks (Cowan et al., 1991). Women assume more of the parenting and household tasks than men, even if they are employed outside the home.

One new mother of a 6-month-old, who is doing more housework than ever before, describes this vividly:

> He wasn't being a chauvinist or anything, expecting me to do everything and him to do nothing. He just didn't volunteer to do things that obviously needed doing, so I had to put down some ground rules. Like if I'm in a bad mood, I may just yell: I work eight hours, just like you. Half of this is your house and half of this child is yours too. You've got to do your share. We planned this child together, and we went through Lamaze together, and Jackson stayed home for the first two weeks. But then—wham—the partnership was over. (Cowan & Cowan, 2000, p. 98)

Most educators agree that children thrive best in a home where some consistency between the parents is present. Significant differences between parents on developmental expectations, discipline, and nurturing styles could signal potential problems for the family. In a recent study, mothers and fathers of young children (ages 1 to 4 years) were asked to assess their own parenting and that of their spouse. Three parenting categories were examined: developmental expectations, discipline, and nurturing (Platz, Pupp, & Fox, 1994). Mothers and fathers had similar developmental expectations for their young children. However, fathers tended to see themselves as having a more disciplinarian approach than mothers. Furthermore, fathers gave mothers higher discipline ratings than mothers gave themselves. Mothers rated themselves as more nurturing than fathers. Mothers gave fathers higher ratings in developmental expectations than fathers gave themselves.

After the First Year

How does the role of parenting change during the second year of life? This is the question asked in a study of fathers and mothers (Fagot & Kavanagh, 1993). Parents with 12-month-old children (infants) reported greater marital adjustment and more pleasure in parenting than parents of 18-month-olds (toddlers).

Meeting the daily hassles of parenting adds to parental strain as children make the transition from infancy to early childhood. Perceptions about the minor daily hassles and inconveniences associated with parenting were studied in families with young children. Three groups of parents were studied: those with children aged 9 to 12 months, 18 to 24 months, and 30 to 36 months. Such things as "continually cleaning up the same messes," "difficulty getting privacy," "being nagged or whined to," "kids resisting or struggling over bedtime," and so on, were rated.

Parental reports of the daily hassles of parenting increased across the age groups—that is, as children grew older, the hassles increased. It seems that as children are developing and gaining more abilities, they may be presenting a greater range of behaviors and situations that parents find stressful. Furthermore, as the daily hassles of parenting increase, life satisfaction and parenting satisfaction decrease.

Daily hassles of Head Start fathers were studied in relation to their play involvement with their children. Fathers reported 2.38 hassles per day related to work, travel, health, family finances, friends, and chance occurrences. For every additional hassle per day, fathers' play interaction with their children decreased by 10 minutes on the same day (Fagan, 2000).

Parenting Styles

Parenting styles are shaped by the values, attitudes, and beliefs of the parents. Diana Baumrind identified three parenting styles that emerge when children are at the preschool stage of family development and continue on through adolescence. These three parenting styles are *authoritarian, authoritative,* and *permissive* (Grobman, 2003).

Authoritarian Parents

The authoritarian parenting style emphasizes total parental control and the obedience of the child. The parent is definitely the person in power; conforming to the parent's standards is required. If necessary, the parent may use physical punishment to force the child to comply. The parent dominates the child by use of rewards and punishment. The child is not allowed to question or given opportunities to discuss directives.

Authoritative Parents

Authoritative parents make use of reasonable limits and controls for the child's behavior, considering the child's stage of development and individuality. Authoritative parenting falls between authoritarian and permissive parenting. In this parenting style, the authoritative parent wants to develop responsible children by allowing input into discussion on rules and responsibilities. Children have some freedom, but not at the expense of rights and responsibilities of others.

Bogenschneider and Small (1997) found that mothers and fathers of teens who saw themselves as being more competent had teens who reported that their parents had more competent parenting behaviors. These parents monitored their teens at a higher level and were highly responsive to them.

Permissive Parents

Permissive parents strive to promote the child's regulation of his or her own behavior rather than regulating the child's behavior by intervening. In this approach,

Case Study

Karen is a 30-year-old working single mother and has three children ages ten, eight, and four. Her former husband has moved to a city some distance from them and sees the children infrequently.

Karen is a working mother (bookkeeper). She loves her children but has little confidence in her ability to parent them. Whereas authoritarian, authoritative, and permissive parents make decisions (consciously or unconsciously) that are coherent with their beliefs about children's needs, Karen has difficulty making any decisions and has no definable goals directing her involvement with her children. Her parenting style might be labeled as laissez-faire.

One might think that doing whatever you want would be seen as highly desirable by children, but they generally feel insecure as well as angry with the laissez-faire parent and try to force them to be more predictable and commanding. Karen's children fight more than most siblings, there is no teamwork, and they don't know what is expected of them. Karen knows that she is an ineffective parent, and her primary response to her lack of parenting skills is tears. The parent and children alike are miserable.

Questions and Considerations

1. Looking at the list of parenting styles (authoritarian, authoritative, and permissive) which would be best for these children? Why?
2. Can Karen be helped to be a better parent? If so, what can be done?

---

the child has more power than the parent. The permissive parent allows a child to regulate his or her own activities as much as possible, avoids the exercise of control, and does not encourage him or her to obey externally defined standards (Grobman, 2003).

Most American parents see themselves as raising their children in an authoritative parenting style. When parents were asked to respond to problems dealing with children's misbehavior, most of the people selected responses that would fit with the authoritative parenting style (Bluestone & Tamis-LeMonda, 1999).

In addition, the popularity of the three parenting styles varies by social class. The authoritarian style is found to be more popular with blue-collar families. They are more likely to insist on obedience and to value teaching children to control their impulses. Middle-class parents are more likely to value explaining rules to the child, using verbal discipline, and prizing the child's individuality; this is consistent with the authoritative parenting style. Perhaps more important than style of parenting is that the parents provide guidance, consistency, and an atmosphere of caring. No matter which parenting style is used, children need parents who care as "parental involvement plays an important role in the development of both social and cognitive competence" (Parke & Buriel, 2006, p. 437).

Reflection...

Which parenting style did your parents use? What would be examples of your parents' discipline behaviors that would support your selection? If you are a parent, what parenting style do you use and why? If you plan to be a parent, what discipline style will you use?

Reflection...

Think of the stresses present in your life. How would these affect your parenting if you were a parent? If you are a parent, how are your life stresses evidenced in your parenting? How could you reduce these stresses?

Parenting Behaviors in Diverse Family Structures

Dual-Employed Parents

Kenneth (36) and Grace (38) are middle-class African American parents with two children, Alicia (12) and Francine (10). They live in a four-bedroom house in a small city in California. Kenneth is an accountant for a large clothing firm and Grace teaches math at a local high school.

Kenneth, Grace, Alicia, and Francine experience a lot of family stress, as do most families in which both parents work. Although Kenneth and Grace value enrichment experiences for their children, these activities do add to the complexities of their family life. The children are busy with Scouts, music lessons, ballet, after-school sports, and family activities. There is never enough time.

Kenneth and Grace, as dual-employed parents, are facing the many challenges of multiple roles: worker, parent, and a marital partner. People who have multiple roles gain benefits from each of their roles (e.g., a sense of accomplishment, financial gains, and enhanced self-esteem). These benefits can help to balance the role strain they also encounter. Role strain refers to the problems, challenges, conflicts, and difficulties one has as a result of being in a particular role and fulfilling the tasks and responsibilities that role requires.

Role Conflict and Conflicting Demands.   Two types of role strain are role overload and role conflict. Role overload is the feeling that there is not enough time to accomplish everything one has to do. Grace teaches school all day and shuttles Alicia and Francine to music lessons, ballet, and Scouts before rushing home to fix supper. After supper, Grace has housework to do, a stack of math papers to grade, and to "catch up" with Kenneth on how his day went. The heavy work schedules of dual-employed families often leave limited time for parenting, the marital partner, household work, and leisure. Role conflict occurs when the demand of one of these roles interferes with doing what needs to be done in another role.

Kenneth's job requires that he be at the office until 6:00 P.M. each weekday. He is thankful that Grace can do the driving so Alicia and Francine can take part in after-school activities. He hates missing Alicia's soccer games and Francine's ballet and piano recitals.

Managing the demands of competing life roles, which Kenneth and Grace do daily, has become a common experience for many American men and women. Grappling with multiple life-role commitments is a key source of stress in dual-employed families, especially those with children in the home. Today dual-employed couples frequently have ambitions and commitments in both the work and family areas simultaneously. Men report career interests intruding on fathering roles. Women say that parenting is interfering with career roles. One first-time mother in her thirties described this conflict as follows:

> For the first time in my life I was having to make tradeoffs—work, to have a child, to be a wife, to take care of a home, and to try to do all of these things well meant that something had to get cheated a little bit in each area. Not enough so that anybody else would notice, maybe, but I did. I noticed it. (Daniels & Weingarten, 1984, p. 224)

Prioritizing Life Roles.   Dual-employed couples' personal expectations concerning occupational, marital, parental, and home-care roles were examined in a study of parents with children (Zimmerman, Skinner, & Muza, 1989). Surprisingly, both husbands and wives independently rated their commitment to four life roles in the same priority order: parental as first, marital as second, home care as third, and occupational as fourth.

Reflection...

Which of your life roles (school, family, work, etc.) do you consider to be most important? How is this reflected in the life choices you make?

Although dual-employed couples agreed on the relative importance of these four life roles, they weighed these commitments differently. That is, wives were significantly more committed to the parental role than husbands, although both groups agreed that this was their highest priority. In contrast, husbands were significantly more committed to the occupational role than wives. Thus, both men and women placed a higher value on commitment to familial roles, particularly parental roles, than other life roles. For example, Kenneth and Grace are committed parents but, as discussed earlier, Kenneth's job prevents him from taking the girls to their after-school activities.

These dual-employed couples were divided into two employment orientation groups, worker and career, based on their education and the type of employment. Worker couples were significantly more committed to marital roles and to home-care roles than career couples. It is interesting to note that worker men, career men, and worker women all valued home-care commitment (e.g., working to have a neat, well-kept, and attractive home) to a greater extent than career women.

Moreover, the scores of career women on occupational commitment were similar to those of both worker and career men. Both groups of men and career women were committed to their occupation significantly more than worker women. One dual-employed father described how he prioritized his life roles in an account about his relationship with his daughter, Lisa.

> I drove a truck for a while and I think it contributed to our being distant. Lisa felt like she didn't have a daddy. I came home and told her to clean something and she said, "You can't tell me what to do. You're not my daddy." That ripped me apart. I don't think it was really meant, but it hurt. I stopped driving a truck really fast and brought myself back home. She was more or less saying, "You should be home." (Dollahite, Hawkins, & Brotherson, 1996, p. 361)

Coping Patterns in Dual-Employed Couples.   What coping patterns do dual-employed couples use to deal with stress from their work–family roles? Several studies have addressed this question. One study of dual-employed parents with children examined the coping patterns parents identified using most frequently (Zimmerman et al., 1989). Coping patterns are a broad range of behaviors used together to manage various dimensions of the dual-employed lifestyle simultaneously (Skinner & McCubbin, 1991). Maintaining a positive perspective on lifestyle and reducing tensions and strains were the most frequently used coping patterns. This pattern includes behaviors that attend to personal needs focusing on reducing individual stress and maintaining an optimistic perspective on the situation. Examples include "maintaining health," "encouraging children to be more self-sufficient where appropriate," and "believing that there are more advantages than disadvantages to our lifestyle."

The second most frequently used coping pattern was modifying roles and standards to maintain a work–family balance. These couples modified their roles and standards by buying convenience foods, leaving things undone, and limiting involvement on the job.

Maintaining and strengthening the existing work–family interface was the third most frequently used coping pattern. The focus of this approach was using organizational skills in meeting family, work, and homemaking demands efficiently. An example would be planning schedules ahead of time.

Schnittger and Bird (1990) have identified the coping strategies that dual-career couples have found successful in dealing with the stresses in family life. Among these coping strategies are encouraging their children to help out whenever possible, eliminating some community activities, cutting down on outside and leisure activities, and lowering household standards. Also, parents find spending time alone with their spouses and making friends with other two-career couples helpful.

Coping with work and family demands by subordinating their careers, compartmentalizing work and family roles, and avoiding some responsibilities are strategies used both by career husbands and career wives. These couples contend with stress by limiting their involvement on the job, saying "no," and reducing the amount of time spent at work. They practice making efficient use of their time at work, plan ahead, and postpone certain tasks.

Single-Parent Families

Joyce Anderson (28) is a single parent. Joyce, her daughter, Beth, a 6-year-old, and Joyce's mother, Helen, are a family. They live in an apartment in a low-income neighborhood in Minneapolis. Joyce has worked at the same minimum wage job for a little more than 2 years. Beth is in first grade in a neighborhood school. One of their chronic problems is lack of health insurance. Although most single-parent families are functional families, their situation has lately become even more precarious than usual. Helen has suffered from a severe respiratory problem for a few years, and her doctor wants her to move to Arizona and live with her other daughter. If Helen leaves, not only will Joyce's resources be greatly reduced, she will have to pay for child care. The stresses Joyce and her family experience are good examples of those experienced by single-parent families.

Financial Concern.   Problems occur in every family type, single-parent families included. Most studies have identified financial problems as a major problem of this type of family. One 35-year-old single mother on welfare described her situation:

> I can't pay rent, I can't buy Keith clothes that will fit him, I don't have enough money for food, furniture, or clothes for Erin and myself. Everything and anything is a burden, right down to buying a roll of toilet paper. Not to mention Christmas . . . things are so bad that the thing the kids want most for Christmas is a kitchen table. (Richards, 1989, p. 398)

Worrying about finances can have a negative impact on parent–child relationships. As one mother said, "The lack of money is a real problem for all of us. My anxiety over not being able to find a job makes it hard to be attentive and concerned with the everyday demands of my children" (Richards, 1989, p. 398).

Other Areas of Concern.   Whereas the lack of money is the single biggest problem reported by single parents, there are a number of other problematic areas. In a study of single parents, lack of money was the number one problem reported by mothers (77%), followed by role/task overload (55%), and the lack of social life (30%) (Richards & Schmiege, 1993). For fathers, role/task overload and problems with the ex-spouse were tied for first (35%), followed by lack of social life and lack of money (18%). In addition, problems with role overload were reported by over half the mothers and a third of the fathers. A mother of three adolescents described role overload in her own words, "In this day and age of childrearing, it sure would be nice to be sharing the responsibility with someone else. I get tired of being a full-time policeman and everything else" (Richards & Schmiege, 1993, p. 280). A single-parent father also mentioned task and role overload. He especially hated cooking and believed role overload affected his parenting. He noted, "I would have to say that I tended to be more lenient than I should have been simply because I just didn't have the energy after I worked all day" (Richards & Schmiege, 1993, p. 280).

Children were also reported as a major source of stress. Most of these stressful encounters (50%) involved negative challenging behavior on the part of the child. These included noncompliance ("my youngest refused to take his nap," "fought with the kids to clean up their room"), irritating behaviors ("my daughter began whining during her nap," "the kids ran in and out all day and made a lot of noise"), defiance ("sassing and rebelling"), temper tantrums, and rule violations. These were followed by sibling conflict, demanding attention, being slow in getting ready for outings, illness, school failure, and misbehavior, as well as stressful interactions with child-care providers (Olson & Banyard, 1993).

In general, the single parent is apt to be closer to children emotionally than are parents in the two-parent families. However, the single parent is likely to have less authority or power than do parents in two-parent families. For example, there is no one to back the single parent, impose the rules, or allow the single parent to take a breather. Thus children may have more power to negotiate the roles (Strong, DeVault, & Cohen, 2008). Single parents, like all parents, have strengths as well as problems. Women often say that their single-parenting experience helped them to build personal strengths and confidence (Jorden, 2003). Single mothers and fathers see themselves as being supportive of their children, being patient, helping children to cope, and fostering independence in their children. They also describe themselves as well-organized, dependable, and able to coordinate schedules in managing their family. In an interview, one mother said of her parenting strengths:

> I think just communicating with my kids and listening to them and letting them make decisions and giving them choices. . . . They're very independent and responsible and they have very high self-esteem. I think I've helped them reach their potential and be good caring kids. (Richards & Schmiege, 1993, p. 281)

When these parents were asked whether single parenting becomes easier or more difficult over time, the majority agreed that single parenting becomes easier over time.

One father said, "Things go more into a routine, so it got a little bit easier that way. . . . You would learn how to do things, and again, I had a lot of support from my parents" (Richards & Schmiege, 1993, p. 282).

Many children in single-parent families spend time with the other noncustodial parent. Shawna, a single-parent mother, is pleased that 3-year-old Tasha has a strong relationship with her father, William.

> And I don't want my daughter to feel that she has to look for love, she has both of her parents' love, although she only lives with her mom. And she knows that because she'll say, "My daddy loves me and my mommy loves me, and I love my daddy and mommy." (Patterson, 2001, p. 191)

A study of rural low-income, single-parent mothers found that they wanted father–child interactions even if the father was irregular in paying child support (Sano, Richards, & Zvonkovic, 2008). These mothers knew that the fathers had limited incomes and few economic opportunities. Although the majority of mothers were frustrated with receiving little or no child support, they were aware that the non-resident father did not have enough money to pay child support regularly. Marlene articulated this desire for father–daughter contact:

> My primary concern is not to get money from him but to make sure that Larisa [her daughter] is safe and happy. She just loves her father, and she wants to see him. My primary concern is to make him behave himself, and be a good father. (Sano et al., 2008, p. 1711)

Two-thirds of the mothers in this study were dissatisfied with the father's lack of contact with the children. Inocencia expressed her frustration:

> I would have to call and say, are you gonna get Lavar [her son] this day? Or, are you gonna do this with Lavar? Or Lavar want to talk to you. He didn't call or come unless I called him. And what I want him to realize is that I shouldn't have to ask him . . . that shouldn't be a question. That should be something he knows well. (Sano et al., 2008, p. 1712)

Divorced Noncustodial Fathers and Mothers

The divorce rate in the United States is high. Half of all marriages in the United States end in divorce and approximately 60% of these divorces involve minor children. Mothers are still much more likely to become the custodial parent than fathers. Relationships between noncustodial divorced fathers and mothers and their children are often strained and interaction may be infrequent.

Umberson and Williams (1993) held in-depth interviews with 45 divorced fathers in Texas to identify the stress involved in noncustodial parenting. They found that visitation and custody issues presented major problems along with relationships with the ex-wife, as well as personal and social identity issues. Child support was also an area that these fathers found to be problematic. The unfairness of the system was pointed to by one divorced father:

> One thing that really irritates me about the court system here is that . . . you can be married for 10 years, and you can be a loving, wonderful father for 10 years. And . . . in my instance, she met this other guy and decided to run off with him, and the minute that she left, I was no longer a worthy father. I got visitation! (Umberson & Williams, 1993, p. 389)

Some fathers in this study described the pain they felt after dropping off their children following a visitation. One father of a 6-year-old son noted:

> I don't perceive any stress from being a single parent. When he's with me, it's not stressful at all. It's just hard bringing him back home. . . . All the way going back home he'll tell me how he wishes he could stay with me, he's going to miss me. (Umberson & Williams, 1993, p. 389)

Other divorced fathers reported that their former wives were good mothers. Knowing that their children are receiving good care is important to many divorced fathers. In the words of one of these fathers: "I think she does a real good job considering all the circumstances and everything" (Umberson & Williams, 1993, p. 392). In a second study, Thompson and Lawson (1994) examined divorced African American fathers in Kentucky and Missouri. These fathers had working- and middle-class jobs. From these in-depth interviews, two themes emerged: fathers seeing their children as the most important reason for marriage, and fathers seeing their children as the most significant reason for not divorcing. Most of these fathers were willing to stay married for the sake of their children. After divorce these fathers did not disassociate or think about disassociating from their children.

Children with noncustodial fathers are found in most classrooms; children with noncustodial mothers are significantly less. However, the number of noncustodial mothers is increasing. The activities of nonresident mothers and fathers with their absent children were studied by Stewart (1999). Overall, 41% of noncustodial parents engage only in leisure activities with their children. Thirty percent have not had contact with their children within the past 12 months. The remaining 29% of noncustodial parents mentioned school or organizational activities among the activities they participate in with their child. Stewart found that nonresident mothers and fathers have a similar pattern of interaction with their absent children. Nonresidential mothers spent 37.9% of their time in only leisure activities. Likewise, 24.8% of these mothers had no contact with their child. Nonresidential mothers spent 37.3% of their activity time with school and organizational activities.

In a study of 13 noncustodial mothers in southwestern Virginia, mothers noted changes in the parent–child relationships following divorce (Arditti & Madden-Derdich, 1993). One 41-year-old mother missed the responsibilities of parenting:

> I don't consider myself a parent any more . . . I mean, I will always be their mother, but I don't look at it as a parent anymore without the day-to-day routine of getting meals, of making sure their homework is done because I am not living with them. (Arditti & Madden-Derdich, 1993, p. 313)

Another mother of 6- and 10-year-old sons discussed discipline as a noncusto-dial parent who only sees her children for a limited time:

> I enjoy being with the kids and look forward to seeing them all the time. Some-times it is hard to discipline them because when I'm with them I don't want to be punishing them. I call them on the phone all the time. (Arditti & Madden-Derdich, 1993, p. 313)

These noncustodial mothers expressed dissatisfaction with custody arrange-ments and indicated that their ex-spouses were very satisfied. One mother ex-pressed discomfort and guilt over the custody arrangements: "It's abnormal—a mother and child not being together. I think it's an injustice that's been done" (Arditti & Madden-Derdich, 1993, p. 313). With the increase in noncustodial mothers, we as educators must inform ourselves as to the needs and special circumstances of this parent population.

Stepparent Families

Challenges of Stepparenting.   Kathy (35) is of European American extraction and the mother of Amy (9) and Jack (14). Both children are from a previous marriage. Robbie (35) is an American Indian who also has children from a previous marriage—Amanda (14), Jim (12), and Fred (7). Kathy and Robbie have been married 4 years and are both custodial parents. They live in a three-bedroom house in a medium-sized community in Colorado.

Robbie and Kathy started their new marriage with five children in the house-hold—a blended family. In addition to working hard to form a strong, marital bond, Robbie and Kathy each had the challenge of performing in new roles as stepparents. Neither the role of stepfather nor stepmother is easy to carry out. Lacking clear role definition and being uncertain about how family roles should be carried out is called *role ambiguity*. Stepparents, such as Robbie and Kathy, frequently become confused and frustrated as they work out the role ambiguity of being a stepparent by the trial-and-error method.

Who Is in Charge?   Although Robbie was experienced in disciplining his own three children, he felt uncomfortable and wondered what he should be doing regarding disciplining Jack and Amy. The disciplining of stepchildren is a major issue con-fronting stepfathers. One study found that stepchildren reject stepparents who engage in discipline and control early in their relationship (Ganong, Coleman, Fine, & Martin, 1999). Even stepfathers who had children prior to stepparenting find it difficult. In one study, 30% of stepfathers believe that it is more difficult to discipline stepchildren than their own children (Marsiglio, 1992). Moreover, it is more challenging when the stepchild is an adolescent. One stepfather complained about his adolescent stepson as showing a "complete lack of any acknowledgment of my right to correct him or have him obey when asked (told) to do something—like clean up his room or be home at a certain time" (Giles-Sims & Crosbie-Burnett, 1989, p. 1071).

Because biological mothers receive physical custody of the children in a large percentage of cases, there are more stepfathers who live with her children than stepmothers who live with his biological children. A stepfather usually joins an already established single-parent family.

Most stepmothers are classified as a nonresidential stepmother. That is, a stepparent who does not live with the children or who lives with them only part of the time, such as weekends and a few weeks in the summer. These nonresidential stepmothers are part-time and their roles can be very ambiguous. They report higher levels of stress than residential stepmothers who have daily contact with the children (Stewart, 2007).

Stepfathers were asked what they would advise a friend about being a stepfather. Here is what they said:

> Live with them first, don't expect to ever replace the natural father in their eyes; win their respect; treat them as your own; love them and discipline them as your own; let nothing come between you and your woman—especially the kids. (Giles-Sims & Crosbie-Burnett, 1989, p. 1071)

A national study of stepfathers who were also natural parents found that the majority disagreed with the notion that it is harder to love stepchildren than their own children (Marsiglio, 1992). However, a third of these stepfathers also reported that they were apt to be more a friend than a parent to their stepchildren although the majority still felt that they had assumed the full responsibilities of parenthood. Kathy was concerned about Jack and Amy's reaction when Robbie tried to discipline them, especially during the first year of marriage. Mothers question how much to rely on the stepfather and how much authority he should have in disciplining the children. Typically, mothers remain in the disciplining role and stepfathers gradually begin assuming more of this role when they feel more comfortable with stepparenting. This is how Kathy and Robbie handled the situation. However, some mothers remain in the disciplining role. One mother related:

> I have never counted on their stepdad to provide discipline, not even to put them to bed. That is not his responsibility. Those children are my responsibility and it is one that I choose to have. He married me, he only has to live with them, not discipline them. (Giles-Sims & Crosbie-Burnett, 1989, p. 1071)

There are indications that stepmothers have a harder time raising stepchildren than stepfathers do (MacDonald & DeMaris, 1996). Stepmothers report greater dissatisfaction with their family roles and higher levels of stress in carrying out family responsibilities than stepfathers (Ahrons & Wallish, 1987). Women are usually more responsible for the daily contact with and management of children. Therefore, they have the daily hassles of making decisions that may be unpopular with the children.

Coleman and Ganong (1997) found that the stepmothers who expressed the most frustration were those who indicated that they had high control needs. These stepmothers "had greater difficulty accepting messes children made, the noise and chaos children created, child's lack of gratitude for assistance, and the vying of the children for their father's attention" (Coleman & Ganong, 1997, p. 113). The husbands appeared to be passive, not wanting to take sides with their wives or to punish their children for the behaviors that caused problems between the stepmother and the children. Over time, these high-control stepmothers said they learned to back off.

Cohabitating Stepfamilies.   Many single-parent-headed households are actually cohabiting stepfamilies. These stepfamilies are more likely to be living with male than female cohabiting stepparents as biological mothers are more likely to gain custody of children (Stewart, 2001). Cohabitating stepfamilies are different than single-parent families. Cohabitating partners live and interact with their romantic partner's children through physical care, conversation, play, discipline, and role setting.

Cohabitating couples with stepchildren sometimes do not see much of a distinction between cohabitation and marriage. A cohabitating stepmother explains:

> There's nothing that we don't do now that is not like being married. I mean our finances [are] together . . . we do for our daughter, he has a little boy that's four by someone else before we got together, we do, I do for him like you know, he's part of the family, even though we're not married. (Manning, Smock, & Bergstrom 2004, p. 22)

Successful Stepparenting.   Six characteristics of adults who have successfully adapted to stepfamily life have been identified by Emily and John Visher, founders of the Step Family Association of America (Visher & Visher, 1990). These characteristics are:

1. These adults have mourned their losses and are ready for a new pattern of life.
2. They have a realistic expectation that their family will be different from a first marriage family.
3. They are a strong, unified couple.
4. Constructive family rituals are established and serve as a basis for positive shared memories.
5. Satisfactory step-relationships have formed (which takes time).
6. The separate households cooperate in raising the children.

Healthy stepfamilies may differ from healthy intact families according to Pill (1990). They are more flexible and adaptable because of the comings and goings of family members, and they allow for differences among family members. For example, they allow their children to decide whether to go on a family vacation or when to spend time with their other birth parent.

Rewards and Satisfactions of Parenthood

Nurturing children and being needed are sufficient rewards for parenthood. But would parents do it again? In one study, 93% of parents said yes—they would have children again. These parents felt that the greatest advantages of having children were the love and affection children bring; having the pleasure of watching them grow;

the sense of family they create; the fulfillment and satisfaction they bring; and the joy, happiness, and fun they bring (Gallup & Newport, 1990).

Research studies on parental satisfaction have shown consistently that an overwhelming majority of parents report being satisfied with their parenting role (Cheng, Taylor, & Ladewig, 1991). For some people, living childless even with a partner one loves is unacceptable. They want children as a creative expression of themselves. These parents find their own lives enriched by having children: to love and to be loved by them.

A more recent study of young parents examined factors that appear to predict attitudes of childbearing rewards and regrets (Groat, Giordano, Cernkovich, Pugh, & Swinford, 1997). Young parents who found childbearing most rewarding were white, were married, and had positive feelings about their first pregnancy. Those holding regretful childbearing attitudes were African American, were materialistic, had three or more children, and expressed negative feelings about their first pregnancies.

In a study of the satisfying aspects of parenting, Langenbrunner and Blanton (1993) conducted in-depth interviews with mothers and fathers. Their statements regarding satisfaction clustered into six major areas: (1) the child's growth and accomplishments, (2) verbal and physical interactions between parent and child, (3) the child showing affection toward the parent, (4) parent–infant attachment processes, (5) positive evaluations of their performance of the parental role, and (6) experiencing a sense of cohesion in their family. Overall, these parents received the greatest amount of satisfaction from seeing their children's developmental accomplishments. One parent described this:

> I also derive a great deal of satisfaction from watching both of them, I have two children now, learning things. It's very interesting for me to see James learn to talk. I have also taken a great deal of satisfaction in seeing James take an interest in books. (Langenbrunner & Blanton, 1993, p. 184)

All the parents in this study expressed the good feelings they felt from physically interacting with and talking with their children. As one father said, "It is surprisingly relaxing to spend time with a small child and for me it is good therapy" (Langenbrunner & Blanton, 1993, p. 184).

The primary source of satisfaction for fathers in this study came from their experiencing a sense of family cohesion or family unity. For these fathers, a feeling of connectedness to the family was very important. As one father concluded:

> Well, I was thinking about it a lot. And the most satisfying times are just "feelings" that I have. There's not really anything happening specifically. But I have a sense of being a family unit or we're sharing our feelings. (Langenbrunner & Blanton, 1993, p. 185)

Part of the parenting reward is being judged as competent and successful as a parent by others. Antoine, a single black custodial father and a widower, recognizes that he is being watched and evaluated. His comments reveal his personal satisfaction and public recognition and standing:

> People always ask me, "Where is your daughter?" [I say,] "I have her" and everybody is like "You do?" I guess they think I'm not going to deal with that. . . . So I would say for me I think it has been rewarding because I know I can take care of her and I'm going to take care of her and I do a good job of it. . . . And then people from the outside, they see you doing it and say "OK, it can be done." Not only can it be done but you can do a great job and the child can grow up to be a respectable person and be successful. (Coles, 2009, p. 1332)

Reflection. . .

How do you think your parent(s) would respond to the question, "What has been the greatest satisfaction in your parenting?" After considering this question, call or write your parents and ask them.

Summary

Becoming a parent involves a major transition for the couple and taking on a new life role. This changes the relationship between the husband and wife. Typically marital satisfaction decreases somewhat in the early stages of the family life cycle when children are in the home. The daily hassles of parenting add to parental strain especially when children are preschool age and younger.

Baumrind identified three parenting styles: authoritarian, authoritative, and permissive. These styles can be seen in the preschool through adolescent years. Working-class parents usually prefer the authoritarian style, whereas middle-class parents prefer the authoritative style. Consistency, guidance, and caring are very important in parent–child interactions (Grobman, 2003).

Dual-employed parents encounter role strain as they try to meet the expectations of their various roles. Role strain includes role overload (having too much to accomplish in a limited time) and role conflict (demands of one life role interfere with meeting the demands of another life role). Dual-employed parents rate their life-role commitments in the following order: parent, spouse, home care, and occupation.

Coping patterns used by dual-employed parents to deal with work–family demands include (a) maintaining a positive perspective on the lifestyle to reduce tensions, (b) modifying roles and standards to maintain a work–family balance, (c) maintaining and strengthening the existing work–family interface, and (d) finding support to maintain the family unit.

Single parents are faced with financial problems, role overload, and the daily hassles of interactions with children. They see their parental strengths as parenting skills, managing a family, communicating, growing personally, and providing financial support. They believe that single parenting becomes easier over time. Divorced, noncustodial fathers report parental role strain due to visitation and custody issues, relationships with ex-wives, and personal and identity issues. They believe that the children are the most important reason for staying married. Noncustodial parents engage in mostly leisure activities with their children, or they have had no contact with them over the past year. Less than a third of noncustodial parents participate in school or organizational activities with their children. The pattern of activity is similar for both noncustodial fathers and noncustodial mothers.

Stepparent families find that the roles of stepfather and stepmother are not easy to carry out and lack clear role definition. They experience role ambiguity. Disciplining children is a major issue confronting stepfathers. Stepmothers report greater dissatisfaction with their family role and higher levels of stress. Healthy stepfamilies differ from healthy intact families. They are more flexible, are more adaptable, and allow for more differences.

Recommended Activities

1. Watch the movie *Parenthood* (with Steve Martin) and analyze the parenting styles of the five families depicted in the film.
2. Invite an attorney, two noncustodial fathers, and two noncustodial mothers to speak to the class about legal and parenting concerns.
3. Put together pamphlets of resources that will help parents in your community with their parenting (e.g., organizations, mental health services, videos on parenting, books) and distribute them.
4. Monitor an evening of prime-time television and document the parenting behaviors you observe.
5. Invite parents from dual-employed families to class to discuss the mechanics of running a dual-employed family. What are the rewards and the stresses?
6. Have various students in the class interview custodial parents, noncustodial parents, a family therapist, and children from these homes, and share the various positions in class.
7. Examine the role of mediation in working out problems between the custodial and noncustodial parent. A panel comprised of a psychologist, family mediator, and an attorney could be helpful in reviewing this topic.

Children's Books

The following children's books are suggested as a way of helping your students consider issues in this chapter.

Mama, Do You Love Me?
Barbara M. Joosse, Barbara Lavallee (Illustrator)
Reading Level: Ages 4–8
Chronicle Books (1991)

Papa, Do You Love Me?
Barbara M. Joosse, Barbara Lavallee (Illustrator)
Reading Level: Ages 4–8
Chronicle Books (2005)

If You Had to Choose, What Would You Do?
Sandra McLeod Humphrey, Dan Barker, Brian Strassburg (Illustrator)
Reading Level: Ages 8–12
Prometheus Books (2003)

Manners at a Friend's Home
Terri Degezelle
Reading Level: Ages 5–7
Capstone Press (2004)

Additional Resources

Parenting

Books

Bigner, J. J. (2010). *Parent–child relations: An introduction to parenting* (8th ed.). Upper Saddle River, NJ: Pearson.

This is an excellent text that covers parenting from a developmental perspective. It has a short, but good, section on the cultural meaning of parenthood and also includes contemporary parenting concerns (e.g., latchkey children).

Brooks, J. B. (2006). *The process of parenting* (7th ed.). Toronto: Mayfield Publishing Company.

This is a superb resource book about parenting. It is thorough and well written. It explores parenting and the life cycle as well as the process of parenting. Brooks then looks at each stage of parenting and examines some special topics (e.g., children with special needs).

Galinsky, E. (1987). *The six stages of parenthood.* New York: Addison-Wesley.

Galinsky points out that parenting has stages just as childhood does. She examines these stages and discusses their implications as they relate to the individual parent.

Organizations

American Association of Family and Consumer Science
Phone: 703-706-4600
www.aafcs.org

National Parent Teacher Association
Phone: 800-307-4782
www.pta.org

National Council on Family Relations
Phone: 888-781-9331
www.ncfr.org

Websites

Family Education
www.familyeducation.com/home

National Center for Fathering
www.fathers.com

National Child Care Information Center
www.nccic.org

National Parent Information Network
www.npin.org

Parenting
www.parenting.village.com

References

Ahrons, C. R., & Wallish, L. (1987). Parenting in the binuclear family: Relationships between biological and stepparents. In K. Pasley & M. Ihinger-Tallman (Eds.), *Remarriage and stepparenting* (pp. 225–256). New York: Guilford.

Arditti, J. A., & Madden-Derdich, D. A. (1993). Noncustodial mothers: Developing strategies of support. *Family Relations, 42,* 305–317.

Bluestone, C., & Tamis-LeMonda, C. S. (1999). Correlates of parenting styles in predominately working- and middle-class African American mothers. *Journal of Marriage and the Family, 59,* 345–363.

Bogenschneider, K., & Small, S. A. (1997). Child, parent, and contextual influences on perceived competence among parents of adolescents. *Journal of Marriage and the Family, 55*(6), 345–362.

Cheng, T. C., Taylor, M. R., & Ladewig, B. H. (1991). Personal well-being: A study of parents of young children. *Family Perspective, 25,* 97–106.

Coleman, M., & Ganong, L. H. (1997). Stepfamilies from the stepfamily's perspective. *Marriage and Family Review, 26,* 107–121.

Coles, R. (2009). Just doing what they gotta do: Single black custodial fathers coping with the stresses and reaping the rewards of parenting. *Journal of Family Issues, 30,* 1311–1338.

Cowan, C. P., & Cowan, P. A. (2000). *When partners become parents: The big life change for couples.* Mahwah, NJ: Lawrence Erlbaum.

Cowan, C. P., Cowan, P. A., Heming, G., & Miller, N. B. (1991). Becoming a family: Marriage, parenting, and child development: In P. A. Cowan & M. Hetherington (Eds.), *Family transitions* (pp. 79–109). Mahwah, NJ: Lawrence Erlbaum.

Daniels, P., & Weingarten, K. (1984). Mothers' hours: The timing of parenthood and women's work. In P. Voydanoff (Ed.), *Work and family: Changing roles of men and women* (pp. 204–231). Palo Alto, CA: Mayfield.

Dollahite, D. C., Hawkins, A. J., & Brotherson, S. E. (1996). Narrative accounts, generative fathering and family life education. *Marriage and Family Review, 24,* 349–368.

Fagan, J. (2000). Head Start fathers' daily hassles and involvement with their children. *Journal of Family Issues, 21,* 329–346.

Fagot, B. I., & Kavanagh, K. (1993). Parenting during the second year: Effects of children's age, sex and attachment classification. *Child Development, 64,* 258–271.

Gallup, G. H., & Newport, F. (1990). Virtually all adults want children, but many of the reasons are intangible. *The Gallup Poll Monthly, 297,* 8–22.

Ganong, L., Coleman, J., Fine, M., & Martin, P. (1999). Stepparents' affinity-seeking and affinity-maintaining strategies with stepchildren. *Journal of Family Issues, 20,* 299–327.

Giles-Sims, J., & Crosbie-Burnett, M. (1989). Adolescent power in stepfather families: A test of normative-resource theory. *Journal of Marriage and the Family, 51,* 1065–1078.

Groat, H. T., Giordano, P. C., Cernkovich, S. A., Pugh, M. D., & Swinford, S. P. (1997). Attitudes toward childbearing among young parents. *Journal of Marriage and the Family, 59,* 568–581.

Grobman, K. H. (2003). Diana Baumrind's parenting styles: Original description of the styles. Retrieved August 24, 2005, from www.devpsy.com

Jorden, D-L. (2003). *How to succeed as a single parent.* London: Hoddler & Stoughton.

Langenbrunner, M. R., & Blanton, P. W. (1993). Mothers' and fathers' perceptions of satisfactions and dissatisfactions with parenting. *Family Perspective, 27*(2), 179–193.

MacDonald, W., & DeMaris, A. (1996). Parenting stepchildren and biological children: The effects of stepparent's gender and new biological children. *Journal of Marriage and the Family, 17,* 5–25.

Manning, W. D., Smock, P. J., & Bergstrom, C. (2004, November). *Children and cohabitation: Lessons from focus groups and in-depth interviews.* Paper presented at the annual meeting of the Association for Public Policy Analysis and Management, Atlanta, GA.

Marsiglio, W. (1992). Stepfathers with minor children living at home. *Journal of Family Issues, 13*(2), 195–214.

Olson, S. L., & Banyard, V. (1993). Stop the world so I can get off for a while: Sources of daily stress in the lives of low-income single mothers of young children. *Family Relations, 42,* 50–56.

Parke, R. D., & Buriel, R. (2006). Socialization in the family: Ethnic and ecological perspectives. In W. Damon & R. M. Lerner (Series Eds.) & N. Eisenberg (Vol. Ed.), *Handbook of child psychology: Vol. 3. Social, emotional and personality development* (6th ed., pp. 429–504). Hoboken, NJ: Wiley.

Patterson, W. A. (2001). *Unbroken homes: Single-parent mothers tell their stories.* New York: Haworth Press.

Pill, C. (1990). Stepfamilies: Redefining the family. *Family Relations, 39*(2), 186–193.

Platz, D. L., Pupp, R. P., & Fox, R. A. (1994). Raising young children: Parental perceptions. *Psychological Reports, 74,* 643–646.

Richards, L. N. (1989). The precarious survival and hard-won satisfactions of white single-parent families. *Family Relations, 38,* 396–403.

Richards, L. N., & Schmiege, C. J. (1993). Problems and strengths of single-parent families: Implications for practice and policy. *Family Relations, 42,* 277–285.

Sano, Y., Richards, L. N., & Zvonkovic, A. M. (2008). Are mothers really "gatekeepers of children"? Rural mothers' perceptions of nonresident fathers' involvement in low-income families. *Journal of Family Issues, 29,* 1701–1723.

Schnittger, M. H., & Bird, G. W. (1990). Coping among dual-career men and women across the family life cycle. *Family Relations, 39,* 199–205.

Skinner, D. A., & McCubbin, H. I. (1991). Coping in dual-employed families: Gender differences. *Family Perspective, 25*(2), 119–134.

Stewart, S. D. (1999). Disneyland dads, Disneyland moms? *Journal of Family Issues, 20,* 539–557.

Stewart, S. D. (2007). *Brave new stepfamilies: Diverse paths toward stepfamily living.* Thousand Oaks, CA: Sage Publications.

Stewart, S. (2001). Contemporary American stepparenthood: Integrating cohabiting and nonresident stepparents. *Population Research & Policy Review, 20,* 345–364.

Strong, B., DeVault, C., & Cohen, T. F. (2008). *The marriage and family experience: Intimate relationships in a changing society* (10th ed.). Belmont, CA: Thomson Wadsworth.

Thompson, A., & Lawson, E. J. (1994). Fatherhood: Insights from divorced black men. *Family Perspective, 28*(3), 169–181.

Umberson, D., & Williams, C. L. (1993). Divorced fathers: Parental role strain and psychological distress. *Journal of Family Issues, 14*(3), 378–400.

Visher, E., & Visher, J. (1990). Dynamics of successful stepfamilies. *Journal of Divorce and Remarriage, 14,* 3–12.

Zimmerman, K., Skinner, D., & Muza, R. (1989). *The relationship of life cycle stage and employment orientation to work–family stress, coping and life role salience in dual-earner families.* Paper presented at the meeting of the National Council of Family Relations, New Orleans, Louisiana.

Chapter Five

Teachers and Parenting: Multiple Views

Judith B. MacDonald
Montclair State University

This chapter begins by identifying why it is important for teachers and parents to be aware of each other's viewpoints and attitudes. A range of perceptions teachers have about parents—from an understanding of their vulnerability to a puzzlement about their indifference to school matters—is presented. In the last section, the attitudes various groups of parents have about teachers and parents are described. We believe students will ultimately benefit when parents and teachers better understand each other's frames of reference. This chapter helps you to:

▶ Describe the similarities and differences of teaching and parenting.

▶ Explain the changing roles of the teacher and the parent in the schools.

▶ Compare teachers' perspectives on parents to parents' perspectives on teachers.

▶ Identify ways for teachers to deal with parents' vulnerability and sensitivity about their children.

▶ Compare and contrast time and work constraints for both parents and teachers.

▶ Identify ways that parents are partners with the teacher in the education of their children.

It is understandable that teachers and parents have been called "natural allies." They share the common goal of wanting children to develop their potential as fully as possible. But despite their similar aims, teachers and parents don't always work comfortably together to achieve them. The complexity of life today makes it hard for teachers and parents to connect with each other at a time when understanding one another may be even more critical than in the past. How teachers perceive parents and how parents view teachers and schools are subtle, but important, elements in providing optimal educational service to students.

When we talk about groups we tend to make generalizations. Although it may be easier or more efficient to talk "globally" about a group, we also know that talking in a general way can mask differences within a group that should be identified to understand its range and complexity. Just as we know that adolescents have certain characteristics and are driven by feelings that are particular to that age and stage of development, we also know how much they can differ from each other. When we talk about teachers and parents in this chapter, we describe the varied perceptions that people from each group have about the other. We explore teachers' views about parents and parents' perspectives on teachers and schools. We also consider how to help beginning teachers prepare for relating to the parents of the students they will teach.

Teaching and Parenting

Similarities

Although teaching and parenting are different experiences, as we have noted, they do share some common elements. We teach and nurture in both roles. The settings we work in as teachers and parents have similarities. The privacy (some teachers have called it loneliness) of the classroom has been compared to "the exile of domesticity." Being a teacher or parent requires an energetic giving of oneself. Just listening to students and children demands a special attentiveness. Last, but certainly not least, is patience, an attribute essential in both teaching and parenting.

Differences

When teaching has been compared to other kinds of work, it is called unique because teachers, unlike other workers or professionals, confront a unique set of difficulties working with inherently changeful materials (Lortie, 2002). But parents also contend with the changeful nature of children and for longer periods of time than teachers. In fact, teachers who are also parents would be the first to say that hard as teaching can be, its challenges can't compete with those a parent faces. The vast number of books on raising children suggests that parents seem to need guidance and support.

In comparing teaching to parenting, the most obvious difference is the feeling of attachment one has to one's child versus one's student. Although the bond between teacher and student can be strong and meaningful, it lacks the elemental and enduring connections that usually develop between a parent and child.

Knowledge of Parents Versus Pedagogical Knowledge

At this point in your preparation to become teachers, you may not yet have thought much about relationships with the parents of your prospective students. You are probably more concerned with issues of classroom management or of academic and pedagogical knowledge. Understanding parents, their views about their children, and those of the school may seem like a "back burner" issue. Without passing judgment on where it belongs in your hierarchy of topics in education, we suggest that knowing a parent's perspective will enrich your understanding of students. Because teaching is so fluid and unprescribed, and because there are concurrent classroom demands for attention, we contend with gaps in understanding students. Learning more about parents and their perspectives is one way of learning more about students.

Teacher Morale

Just as it is useful for you to know about parents, the parents should know about the challenges inherent in teaching. We know that parent attitudes affect teacher morale. Feeling valued and respected is crucial for teachers (and for most people), and its absence is the chief cause of teacher burnout or depression. A major cause of teachers leaving the profession is their perception of a lack of respect from parents.

Rob is an example of a teacher who became disenchanted with teaching due to a sense of growing disrespect from parents (and students). He teaches social studies in an ethnically, racially, and religiously diverse middle school. Rob is 42 years old, is married, and has two adolescent children. He has taught for 20 years and enjoyed teaching until the last 5 years. Rob told me that in recent years the parents in his school treated him as if he were their employee rather than a respected member of a profession.

> I had a student say to me, "Hey, take it easy, I'll have my mother get you fired". . . . So that lack of respect, the lack of returning the caring attitude that I have for them is very demoralizing. (MacDonald, 1994, p. 60)

We know that teachers are less valued in contemporary society than in the past. Reasons for this change in attitude deserve more analysis than we can provide here. But we do know that if teachers are to function effectively, efforts must be made to correct the misunderstandings that exist between parents and teachers who feel disrespected.

Changing Role of Parents in Schools

It is helpful in understanding how teachers perceive parents to note how the parent's role in schools has changed. In the first quarter of this century when "children were to be seen and not heard," parents, too, were not very visible or vocal in schools. Parents viewed teachers as experts and accorded them the respect appropriate to their position. Until the 1960s parent participation in schools was mainly confined to attending PTA meetings and was limited to those parents who were interested in school issues. Today, PTA events are still mainly supported by groups of interested parents, but most schools would welcome more parent involvement. A recent Gallup poll showed that the lack of parental interest and support is a primary factor contributing to teacher dissatisfaction (Bushaw & Lopez, 2010).

Reflection...

Consider the responsibilities of working parents. Many parents' home and work responsibilities are such that they don't have enough time for everything they must do. Make a list of these responsibilities and consider the time required for each.

At the same time that teachers want parent support, they are also wary of activist parents who have become more numerous since the 1960s and who act as if the schools belong to them (Newman, 2006). According to one study of teachers (Lortie, 2002), "the good parent" is one who doesn't intervene and also supports teacher's efforts or acts as a "distant assistant." It is obvious there is a range of attitudes that teachers have toward parent involvement. It is a bit of a paradox that as parents have more opportunities to make educational choices—through the development of magnet schools and, in some systems, of school vouchers—they have less time to make use of the expertise of teachers. Parents' stressful, busy lives and work schedules often prevent them from consulting with teachers on issues with which they could provide assistance.

Teachers' Perspectives on Parents

Teachers develop ideas about parents based on their interactions with them. As we consider teachers' perspectives, you will note the variety of opinions teachers seem to have about parents.

The Perspectives of Teachers Who Are Also Parents

It may surprise you to learn that more than 70% of teachers in the United States are also parents. Teaching parents are a useful source of knowledge about parents. Their perspective is especially instructive if they taught before becoming parents—which is the case for most teachers—and can compare their attitudes toward parents before and after being a parent.

Teaching parents find that a main effect of the dual role is an increased empathy for parents. They understand the complexities of the role of parent when they become parents themselves, and this positively affects their relationships with parents of students (MacDonald, 1994).

We think that sharing some of the attitudes teaching parents have about parents will be useful to you. Perspectives of teachers who are not parents are also presented in this section.

Attachment to Children

When teachers become parents, they understand the profound attachment parents can have to their children. Although you may lack actual experience as a parent, awareness of a parent's attachment to a child may help you understand how it can affect the parent's perspective.

Consider Max, a 48-year-old elementary school principal who began his career as a kindergarten teacher. He has a 10-year-old son and has been teaching and working in elementary education for more than 20 years. Max is the principal of a suburban school outside of New York City. Parents in this community are high achievers academically and economically, and, as Max said, "They are quite ambitious for their children. . . . You understand a parent's investment in their own child and how attached parents can be to their children. . . . As a parent you can understand why somebody would want everything for their child." So having his own child and feeling what he calls "that inexplicable love" helped Max, as a principal, understand and better cope with "irrational" attitudes of parents.

Understanding Limitations in Parents' Power

It goes without saying that parents are responsible for their children. Parents' values and priorities determine how they raise their children. Clearly they have the responsibility of setting rules and limits. Yet, there are situations in which a parent lacks control. For example, you might want your child to study for a test before doing something more enjoyable. Alice, a science teacher with two young children of her own, found that she could not actually force her child to study for a test. Alice teaches science in a white, middle-class school. She says she loves teaching science although, as a single mother and conscientious teacher, she is exhausted at the end of a school day. She said, "Prior to having my own children, I wouldn't understand how a parent couldn't make a child do his homework. Now I understand you can't force Johnny to study for a test; you can't force your kid to get A's."

Stanley is the father of three adolescents. He teaches English in a middle school that is ethnically, racially, and religiously diverse. He said, "You become sensitive to some of the problems that parents have. Before being a parent I thought 'well, you're the parent, you're in charge, why don't you do something about it.'" But Stanley also talked about parental responsibility:

> On the other hand being a parent also gives you the sense of what it is that parents *aren't* doing that they should be doing. You see children who come to school whose parents aren't involved in their lives, and that makes you wonder and get angry. So I think I'm more sensitive to that as well because I know what goes into parenting.

Awareness of Vulnerability, Sensitivity, or Defensiveness

Teachers who realize how vulnerable and sensitive parents can be about their children will have an easier time communicating with parents. It is hard for parents to hear negative news about their child even when they ask you to tell them the truth.

Selma is an experienced 50-year-old fifth-grade teacher in a suburban elementary school. She was very puzzled by her student Collin's lack of interest in school and lack of connection with the other students. Collin's mother is a well-educated woman in her forties who seemed worried about her son's lack of well-being and inability to fit in to the school. During a conference with Collin's mother, Selma focused on Collin's positive aspects. (He was a kind, sweet-natured boy who loved music.) The atmosphere Selma created encouraged Collin's mother to ask direct questions about Collin's adjustment to school. Selma was able to share more of the truth about Collin than if she had started the discussion with her very real concerns about him. Because the conversation was an honest sharing of knowledge about Collin, both the teacher and mother felt good about it and made plans to meet again.

We think it is useful to realize that if a student is not happily engaged in school, the parent may know it but may not know what to do about it. When a teacher is aware of the pain that a child's unhappiness causes the parent, the teacher is seen as an ally and not a judge. Together they can take steps to address the problem.

Maureen teaches elementary school and has four children. A parent of one of her students who had a learning disability was "resisting referral," as Maureen put it. After Maureen told the parent about her own learning-disabled child and how hard it was for her to face what she felt was the shame of this condition, the parent agreed to have her child evaluated.

When parents are hurting, it is hard for them to use their usual common sense. Parents feel vulnerable when school life isn't going well for their child. Parents of children with difficulties in school, such as learning disabilities, can be defensive about their child's condition, often denying it and thereby depriving the child of better educational alternatives.

Just as teaching isn't formulaic, there is no formula for helping parents see their child impartially. We suggest that you be aware of how sensitive parents of children with problems can be. It may be helpful to remember situations in which you felt vulnerable so as to become attuned to the parents' feelings. You may need to give them time to reveal their concerns, and you may often find it is useful to talk first about less sensitive issues.

Reflection...

Why does there appear to be an uneasy tension between teachers and parents? Why can't teachers and parents trust each other to have children's best interests at heart?

Awareness of Insufficient Time, Being Overworked

Parents today, and especially mothers, have layers of responsibility. Many women work outside the home and have to attend to children and their activities, as well as take some if not all responsibility for household duties. Women who don't work outside the home may have other obligations such as caring for their parents.

Walter is a math teacher in an urban high school. He is in his early forties and has two children in elementary school. When his wife went back to work, he gained a new perspective on working women:

> When my wife went back to work, I really appreciated how hard it is for women who work. . . . You work all day just to come home and make the dinner, correct papers, and prepare for the next day's classes, and make lunches for the next day, and pretty soon it gets to be 10:00 at night.

We know that people today have less leisure time than their parents did despite the labor-saving devices that many families have. Mothers with young children have the least free time and seem to have profited least from advances in labor-saving technology.

An awareness of parents' lack of free time will help you understand the constraints and stresses they contend with. Parents may not have the time to help with homework or other school-related tasks. Knowing the time limitations of parents may affect your decisions about what schoolwork should be done at home.

The Educated and/or Affluent Parent

This section describes the negative attitudes teachers have reported that some educated and/or affluent parents exhibit (Kohn, 1998). These behaviors clearly don't apply to all educated or affluent parents. New teachers, in particular, feel uneasy teaching students of highly educated parents who may lack the sensitivity to understand the vulnerability of a new teacher. You might expect that the parent who is as educated as or more educated than you would be your natural ally in school. Unfortunately, this isn't necessarily so. Teachers have varying perspectives about educated parents. They are clearly valued when they share an understanding of the teacher's educational objectives, but teachers also report that educated parents can be demanding and aggressive.

Experienced teachers claim that parental respect has declined in the last 10 to 15 years. Two groups in particular, educated and affluent parents, seem to be the culprits. Affluent parents can undervalue the teacher if they assess accomplishment in strictly monetary terms.

We know it is difficult to work in a community where you expect educated parents to support your efforts but instead perceive themselves as experts and question your professional expertise. It is important for teachers, and especially beginning teachers, to realize that their professional knowledge is distinct and not interchangeable with the knowledge that educated parents may have. It may be a misnomer to call parents "educated" when they are disrespectful of teachers. We alert you to the existence of these parents but also reassure you that the truly educated parent will value and respect you as a teacher.

The Indifferent Parent

Teachers have found it frustrating to work with a parent who seems indifferent to their efforts. It is hard to understand why a parent wouldn't be responsive to a teacher's overtures for contact. We are usually not privy to the origins of a parent's indifference, although knowing why a parent seems apathetic might help you better connect with her or him.

Consider Melinda, a 30-year-old kindergarten teacher who teaches in Newark, New Jersey, a large city with many urban problems. She has felt frustrated over the parents' lack of involvement and interest in their children's development and school-work. She feels it diminishes her job as a teacher when she cannot follow through on her commitment to children by connecting with parents.

We know that "back to school" nights usually draw the parents who don't need to come. That, too, is frustrating for teachers because it deprives them of the chance to interact with parents whose children they want to know more about. You should realize that the appearance of indifference may be masking other conditions. We know that life can be complicated for parents. They may be unable to come to school due to work or other familial obligations. They may feel uneasy in a conference situation. They may have unpleasant associations with school based on their own educational experience.

What can you do? Generally speaking, parents sense a teacher's earnestness. If you send home a note or make a telephone call that reveals your commitment to reaching the parent, that is an important step in connecting. We realize that you may ultimately have to accept the fact that, despite your efforts to reach out to parents, some will not be there for you.

The Bewildered Parent

Being a parent has never been easy. Parenting is one of the few jobs for which there is no preparation. Parents today may be more isolated and vulnerable than in previous generations. The extended family, which provided psychological support, has largely disappeared. In most two-parent households both parents work. In single-parent families, the parent bears even more responsibility. Today's parents may be more enlightened about child rearing than their parents were. They clearly have access to more literature on the subject. But they have less firsthand knowledge of children. When both parents work, they not only have less time with their children, but also have less familiarity with their children's friends, and so have limited knowledge of the range of normal behavior. Teachers today are often called upon to provide support for bewildered parents.

Teachers express a range of opinions about bewildered parents. Rachel teaches English to special education students in a large, racially mixed suburban high school.

She loves teaching and enjoys her students. However, she is appalled by the lack of maturity on the part of parents: "They simply don't know how to be parents. They don't know how to set limits; they don't know the importance of consistency." Her reaction to what parents didn't know was one of annoyance with what she felt was a lack of parental responsibility. She felt her students were being short-changed because of the parents' ignorance about their responsibilities.

Linda, a third-grade teacher in a suburban school, strongly believes that parents today need parenting skills. She was astonished at the lack of know-how a professional couple demonstrated regarding their child. They seemed to not know when a third-grader should go to bed, let alone the kinds of limits and responsibilities they should set. Linda is troubled by the parents' fundamental lack of common sense.

Other teachers are more empathic toward parents who are unsure about how to cope with their children. Alex teaches social studies in a middle-class middle school. He empathized with parents who had adolescent children and found it "hard to know if you're doing the right thing." He understood how peer pressure can make life very difficult for parents as well as for children.

Reflection...

What is so difficult about parenting? Isn't it better we learn from our parents? If not, where do we learn how to parent and why do some parents seem to have such a hard time with parenting?

Max, the elementary school principal whom we described earlier, empathized with parents of preadolescent children, because he was going through the throes of that experience himself. He said:

> I feel for parents who are confused. My son is a pre-adolescent . . . he wants to be a baby one minute and the next minute he wants to be the independent teenager going off on his own and not wanting any questions asked of him. I know this is typical adolescence, but it's my first and only child, so the first time it hits you, it's a growth experience for the parent.

Being a parent means that you contend with uncertainty and change. Max enjoyed the challenge of growing as a parent and understood that parents must adapt to the stages their children go through. Alex understood the dilemmas of adolescents and their parents. Rachel and Linda are disturbed by what they perceive is a lack of parental responsibility where they believe it is sorely needed.

Case Study

John is a single father with two children, Sherrie (11) and Natasha (9). They both attend the same elementary school and until recently both were excellent students. Sherrie lately has been having some difficulty with her math.

Unlike his usual behavior John has been putting off visiting school. He has always been generous with his time and has served on committees, helped build a loft for the kindergarten room, and accompanied his daughters' classes on field trips. He genuinely enjoys his involvement with his daughters' school and appreciates their teachers. However, lately he makes excuses not to go to school and has not even answered the notes and calls from Sherrie's teacher.

However, school has not always been such a positive place for John. Elementary school was a demoralizing experience both socially and academically. He is now a successful businessman and a respected member of his community.

Questions and Considerations

1. What could be some explanations for John's change of behavior?
2. Suggest possible solutions.
3. Who does his behavior affect and how?

The Parent as Partner

Teachers find particular satisfaction when they encounter parents who seem to profit from a relationship with them. These parents defy categorization in terms of age or socioeconomic status. What they seem to have in common is open-mindedness, respect for the teacher's knowledge, an eagerness to learn from the teacher, and a feeling of being at ease in a school setting.

Dorothy, a second-grade teacher, enjoyed having Jessica assist as a mother: She was so involved with all the kids, not just her own. Of course, we tell parents who come on trips with us or come to school to help out that those are the rules of the game—that you are there for all the children. But Jessica *really* was interested in all of them and in my behavior with them. She watched me very closely and was very interested in picking up on my routines. She asked me a lot of questions. I could tell that she was storing away what she saw for use at home. I love having parents like that around because I do think after thirty years I know a lot and I wish I could share what I know more specifically with the parents. Jessica is like a sponge and I get such pleasure from sort of teaching her, too.

Dorothy isn't the only teacher to experience the satisfactions of developing a relationship with a parent. One of the pleasures of teaching is sharing what you know or have learned, and a likely recipient of this knowledge is a parent. But the parent has to be ready to receive and use this knowledge.

Understandably, teachers develop a perspective about parents based on the nature of their experiences. They feel frustrated with parents they cannot reach, and they also know the satisfaction of connecting meaningfully with parents who need their help. We believe that in general parents want to do the best they can for their children. We think it is useful to have some familiarity with the perspectives teachers have about parents. These perspectives are presented to show the variety of ways parents present themselves to teachers, although parents may not be conscious of the effect they have.

As you know, teaching is more than teaching subjects. Who the students are and what they contend with at home affects the attitudes they bring to school. It may be helpful for you to think of your students as someone's child who goes home to a family after being in school and blends the school experience with the realities of home life.

Teachers are required to take on many roles today. We don't suggest that your teaching world extend to the home life of children. But we do believe that the parent is your partner in education, and you can learn from and teach each other—for the benefit of your students.

Parents' Perspectives on Teachers and Schools

For some people, one of the perks of growing up is not having to go to school anymore. But that advantage ends when you become a parent and your child goes to school. The discomfort you felt as a student can return when you are in an environment you never liked in the first place. Why talk about negative feelings as we begin to consider parents' perspectives on teachers and schools? Because many of us have them. Just walking into a school can suddenly make you anxious, remembering the tests on Friday and the Sunday night feeling that Monday was coming.

Are we exaggerating? Yes and no. For many people school was a haven—a place to learn, be with friends, and be nurtured intellectually and emotionally. For others, it was a place where they felt genuinely uncomfortable. The reasons vary. They may have been the victims of poor teaching; they may have had difficulty learning; they may have had problems with social adjustment. As we consider parents' perceptions about teachers and schools, we should remember that parents vary greatly, and the more we know about the range of their attitudes, the better we can address their needs.

Why Should Parental Perspectives Be Considered?

There are two principal reasons to pay attention to parents' feelings about school. First, their attitudes toward school influence their children's attitudes and affect their behavior in class (Moore, 2008). Second, when parents demonstrate a supportive attitude about school, it has a beneficial effect on teachers. It makes them feel valued and contributes to keeping them in the profession (Newman, 2006).

Shift in Parents' Attitudes

We have already noted that before the 1960s most parents were not active in school affairs. School was the domain of teachers and children. Children went to school either knowing implicitly or being told explicitly that they should cause their parents no shame. Nowadays, however, according to one 50-year-old teacher, "The parent is likely to blame the teacher for what the child hasn't taken the trouble to learn." Although this shift in parent attitude is not universal, it is sufficiently widespread to concern teachers.

Defining Parental Perspectives on Teachers and School

It can be difficult to assess parents' attitudes about school, and that isn't your primary task as a teacher. Still, if you have some sense of the feelings parents bring to school, you will better understand them and the environments from which your students come. We present viewpoints parents have about teachers and schools to make you aware of the array of feelings and beliefs parents can have on these issues. The circumstances of parents' lives—whether they are single parents, working parents, or stepparents, for example—will also affect their relationships with teachers and schools.

When we describe parents of a particular group, we don't mean to imply that all parents will have the attributes we have used in our example. We are identifying tendencies that people in a specific group may have.

Negative Feelings

Parents with a "Good Old Days" Mentality.   This view represents the belief that teachers are not as dedicated as they were in the past. These parents believe that teachers don't work as hard as they used to and that teaching isn't the "calling" that it once was. Parents assert that the caliber of people entering the profession has declined. They contend that teachers are in the profession for the security it provides and that they don't care sufficiently about students.

Parents who have these beliefs can undermine their child's education by their lack of support for the teacher. It is confusing to a child to hear his or her parent denigrate teachers. A student's success in school can be hampered by a parental attitude of alienation from school. We identify this attitude because you may encounter it. We think the mindset of these parents can be altered as their children have positive school experiences.

Feelings of Discomfort Due to Disliking School.   As we have said, not everyone liked school as a student, and these feelings can reemerge as a parent. Consider Joyce, who never enjoyed school. She saw it as a chore she had to get through. When her daughter, Beth, began going to school, Joyce felt the old apprehensions about school return. Fortunately, Beth seems to enjoy school and this pleases Joyce because of the potential for the better life education can give Beth. Joyce's jobs have been confined to minimum wage work from which she derives little satisfaction.

One of Joyce's lingering worries is that because she wasn't a good student, she will be unable to help Beth when she gets into higher grades. Being a single parent, she sees herself as having sole responsibility for helping Beth at home. In a conference setting, a teacher can usually sense a parent's uneasiness. Joyce would feel reassured learning how well Beth was doing in school. Beth's positive adjustment is likely to contribute to Joyce's level of comfort in school. With reduced anxiety about school, Joyce could get the help she might need to assist Beth if or when she will need it.

Effects of Feeling Discomfort in School.   It may be hard to understand how a parent's discomfort about school could be more important than attending to his or her child's problems. But there are such parents. Linda is an educated woman, but she is also depressed by the emotional aspects of her life. She is not a joiner and has avoided school and parent association events. She has a son with learning difficulties and, despite being an educated person, she feels a sense of shame about her son's condition. Her uneasy feelings about school, coupled with an unwillingness to face her child's problems, interfere with finding an appropriate course of action for her son's problems.

A teacher cannot know a parent's frame of mind. We include Linda in our example of parents because, as we said earlier, parent vulnerability is a subtle but frequent condition. With parents such as Linda, listening to them in a nonjudgmental, supportive way is a first step toward making them less anxious in school.

Positive Feelings

Single Parent–Child's Advocate.   As you might expect, not all parents of children with disabilities are vulnerable and take a "head in the sand" approach to solving problems. Louisa is a 40-year-old single mother of two elementary school–age daughters. The family lives in an integrated suburb. Louisa has sole responsibility for her children and is also working toward a college degree. One of her daughters has learning difficulties in math and reading. Louisa sees herself as the child's advocate and maintains frequent contact with the teacher. Although she describes herself as having emotional problems, she has the focus and the energy to get what is best for her child.

Maria is a single mother of three children, one of whom is severely learning disabled. Like Louisa, she does not shy away from finding solutions for her son. She has an optimistic outlook about what school can do for her son. She sees teachers as being on her side and feels nurtured by the efforts they have made for him.

Effects of Feeling Comfortable in School.   Parents who feel comfortable in a school setting tend to take leadership roles in parent–teacher associations. They are in a good position to use the school beneficially for their children.

Jean has three children. Her two daughters were very school oriented, but her youngest child, Tim, was not interested in school. Jean did not work outside the home and so was fortunate in having the time to talk to Tim's teachers about him. She felt that informing teachers about one's child makes an important difference in their understanding of a puzzling student. Besides having the time to talk to Tim's teachers, Jean also had the inclination to work with them. She felt at ease in school and with teachers and so was able to help them address Tim's needs. She felt it was her obligation to share what she knew about Tim with his teachers.

Blended Family Perspectives

Blended families have many adjustments to make at home. Sometimes the school can be a haven of retreat from family conflicts. In other cases, family problems demand more solutions than the school can successfully provide. Gail was a 38-year-old teacher with a 5-year-old son and 3-year-old daughter when her husband died of a heart attack. After a period of 3 years, she married a widower, Martin, who was 10 years her senior. He had three children—daughters aged 18 and 8 and a son aged 15. When they married, Gail moved into Martin's house. There were marked differences in Gail and Martin's style of parenting. Gail set very clear limits and was consistent, whereas Martin was unable to deny his children anything. Martin's children were unaccustomed to rules, which made home life very hard for everyone.

Gail's children adjusted well to school because the orderliness their mother provided at home resembled the structure of school. Martin's children, however, were poorly adjusted at school (and at home). They no longer had the freedom at home that they were used to, and they were not involved at school.

With the help of psychological school services and family therapy, Martin's children began to function in school. They were moved to smaller schools where they could get more professional attention. Gail's children functioned well in their regular school but continued to have conflicts with their siblings at home.

As you can see, the different and conflicting parenting perspectives of Gail and Martin had an impact on their children at school as well as at home.

Teaching–Parenting Perspectives

It goes without saying that parents who also teach are comfortable in schools although they may not necessarily be in total agreement with a teacher's method of teaching. In general, though, parents who also teach feel a rapport with teachers and view them as colleagues and allies. Paula and Larry are both teachers and have three adolescent children. Paula said both she and Larry are very sympathetic to teachers. She described the atmosphere of her children's schools as "comfortable, inviting, and homey." She acknowledged that she and her husband are on the same economic and social level as the teachers, which she feels adds to the ease of communicating with them. She and Larry hold teachers in high regard and believe that most teachers work hard and seek to improve their teaching by taking courses to keep up with educational innovations.

Ruth is an example of a teacher-parent who is less contented with her children's teachers than Larry and Paula are. She has two preadolescent children and said:

> On several occasions my children have had teachers who were, in my judgment, doing a very poor job. Teachers who are parents must be very careful in the way they approach their own child's school and teachers. Over the years, I have felt uncomfortable at times having to walk that very thin line. To remember my place and then when necessary to "go to bat" for my child.

Being a teacher and parent gives a parent the opportunity to interact as a colleague with the child's teacher. The success of the relationship depends on having similar educational goals. As we know, not all teachers share a common perspective. So although being an insider as a teacher is beneficial for a parent, it doesn't guarantee the parent the understanding he or she might expect.

Reflection...

How can teachers enable parents to better understand the complexities of teaching? How can parents help the nonparent teacher understand the total responsibility of parenting?

The Parent as Learner and Partner

We have referred to the parent, Jessica, in the section on teachers' perspectives, as someone who the teacher, Dorothy, perceived as benefiting from being in her classroom. Jessica valued what she learned from the teacher, such as routines and consistency, which she had not learned elsewhere. She sees the classroom as a unique setting in which to learn about children and then to use this knowledge as a parent. It is both instructive and nurturing for her. From Jessica's perspective, the school and teachers are sources of learning and collaboration.

Summary

We have presented a range of attitudes parents have toward teachers and schools. Despite the differences in their feelings about school, parents have a common desire for their children to succeed there.

We see the school as a place for teachers and parents to exchange knowledge and perspectives. The expertise of teachers should not be confined to the classroom. Most teachers have a natural desire to communicate what they know, and this knowledge can be used by parents. Teachers have honed their skills in the laboratory setting of schools, and parents can adapt these skills for use at home. Classroom techniques, such as questioning to stimulate thinking and giving students (children) time to think and respond, could be used by parents if they aren't engaging in these practices.

We believe parents should know more about what it is like to be a teacher in today's society. Parents may not be sufficiently aware of the varied roles teachers are required to assume (e.g., social worker, surrogate parent) and the impact of these responsibilities on their teaching lives. We think that if parents better understood the complexity of teachers' professional lives, it would positively affect their relationships with them.

Schools where the development of teacher–parent collaboration and trust is given priority produce students who take learning seriously and enjoy school. (Note: Two examples are James Comer's work in schools in New Haven, Connecticut, and Deborah Meier's in the Central Park East schools in New York City.) We hope this trend will grow, and as teachers you will contribute to it.

Recommended Activities

1. Invite a panel of parents into class to discuss, from their perspective, the relationship between the parent and teacher. Make sure to include parents of children in preschool, elementary, middle, and high school classes.
2. Invite a panel of teachers into the class to discuss, from their perspective, the relationship between the teacher and parent. Make sure to include teachers from preschool, elementary school, middle school, and high school.
3. Interview teachers and/or administrators who have been teaching for over 20 years. Ask them to compare teaching today with teaching 20 years ago. Ask them specific questions about changes they see in the roles of teachers, parents, and children. What do they see as changes that are positive as well as negative?
4. Have a teacher-parent come into class and discuss the types of questions he or she hears from parents about parenting issues. How do these questions relate to teachers?
5. Identify various parenting blogs on the Internet. Describe the different groups and the emphasis of their discussions. Ask parents you know if that is the type of format they would like to have available to answer their questions or if they prefer face-to-face contact.
6. Interview parents and teachers and ask them what they perceive the role of the parent to be in the school. If they identify roles, ask them to describe the differences they see with parent involvement in schools today compared to when they were growing up.
7. Survey children of different ages to determine what kind of role they would like to have their parents play in schools. Make sure to survey different age groups from 4-year-olds to 17-year-olds.

Children's Books

The following children's books are suggested as a way of helping your students consider issues in this chapter.

Thank You, Mr. Falker
Patricia Polacco, Patricia Gauch
Reading Level: Ages 6–9
Penguin Putnam Books (2001)

Hooray for Diffendoofer Day!
Dr. Seuss, Jack Prelutsky, Lane Smith (Illustrator)
Random House (2001)

My Teacher Sleeps in School
Leatie Weiss, Ellen Weiss (Illustrator)
Reading Level: Ages 5–7
Penguin Putnam Books for Young Readers (2009)

Teacher from the Black Lagoon
Mike Thaler, Jared Lee (Illustrator)
Reading Level: Ages 4–6
Scholastic, Inc. (2008)

Additional Resources

Parental Participation

Books:

Lawrence-Lightfoot, S. (2004). *The essential conversation: What parents and teachers can learn from each other*. New York: Ballantine Books.

McDermott, D. (2007). *Developing caring relationships among parents, children, schools and communities*. Thousand Oaks, CA: Sage.

Rudney, G. L. (2005). *Every teacher's guide to working with parents*. Thousand Oaks, CA: Corwin.

Tutwiler, S. W. (2005). *Teachers as collaborative partners: Working with diverse families and communities*. New York: Routledge.

Articles:

Valli, L., & Buese, D. (2007). The changing roles of teachers in an era of high-stakes. *American Educational Research Journal, 44*(3), 519–558.

Organizations:

National Association for the Education of Young Children (NAEYC)
Phone: (202) 232-8777
www.naeyc.org

Parents as Teachers National Center
Phone: (314) 432-4330
www.parentsasteachers.org

Parental Rights
Phone: (540)-751-1200
www.parentalrights.org

DVDs:
Conducting Parent–Teacher Conferences: A Partnership in Progress

Examines how to improve communication between teachers and parents when they meet at parent–teacher conferences to better serve the student. 2007. (30 minutes)

Websites:

Parent Teacher Association (PTA)
www.pta.org

Parent Zone
www.parentzone.org

Teacher/Parent/Trainer Site List
www.edpro.com

Parent Teacher (Turning parents into volunteers)
www.parentteacher.net

Teachers and Families
www.teachersandfamilies.com/index.html

References

Bushaw, W., & Lopez, S. (2010, September). A time for change: The 42nd annual Phi Delta Kappa/Gallup Poll of the public's attitudes towards the public schools. *Phi Delta Kappa, 92*(1), 9–26.

Kohn, A. (1998, April). Only for my kid: How privileged parents undermine school reform. *Phi Delta Kappa*.

Lortie, D. C. (2002). *Schoolteacher* (2nd ed.). Chicago: University of Chicago Press.

MacDonald, J. B. (1994). *Teaching and parenting: Effects of the dual role*. Lanham, MD: University Press of America.

Moore, K. (2008). *Effective instructional strategies: From theory to practice* (2nd ed.). Thousand Oaks, CA: Sage.

Newman, J. W. (2006). *America's teachers: An introduction to education* (5th ed.). New York: Allyn & Bacon.

Chapter Six

Parent–Teacher Communication: Who's Talking?

Sara Fritzell Hanhan
University of North Dakota

Yuliya Kartoshkina
University of North Dakota

Communication is a critical component in any parent, teacher, and community education setting. Communication has taken on a much larger meaning with the increase in technology. The purpose of this chapter is to help the reader:

▶ Identify principles for establishing two-way communication with parents.

▶ Identify significant barriers to good home–school communications and how to overcome them.

▶ Describe a variety of ways of communicating with families.

▶ Identify ways technology has changed over the past 10 years and the effect those changes have on parent–teacher communication.

Importance of Communication Between Teachers and Families

Although many of you may believe strongly that parents and schools should form true partnerships in order to maximize the benefit of parent involvement, this is not always easy to achieve. It requires mutual commitment, action, trust, and understanding on the part of both parents and school personnel. One of the first steps teachers can take toward successful parent involvement and the possibility for true home–school partnerships is to learn the ins and outs of communicating with parents. This is not so different from skillful communication with anyone else, of course, but there are some purposes and nuances that can be particular to parent–teacher relationships.

In many teacher education programs, students are required to take a course in communication, usually a course in fundamentals of public speaking. When a rationale for the requirement is offered, it is usually that teachers need to learn to feel comfortable speaking in front of a group and to make an organized and articulate presentation. Although there are few occasions for teachers to give formal speeches to groups of parents, the direction of much parent–teacher communication nonetheless tends to be one-way, flowing from teacher to parent, with an expectation or perhaps even a hope that parents will receive teacher wisdom passively. Some of the most common methods teachers use to communicate with parents are newsletters, parent handbooks, orientation meetings, and report cards, which typically involve the teacher *telling* parents about activities, school policies and procedures, student progress, curriculum, and so on. Even parent–teacher conferences are sometimes viewed as opportunities to *tell* parents how their children are doing in school. The idea is to have parents informed.

Although just as important as the teacher education emphasis on speech, courses on *listening* not only are not required for teacher certification, but are seldom even available at any college or university in the country. Teachers, in other words, despite rhetoric about the importance of good home–school communication, are taught to talk rather than to listen to students and parents. To reap the benefits of parent involvement, however, parents too must speak and be heard. Communication must flow in at least two directions (National PTA, 1997), and for this to happen both parent and teacher need to consider each other as equals.

In most cases teachers need to take the initiative to make this happen. Problematic for a parent–teacher relationship based on equality is the inherent inequality of the relative positions of teacher and parent within the school. For many parents, their own children's initial school enrollment is their first contact with teachers and schools since they themselves were students, and school memories for adults are not always pleasant. Whether or not memories of school are pleasant, however, parents' childhood relationships with teachers were inherently unequal, and for many the nature of that relationship lives on, even though they are now adults. Teachers must also keep in mind that in some cultures parents cannot even imagine the idea of a parent–teacher partnership. In these cultures the expectation is that the teacher is always right and that it is best for the child and the parent to remain quiet about concerns they might have.

Reflection...

Think about your teachers from elementary or secondary school. Which teacher would you look forward to having a frank conversation with—and which would you not? What makes your memories of these teachers different?

In addition to a perceived inequality between teacher and parent, parents are also keenly aware that they have placed the welfare of their children in the hands of teachers and that each teacher potentially has the power to make children's school lives either comfortable or difficult. For this reason, many parents tread lightly within the parent–teacher relationship, unwilling from their perspective to upset the child–teacher relationship for fear that the teacher might take it out on the child.

Finally, an important idiosyncratic quality of the teacher–parent relationship is that the stakes are so high. To be sure, this is true of some other relationships that rely on good communication as well, but in this case the quality of the relationship may affect what happens to a child's life—something that for many of us is of ultimate importance and bears a heavy weight of responsibility.

Building Relationships

Building true partnerships is a process that requires both teachers and parents to create a shared meaning about education. However, it is not an easy process to create shared meanings. Many differences exist between teachers and families, such as socioeconomic status, education, cultural background, group affiliation, and others (Shalaway, 2005). Teachers have developed their own unique set of ideas, customs, traditions, and methodologies through their own education, experience, and environments. Professional educators must remain aware that cooperating with families brings different knowledge bases and ideas to the relationship. Teachers and parents should not forget that they are united by a common goal—to help children develop the knowledge, skills, and abilities that will assist them in finding their personalities and fulfilling their roles as members of society. Teachers need to recognize that each child has a unique personality, family situation, and environment that shape the learning process. Children can be introverted or extraverted, brave or hesitant, respectful or rude, enthusiastic or passive, patient or impatient. Students will have varying inclinations toward art, sports, music, and extracurricular activities. Their families may have recently immigrated or struggle with poverty. Some children are led by a single parent or by parents who are remarried, and there are many other unique situations in which children find themselves today. Children's environments can vary from rural to urban, quiet to noisy. They may have limited access to outdoor activities. Some children are surrounded by a rich community of extended family, whereas others have only a few immediate family. By learning about the context in which their students live, teachers can better understand the families that they are working with. Ultimately, teachers begin to develop personal relationships that are based on the child's unique experience. Some teachers use their own cultural lenses to interact with culturally and linguistically diverse parents, and this may cause a disconnect in relationships with these parents (Colombo, 2004). To address this, teachers can take time to reflect on their own culture and its limitations, seek information on cultures represented in their classrooms, and develop activities that will welcome diversity. Teachers can invite speakers from the community to talk about their cultural backgrounds, and they can celebrate various cultural holidays in the classroom. They can also try to understand the difficulties faced by immigrant parents. By learning about the unique culture of every family, teachers will be able to understand their students better and also reflect on their own cultural background.

Although it takes time and motivation to nurture student respect, establish trust, and find that common ground, this effort will harvest rewards in children's futures.

Reflection...

Write down the values that are important to you as a teacher. Think about why you have those values and how you developed them. Do you know other cultures that might have different educational values?

Communication Barriers and Ways to Overcome Them

Establishing strong communication between teachers and families is not an easy task. There are several barriers that may interfere with the creation of shared meanings and responsibilities.

Parents' Perspectives

It is important to be aware that parents may be prone to criticize teachers for ineffective communication. Many parents believe that it is the teacher's obligation to make the initial contact and report on a child's performance at school. These parents are waiting for teachers to make the first step in establishing communication. Therefore, it is crucial that teachers understand this expectation and begin to lay the foundation for a partnership with parents as soon as they receive their student rosters (Hoover-Dempsey et al., 2005).

Another common critique from parents is that teachers wait until issues become severe and fail to contact parents when the issue first appears (Hawes, 2008). Many parents also argue that feedback should be provided on a continual basis for both positive and negative events and communication should be constant throughout the school year (Montgomery, 2005). For all the reasons stated, it is good practice to contact parents before you become concerned about a child's academic progress or behavior. The sooner a parent is involved, the easier it will be to develop a mutual understanding of the problem and collaborate on possible solutions.

Although parents want their children to succeed in school, many also believe that it is the school's responsibility to teach students the most important skills (Montgomery, 2005). Some parents question the amount of work that their child is asked to do at home. Researchers have found that parents tend to forget the advanced instruction and considerable homework that was an essential part of their own learning as schoolchildren. Make it a priority to explain to parents your expectations at the beginning of a school year. Offer them a variety of avenues in which they can become involved in the educational process of their children.

Teachers should be sensitive to research that shows parents report confusion and insecurity about their roles and responsibilities as partners with teachers (Yerger, 2010). Parents might view teachers as experts in teaching and learning, and feel intimidated to approach them as authority figures. All too often, teachers use educational jargon that confuses parents and presents an obstacle to establishing rapport.

Parents appreciate teachers who take the time to explain and discuss with them the learning process and how their children are progressing at school. By knowing what is expected of their children at school—and how these expectations lead to academic success—parents become more involved in the educational process. Parents are then motivated to assist their children with homework and may inspire them to study (Hoover-Dempsey et al., 2005). As children often behave differently at home and school, this dialogue between parent and teacher benefits parents by giving them access to another side of their children's lives. By communicating with teachers, parents will understand their children better by discovering how their children think, learn, and behave outside of the home.

Finally, many parents have restrictions that keep them from interacting with their child's school as much as they would like to. Some of them report a lack of time due to their work commitment, reliable transportation, technology, and skills to communicate as frequent as they want. Some of them might also have physical and mental disabilities (Montgomery, 2005). To address these issues, teachers can survey parents at the beginning of the year to learn about possible challenges in communication and inquire about parents' schedules and availability. This helps teachers to understand unique family situations and develop ways to work with them. Some adjustments might include organizing home visits for those parents who cannot come to school, providing transportation and dinner for some after-class events, or organizing classes to teach technology skills.

Reflection...

Describe how you would establish effective communication between yourself as a teacher and a family. Do you think your feelings about home–school communication would change if you had children in school and were teaching?

Teachers' Perspectives

Some teachers are convinced that many parents often place their careers and social events before involvement in their child's education. If this is actually the case, it leaves both instruction and the majority of moral support on teachers (Sirvani, 2007). Some think that parents do not provide the quality of character education and guidance they did in the past. Thus, teachers have to do the parental work of teaching rules of social interaction in addition to following state curriculum. Teachers also report that they are not happy with declining parental involvement in the school and community in general. Before blaming parents and comparing their involvement with the old days, however, teachers need to remember that the pace of life has changed, and socioeconomic pressures on parents have increased. In the past, more parents could stay at home and not work, whereas now many do not have that luxury. As a result, teachers need to concentrate on what can be done to accommodate the needs of parents who live, work, and raise children in a modern, fast-paced society (Xu & Gulosino, 2006).

In addition, many teachers believe that parents need to update their memories of fundamental knowledge and skills, especially in mathematics and reading, so they can help their children with homework. It may be helpful to provide parents with an opportunity to take classes to refresh old skills and learn new ones, such as using a computer and other new technologies (Scott, 2007). By providing these opportunities, schools empower parents and increase their involvement in their child's learning process. For example, in one school in Great Britain, parents enrolled in a review program to refresh mathematical skills that resulted in better performance for their children in math classes (Andrews, 2008).

Some teachers feel that they do not have sufficient training for establishing communication with parents and family involvement. Many teacher-education programs do not offer necessary classes on interpersonal communication and family involvement. According to Yerger St. George (2010), professional development initiatives for teachers can help improve their communication skills, educate them about the value of including parents, and provide practical ideas on how to accomplish that.

Significant Barriers to Good Communication

Language

In addition to the barrier of perceived inequality, language itself poses a number of stumbling blocks for those teachers and parents who wish to establish open and two-way communication. Teachers need to think about what language to use with parents (Graham-Clay, 2005). It can be ambiguous. Mutual understanding requires both clear articulation on the part of the speaker/writer and accurate interpretation on the part of the listener/reader. The very acts of speaking, listening, writing, and reading, however, leave much room for misinterpretation. Teachers may, for instance, in the hopes of lessening parental disappointment, couch what they have to say about children in gentle terms, which in turn may be interpreted by one parent as teacher satisfaction or by another as a cover-up of serious problems. Another example that illustrates the importance of specificity and clarity comes from a first-grade parent–teacher conference. The teacher told the parent in this conference that her child was "what we call immature." When the parent inquired further about her immaturity, the teacher offered that "she was reluctant to try new things." The parent in turn asked what she was reluctant to do. The teacher said that the child was unwilling to climb some bleacher-like stairs. At this point, the teacher's comments made sense to the mother because she knew of her daughter's fear of heights; only now could she be of some help to the teacher in offering both an explanation and the beginnings of a solution.

Although there is ambiguity in cases such as the above example, parents at least have the background to make some interpretation. When educational jargon is used, however, parents can be left feeling inept, ashamed, or even stupid or embarrassed to ask for an explanation. What does it mean to have an "auditory processing problem" or good "visual–spatial abilities" or "learning disabilities"? It seems best for teachers to forgo jargon of all kinds in favor of using everyday language that is as descriptively specific and as free of value judgments as possible. This also holds true for parents whose native language is not English, but there is even more risk of misunderstanding when everyday language may be difficult to understand. In such cases, if the school cannot provide a translator, it may be wise to invite the parent to bring in someone with whom he or she feels comfortable and who can help translate for both the teacher and the parent.

Body Language

The influence of nonverbal messages can also complicate the communication process. Body positions (e.g., arms and legs folded tightly), gestures (e.g., a shrug of the shoulders), facial expressions (e.g., a quivering lip or flaring nostrils), voice intonation or rate of speech (e.g., a firm and monotone voice), or an involuntary behavior (e.g., a quick inhale of breath) can all carry signals to the listener. If your nonverbal behaviors do not correspond with the message you wish to convey, or if

TABLE 6.1   Nonverbal Communication

Attitude	Nonverbal Cue	Attitude	Nonverbal Cue
Openness	Open hands Unbuttoned coat	Nervousness	Clearing throat "Whew" sound
Defensiveness	Arms crossed on chest Crossing legs Fist-like gestures Pointing index finger		Whistling Picking or pinching flesh Fidgeting in chair Hand covering mouth while speaking
Evaluation	Hand-to-face gestures Head tilted Stroking chin Peering over glasses Taking glasses off, cleaning Earpiece of glasses in mouth Pipe smoker gestures Putting hand to bridge of nose		Not looking at the other person Tugging at pants while seated Jingling money in pockets Tugging at ear Perspiration, wringing of hands
		Frustration	Short breaths "Tsk" sounds Tightly clenched hands
Suspicion	Arms crossed Sideways glance Touching, rubbing nose Rubbing eyes Buttoning coat—drawing away		Wringing hands Fist-like gestures Pointing index finger Rubbing hand through hair Rubbing back of neck
Insecurity	Pinching flesh Chewing pen, pencil Thumb over thumb, rubbing Biting fingernails Hands in pockets	Cooperation	Upper body leaning forward Open hands Sitting on edge of chair Hand-to-face gestures Unbuttoning coat Tilted head
		Confidence	Hands behind back Back stiffened Hands in pockets with thumbs out Hands on lapels of coat

you are unfamiliar with the meanings of nonverbal behaviors in other cultures, these behaviors can become obstacles to clear and sensitive communication.

Body language can provide information about a person's emotional state (see Table 6.1). The person who folds his or her arms and quickly turns away is most likely upset. This can be useful information. On the other hand, you do not want to overinterpret every movement. Some people are more comfortable sitting with their legs or arms crossed, and it is their desire for comfort, rather than a nonverbal message, that may be the reason for the position.

You need to be aware of clusters of behaviors that seem unusual for that person. You can then use this information to help rethink how you can best deal with the situation. It is also a good idea to monitor your own body language when dealing with parents—especially if it is a tense moment. What is it saying about you? Are you demonstrating defensiveness?

In addition, teachers sometimes must deal with parents who are exhibiting contradictory nonverbal messages. Most seasoned teachers have had the experience of talking with a parent whose voice is calm, and face smiling, but who has tears running down his or her face. In situations such as these you can say something such as, "I noticed that while we were talking about Beth's reading scores you were upset." It is then important to give them a few moments to think about what they are going to say about this emotional topic. This is also just as necessary with the parent whose body language suggests anger and hostility.

Still other barriers to effective two-way communication include such things as fatigue, lack of time, ego involvement (often manifested in defensiveness), differences in personality or communicative pace (most of us can think of people who speak annoyingly slowly or quickly), preoccupation with personal circumstances or other distractions, differing communicative purposes, or simply differences in status, age, gender, race, or culture. Obviously no matter how hard an individual teacher tries to establish a communicative flow that is two-way, there may be other contributing factors that make it impossible. But there are strategies that can be used successfully to lessen the impact of such factors.

Significant Aids to Good Communication

Active Listening

Using everyday, but descriptive, language to clearly articulate ideas in nonjudgmental ways is obviously important for conducting effective two-way communication; but even the most gifted speaker will not support a reciprocal conversation if he or she does not listen. A key to establishing a relationship in which two (or more) people communicate effectively is *active listening*. If you think of someone you consider a good listener, you can probably identify some of the visible outward characteristics that communicate close listening. Active listeners tend to maintain eye contact with the speaker; their posture communicates attentiveness, often with a forward lean; they may encourage the speaker by nodding, raising eyebrows, or smiling appropriately in response to what the speaker is saying; they ask pertinent questions, sometimes to check their perceptions; they get rid of or ignore potential distractions; they acknowledge the feelings of the speaker; and mostly, they stop talking.

These are behaviors that are practicable and learnable, but active listening is more than just outward behavior; it is an attitude. The active listener *wants* to hear what is being said, and he or she listens with the goal of hearing—and empathetically understanding—what the speaker is saying; he or she is nonjudgmental. Active listening on the part of a teacher can communicate a wish to engage in real two-way communication, and this in turn begins to equalize the position of those in the relationship. When the teacher begins to listen and respond with empathy and understanding, mutual trust and respect begin to develop, and the parent(s) are able to speak out (and to listen actively and intelligently themselves). Communication begins to flow two ways, with each party truly hearing the other and therefore responding appropriately.

Honesty

In addition to a context of mutual respect and trust, active listening, and the use of descriptive and nonjudgmental language, communication must be based on a commitment to openness and honesty. If parents (and teachers) feel they are being manipulated or lied to, communications will break down. All of these qualities simultaneously interact to provide the atmosphere in which true partnerships can be developed and maintained. The foundation for the success of the following kinds of teacher–parent communication is the early establishment of relationships that embrace and enact the above qualities.

Types of Communication

There are many ways of initiating parent–teacher relationships, and each of them should be planned with an eye to establishing a context in which teacher and parent are coequal, leading, in turn, to the establishment of communication that is two-way, respectful, honest, and productive. The most common types of communication between teachers and parents can be categorized as verbal (oral) communication, written communication, communication through technology, and communication on special occasions.

Reflection . . .

Describe how you would establish effective communication between yourself as a teacher and family. Do you think your *expectations* about home–school communication would change if you had children in school and were teaching?

Verbal (Oral) Communication

Verbal communication requires strong interpersonal skills from teachers and a desire to listen and understand. Teachers who project warmth, friendliness, honesty, and respect have fewer difficulties establishing good relationships with parents than those who talk to parents in a cold, professional tone.

Initial Interview

Some schools or centers have initial (intake) interviews for parents when they enroll their children. These interviews should be viewed as opportunities for parents to ask for and receive information about the school and for the teachers and administrators to learn about the child from the parents. For instance, parents might share with teachers their child's interests or preferred ways of spending free time, as well as the family's linguistic, religious, and cultural background. They can provide medical information that could be relevant for teachers, especially in emergency situations. The name and phone number of the child's doctor, food allergies or other diet restrictions, medical conditions that might require special responses or that might affect the child's school performance are a few examples. Teachers and administrators, in turn, can introduce parents to the physical spaces, rules, and expectations of the school or center. During intake interviews, parents and teachers have an opportunity to talk about the meaning and value of education in the children's future. Information received at the interviews can allow teachers to build a curriculum responsive to children's background, interests, and needs.

Initial information from and to parents might be made in writing (e.g., an enrollment form to be filled out by the parents or a policy manual for parents to take home), or the information might be offered and received verbally. Many educators advise using both an oral and written method of communicating initial information—oral because it is more personal and written because there is no guarantee verbally stated information will be remembered. And in the case of the school receiving personal information about children, the sheer number of children precludes the possibility of a person remembering details for each child with any accuracy.

Although intake interviews are usually conducted by principals or directors, it is important for teachers, if at all possible, to attend them to initiate communicative and two-way relationships early. In the event that teachers cannot attend such interviews (often the case, as teachers have class preparation to attend to and initial intake interviews most logically complement the administrative processes of registering), there are many other kinds of activities that can help establish early relationships both with families and among families, and with students. Some that we've heard about or used ourselves include a beginning-of-the-year family picnic, a personal phone call to welcome each family to the school, a welcoming postcard sent prior to the beginning of school, a home visit by the teacher, a family–teacher start-of-the-year social, or an invitation to families and students to visit the classroom together. Such activities can take many forms, but the objective should be to exchange information and to initiate personal attention from the teacher to lay a foundation for two-way communication.

Home Visits

Teachers in some schools and educational programs such as Head Start visit parents in their homes for a variety of reasons. Although a frequently cited reason for such home visits is that they allow teachers opportunities to see the home contexts of children as a way of understanding them better and gaining some empathy for their families, other reasons may be just as compelling. Many teachers say that home visits strengthen home–school partnerships, improve communication with the parents, as well as help them understand the child better by observing the child's home environment (Meyer & Mann, 2006). Home visits at the beginning of the school year can establish an early context for two-way communication. Parents generally appreciate the teacher's efforts to come to their territory—a place where they are in charge and where the teacher is a guest. Making a home visit can signal to a parent that the teacher is interested in the family and a partnership, and when this occurs, parents often start the year ready to work together rather than spending valuable time trying to find their role with the teacher (Burian, Haveman, Jacobson, & Rood, 1993). In addition, children are often quite taken by the presence of their teacher in their home, and they too start the school year more enthusiastically. The relationships in these cases are already initiated before school even gets started.

There is need for some caution related to home visits as well. It is important to allow parents to refuse a home visit. They may be self-conscious about the conditions of their home, or they simply may not be individuals who are pleased to welcome others into their home. Also, some teachers recommend doing home visits in pairs, both to help collect multiple perspectives and to guard against the possibility of a threatening visit. It should be noted, however, that each additional person from the school upsets the balance of equality. Unfortunately, lack of funding often means that teachers cannot be paid to conduct home visits, but many teachers, after experiencing the good will that comes from them, are willing to do them on their own time.

Informal Communication

The most common method of regular communication, especially with families of young children, is the casual conversation parents have with teachers while dropping off or picking up their children from school. For parents who do this, this may, in fact, be the most important place for tone setting. A casual conversation, if done with respect and with genuine interest in the parent's child, can go a long way simply because it does not occur in a more formal setting, such as a parent–teacher conference where parents may feel as if formal feedback is what goes on record. In the daily conversations parents have with teachers, feedback (two-way) is generally considered more helpful than threatening, more flexible than permanent.

For parents of children who are old enough to get themselves to school or for parents who are too busy or unable to make daily trips to the school or whose children ride buses, other means of regular informal communications can substitute. Perhaps one of the most common is the phone call. Although teachers may view this as an imposition on their personal time, a call to a parent of each child, well-spaced over the course of the first month of school, can be a key to parents realizing that the teacher is approachable and genuinely concerned about children and parental opinions. You should be warned, however, that despite many classrooms now having their own phones, most teachers do not do this, and as a result a phone call out of the blue from a teacher may initially be frightening to parents. If no one has ever called the parent from school or there have only been calls when something is wrong (the child is sick or misbehaving), it may take more than one call to convince the parent that you are calling just to check in or to describe an interesting event. It is for this reason that we recommend that the first call of the year be a positive one. If this is the case, later calls that might not be so pleasant will be received much more willingly.

Parent–Teacher Conferences

Although there was a time when parent–teacher conferences were not used except when there was trouble afoot, they are now probably the single most frequently used (and most institutionalized) method of parent–teacher communication in schools and other educational settings. The parent–teacher conference may vary in its frequency, length, and even purpose, but most often it occurs twice a year, lasting about 15 or 20 minutes, largely for the purpose of informing parents of their child's progress in school. Perhaps one reason that it has become such a stable method of home–school communication is that it has been relatively successful. For the most part, parents appreciate a time to talk to the teacher about their child's school life, and when done at regular intervals, with administrative time and support, it affords teachers an organized means of ensuring that each family has an opportunity to be personally informed. It is also interesting to note, however, that many teachers come to view these conferences as a chore rather than an opportunity and that both teachers and parents report some nervousness about them. The conferences can be emotionally draining for teachers and parents. Parents and teachers further complain that there is usually not enough time for meaningful conversation, and teachers often note, with regret, that the parents whom they most need to see do not come.

Even though it is improbable that parent–teacher conferences on their own can create two-way communication patterns between teachers and parents, there are a number of strategies that can be brought to bear at conferences that will maximize their potential for supporting other efforts at good parent–teacher communication. They can be scheduled, for instance, to accommodate parents' work schedules. Many schools now have parent–teacher conferences scheduled during one evening as well as during the day. It can also be helpful to parents to schedule conferences for siblings back-to-back, so that one trip to school will suffice to see the teachers of all the children in the same family.

The conference environment can be made less threatening as well. Seating parents next to the teacher at a table, rather than on the other side of a desk, can reduce the perception of unequal positions. Making parents comfortable with adult-sized chairs can help put them at ease. When possible, not keeping parents waiting and getting up to greet them at the door can communicate care and interest and help make parents feel welcome and valued. Engaging in a minute of small talk before addressing the conference agenda can also help put parents at ease and make the atmosphere more friendly.

Although 15 or 20 minutes is a very short time to accomplish much in the way of communication, there are other things that can be kept in mind that can help maximize the success of the conversation itself. Experts recommend, for instance, that discussion about the child start out and end with something positive. If there is a concern to be communicated, it is best done in the middle of the conference (Rockwell, Andre, & Hawley, 1996). It is also important to limit the number of areas of concern expressed at any one time, especially if the advice and help of the parent is desired, as it is difficult for anyone to effectively deal with a litany of concerns at once. It is also important and very effective to be able to describe something about the child that shows the parent that you know the child in ways that go beyond grades on tests and academic performances. What engages her in class? Who are his friends? What role does he play in a group project? How does she express herself?

Two controversial activities related to parent–teacher conferences are note taking and parents bringing others to the conference. Although there are some advantages to either a parent or a teacher taking notes at conferences, there are also disadvantages. Note taking both helps the note taker remember what has been said and conveys to the other person that he or she takes what is said seriously. On the other hand, note taking can convey an impression that the note taker is creating a written record that could be used against the speaker. This becomes a particularly touchy issue in a litigious time and culture such as ours. Whatever your inclination, however, permission to take notes should be requested before doing so.

Although some teachers react strongly to the presence of anyone but the parents in a conference, parents do have a right to bring others with them, and sometimes there are sound reasons for doing so. Especially when issues such as special education diagnosis or placement are being discussed, it helps to have a second pair of ears. When we take in difficult or disappointing information, we tend to focus on only the most shocking elements of the conversation. We can miss such things as suggestions for action or possible alternative interpretations. For this reason, we should welcome friends or relatives who come to help parents hear. We should also welcome child caregivers when parents have invited them to be part of the conference, as they often have as much information to contribute to the conversation as the parents do. For non-English-speaking parents, a friend can serve as a translator and is often a welcome relief for both teacher and parent. If, however, parents have been accompanied by someone and they seem to be uneasy about the person's presence, or if a neighbor has just come along for the ride (and may be a possible gossip), it is appropriate to request that such individuals wait outside while you confer with the parent(s). Decisions about children attending their siblings' conferences depend on the preferences of the teacher and the parent, the age of the children, and the purpose for their attendance, and need to be determined on an individual basis. Similarly what happens if the parents are divorced or separated? Frequently the teachers, when presented with those situations, will hold separate conferences with the parents.

Reflection...

How would you make sure fathers are included in conferences? What if both parents were female (a lesbian relationship)?

These suggestions can help make the parent–teacher conference pleasant and productive, but they don't go very far toward increasing the reciprocal nature of information flow. It's important to save time for parents' questions and discussion of any agenda they might bring to the conference. And if time runs out during the regularly scheduled conference, arrangements should be made for a second conference. In fact, parents need to feel that they can request a conference with the teacher at any time during the year, without suspicion.

Effective parent–teacher conferences require planning, thoughtful action, and timely follow-up on the part of the teacher and the parent. Table 6.2 offers a helpful

TABLE 6.2 Conference Checklist

Pre-Conference

_____1. Notify
    –Purpose, place, time, length of time allotted
_____2. Prepare
    –Review child's folder
    –Gather examples of work
    –Prepare materials
_____3. Plan agenda
_____4. Arrange environment
    –Comfortable seating
    –Eliminate distractions

Conference

_____1. Welcome
    –Establish rapport
_____2. State
    –Purpose
    –Time limitations
    –Note taking
    –Options for follow-up
_____3. Encourage
    –Information sharing
    –Comments
    –Questions
_____4. Listen
    –Pause once in a while!
    –Look for verbal and nonverbal cues
    –Questions
_____5. Summarize
_____6. End on a positive note

Post-Conference

_____1. Review conference with child, if appropriate
_____2. Share information with other school personnel, if needed

Source: Modified from material developed by Roger Kroth and the Parent Involvement Center, University of New Mexico.

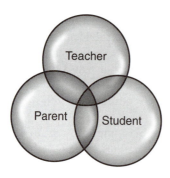

Figure 6.1   Three-Way Conferences

checklist for teachers as they engage in their parent–teacher conferences. Of course the most important element in supporting parental participation in a conference is to stop talking and start listening!

A popular model for conferences includes the student in the conference. This model can be used from first grade on. In this case, the creation of shared meanings must involve all parties—teachers, parents, and students (see Figure 6.1). In this way, all stakeholders have an opportunity to express their opinions and share knowledge, experience, and understanding. All voices are valued.

There should be a dialogue about expectations and the value, process, and outcomes of learning. This will help students to receive support from both school and family and understand what is expected of them in the learning process. By knowing what is necessary to learn at school and why, children will continue to develop their natural curiosity and positive attitudes will form as they learn new skills and material.

There are several methods of conducting this type of conference and numerous variations. The following are three possible scenarios.

Beginning of the School Year.   Meet during the first weeks of school to set goals for the school year and discuss how these goals will be met. At this time the responsibility of each participant should be determined and written down for future reference. The time and date for the next conference might also be determined.

Midyear.   This conference should begin with a collective evaluation of the success of the previously set goals. At this time, adjustments to the goals and responsibilities should be made as needed. These adjustments might involve knowledge not available to the participants earlier in the semester. An appointment might be made for the next conference.

Final Conference.   Again, it is important to review the original goals and the modifications made during the second conference. This is a time to evaluate the year's progress. It is important that all areas be evaluated—areas of strength as well as areas of concern. It is also a time for parents, teachers, and students to enjoy the successes of the year.

Both teachers and parents have reported this as a productive format. By including students in the conferences, the responsibility for a team effort includes not only parents and teachers, but also students. The number of conferences may vary according to individual need and school policy.

Case Study

Conferences have just concluded and Julie, a third-grade teacher, is disappointed that Todd's parents didn't attend. They had returned the conference request slip indicating that they would be there. Julie was particularly anxious to meet with Todd's parents because he has both academic and behavioral problems. Julie has sent notes to Todd's parents and left several messages on their answering machine but has not heard from them.

Questions and Considerations

1. What are some possible reasons for Todd's parents not attending the conference, answering the phone messages, or acknowledging Julie's written communications?
2. List other ways Julie might communicate with these parents other than the traditional school meeting.
3. Who else (school personnel) might be of assistance to Julie?

Written Communication

Written communication has a permanence about it that demands a particular kind of attention. Although it can take many forms and can be informal or formal, teachers are expected to write in proper English with correct spelling and use clear language. When this is not the case, negative judgment of the teacher may occur, interfering with expectations of coequality. Likewise, teachers need to guard against negative judgment of parents who have poor writing skills or who are illiterate, lest this too interfere with a coequal relationship. The goal of written communication is to organize concise and accurate information so that parents are able and willing to read and understand it (Graham-Clay, 2005). However, many forms of written communication have a potential for fostering one-way communication and perpetuating the distance between parents and teachers. It is possible, however, to turn such attempts into two-way communications and involve parents not only in reading but also in contributing to them. The following are the most common types of written communication used by teachers at different school levels.

Welcoming Letters

It is very important for teachers to initiate communication with parents. Sending a welcoming letter before school starts will show parents that you are interested in meeting their child, help them prepare for your expectations in the classroom, and inform them of how they can become involved. The length of this letter varies from teacher to teacher and depends on how much information a teacher wants to share. Here are some things a welcoming letter might include:

About the teacher
- Information about your background and experience
- The best way and time to contact you

About the school/class/center
- The stated philosophy or principles of the school or center
- The school year schedule
- School or center policy around attendance, etc.

For parents
- Ways parents can be involved in their child's education
- A sincere invitation for parents to share their concerns, visit the classroom, and provide support
- Description of communication tools that you will be using throughout the year (a regular newsletter, homework folder, classroom website, etc.)

Feedback
- A form through which parents can express how they would like to communicate with you, indicate how they want to be involved, and share their expectations for their child

Parents will appreciate you taking the time to share this information with them and if they sense your sincerity may be more willing to collaborate with you.

Newsletters

One of the most common forms of written communication with parents is the *newsletter*. This is a regular written publication that most often informs parents of the events in the classroom either prior to or following the events themselves. Most newsletters are sent biweekly or monthly, but how often they are published is up to the individual teacher or school. There should be consistency of format whereby all newsletters have the same color, fonts, paper size, and quality. The most important elements of a newsletter include student-oriented materials, family involvement materials, informational materials, and most importantly, a place for feedback.

Student-oriented materials provide you with an opportunity to share with parents the exciting things that are occurring in the classroom. It is important to include students' work and pictures when they are working on projects. Make certain that every student is mentioned several times during a school year. Inclusion of students' work provides children with pride and ownership and can entice even reluctant parents into reading them.

Family involvement materials provide parents with the opportunity to feel connected with their children's lives in the classroom and to become a source of support for their school success. They give parents ideas on how to connect their home activities with classroom material, open up involvement in the classroom, and increase parent-to-parent communication. By inviting parents' involvement in and outside of the classroom and by opening up communication through newsletters, teachers can also develop a better understanding of students' broader sociocultural background (Jensen, 2006). For convenience, a copy of a current newsletter can be located on a classroom website. To assess the needs of individual families, teachers can have newsletters in languages other than English available on their websites.

Informational materials keep parents knowledgeable about what their children are doing and learning in the classroom. By being informed, parents will be able to talk to their children about school activities at home and extend students' learning and exploration beyond the classroom. Teachers can share books they are reading with students, strategies used to explain math assignments, and many other activities that are taking place in the classroom. Parents can feel empowered by this knowledge and may be more willing to be involved in classroom activities.

The following is a list of possible newsletter items:

Student-oriented materials
- Samples of students' work (writing samples, art projects, etc.)
- Relevant quotations from students about their work and experience in the classroom
- Pictures of students at work

Parent involvement materials
- Requests for needed materials
- Out-of-classroom resources related to current classroom activities
- Strategies to practice classroom material at home
- Requests to submit photographs, drawings, and written materials on various topics (family trips, cultural holidays, etc.)

Informational materials
- Important dates to remember
- School and community announcements
- Short articles that might be of particular interest to parents
- Thank you notes to parents who have helped in the classroom in various ways
- Suggested books and websites for children and parents
- Suggestions of things parents and children can do together
- Welcome messages to new class members and their families
- A brief synopsis of what is being studied in class
- Articles or notes from parents for other parents

Computers have made the production of newsletters easier than ever, particularly if you use the same format each time. Newsletters should not be more than two pages long. Parents are very busy and may feel put off by a multipage document. Unfortunately, most newsletters are a method of teacher-to-parent communication, which by itself is no problem, but when put together with other one-way communication has the potential for perpetuating the distance between parents and teachers. As teachers, you might want to consider how to involve parents in writing and planning part of the newsletter. This not only opens up possibilities for parental involvement in the program, but also opens up possible parent-to-parent communications; may identify items more parents would like to see; and has the potential for lightening your own workload. It is also important to find a way for parents to provide their *feedback* through a newsletter. A tear-off portion within a newsletter inviting comments, questions, or concerns may work for the parents. A classroom website address can be offered as an alternative for parents to provide feedback (as well as a place to find copies of previous newsletters).

Newsletters can also be used as teaching tools (Jensen, 2006). By including activities, books, websites, and community resources, children have an opportunity to extend their learning of classroom material and expand their interests beyond the classroom. Often teachers do not have enough time to spend on a topic, and newsletters can provide resources for the family and children to explore topics more deeply if they wish. Teachers can make students responsible for part of or for the entire newsletter, depending on the grade. Students can sharpen their critical thinking skills when choosing what information to include; they can sharpen their reading, writing, and editing skills; and they can learn how to navigate through various computer programs and to pay attention to layout and design.

A newsletter creates a valuable opportunity for parents to be involved in their children's learning, strengthen their feeling of connectedness with teachers, and feel a source of support for their children's success.

Progress Reports

Report cards are traditional methods of sharing information about students' academic progress. Teachers evaluate and record students' grades and then write comments regarding students' weaknesses and strengths. There is usually a limited space provided for comments, however, and it is very hard to avoid generic comments. Another means of describing to parents the child's life in school is through *narrative reporting*. Although many parents cling to the traditional report card as a way of comparing their children with others, teachers who write narrative reports for parents are often rewarded for their time and effort with increased parental appreciation and support. It is important, however—especially because such reports are time consuming for teachers—that the reports speak to the child's unique presence in the classroom. Comments such as "great student" or "needs some work" tend to be so generic that they are not helpful to parents. Nor do such remarks give specific enough information to enable the parent's helpful response. A good narrative report is one that describes only one child and is therefore not interchangeable with or substitutable for narrative commentary about other children. It is descriptive and sufficiently detailed to make the child's classroom work come alive for the reader.

When filling out a traditional report card or writing a narrative report, teachers need to write in clear and easy language for parents to understand. At the end of the report, it would be good to invite parents to provide feedback about their child's progress. This can be done in written form or discussed at a face-to-face meeting or at a parent–teacher conference. To avoid confrontation from parents, teachers need to make sure that the report card is not the first communication that happens about a sensitive issue. Personal contact by phone or e-mail may be more effective since it gives the opportunity for parents to discuss the issue with the teacher and think through ways the issue can be resolved before report cards are sent. Davern (2004) notes that it is important to recognize when to send a written note and when to set up a face-to-face meeting about an issue.

Another form of progress report is a recognition card or certificate (sometimes called a happy gram) where teachers simply write the child's name and achievement. These cards need to be personal and never sent out *en masse* because there will be nothing special in them if everybody gets one. Teachers can keep notes on when they sent them and to whom (Shalaway, 2005). They can also be used to thank parents for their efforts. The format of these cards needs to be bright and colorful so children can proudly show them at home and even put them on home display.

School–Home Folders and Journals

Teachers can create weekly communication folders that students regularly take home and then return to school. This is an easy and inexpensive way to reach parents. Teachers usually choose one day of the week to send the folder home with students. These folders can include homework assignments, in-class work, a feedback form for parents, announcements of upcoming events, notes to parents, or any other materials you consider important. Some teachers choose Wednesday as a day for regular communication because it allows two days for them to collect the folders before the weekend. This type of communication also develops a sense of responsibility in students who can remind their parents to read the folder.

A form of two-way written communication, used most often for children with special needs, is the *school–home journal*. This is especially helpful when parents do not or cannot visit the school on a daily basis. It consists of a notebook in which teachers make comments about the child's school day on a regular basis. It is then sent home with the child, and the parent(s) respond to what the teacher has said and comment on the child's day at home. Of course, its success depends on the diligence of both the parent and the teacher, but you should not get discouraged easily. A parent may not be able to write in the journal every day but may find the time to do so once or twice a week. Encouraging the child to write or draw his or her own occasional entry may also perk up the parent(s)' or the child's interest (and children can then help remind parents and teacher about their commitment to the journal).

Parent Bulletin Boards

Still another vehicle for communicating with parents is a *parent bulletin board*. Strategically placed so that parents see it when they are at the school or center, a bulletin board containing attractive and interesting information for parents can be an effective way to communicate with parents. Unfortunately, depending on the program, all parents may not come to the school or center, and the communication on bulletin boards moves from displayer to onlooker, generally not in the other direction. This kind of communication tends to be one-way. Nonetheless, there are strategies that can be employed to encourage both parent attention and parent participation. One key to interesting bulletin boards is relevant and attractive displays of information. Interesting information for parents might include pictures and documentation of children's work at school (both product and process) (Edwards, Gandini, & Forman, 1993); information about parenting; notices of community events that might be interesting for parents, children, or families; interesting (and positive) news clippings about the parents; announcements about school events; and so forth.

To ensure continued attention over time, the bulletin board needs to be changed on a regular basis. Although using a bulletin board for parents to communicate to teachers is probably inappropriate, given other more direct modes of communication, using the bulletin board as a place for parents to communicate with one another is certainly possible. The bulletin board then becomes interactive, not passive. If a section of the bulletin board were set aside for parents' use, they could bring in items that they know would be of interest to other parents, which in turn could lead to more parental interest and ownership as well as the establishment of a vehicle for parents to find and communicate with others who share similar interests and concerns related to their children in school.

Communication Through Technology

In recent years, teachers have experimented with integrating various technologies to establish successful, time-efficient communication with parents. Classroom phones, voice mails, classroom websites, e-mails, integration of photography, and video technology are just some of the mostly commonly used methods.

When choosing an appropriate technology for communicating with parents and students, teachers need to make sure that parents have access to that technology. This can be done at the initial contact (interview, feedback page after the first letter, an introductory survey, etc.).

E-mail

E-mail communication has become an increasingly prevalent form of communication between teachers and students or parents and will continue to grow in the future. There are many advantages to using this type of communication: timeliness, accessibility, convenience, and ease of response. E-mailing is free (as long as the hardware is available), can be sent to a large number of recipients at the same time, and decreases the amount of paper consumed. E-mail can be used for regular communication with some parents, either between parent and teacher or among parents.

Because e-mail messages may be written at convenient times, this may increase the frequency of communication, but should not completely replace face-to-face communications. After conducting research on parent–teacher e-mail communication, Thompson (2009) summarized several important concerns connected with using e-mail as a frequent tool for communication.

First, parents and teachers complained that they did not always understand each other well because of the language used in an e-mail, negative content (for example, student misbehavior), not knowing each other, and so on. Teachers and parents can avoid misinterpretations by keeping messages short, getting to know each other better before writing concerned e-mails, and using verbal communication for complicated issues, including positive messages to balance out the negative messages.

Second, many teachers reported decreased face-to-face communication when e-mail communication increased, including less participation in parent–teacher conferences and fewer phone conversations. To avoid this trend, teachers and parents need to agree on the parameters of the topics and situations that can and cannot be discussed through e-mail.

Third, e-mails created new boundary issues that could negatively affect pedagogical practices. For example, students were blaming teachers for e-mailing their parents about their behavior and grades, which resulted in frequent punishment at home. Frequent parental e-mail communication can also hinder the development of student responsibility for their educational progress and behavior. Teachers and parents need to make sure that students are given the opportunity to take personal responsibility first and use e-mails only when needed.

Teachers and parents both need to be aware of the benefits and dangers of using this communication medium on a regular basis.

Classroom Website

Many teachers have classroom websites where they share important information about their classroom teaching and provide important resources for parents and students.

Teachers create their websites according to their technological skills and the purpose they want their website to serve. Your website can be as informative and as interactive as you want it to be. Some teachers prefer to have it only for informative purposes, whereas others include an interactive part for feedback and discussion. Before beginning, you need to decide the advantages of a website and what you might include. Free Teacher Website (2005) suggests the following:

- Your portfolio and résumé
- Information for students and parents
- School information
- Classroom projects
- Student web pages
- Student work
- Lesson plans and ideas
- Ideas and links for teaching units
- Anything related to teaching and education

Most classroom websites include the following pages:

1. *Home page*. This page introduces you as a person and a teacher. It needs to have a title, a theme, and graphics that will be repeated in the rest of the site. Make sure it is not too busy and distracting but enjoyable and easy to navigate. Here you can include your picture, teaching philosophy, contact information, and any other additional information that you would like to share.
2. *Pages for students*. These pages might include the classroom schedule, classroom activities, policies and expectations, homework activities, lessons plans, and any other resources that are connected to the topics that you cover in class. Here

you can showcase students' work, display their online portfolios, and report student progress.

3. *Pages for parents.* These pages need to inform parents about what is happening in your classroom, provide various resources on how to support children in the learning process, and give parents an opportunity to provide feedback. Some of the pages might include a calendar of upcoming events at school and in your classroom, an online chat room where parents can talk to you and other parents, an online version of a newsletter, and links to additional resources on education and parenting.

4. *Teacher's professional page.* This page can serve as your teaching portfolio with professional materials and accomplishments, conferences that you attended, and presentations you made.

5. *Community pages.* Here you can write about the school community, list activities for parents' and children's involvement in community life, and showcase activities that parents and children are already doing in the community.

Also, the suggestions made for newsletters (pp. 118–120) are appropriate for your website—particularly pictures of your students and comments on their activities. Since your website is available to people outside of your educational community, don't use students' last names, phone numbers, or addresses. Also, check to see whether your school or district has a policy dealing with teacher websites.

Make sure that the information on your website is up to date, especially if you have time-sensitive information such as a school calendar, classroom calendar, or classroom blog. When creating a classroom website, think about how much time and effort you would like to invest in it. Think about the purpose. It needs to assist you in communicating with parents and students but not distract or overload you.

Potential problems with the use of websites include the availability of computers and the interest of the parents of your students. If a significant number of them lack access to this technology, then you need to consider other ways you can communicate with them. You may also wish to include your e-mail address on your website. This can turn one-way communication to two-way communication.

Homework Hot Line

Parents often feel intimidated by their child's homework. They may have found a subject difficult when they were in school, not have been exposed to the material, or have forgotten it—after all, it has been a number of years since these parents were the age their children are presently. Whatever the reason, parents and students may need additional help. Schools that have implemented *homework hot lines* have found this a positive way to help both parents and students. They enable students and parents to call for help during evening homework hours or to access assistance through e-mail.

Homework hot lines can be used in a variety of ways. For example, they could be used to assist callers with their assignments or to verify homework assignments. The following is a list of guidelines for running a successful homework hot line. It is important to remember that there are many variations of this program and that a school must tailor it to meet its own needs.

- Determine what the greatest homework need is for your school and for students. Include parents and students in planning efforts. In most schools, it is math—particularly pre-algebra and algebra. The second most common need pertains to writing skills and is very broad in nature—everything from punctuation and grammar to how one structures a term paper. After determining your needs, decide how you are going to meet them.
- How often is this service going to be available? Mondays through Thursdays are generally busy homework nights for middle school students. Remember that it is usually better to start small and increase the service as needed.
- Who is going to staff the homework lines? Some schools use volunteers as "homework helpers" and some use paid personnel. Those programs that pay "helpers" tend to be the most successful. If volunteers are the most practical option for your school, then consider hiring a part-time coordinator who will set up schedules, find replacements for those helpers who cancel, and so on. If this program becomes an added burden for busy teachers and/or administrators, it will fail.
- After the program is planned, determine how to best inform parents and students about the homework hot line.
- Have regular meetings of the hot line staff to identify problems and improve the service.
- Give the program time before trying to determine its success. It generally takes a while to build a clientele for any program of this nature.

Communication on Special Occasions

Initial communication and regular communication are important contexts for parent–teacher communication, as they first set the stage and later work toward maintaining relationships that are open and productive for all concerned, especially for the students. There are, however, times that require other strategies for other kinds of communication.

Communication with Groups

There are occasions when those required classes in public speaking can come in handy. Parent nights, parent education classes, school programs, and even school orientation programs all are events at which teachers may be asked to speak to groups of parents *en masse*. When such opportunities arise, however, there must also be room for parents' voices to be heard. Whenever such meetings occur, for instance, there needs to be ample time for parents to ask questions and to give their opinions. Parent speakers might share the podium with teachers and other school personnel. Structuring the schedule for parent or parent–teacher discussion groups can help parents feel ownership in the events and know that their opinions also have weight.

Times of Crisis and Truly Difficult Parents

Even given the most successful and productive efforts at open and effective parent–teacher communication, there are both times and individuals that can test the commitment of the most well-meaning teacher. Despite parents who are generally co-operative (if sometimes or initially reluctant) about working with the teacher in partnership, a few, no matter what the teacher does, cannot easily be reached. Some examples are the very irate parent or the chronic complainer. Parents who are irate are obviously unhappy people, but frequently they are people who have had trouble getting themselves heard. If a parent is irate, one strategy is to swallow your pride and your defensiveness and concentrate on listening alone, without responding. Try, in such instances, to hide your own emotions, take out pencil and paper and concentrate on writing down every complaint the parent has. Do not interrupt with explanations or even apologies. Simply write. When they begin to slow down, ask if they have anything else to add. Continue this until they exhaust their list. Doing this will generally have an effect on their demeanor. Anger will usually dissipate, and in the meantime, you have a clear record of what the complaints are. When you have everything recorded, calmly read to the parent(s) what you have listed and assure them that you will look into the issue(s) and then get back to them. Give yourself some time, and then return to the list when you have more emotional distance from it (usually overnight will do). Confer with others who can help you think about the course of action you can take, changes you can make, and principles on which you wish to take a stand. Be prepared and calm when you get back to the complainer. Chances are, he or she will be much more willing to hear your thoughts on the matter now.

Chronic complainers can also benefit from knowing they are being heard, but sometimes such individuals continue looking for problems no matter how many you've solved for them. One strategy for working with such parents is to invite them into the classroom to observe and participate, as appropriate, in classroom activities. (They can, for instance, be invited to read to children.) When they become part of the inside, rather than staying on the outside, and when they discover the difficult and complicated nature of teaching and learning, they often become the teacher's best allies, spreading the word to other parents about the teacher's good work.

We, as educators, work toward a cooperative environment where individuals are respected. We work with students to resolve their problems in nonconfrontational ways. In fact, many schools employ conflict resolution as a way of dealing with conflict. Consequently, we often feel uncomfortable with discord. Table 6.3 provides some guidelines for working with aggressive people. It also helps you to be less defensive and more centered on solving the problem at hand.

These strategies take practice. Our first reaction is almost always anger or hostility, and these only serve to make matters more volatile. Also, remember that all of us have, on occasion, acted in an angry, inappropriate way and usually wish we had behaved with more temperance. Give the parent the same understanding that you would like to receive.

Some parents prove difficult for teachers because they come to rely on their listening skills *too* much. For some parents, you will be the only other adult who cares

TABLE 6.3 Tips for Dealing with Aggression

Do	Don't
1. Listen–without interruptions.	1. Argue.
2. Write down main points of what has been said.	2. Defend or become defensive.
3. When they slow down, ask if anything else is bothering them.	3. Promise things you can't produce.
4. Exhaust the list of complaints.	4. Own problems that belong to others.
5. Ask for specific clarifications when complaints are too general.	5. Raise your voice.
6. Show them the list of complaints.	6. Belittle or minimize the problem.
7. Ask for suggestions in solving the specific problems and write down the suggestions.	
8. As they speak louder, you speak softer.	

Source: Modified from material developed by Roger Kroth and the Parent Involvement Center, University of New Mexico.

about them enough to listen to their problems. You, after all, have a mutual concern for their child, and you may have chosen this profession to be of help to others. Although such parental trust can be helpful for two-way communication, if it gets out of hand and becomes excessive, the teacher may feel (uncomfortably) as if he or she is expected to be a counselor to the parent. Under such circumstances it is important to remember that you have been trained as a *teacher*, not as a counselor. Having knowledge of community resources is helpful in such situations, as the most appropriate help you can give such individuals is probably to refer them to professional services that meet their counseling needs.

Summary

Working with parents can be very rewarding—for you, for parents, for your school or center, and especially for the children who are under your care and tutelage. For this work to be most fruitful for all concerned, a concentrated effort at open and two-way (and sometimes three-way) communication is required. Without communication, mutual goals are less likely to be met. Here is a list of some principles to keep in mind when planning for effective communication with parents:

- Choose or create an environment that puts parents on an equal footing with you.
- Care about the parent(s)' child. Ask about him or her.
- Care about the parent(s). Ask about him or her.
- Listen to understand.
- Use descriptive, rather than judgmental, language when relating a child's school life. Avoid educational jargon.

- Don't talk about other parents or their children. Respect the confidentiality of all families.
- Take the initiative to establish a coequal relationship. Don't be discouraged by limited initial success.
- Establish communications early in the school year, before problems occur.
- Find time to spend with parents.

Recommended Activities

1. Think of a time when you know you were not being listened to. How did you know? What was the behavior of the person to whom you were speaking? How did you feel? What was your response?

2. Ask three friends to think about a person they consider a good listener. Interview them about the qualities this person demonstrates as a good listener. Make a list of these qualities and compare them with what you know about yourself as a listener.

3. Interview three teachers. Ask them about the principles and the techniques they use for communicating with parents. Where appropriate and possible, obtain examples of written communications, such as newsletters. Analyze what was described and given to you for communicative flow. Note especially where parent voices were heard.

4. Interview three parents of school-age children. Ask them about parent–teacher conferences. How do they prepare for them mentally and emotionally? Ask them to describe the worst and best conferences they have had with teachers.

5. Interview three teachers. Ask them about parent–teacher conferences. How do they prepare for them mentally and emotionally? Ask them to describe the worst and best conferences they have had with parents.

6. Ask teachers about the role technology—other than the telephone—plays in their communication with parents.

7. Interview teachers to discuss how report cards or narrative reporting is being done. Does it change from grade to grade? If so, how does it change?

Additional Resources

Websites

Center for Effective Parenting
www.parenting-ed.org

Parenting-Healthy-Children.com
www.parenting-healthy-children.com

Teacher Communication Suite
www.teachercommunicationsuite.com

Helping Children Succeed in School
www.urbanext.illinois.edu/succeed/
    communication.cfm

Management Ideas for Teachers
www.mspowell.com

Teachnology
www.teach-nology.com/ideas/parent_
    communication/

Parent Communication
www.mandygregory.com/Parent%
    20Communication.htm

References

Andrews, C. (2008). Add parents, subtract confusion. *Times Educational Supplement, 4770*, 56–57.

Burian, B., Haveman, S., Jacobson, M., & Rood, B. (1993). Implementing a multi-age level classroom: A reflection on our first year. *Insights into Open Education, 26*(2), 23–32.

Colombo, M. W. (2004). Family literacy nights . . . and other home–school connections. *Educational Leadership, 61*(8), 48–51.

Davern, L. (2004). School-to-home notebooks: What parents have to say. *Council for Exceptional Children, 36*(5), 22–27.

Edwards, C., Gandini, L., & Forman, G. (Eds.). (1993). *The hundred languages of children: The Reggio Emilia approach to early childhood education*. Norwood, NJ: Ablex.

Free Teacher Website. Inspiring Teachers Publishing. Retrieved July, 2005, from www .inspiringteachers.com/community/webpages .html

Graham-Clay, S. (2005). Communicating with parents: Strategies for teachers. *School Community Journal, 16*(1), 117–129.

Hawes, K. (2008). Parents are not the enemy: Ten tips for improving parent–teacher communication. *Mathematics Teacher, 101*(5), 328–331.

Hoover-Dempsey, K., Walker, J., Sandler, H., Whetsel, D., Green, C., Wilkins, A. , Closson, K. (2005). Why do parents become involved? Research findings and implications. *The Elementary School Journal, 106*(2), 105–130.

Jensen, D. (2006, October). Using newsletters to create home–school connections. *The Reading Teacher, 60*(2), 186–190.

Meyer, J. A., & Mann, M. B. (2006). Teachers' perceptions of the benefits of home visits for early elementary children. *Early Childhood Education Journal, 34*(1), 93–97.

Montgomery, D. J. (2005). Communicating without harm: Strategies to enhance parent–teacher communication. *Teaching Exceptional Children, 37*(5), 50–55.

National PTA. (1997). *National Standards for Parent/Family Involvement Programs*. Chicago, IL.

Rockwell, R. E., Andre, L. C., & Hawley, M. K. (1996). *Parents and teachers as partners*. Fort Worth, TX: Harcourt Brace.

Scott, P. (2007). Successfully bringing parents into the classroom. *Education Digest, 73*(2), 47–49.

Shalaway, L. (2005). *Learning to teach . . . Not just for beginners* (3rd ed.). New York: Scholastic.

Sirvani, H. (2007). The effect of teacher communication with parents on students' mathematics achievement. *American Secondary Education, 36*(1), 31–46.

Thompson, B. (2009). Parent–teacher e-mail strategies at the elementary and secondary levels. *Qualitative Research Reports in Communication, 10*, 17–25.

Xu, Z., & Gulosino, C. A. (2006). How does teacher quality matter? The effect of teacher–parent partnership on early childhood performance in public and private schools. *Education Economics, 14*(3), 345–367.

Yerger St. George, C. (2010). How can elementary teachers collaborate more effectively with parents to support student literacy learning? *The Delta Kappa Gamma Bulletin, 76*(2), 32–38.

Chapter Seven

Family Involvement in Education

Soo-Yin Lim

University of Minnesota, Crookston

Children learn and grow in three influential contexts: family, school, and community. There is a strong connection on the positive effects for the children, families, and school when schools reach out to parents and actively involve parents to support and encourage their children's learning and development. This chapter helps you to:

▶ Define parent involvement.

▶ Identify and explain the benefits of parent involvement for children, parents, teachers, and school.

▶ Describe ways schools and teachers can involve parents.

▶ Identify and explain the basic foundations of planning and implementing a successful parent involvement program.

Defining Family Involvement

Family involvement is a widely used term, which among educators is sometimes used synonymously with terms such as *family engagement, parent involvement, parent participation, partnership, parent power,* and *school, family, and community partnerships* (Epstein, 1996; Weissbourd, Weissbourd, & O'Carroll, 2010; Wolfendale, 1989). Throughout this chapter, the terms *families* and *parents* mean significant adults who have primary responsibilities for the children you teach. Examples include parents, stepparents, grandparents, extended families such as aunts and uncles, foster families, and other household members.

What is family involvement? According to Moles (1992), parent involvement may take a variety of forms and levels of involvement, both in and out of school. It includes any activities that are provided and encouraged by the school and that empower parents working on behalf of their children's learning and development. Epstein and her colleagues (1996, 2009) extended the term from *family involvement* to *school, family, and community partnerships* to describe how children learn and develop in these three main contexts: school, family, and community. Therefore, these three influential contexts need to be integrated into every facet of children's education and development.

The concept of family or parent involvement is not new to the field of education and has played a significant role in U.S. education. Friedrich Froebel, who made primary contributions to the establishment of U.S. kindergarten programs, commented:

> All are looking for reform in education. . . . If building is to be solid, we must look to the foundation—the home. The home education of rich and poor alike must be supplemented. . . . It therefore behooves the state to establish institutions for the education of children, of parents, and of those who are to be parents. (cited in White, Taylor, & Moss, 1992)

In 1994, the U.S. Department of Education launched GOALS 2000 so that "every school will promote partnerships that will increase parental involvement and participation in promoting the social, emotional, and academic growth of children" (Schulman, 2000, p. 64). Congress also encouraged school and community collaboration to assist families in supporting their children's success in education. The No Child Left Behind Act (NCLB) of 2001, which reauthorized the 1965 Elementary and Secondary Education Act (ESEA), imposes major requirements on the states that have an impact on school districts. One of the major requirements is that school districts are required to have written parent involvement policies and plans, including a plan that implements effective parent involvement activities whereby families, educators, and communities come together to improve teaching and learning (National PTA, 2010; Sheldon, 2005; U.S. Department of Education, 2004). Recently, the U.S. Department of Education proposed a revision to the reauthorization of ESEA to include (a) the need for transparency and accountability by providing better information for families to help them evaluate and improve their children's schools, including information on teachers' and principals' effectiveness; (b) the investment in family and community engagement in order to provide a comprehensive approach in meeting the needs of students and providing successful, safe, and healthy learning environment; and (c) the support for teachers, principals, and leaders in engaging families more effectively through professional development (U.S. Department of Education, 2010). This revision prompts schools across the United States to examine and revise their current policies, practices, and programs on family involvement. To achieve this goal, school, family, and community must see their interconnectedness with each other, come together to build a shared vision, and understand their individual roles in relation to the roles of others. Such cooperation is necessary to ensure that all children receive the support and services they need to succeed in school.

The Benefits of Family Involvement: What Research Has to Say

Researchers have evidence for the positive effects of family involvement on children, families, and school when schools and parents continuously support and encourage the children's learning and development (Henderson & Mapp, 2002; National PTA, 2007; U.S. Department of Health and Human Services, 2006). According to Henderson and Berla (1994), "the most accurate predictor of a student's achievement in school is not income or social status but the extent to which that student's family is able to:

1. Create a home environment that encourages learning
2. Express high (but not unrealistic) expectations for their children's achievement and future careers
3. Become involved in their children's education at school and in the community" (p. 160)

Decades of research studies have documented the comprehensive benefits of family involvement in children's education (Henderson & Berla, 1994; Henderson & Mapp, 2002; Houtenville & Conway, 2008; National PTA, 2007). Studies also show that family involvement activities that are effectively planned and well implemented result in substantial benefits to children, parents, educators, and the school.

Benefits for Children

- Children tend to achieve more, regardless of ethnic or racial background, socioeconomic status, or parents' education level.
- Children generally achieve better grades, test scores, and attendance.
- Children consistently complete their homework.
- Children have better self-esteem, are more self-disciplined, and show higher aspirations and motivation toward school.
- Children's positive attitude about school often results in improved behavior in school and less suspension for disciplinary reasons.
- Fewer children are being placed in special education and remedial classes.

- Children from diverse cultural backgrounds tend to do better when parents and professionals work together to bridge the gap between the culture at home and the culture in school.
- Junior high and high school students whose parents remain involved usually make better transitions and are less likely to drop out of school.

Benefits for Parents

- Parents increase their interaction and discussion with their children and are more responsive and sensitive to their children's social, emotional, and intellectual developmental needs.
- Parents are more confident in their parenting and decision-making skills.
- As parents gain more knowledge of child development, there is more use of affection and positive reinforcement and less punishment on their children.
- Parents have a better understanding of the teacher's job and school curriculum.
- When parents are aware of what their children are learning, they are more likely to help when they are requested by teachers to become more involved in their children's learning activities at home.
- Parents' perceptions of the school are improved and there are stronger ties and commitment to the school.
- Parents are more aware of, and become more active when they are requested by school to be part of the decision-making team regarding policies that affect their children's education.

Benefits for Educators

- When schools have a high percentage of involved parents in and out of schools, teachers and principals are more likely to experience higher morale.
- Teachers and principals often earn greater respect for their profession from the parents.
- Consistent parent involvement leads to improved communication and relations between parents, teachers, and administrators.
- Teachers and principals acquire a better understanding of families' cultures and diversity, and they form deeper respect for parents' abilities and time.
- Teachers and principals report an increase in job satisfaction.

Benefits for the School

- Schools that actively involve parents and the community tend to establish better reputations in the community.
- Schools also experience better community support.
- School programs that encourage and involve parents usually do better and have higher quality programs than programs that do not involve parents.

Six Types of Family Involvement

If there are so many benefits to the teacher, child, and family, why is it so difficult to establish a detailed building or district family involvement plan? Why don't schools or districts target a percent of volunteers they want on an annual basis?

It is clear and beyond dispute that family involvement has significant and wide-ranging positive effects. Most educators and schools agree and embrace the concept of family involvement and its impact on children from birth through high school. Programs and schools can no longer focus only on working with children, but must also recognize the value of engaging and investing family engagement to ensure their child's optimal learning and development (Chang, 2010; Weissbourd et al., 2010). Therefore, educators need to transfer their knowledge or beliefs into plans, plans into practice, and practice into results (Gestwicki, 2009; Simon, Salinas, Epstein, & Sanders, 1998). Few parents understand or are aware of the resources of their children's school system, specifically, the programs and activities available for their children (Anderson & Minke, 2007; Epstein, 1996). Many studies indicate that parents are interested in participating at all levels from playing the role of an audience to decision making. Unfortunately, many parents often do not know how to get involved. Thus, it is the parents' lack of knowledge and/or skill, not lack of interest in supporting their children's education that prevents them from participating (Anderson & Minke, 2007; Hoover-Dempsey et al., 2005). Even though everyone agrees that family involvement is beneficial, it cannot be achieved until there is real agreement about its value and a shared understanding of the complementary roles of the parents and educators in the entire educational process.

The National Network of Partnership Schools established by Joyce Epstein and her colleagues at Johns Hopkins University responded to the challenge by developing six types of parent involvement based on the theoretical model of "overlapping spheres of influence." This model indicates that children do not learn and grow in the context of home alone or school alone, but in three influential contexts—home, school, and community. There is no one single formula or blueprint that will create a successful home–school–community partnership. However, there are basic guidelines for schools, districts, and state departments to create meaningful, positive, and permanent programs that actively involve families in their children's education.

Each of the six types of involvement consists of many different activities that promote or enhance partnership and family engagement. Each will likely yield different results for children, parents, teachers, and the school, depending on how well the activities are designed, planned, and implemented, thereby leading to either positive or negative results. Schools may choose to use the framework of six types of parent involvement developed by Epstein. But each school must be aware of the local needs of its families and children while designing its own family involvement program (Epstein, 2001, 2006; National PTA, 2007).

Type 1: Parenting

The most basic involvement of parents is their continuous responsibility for raising their children and providing them with food, clothing, shelter, health, and safety. The

National Education Goals for Year 2000 indicate that "all children in America will start school ready to learn" (Schulman, 2000, p. 63). What does "ready to learn" mean? It goes beyond teaching children across the nation their basic ABCs and numbers. It means parents should form the foundation for their children's success in school by providing and maintaining a positive home environment that is conducive to learning and the development of physical, intellectual, social, and emotional skills and values. This is a continuous process of teaching and guiding children throughout their school years and helping them build self-confidence and self-esteem (Gonzalez-Mena, 1998; National PTA, 2007).

Parents vary in their experiences and parenting skills. Thus, schools will have to take an active role in assisting parents with parenting and child-rearing skills, helping in understanding child and adolescent development, and providing ideas for creating a home environment that supports children's learning at each age and grade. Research indicates that families want to learn and receive ongoing information on how to help their children succeed and excel in school. Concurrently, teachers and administrators need the families to assist schools in becoming better informed about their children and families. Information about children and family backgrounds, cultures, needs, interests, goals, and expectations can be provided by families. Therefore, Type 1 involvement consists of a combination of information *for* parents and *from* parents about children and families (Epstein et al., 2009).

Sample Activities That Support and Assist Parents in Parenting and Child-Rearing Practices

1. Provide ongoing information to all parents in a variety of ways:
   - workshop, parent education, and grade-level meetings
   - newsletters and pamphlets
   - videos and audiotapes
   - school websites and e-mail
   - computerized phone messages
2. Establish a parent resource room—a family-friendly center where parents can come together and discuss parenting issues and check out resources and materials.
3. Organize a family support program—encourage parents to organize a parent-led support group where families can connect and share their experiences and their knowledge with each other. This can also be done through an online discussion forum through the use of school or program websites. All websites should be password-protected and secure limited access.
4. Provide home-visit opportunities for teachers to learn and to become more aware of the families, as well as for the families to understand school expectations.
5. Provide information on community services, such as free immunizations and clinics, workforce development and financial services, health insurance, services offered by social services, community parent education, parent–child community activities, and religious services (Chang, 2010; Epstein et al., 2009; National PTA, 2007).

Tips on Successful Planning and Implementation of Parenting Activities

1. *Select relevant and meaningful topics.* It is critical that topics selected are relevant and meaningful for parents regarding the age or grade level of their children. An ongoing survey of needs and wants from parents is highly recommended throughout the year. The survey allows the parents to be a part of the decision-making process when their topics of interest are selected and presented.

2. *Disseminate information to all families.* Information should be distributed to all parents regardless of whether they are able to attend workshops or parent meetings. Workshops should not be limited to school premises; instead, the content of topics discussed can be viewed, heard, or read at times and locations that are convenient for the families (Epstein et al., 2009). For example, the workshops can be videotaped or audiotaped, allowing families to receive the information at their convenience. Workshops can be summarized and put in a variety of forms, such as newsletters, school websites, or computerized phone messages. Parents can read them at home, in the school's parent room, or at the public library. Allow parents who were unable to attend meetings or workshops to discuss them online with other parents and speakers.

3. *Provide sufficient notice to parents.* Workshops or meetings that require parents to come together at the same time and place need sufficient notice. Such notice should include location, date, and time of the meeting; a brief description of the topic; and the name of the presenter of the workshop.

4. *Vary the location.* Workshops may be offered at the school building as well as other locations in the community that represent families' neighborhoods.

5. *Vary the time schedules.* Workshop information should be made available at various times rather than one scheduled time. Additionally, families have other obligations; therefore a conscious effort to start and end on time is critical.

6. *Provide concise, clear, and easy-to-understand information.* Ongoing verbal and written information on parenting should be concise and clear and should use plain language that is free from educational jargon. Translation of information is needed for families whose first language is not English, and alternate formats are needed to meet the needs of parents with disabilities (Epstein et al., 2009; National PTA, 2007).

Type 2: Communicating

Effective communication is essential for building a successful partnership between school and home. It requires the school to build two-way sharing of information, with conscious efforts from the school to engage in give-and-take conversations, establish common goals, and follow up with consistent interactions between school and home (National PTA, 2007). Without good two-way communication between the school and the family, other levels of involvement are made much more difficult to achieve. Children often play an important role in the success of Type 2 involvement when children are involved as couriers in taking messages from school to home and bringing them back to school from home.

The school's basic obligation is to consistently and effectively provide information about school programs and children's progress through school-to-home and home-to-school communications. When successful, this reduces the potential for conflict and stress between all parties involved. A common practice used by many schools is to share information about their programs and children's progress through school and class newsletters, report cards or narrative progress reports, parent–teacher conferences, and phone calls. With the advance of technology, schools are increasingly using e-mail to communicate with families and using voice mail and the school's website to relay messages to parents.

Sample Activities That Are Effective in Establishing Two-Way Communication

1. Create newsletters and bulletin boards that are interactive, through which parents are able to respond to teachers, administrators, and other parents. A few examples are to include a question for parents to respond to and then provide the responses or answers in the next newsletter and to provide a venue for interaction between parents regarding carpooling, exchange of outgrown clothing, weekend child care, recipes, a source of "take-away" coupons, and parenting articles.

2. Send weekly or monthly folders of children's work home for parents to review and comment on their child's progress.

3. Establish online discussion with teachers and administrators. The purpose is to exchange and clarify information and perceptions; to support parents, teachers, and administrators; and to provide suggestions or ideas. Many schools and programs have their own websites, within which teachers can create their own classroom websites. In addition, Google sites and Facebook are free and allow teachers to create their own website. It is strongly recommended that the websites be password-protected and of limited access (Mitchell, Foulger, & Wetzel, 2010).

4. Include e-mail addresses of school staff in the school handbook as well as on the school's website. Send positive messages about their child's activities.

5. Place a suggestion box or create an online suggestion box to encourage parents to ask questions and offer ideas. Encourage conversations that will help their children's learning. Encourage parents who speak other languages and have limited English skills to write in their own language.

6. Conduct parent–teacher conferences with follow-ups as needed. Provide language translators for written and verbal communication to assist families who do not speak English. Arrange and plan for phone conferences when parents are unable to come to school for the conferences.

7. Provide clear information about school policies, roles, and curriculum, as well as responsibilities of the school, family, and community in school or parent handbooks. Provide easy two-way communication for parents to make comments and ask further questions after reviewing the handbook. This can be implemented through a short open-ended questionnaire at the back of the handbook or by encouraging parents to drop a note in the suggestion box.

8. Establish a regular schedule of distributing notices such as school and classroom newsletters, calendars, and other communication activities that notify parents about important school dates, school events, parent–teacher conferences, parent meetings, and other important information.

Tips on Successful Planning and Implementation of Two-Way Communication

1. *Provide clear, readable, and useful information.* Periodically review all written communication to make sure that content is current, clear, understandable, relevant, and meaningful to families.
2. *Provide special consideration for families who do not speak or read English well.* A language barrier between educators and families presents the greatest obstacle to effective communication. The challenge increases when there are several different languages spoken within one school. This makes school and parent–teacher meetings difficult. Stenomask or TALK System (TS) allows translators to translate what is being said and then transmit to the audience members with receivers and earphones. This system can accommodate five different translators at the same time (National PTA, 2007).
3. *Provide a variety of ways for parents to communicate with the school.* Communication methods such as notes, journals, e-mail, websites, computerized messages, and voice mail allow parents to access messages at their convenience. This gives flexibility to parents who work irregular shifts or have difficult schedules.
4. *Develop "telephone trees" or family directories.* These would include phone numbers and e-mail addresses of school staff (teachers, administrators, counselors, family coordinator, nurses, class parents, and parent organizations) and serve as a great reference for the families.

Type 3: Volunteering

The typical activities in this category are parental assistance to teachers and administrators in supporting the school program and helping with children's schoolwork and activities, including field trips, class parties, and class performances. Volunteering ranges from low to high levels of participation. Parents can either act as audience with minimal commitment in advocacy, or they can act in decision-making roles with higher levels of commitment.

Many schools face the challenge of having too few volunteers. Often the same group of parents repeatedly does the volunteer work. Epstein (2007) reported that approximately 70% of parents have never helped the teacher in the classroom, and only 4% of the parents (about one or two parents per classroom) were highly active at school. Families that are white and middle-income are more likely to participate and be better informed on how to help their children at home (Swick, Head-Reeves, & Barbarin, 2006). Therefore, educators need to be aware and make extra effort in engaging all families of different racial, socioeconomic, and educational background. This is one way of addressing the achievement gap between children of color growing up in poverty and their affluent white peers (Bredekamp, 2011). The number of children with parents working full-time or part-time during school hours has dramatically increased. More than 60% of children under age 6 and 70% of school-age children have all parents in the workforce (Children's Defense Fund, 2010). To meet this challenge, there is a need to redefine volunteerism to include parents' supporting school goals and children's learning in any place and at any time.

Schools need to provide flexibility in time and place to enable parents to volunteer their talents and interests. For example, parents can volunteer in schools, at home, or in other community locations, and at convenient times such as evenings, weekends, and during school closing or vacation days. Schools that created flexibility for families found an increase in the number of parents and others who volunteer. Flexibility also allows regular and occasional volunteers to come together to work on common goals for the school program, share common interests, and acquire other talents while providing volunteers with the opportunity to work in various areas of the school.

Sample Activities for Volunteering in and out of School

1. For teachers:
   - *Volunteers in the classroom.* Listen to a child read and encourage a child to write; assist in a computer laboratory; serve as chaperones for field trips, school dances, class parties, or sporting events; share hobbies and cultures by integrating them into curriculum; celebrate diverse cultures represented in the class, school, and community.
   - *Volunteers outside the classroom.* Translate children's books or written communication such as newsletters; update classroom website or search for Internet links that support children's learning; lead cooking or craft activities at home; contribute to long- and short-term projects such as making costumes and plots for dramatic play centers or a school play; gather necessary resources or materials for special events; be coaches, tutors, or mentors for middle or high school students.
2. For administrators:
   - *Volunteers in the school.* Encourage parents to come to school for their light exercise by walking around middle and high school hallways. This increase of adult presence will decrease behavioral problems. In addition, parents can volunteer as chaperones at school dances, sporting events, and school plays or join advisory committees such as PTA, PTO, or other groups.
   - *Volunteers outside the school.* Create and maintain school websites; take or compile pictures or videos of students and develop presentation for school use; organize letter-writing campaigns on education issues; plan and organize school exhibits (such as art, science, clubs) at local malls or stores; compile "yellow pages" of parent resources regarding family hobbies, expertise, special interests, and places of work; recruit, train, and organize recognition ceremonies for volunteers.
   - *Volunteers as audience.* Attend school or class events, sporting events, open houses, and recognition and award ceremonies.

Tips for Successful Planning and Implementation of a Volunteering Program.   To implement and maintain Type 3 involvement (volunteering) successfully, schools need to include ongoing activities such as recruitment, training and supervision, and recognition.

1. *Recruitment.* In general, there are two important issues that relate to recruitment:
   - *Identify potential volunteers.* Volunteers should not be limited to parents of children who attend the school. Instead, volunteers should represent parents and people from the community that cut across categories of age, sex, education, socioeconomic status, race, ethnicity, religion, occupation, and various neighborhood communities. Volunteers may be recruited by exploring a variety of places in the local community. Such locations include colleges, senior citizen or retirement communities, television and radio stations, businesses, museums, libraries, parks, and churches.
   - *Strategies for finding people to volunteer.* The methods of recruitment depend on the size of the school and number of volunteers needed. Schools need to reach out to the community and communicate the what, why, and how of volunteer service in schools. The school can arrange to speak at different community events and local meetings such as senior centers, retirement communities, businesses, agencies, committees, and organizations. This kind of recruitment elicits discussions, answers questions, and clarifies information. Other recruitment methods include:
     - Working with local media such as television, radio, and newspapers to promote the school's volunteer programs
     - Developing brochures, posters, and fliers that can be posted and distributed in retirement communities, hospitals, social service agencies, banks, churches, and grocery stores
     - Setting up booths in local malls or community fairs
2. *Training and supervision.* Even before recruiting volunteers, schools need to assess and review their needs for volunteer services. During the assessing and reviewing process, school staff, including teachers, counselors, coaches, club advisors, janitors, secretaries, and administrators, should help in identifying the needs of the school. Similarly, the need for volunteers in classrooms of a specific age or grade level or on a particular subject matter can be assessed and reviewed. When a list of needs is identified, it can be translated into a clear and concise job description for volunteers (see Figure 7.1) and placed in the classroom.

It is highly recommended that before being accepted, all volunteers should be interviewed to assess their skills, interests, and placement. Program orientation and ongoing training are crucial for the success of volunteer programs. Orientation sessions should include the following:

- *Taking a tour of building.* Provide a map and tour of the facility (both internal and external), highlighting key places such as bathrooms, main office, library, lounge, and space for volunteer workers to store their personal belongings.

Figure 7-1   Sample Job Description for Classroom Volunteers

Classroom Volunteer Job Description

Teacher: Lisa Myers   **Grade:** Preschool I

Job Responsibility: Supervise painting area

Time and Day Needed: 10:00–11:00/3:00–4:30 (Monday through Friday)

Volunteer roles:

- Help children put on aprons if they are painting. First, encourage them to do this themselves.
- Discuss colors, mixing of colors, shapes, sizes, etc. with children. Some children like to tell you about their painting, but do not insist on this. You may ask, "Would you like to tell me about this?"
- Write child's name on the upper left corner or ask child where he or she wants it. Use upper- and lowercase letters (e.g., John).
- Help children put their work on the drying rack, put their aprons away, and wash their hands.
- Extra paints are in the art cupboard (above the sink) if needed.
- Wash brushes and containers as needed.

Helps develop the following:

- Concepts of colors, shapes, sizes, and textures
- Hand–eye coordination
- Expression of ideas and feelings

- *Reviewing policies and procedures.* Provide a school handbook for volunteers to refer to when needed. Discuss the school's philosophy and mission, operating policies and procedures, children's guidance and discipline, confidentiality, ethics on working with students and school staff, attendance, and dependability.
- *Meeting with school staff.* Introduce volunteers to school staff such as administrative and office staff, teachers, and cafeteria and custodial staff.

Orientation should lead into training that is ongoing and can be done on the job or through individual or small group sessions. Training sessions should be informal (friendly and supportive), hands-on, clear, and relevant to the specific skills and responsibilities of each volunteer. All volunteers should have their job description and expectations to refer to when needed. Effective training will reduce conflict between school staff and volunteers, such as communication problems and confusion over expectations and responsibilities. It also eases fear and anxiety for the volunteers and increases a positive and cooperative relationship with school staff.

Supervision is needed for all volunteers. Volunteers are entitled to receive feedback from supervisors. This also provides opportunities for volunteers to share their experiences and to provide input on the work they performed. This initiates an informal evaluation, and such systematic evaluation allows for volunteers to self-evaluate their contributions to the program, for school staff to evaluate volunteers, and for the program to evaluate whether the goals and objectives are being met.

3. *Recognition.* Regardless of the amount of time each volunteer contributes to the school, every volunteer should receive recognition of his or her commitment and services. Individual staff that works with a volunteer must make a continual effort to regularly acknowledge and express appreciation for work done. A year-end acknowledgment such as a reception, dinner, or recognition night should be held to recognize all volunteers who have made a difference for the school program and children's education. There are numerous ways of recognizing volunteers throughout the year. For example:

- *Create a special, visible area in the school dedicated to volunteers.* Display pictures of volunteers working in different projects and places. Include names of volunteers, number of hours volunteered, and brief descriptions of their contributions.
- *Provide incentives.* Issue coupons in exchange for hours volunteered that can be redeemed at "volunteer store" to "purchase" donated materials, such as household and personal products, nonperishable food, greeting cards, and gifts.
- *Publicize volunteers.* Recognize volunteers in monthly newsletters, school websites, or stories in local newspapers (National PTA, 2000; Rockwell, Andre, & Hawley, 1996).

Type 4: Learning at Home

In the field of early childhood education, a basic belief is that parents are their children's first and most influential teachers. Parents have influence over what children do at home—the amount of time and type of programs children watch on television, amount of time spent playing video games, types of music they listen to, and amount of time spent studying and doing their homework. When children reach school age, the amount of time spent at school is less than that spent at home and in child care combined. Thus, the amount of time spent away from school is valuable for learning and building positive attitudes about education.

Home-based learning not only enhances children's learning experiences, but also serves many purposes. It "should reinforce, support, and strengthen learning that has been introduced and shared at school" (Trahan & Lawler-Prince, 1999, p. 65). It involves families with their children via gamelike activities, homework, and curriculum-related activities such as mathematics, science, and social science. This also includes parents assisting their high school children in setting goals for the school year or for the future and making joint decisions on what courses to take. These activities may or may not have directions or suggestions from the teacher. Activities typically cover general skills or behaviors and specific skills. General skills activities are those that promote critical-thinking or problem-solving skills, promote language skills, enhance social and emotional skills, or reinforce certain behaviors using consistent child-guidance techniques agreed on with the teacher. Specific skills activities are those that involve families in helping children to review, complete, or extend skills that the student is working on with the teacher in class. Specific skills activities occur more often for children in grade school.

Most parents help their children through their past school experiences and knowledge of school subjects. Most parents across all grades want more information about their children's homework, homework policies, and tools for helping their children (Epstein, 2007). According to Epstein, 85% of parents spent 15 minutes or more helping their children at home when requested by teachers. These parents stated that they were willing to spend an average of 40 minutes with their children if they had directions from the teacher about how to help their child.

Sample Activities for Involving Parents in Children's Home-Learning Activities

1. *Backpack reading.* Children bring home a book each night for parents to read or listen to their child read. Materials include a book, directions on how to make reading interactive, and an inventory list for parents to complete.
2. *Mobile learning centers.* Each bag includes two or three hands-on activities to either promote several developmental areas or a specific skill. Each bag consists of a letter to the parents, directions for each activity, parents' feedback journal, and materials needed for the activities. The activity bags are sent home with each child for a week or two and then returned. The teacher replenishes the materials and prepares the activity bag to go to the next child.
3. *Home kits.* Activities are theme based, and the kit includes a book with follow-up hands-on activities. Each home kit consists of a letter to the parents, directions for each activity, parents' feedback journal, and materials needed for the activities. Kits are checked out by the child for a week.
4. *Home learning enablers* (HLE). This is an inexpensive way of promoting parents' involvement with their children's learning by showing them how to use household materials to teach children without having to spend a large amount of money on materials. Each week HLE activities are sent home with the child. An activity card includes the name of the activity, the purpose of the activity, materials needed, directions on how to do each activity, time needed for completion, adaptation ideas, and an evaluation form for parents to complete.
5. *Family lending library.* Parents have the opportunity to check out books, materials, and audio- and videotapes in which teachers demonstrate or model a certain skill or activity. Children also have the opportunity to check out books, magazines, toys, and home-learning activity kits.
6. *Interactive homework.* This is geared more for older children in elementary, middle, and high school. Interactive homework is directly linked to course objectives and requires children to interact and communicate with family members or community members (Epstein, 2007; Shoemaker, 1996; Trahan & Lawler-Prince, 1999).

Tips for Successful Planning and Implementation of Home Activities

1. *Provide information and training sessions.* The goal is to explain what home-learning activities entail early in the year, such as during an open house or parent

meeting. Training sessions are offered throughout the year to provide opportunities for teachers to demonstrate sample activities and for parents to practice the strategies. This also allows teachers and parents to share ideas.

2. *Incorporate activities into the family's schedule.* Activities are designed to be completed in short periods of time. For families with very young children, design activities that can be incorporated into the child's daily routine, such as mealtime, bedtime, and bathtime.

3. *Make homework interactive.* Create homework that requires interaction and discussion with parents, family and extended family members, or community members.

4. *Provide easy access of activity resources or materials.* If materials are not provided for parents, then the materials should consist of common household items with special precaution for safety and age-appropriateness of the materials used.

Type 5: Decision Making

Parent involvement in decision making takes a variety of forms, such as choice of school, review and evaluation of school program, review of fiscal budget, hiring of personnel, advisory role for school committees, and advocate for school, families, and children. The types of decision-making practices each school has depend on the school's philosophy and family involvement goals and policies. Decision making involves a partnership process in which parents and educators come together and share their ideas and views, solve problems, and take actions toward a shared vision that contributes to school goals and policies.

Case Study

Nancy has two children and three stepchildren enrolled in Smith Elementary School. She and her husband have been married about 18 months and have just recently moved to a new home in the Smith Elementary School area. Since Nancy is now going to work only half time she is hoping to be able to be involved in her children's school. Previously, as a single mother who worked full time, she wasn't able to be active in her children's school. Also, Nancy is hoping that this will help her better get to know her stepchildren as there has been a lot of tension in the home since the marriage.

Questions and Considerations

1. What sorts of school activities would be an appropriate fit for Nancy? Why?

2. What would be some of the advantages of parental activities for Nancy?

3. Just as this chapter examines parents' opportunities to assist the school, it also looks at ways in which the school can help the parents. How could Smith Elementary School help Nancy?

Parents can act as leaders for other parents by representing their opinions, ideas, and concerns on behalf of their children's learning and development. Equally important is that parent leaders take the information about school decisions and policies back to the families. For parents to act as true leaders, teachers and administrators will need to provide the necessary background information and training for parents to effectively carry out their responsibilities and make sound decisions.

Parents can also participate as advocates for the school, families, and children. In subtle ways, most parents, individually, have acted as advocates for their children. An example is when parents stand up and voice their views and ideas to improve their children's experiences in school. Another level of advocacy is to have parents come together as a group to represent group objectives on issues that affect the quality of school and improve children's education and families' lives. Parents can be seen as advocates at the local, regional, state, and national levels. To become advocates, parents and educators need to work together to identify an issue, research it, disseminate the information researched, attend meetings to discuss the issue, find solutions and identify strategies, provide updates, and last but not least, recruit and train advocates to write and articulate their messages to lawmakers, media, and community members (National PTA, 2007).

Sample Activities for Involving Parents in Decision Making

1. *Parent organizations, advisory committees.* Advisory committees can be long- or short-term projects. Short-term committees are parents and educators coming together to work on short-term projects, such as selecting a math curriculum, reviewing and developing school evaluation forms and processes, forming a student club, selecting materials for a parent room, or organizing a specific school event such as an open house, a school dance, or an awards and recognition ceremony for students and volunteers. Long-term committees (e.g., PTA/PTO) entail parents and educators meeting regularly to discuss issues pertaining to school plans and policies, fiscal budget, school curriculum and activities, and personnel.
2. *Advocacy groups.* These groups target specific activities that educators and parents work on together to lobby for school, children, and family improvement on a local, regional, state, or national level. Issues include teacher–child ratio in the classroom, safety and health regulations, services offered to children with or without disabilities, teachers' salaries, and need for new building expansion.
3. *Town meetings.* These meetings are set up in the community not only inviting other parents and school staff, but also involving and networking with other community members to discuss issues on school goals, children's education, and family needs.
4. *Training sessions for parents and educators.* Parents, educators, and community members are invited to assist in identifying training needs; they then develop and offer training sessions that will help parents and educators to effectively implement their various responsibilities in decision making and advocacy.

5. *Classroom committees for parents and teachers.* Parents and teachers get together to discuss and plan curriculum-related activities for school and home, plan summer learning packets or activities, plan special events and celebrations, and address children's needs and experiences.

Tips for Successful Planning and Implementation of Decision-Making Involvement

1. *Ensure that the number and diversity of parents represented within a committee is adequate.* Parental representation should equal or exceed that of educators. A diversity of parents representing voices for families and schools should come from a balance of age or grade levels, racial and ethnic groups, fathers and mothers, different neighborhoods, and special interests.
2. *Provide information to make sound decisions.* Educators need to consistently provide relevant and clear background information for parents so that they can effectively contribute to any decision making. Teachers should allow parents sufficient time to read any information sent home and to review and reflect on issues to be discussed during the next meeting.
3. *Provide continual training for parents.* Parents need training in a variety of skills that allow them to effectively play their role as leaders and team members, contribute to the decision-making process, and advocate at different political levels.
4. *Establish regular meetings.* Regular meetings allow committee members to form a closer teamwork relationship, stay focused on important issues, and spend less time updating and recalling issues discussed. Meeting times and locations should be flexible to meet parents' needs and other family obligations.
5. *Develop and maintain collegiality between and among educators and parents.* Some educators believe that there should be a boundary between parents and professional educators in order to "preserve the power and authority gained through formal training and experience" (National PTA, 2000, p. 117). Although the professional training and expertise of administrators and teachers is crucial to provide quality education and a safe environment for children, parent involvement activities and practices should not be seen as a threat to teacher authority. Parents actively involved in PTA/PTO "may be perceived by administrators (and other parents not in PTA/PTO) as insiders who are interested in school matters" (National PTA, 2000, p. 118). This creates boundaries between parents, and parent leaders need to make extra efforts to include all parents so that they feel that ideas, insights, and concerns of all parents are welcomed.

Type 6: Collaborating with the Community

Since 1970, the family and social structure in the United States has dramatically changed in complex ways that can have an impact on families and can create stress in families. Families are increasingly facing several difficult issues such as financial concerns, an increase in single parenting, the absence of extended families for assistance and support, and an increase in families that are in the "sandwich generation" providing care for their own children as well as their elderly parents (U.S. Census Bureau, 2008). There is interconnectedness between quality of family life and children's development and learning. When families are struggling and in crisis, schools will need to step in by networking and collaborating with the community to gain access to services and resources to strengthen families and children's success in learning.

As the African proverb says, "It takes a village to raise a child." Schools and teachers need to see the community in a broader context by including community members in improving the quality of education and responding to the needs of the children and families. Community members can provide the schools with materials, people, and natural resources; therefore, schools need to make connections with various community members such as large and small businesses, faith-based communities, cultural groups, government agencies, and other organizations. Colleges and universities usually offer service learning to encourage college students to share their talents and assist in school and community needs (Epstein et al., 2009).

Sample Activities in Collaborating with the Community

1. Provide information and promote awareness to parents and school staff on the availability of community resources and services in a variety of ways:
   - Create yellow pages of community resources and services that are interested in helping families, children, and schools. Include the names of agencies, addresses, telephone numbers, e-mail addresses, and websites if available, and a brief description of resources or services available from each (e.g., free sessions such as parenting, financial and asset-building resources that help families plan their financial future to avoid predatory lending; tax preparation; ESL and GED programs; and leaders that can help families navigate across different cultures and languages).
   - Inform, encourage, and support individual families to access available services or resources needed.
2. Regularly seek, network, and collaborate with community businesses, agencies, organizations, and groups to strengthen the other types of involvement mentioned previously (Types 1 through 5).

Reflection...

As you read about the six types of parent involvement, which one(s) do you think would be the hardest to implement? Which ones would be easiest? Please explain your answer.

Foundations of Planning and Implementing a Successful Family Involvement Program

Parents, regardless of their income level, educational background, family structure, or past experience with schools, want to be actively involved with their children's education. They would like the schools to show them how to get involved (Epstein et al., 2009; Epstein & Sanders, 1998). Educators are increasingly aware of parents' desire to communicate with their children's teachers, receive frequent feedback on the children's academic progress, and have the opportunity to share in decision making that affects their children's education. Once administrators and teachers decide to form collaborative relationships with families and share responsibilities in providing quality education to the children, the first step is to create a partnership (Gestwicki, 2009). Following are some common factors found in programs that are successful in reaching out to families and forming productive school–family partnerships.

1. Positive School Climate

For schools to successfully reach out to parents, the first and foremost step is to create a positive social atmosphere and culture in the school and classrooms. The school climate has a direct effect on the extent to which parents are involved in the school and their children's education (Comer & Haynes, 1991; Gonzalez-Mena, 2010; Weissbourd et al., 2010).

Administrators should be leaders in creating an environment in which teachers and staff demonstrate to parents a sense of full partnership. Administrators should also develop an organized, well-structured plan that allows active, meaningful participation by parents. For schools to have and maintain positive climate and attitudes, all school personnel (office staff, custodial staff, cafeteria staff, administrators, and teachers) should be examined. Below are some examples of attitudes and behaviors that facilitate positive school climate:

- *Friendliness and approachability.* Greet visitors and answer the telephone in a friendly and professional way.
- *Openness and enthusiasm.* Provide parents a sense that "we are all in this together" and make time to listen to concerns, ideas, and questions of family members.
- *Empathy, compassion, and patience.* Acknowledge and recognize parental time and other family obligations, show patience while developing relationships with parents, and be sensitive to the uniqueness of parents' reactions and feelings.
- *Respect for others.* Understand and show tolerance and respect for students and families with diverse cultural values, child-rearing practices, diet, views, values, and so on.

2. Regular Communication

Communication is one of the most crucial components for creating and maintaining a constructive partnership with families. A regular, ongoing, two-way communication from school to home and home to school is needed. All families have different reading abilities and ways to communicate. Not all families are available during school hours because of different work schedules and familial obligations. Schools need to use a range of communication techniques that enable schools and families to share information. Some examples are:

- Teachers setting flexible time options that meet parents' schedules. Options include prearranged phone conversations, evening conferences, and teachers being available during drop-off and pick-up times.
- Administrators compensating teachers who need to meet parents after hours, such as in the evening or early in the morning.
- Teachers using print and nonprint communications, including school or classroom newsletters and parent education newsletters that can be transferred onto video- or audiotapes if needed.
- Exploring technological possibilities such as voice mail, computerized phone messages, e-mail, and school websites. This allows parents to access information or leave messages for the teachers or schools at any time and any place.

Schools and teachers need to make special efforts and considerations when communicating with families in which English is not the first language and/or who have little formal education. Articles or any print resources sent to families should be translated to the family's native language. Transferring information onto audiotapes/videotapes or summarizing articles to lower reading levels is needed for families with lower literacy levels. School staff and teachers sometimes may need to read to the family and ask questions to make sure that they understand. This may take time, but it reduces conflict and promotes and enhances positive relationships between home and school.

3. Diversity

An inclusive family involvement program requires schools and teachers to understand and recognize the diversity of children and families that are represented in their schools and classrooms. Families differ in their structures (two- or one-parent homes; teenage or young parents; gay and lesbian parents; working, nonworking, or unemployed parents; families of children with disabilities), economic status, racial and ethnic backgrounds, and educational backgrounds. Awareness of students' and families' beliefs, attitudes, and cultural customs and values is also essential for the effectiveness of the planning and implementation of parent involvement (Bradley & Kibera, 2006). Acknowledging the presence of family diversity goes beyond visual representations of culturally diverse materials in the school or classroom settings. It includes but is not limited to the following:

- *Reaching out to families from diverse backgrounds.* An effort is needed to encourage and support parents of minority groups to actively participate in all types of parent involvement activities, from leadership roles in decision making to attending parenting classes and assisting their children's learning at home.

- *Listening and looking for clues and cues of individual families.* Educators must encourage families to share their cultural backgrounds that have significance for their parenting and child-rearing practices, diet, communication styles, and education beliefs.
- *Instilling a sense of belonging in children and families.* Educators must seek and involve families and other elders and cultural community experts to help incorporate children's home cultures into school curriculum.
- *Involving parents in assessment and recommendations for children.* Assessment of children should not be limited to standardized tests or formal checklists but should include observations of children's work by teachers and parents. When schools actively include parents' feedback and suggestions during recommendations for remediation, it results in appropriate recommendations that match with the children's home culture and social practices.
- *Ensuring that written and verbal communications to parents is meaningful.* Schools and teachers need to be sensitive and responsive to families' cultural and educational backgrounds when talking to them or writing messages and sending informational materials to parents.
- *Respecting the individuality of families.* Educators need to be aware of different cultural groups but at the same time must avoid generalizing families into their distinct groups, such as low-income families, single-parent families, or American Indian families. Families within the same cultural group can also have individual differences (Coleman & Wallinga, 2000; Hoover, 1998; Walker-Dalhouse & Dalhouse, 2001).

Reflection...

If you have a diverse classroom, would your expectations be the same or different than if you had a more homogeneous classroom?

4. Training for Educators and Parents

Administrators need to support teachers, school staff, and parents in order for them to effectively carry out a productive home–school partnership. Administrators will have to provide emotional and social support, as well as seek and secure funds to provide adequate training for teachers, school staff, and parents.

For Educators.   Provide frequent and regular professional development for administrators, teachers, and school staff that will adequately allow them to plan and implement family involvement activities, improve communication skills and parent–teacher relationships, become aware of and work effectively with diverse students and families, and identify and respond to parents' needs and interests. When educators have adequate training in establishing positive home–school partnerships, it will significantly improve the climate of the school.

Administrators will need to have organized and well-structured plans and implementations of parent involvement in order to communicate effectively with school staff and teachers and provide a consistent approach to family involvement practices.

For Parents.   Parents need ongoing guidance, training sessions, and information on how to become actively involved in their children's education by working as team and parent leaders and contributing to school goals that require decision-making efforts.

5. Providing Comprehensive Parent Involvement Programs

When schools develop parent involvement programs that are comprehensive and offer a variety of different types of involvement, they acknowledge the diversity of parents served in the school. All parents have different skills and abilities, interests and needs, schedules and family obligations, and ages and grade levels of children. Therefore, all parents and families will respond differently to requests for involvement in their children's education. Some parents are able to participate at the school during school hours, yet many will have to choose activities that allow them to stay at home. This comprehensiveness and flexibility acknowledges the parents' needs and interests and allows parents to build on their strengths and resources. All this will affect the amount and type of parent involvement in the school.

Recommended Activities

1. Form a parent involvement panel; invite principals and teachers from different levels of education (e.g., early childhood, elementary, middle, and high school) to speak about best practices in parent involvement activities. Look for the differences and similarities between practices in each level of education.

2. Form a panel and invite parents who have children at different age and grade levels (e.g., infants and toddlers, preschool, elementary, middle, and high school) to discuss their roles in their children's education and how schools can support their roles. Compare and contrast parents' roles for children of different age groups.

3. Visit a Head Start program (center-based) and Early Head Start program (home-based) and interview the parent coordinator to investigate and understand their family involvement programs.

4. You are a classroom teacher. Choose an age or grade level and design your own family involvement program for the school year.

5. You are an administrator for a school. Choose a level of education and design a parent involvement program for your school.

Additional Resources

Books

Epstein, J., Sanders, M. G., Sheldon, S. B., Simon, B. S., Clark Salinas, K., Rodriguez Jansorn, N., et al. (2009). *School, family, and community partnerships: Your handbook for action* (3rd ed.). Thousand Oaks, CA: Corwin Press.

Gonzalez-Mena, J. (2010). *50 strategies for communicating and working with diverse families* (2nd ed.). Upper Saddle River, NJ: Pearson.

Washington, V., & Andrews, J. D. (2010). *Children of 2020: Creating a better tomorrow.* Washington, DC: National Association for the Education of Young Children.

Videos

Building a Family Partnership

This video explains the beginning techniques of family psychotherapy. It emphasizes conversation with family members about important topics related to their child's needs and development. It is produced by the Listening to Families Project AAMFT Research and Education Foundation with funding from the Office of Special Education Programs, U.S. Department of Education.

> Child Development Media, Inc.
> Phone: 800-405-8942
> www.childdevelopmentmedia.com

Communicating Between Cultures

Some cultural assumptions lead to communication breakdowns that cause embarrassment, frustration, or even discrimination. This program shows how to improve communication in a series of eye-opening cross-cultural situations.

> Learning Seed Company
> Phone: 800-634-4941
> www.learningseed.com

Conducting Parent–Teacher Conferences: A Partnership in Progress

> Films for the Humanities & Science
> Phone: 800-257-5126
> http://ffh.films.com/

Diversity and Conflict Management

This video presents information on a variety of topics on family issues and is designed for early childhood educators, caregivers, and students.

> Magna Systems Inc.
> Phone: 800-203-7060
> www.magnasystems.com/default.aspx

Helping Parents Flourish

The National Association for the Education of Young Children provides resources for teachers of young children, families, and other professionals.

> NAEYC
> Phone: 800-424-2460
> www.naeyc.org

IEP Meeting: Roles and Responsibilities

This video presents a team discussion of an IEP meeting demonstrating the team approach to setting goals for a first grader having difficulties in the classroom. Observe parent involvement, parent–teacher conflict, teaming partnerships, and coercion with the parent, teacher, special education administrator, speech therapist, and other support staff.

> Child Development Media, Inc.
> Phone: 800-405-8942
> www.childdevelopmentmedia.com

Parent Involvement

This video examines techniques for encouraging parents to become more involved in their children's education. It makes some very specific suggestions. With the busy schedule of today's parents, this video is most timely.

> Films for the Humanities & Science
> Phone: 800-257-5126
> www.films.com

Reading Rockets: Empowering Parents

Empowering Parents, a new PBS television special hosted by Al Roker, visits schools in Huntingtown, Maryland, and Portland, Oregon, to help families identify early signs of reading problems and find ideas for getting their kids the help and support they need.

WETA
Public Television & Radio
Phone: 703-998-2600
www.weta.org/

Organizations

Center on School, Family, and Community Partnership
Johns Hopkins University
Phone: 401-332-4575
E-mail: jepstein@csos.jhu.edu (Dr. Joyce Epstein)
www.csos.jhu.edu/p2000/center.htm

National Coalition for Parent Involvement in Education (NCPIE)

www.ncpie.org
National Parent Teacher Associations
E-mail: info@pta.org
www.pta.org

National Network of Partnership Schools (NNPS)
Johns Hopkins University
Phone: 410-516-8890
E-mail: nnps@csos.jhu.edu
www.csos.jhu.edu/p2000

U.S. Department of Education
1-800-USA-LEARN (1-800-872-5327)
www.ed.gov

North Central Regional Educational Laboratory
Pathways to School Improvement
E-mail: info@ncrel.org
www.ncrel.org/sdrs/

References

Anderson, K. J., & Minke, K. M. (2007, May/June). Parent involvement in education: Toward an understanding of parents' decision-making. *Journal of Educational Research, 100*(5), 311–323.

Bradley, J., & Kibera, P. (2006, January). Closing the gap: Culture and the promotion of inclusion in child care. *Young Children, 40,* 34–39.

Bredekamp, S. (2011). *Effective practices in early childhood education: Building a foundation.* Upper Saddle River, NJ: Pearson.

Chang, H. N. (2010). Two-generational approach. In V. Washington & J. D. Andrews (Eds.), *Children of 2020: Creating a better tomorrow.* Washington, DC: National Association for the Education of Young Children.

Children's Defense Fund. (2010). Yearbook 2010: The state of America's children. Washington, DC: Author. Retrieved July 5, 2010, from www.childrensdefense.org/child-research-data-publications/data/state-of-americas-children-2010-report.html

Coleman, M., & Wallinga, C. (2000, Winter). Teacher training in family involvement: An interpersonal approach. *Childhood Education, 76*(2), 76–81.

Comer, J., & Haynes, N. (1991). Parent involvement in schools: An ecological approach. *Elementary School Journal, 91*(3), 271–278.

Epstein, J. L. (1996). Improving school–family–community partnerships in the middle grades. *Middle School Journal, 28*(2), 43–48.

Epstein, J. L. (2006, January). Families, schools, and community partnerships. *Young Children, 40,* 37.

Epstein, J. L. (2007, October). Connections count: Improving family and community involvement in secondary schools. *Principal Leadership, 8,* 16–22.

Epstein, J. L., Sanders, M. G., Sheldon, S. B., Simon, B. S., Clark Salinas, K., Rodriguez Jansorn, N., et al. (2009). *School, family, and community partnerships: Your handbook for action* (3rd ed.). Thousand Oaks, CA: Corwin Press.

Epstein, J. L., & Sanders, M. (1998). What we learn from international studies of school–family–community partnerships. *Childhood Education, 74*(6), 392–394.

Gestwicki, C. (2009). *Home, school, and community relations* (7th ed.). New York: Delmar Cengage Learning.

Gonzalez-Mena, J. (1998). *The child in the family and the community* (2nd ed.). Upper Saddle River, NJ: Prentice Hall.

Gonzalez-Mena, J. (2010). *50 strategies for communicating and working with diverse families* (2nd ed.). Upper Saddle River, NJ: Pearson.

Henderson, A. T., & Berla, N. (1994). *A new generation of evidence: The family is critical to student achievement.* Washington, DC: National Committee for Citizens in Education.

Henderson, A. T., & Mapp, K. L. (2002). *A new wave of evidence: The impact of school, family, and community connections on student achievement.* Austin, TX: Southwest Educational Development Laboratory, National Center for Family & Community Connections with Schools.

Hoover, J. (1998, Winter). Community–school alliances: The road to successful learning. *Winds of Change, 13*(1), 28–31.

Hoover-Dempsey, K. V., Walker, J. M., Sandler, H. M., Whetsel, D., Green, C. L., Wilkins, A. S., et al. (2005). Why do parents become involved? Research findings and implications. *The Elementary School Journal, 106*(2), 105–130.

Houtenville, A. J., & Conway, K. S. (2008). Parental effort, school resources, and student achievement. *Journal of Human Resources, 43*(2), 437–453.

Mitchell, S., Foulger, T. S., & Wetzel, K. (2010). 10 tips for involving families through Internet-based communication. *Spotlight on Teaching Preschool, 2*, 56–59.

Moles, O. (1992). Synthesis of recent research on parent participation on children's education. *Educational Leadership, 44*.

National PTA. (2000). *Building successful partnerships: A guide for developing parent and family involvement programs.* Alexandria, VA: Author.

National PTA. (2007). *PTA national standards for family–school partnership: An implementation guide.* Alexandria, VA: Author.

National PTA. (2010). *State laws on family engagement in education.* Retrieved on July 5, 2010, from www.pta.org/State_Laws_Report.pdf

Rockwell, R., Andre, L., & Hawley, M. (1996). *Parents and teachers as partners: Issues and challenges.* Orlando, FL: Harcourt Brace.

Schulman, K. (2000). *The high cost of childcare puts quality care out of reach for many families.* Washington, DC: Children's Defense Fund.

Sheldon, S. B. (2005). *Getting families involved with NCLB: Factors affecting schools' enactment of federal policy.* Paper presented at the Sociology of Education Section *No Child Left Behind* Conference at the annual meeting of the American Sociological Association, Philadelphia.

Shoemaker, C. J. (1996). Home learning enablers and other helps: Home learning enablers for ages two to twelve. *Program Enrichment Paper.* (ERIC Document No. ED 394 694)

Simon, B. S., Salinas, K. C., Epstein, J. L., & Sanders, M. G. (1998). Proceedings of Families, Technology, and Education Conference, Chicago, IL, October 30–November 1, 1997. See PS 027 175.

Swick, D., Head-Reeves, D., & Barbarin, O. (2006). Building relationships between diverse families and school personnel. In C. Franklin, M. B. Harris, & P. Allen-Meares (Eds.), *The school services sourcebook: A guide for school-based professionals.* New York: Oxford University Press.

Trahan, C., & Lawler-Prince, D. (1999). Parent partnerships: Transforming homework into home–school activities. *Early Childhood Education Journal, 27*(1), 65–68.

U.S. Census Bureau. (2008). *America's families and living arrangements.* Washington, DC: U.S. Department of Commerce.

U.S. Department of Education. (2004). *No Child Left Behind: A toolkit for teachers.* Retrieved December 20, 2005, from www.nclb.gov

U.S. Department of Education. (2010). A blueprint for reform: The reauthorization of the Elementary and Secondary Education Act (ESEA). Retrieved July 8, 2010, from www2.ed.gov/policy/elsec/leg/blueprint/blueprint.pdf

U.S. Department of Health and Human Services. (2006, April). *Early Head Start benefits children and families: Research to practice.* Retrieved July 8, 2010, from www.acf.hhs.gov/programs/opre/ehs/ehs_resrch/index.html

Walker-Dalhouse, D., & Dalhouse, M. (2001, July). Parent–school relations: Communicating more effectively with African-American parents. *Young Children, 56*, 75–80.

Weissbourd, B., Weissbourd, R., & O'Carroll, K. (2010). Family engagement. In V. Washington & J. D. Andrews (Eds.), *Children of 2020: Creating a better tomorrow*. Washington, DC: National Association for the Education of Young Children.

White, K. R., Taylor, M. J., & Moss, V. D. (1992). Does research support claims about the benefits of involving parents in early intervention program? *Review of Educational Research, 62*(1), 91–125.

Wolfendale, S. (1989). *Parental involvement: Developing networks between school, home, and community.* London: Cassell Educational Limited.

Chapter Eight

Families and Their Children with Disabilities

AmySue Reilly
Auburn University

Dennis Campbell
South Alabama University

Kari Chiasson
University of North Dakota

The lives of families with children who have special needs are the same as other families and, at the same time, very different. Family love, affection, and pride are similar, but families of children with disabilities often experience variable stresses not usually a part of other families' lives. This chapter examines the dynamics of these special families and helps you explore the:

▶ Role of families in shaping public policy for individuals with disabilities.

▶ Reaction of family members upon learning of their child's disability.

▶ Impact of the disability on family.

▶ Accommodations and adjustment made by the family.

▶ Adjustment of fathers, siblings, and mothers.

▶ Supports for families.

Families of children with disabilities are no different from other families in wanting their child to have an opportunity to develop, learn, and socialize with friends while enjoying life as a part of their community. To enhance these possibilities, families and professionals must work together to ensure that these children are provided the necessary experiences to grow through exploration of the world around them.

This chapter familiarizes the reader with the dynamics surrounding families who have a child with a disability. By way of introduction, a useful synopsis of the progression of integrating individuals with disabilities into homes, schools, and community settings is provided. This is followed by a summary of relevant legislation and a statistical overview of the numbers of students with special needs being served in recent years. Finally, the perspectives of various family members are offered.

Historical Perspective

Historically the fate of individuals with disabilities and their families was rather bleak. Many early societies' attitudes toward individuals with disabilities were that of fear, "fear of catching it," like the plague; disgust, contempt, and shock of the individual's condition as a result of the disability; or believing the individual's disability was a result of demonic possession, resulting in zealots' cruel and inhumane treatment to rid them of these demons. Consequently, families became outcasts from their homes and villages, forced to fend for themselves due to their child's disability. The exiled families' survival was grim especially without the additional support and resources of their extended family and community. These families were banished and left alone, solely because of their child with a disability. This ignorance was due to society's lack of knowledge and understanding of various disabilities. Understandably, we fear and often shun what we do not understand.

Ancient Times

Interestingly, two significant visionaries of ancient times spoke of a more humane social treatment of these individuals with disabilities. Hippocrates (physician, c. 460–377 B.C.) believed that emotional problems were a result of natural forces rather than supernatural powers. Likewise Plato (philosopher, c. 427–347 B.C.) hypothesized that people who were mentally unstable were not accountable for their behaviors. Unfortunately this humane consideration was short lived during this time period yet would arise again during the mid-20th century.

During the Middle Ages, families and their child with a disability were forcibly separated. A limited number of religious orders provided individuals with disabilities, removed from their families, basic care and menial labor in exchange for shelter in the monasteries. These were the early beginnings of institutionalizing and segregating individuals with disabilities from society, and these practices continued through the 20th century. Yet there were major societal changes on the horizon; families and their children with disabilities began to collectively speak and share their individual stories of trials and tribulations. This, in turn, encouraged and facilitated the growth of families' active involvement, which, in turn, empowered other families, legislative changes, and improvements in overall services for their children with disabilities.

20th-Century Inspirational Figures with Disabilities

In the early 20th century, Helen Keller wrote a powerful and incredible story, *The Story of My Life*, which was published in 1905. Her autobiography was one of the first books about a young woman with a disability that defied monumental odds. It's a story of a family's determination to find the solutions for their daughter's disability. As a young child of 19 months, Helen contracted a high fever from an unknown source that resulted in her deafness and blindness. Helen's mother read Charles Dickens's book *American Notes*, written in 1842 about another child who was deaf and blind yet was educated. Mrs. Keller was so encouraged by this story that she sought out a specialist for advice regarding Helen's condition. This doctor confirmed that Helen's condition was permanent but encouraged them not to give up hope, because he felt Helen could learn. The family was referred to an expert working with children who were deaf, Alexander Graham Bell. Bell suggested that they contact the Perkins Institute to request a teacher for Helen. This determined family defied all odds and sought out the best possible services for their daughter no matter how hopeless they may have felt at times with Helen's initially scary, violent, and destructive behaviors. Through the perseverance of Helen, her family, and her teachers, Helen earned a Bachelor of Arts degree, cum laude, in 1904. Her autobiography was one of the most powerfully inspirational books for both families and individuals with disabilities because of the triumph over horrendous obstacles related to her disabilities. Hope and perseverance was the key to open doors for Helen to learn, thrive, and grow—and an encouragement for other families. What was once thought to be impossible now became possible; doors were opened up to her world.

The children's book *The Secret Garden* (1911), by Frances Hodgson Burnett, was about Mary Lennox, a sickly child who became an orphan when her parents died of cholera. Mary was taken in by her wealthy uncle in England who was physically disabled. As the story unfolds, Mary's health improves as she explores the manor's grounds and gardens. On her daily adventures, Mary meets Martha, a maid at the manor, and her odd brother, Dickon, who seems to talk to the animals and has a prolific green thumb. Mary also meets Colin, her cousin, who has given up the will to live, doomed to be a "hunchback" like his father. Since Mary has recovered from her illness, crediting her outdoor adventures, she decides change Colin's pessimistic attitude. Mary initially abducts an unwilling Colin to join her in the gardens, and he is soon eager to go on their exciting adventures. This 1911 publication was one of the earliest children's book positively depicting a child with a disability and a strong friendship that was forged through one's persistence. Mary and Colin's story provided encouragement for parents and children with various disabilities about developing friendships, overcoming obstacles, and persevering. Their story illustrated the power of one individual to make a difference.

Considered a classic book that is shared among families of children with mental retardation, Pearl Buck's *The Child Who Never Grew* (1950) is a heartfelt story about raising a child who was cognitively challenged yet never diagnosed with a specific disability. Buck's frank account of her family's life was one of the first that provided inspiration and support to those parents with similar children. By sharing her personal joys and sorrows, she helped many parents of children with disabilities feel comfortable sharing their families' stories thus fostering the early beginnings of parental support groups, commonality among friends.

My Left Foot (1954) is a compelling autobiography by Christy Brown, born in 1932 to a working-class family in Dublin. His mother noticed at 4 months that Christy, the tenth of 22 children, was not developing like his siblings. Due to her grave concern about Christy's poor development at the age of one, she took him to the doctor, who diagnosed him with severe cerebral palsy. His doctors reiterated that Christy's overall physical and mental prognosis was hopeless since he was unable to communicate or control his movements. Though poor, his family had a wealth of love, encouragement, and time. Christy's mother never believed the doctors' diagnosis that he was mentally retarded. Through her tenacity, she taught him to write the alphabet, spell, and read using his left foot. His brothers and father created many ingenious ways to include Christy in all their daily activities and to teach Christy what they learned in school. Using his left foot, his only controllable limb, Christy eventually became a proficient writer, poet, author, and impressionistic painter. Christy's powerful story of his family's and his own determination and tenacity that, in the end, triumphed over insurmountable odds teaches us not to "judge a book by its cover," but to open it to see what's inside because that's what matters most.

Leaders with Disabilities or with Family Members with Disabilities

The mid-20th century was also distinguished by an inspirational international leader with a disability. President Franklin D. Roosevelt demonstrated through his own perseverance that he could effectively perform his presidential duties despite his polio-afflicted legs. He assumed the presidency during the Great Depression and brought hope to a desperate nation, demonstrated by his own example that one could overcome great barriers despite one's limitations of physical, emotional, or financial hardships. Roosevelt was a very active chief executive despite performing the majority of his duties from a wheelchair. He was a powerful role model for millions of individuals who now could aspire to become what they dreamed to become. If President Roosevelt overcame his limitations, then anyone with a disability could be encouraged to fulfill their dreams and aspirations. Roosevelt's determination and success, and the support of his family, demonstrated that one could accomplish a great deal.

The power of families who were determined to speak out continued with another great man and his family's impact on society. President John F. Kennedy grew up with a younger sister, Rosemary, who was mentally retarded. As a result, the Kennedys and their extended family took on the responsibilities of many causes of individuals with disabilities. While he was in office, President Kennedy established in 1961 the President's Panel on Mental Retardation in honor of Rosemary. The following year that panel presented its report, Proposed Program for National Action to Combat Mental Retardation. This report led to significant bills being introduced in Congress that would and still influence our government's commitment to individuals with disabilities. Kennedy's political agenda was shaped by his personal family experience, and he made significant societal changes that still impact us today when he established the Bureau of Education for the Handicapped (now the Office of Special Education Programs). President Kennedy had strong convictions regarding the right to full attainment of human and legal rights as well as the opportunities for individuals with mental retardation (and eventually to all other disabilities) to receive an appropriate education. These were the initial foundations for families and their children with disabilities to move through previously closed doors into the mainstream of society. Kennedy's leadership led to the development of special education and rehabilitation of individuals with disabilities, giving individuals of various ages with disabilities status equivalent to their nondisabled peers. These legislative changes would later lead to the development of the Americans with Disabilities Act, which would greatly affect the workforce by including those individuals with disabilities as productive, contributing, and valued employees.

In the early 1970s, the daughter of then Senator Hubert Humphrey took her little girl with Down syndrome to her neighborhood school to register for kindergarten. She was met at the door by the principal, who informed her that her daughter would not be registering for kindergarten because she was retarded. Quite shocked by her daughter's rejection to attend kindergarten, Victoria told her father. Senator Humphrey was working in Congress on the Rehabilitation Act of 1973. As a result of his granddaughter's denial to attend school because of her disability, Humphrey put in a section (Section 504) that would protect children with disabilities from being discriminated against. Congress passed this civil rights legislation but with no funding. Once again the power and influence of a family that has a child with a disability make monumental strides for individuals with disabilities. Humphrey's strong interest in early education for very young children with disabilities was based on his granddaughter's experiences. Humphrey also supported the notion that early stimulation would provide a youngster the additional learning opportunity necessary to progressively acquire skills later in life. Families can make a difference.

Another contemporary public official who supported the development and passing of landmark legislation was Connecticut Senator Lowell Weicker, whose son had a disability. The Education for All Handicapped Children Act, known as Public Law 94-142, was implemented in 1975, and in 1986 Public Law 99-457 laid the groundwork for this country's educational reform and commitment to infants, toddlers, children, youth, and young adults with disabilities and their families. Family involvement and their rights were key components of this landmark legislation.

Behind each of these politicians and legislative movements were dedicated parents and parent support groups advocating on their children's behalf. They, like all parents, wanted what was best for their children and advocated with legislators for including them in the public education system. The United States provides a public education to all students. However, in the mid-20th century many students with the most significant disabilities were excluded because schools argued they did not have a program for them or they were simply uneducable. Parents formed organizations such as the Association for Retarded Citizens (now known as the ARC), the Autism

Society, United Cerebral Palsy, and TASH to provide them a stronger advocate voice. The efforts of these early parent groups led to laws such as the Education for All Handicapped Children Act (discussed in Chapter 10), which guaranteed the right to a free appropriate education for all children. Even with this legislative mandate, students with significant disabilities were typically taught in separate programs. These students, however, should have been afforded an education that allowed them to learn as their abilities allowed and provided them with the greatest quality of life. Parents wanted their children to experience school beyond the special education classroom. This led to mainstreaming students with disabilities in general education classrooms, thus providing them proximity to their nondisabled peers.

Mainstreaming provided the access to learn with students without disabilities, which is critical for children to learn to live successfully in our society. We know that children learn much more about how to function in their peer group from each other while learning social skills than they learn from adults. In segregated classrooms, their primary role models were other children with disabilities, which made it difficult to learn appropriate behaviors. Mainstreaming gave them access to their nondisabled peers but often without the support needed to be successful, which was important to facilitate a student's learning. Mainstreaming was the precursor to inclusion.

Rationale of Inclusion

Inclusion is a term generally applied to educating students with and without disabilities within the regular class in neighborhood schools. The Individuals with Disabilities Education Act (IDEA) addressed specialized instruction for students with disabilities, stating that a free appropriate public education and inclusion in education with their nondisabled peers, to the maximum extent possible, be provided to these students. Public Law 99-457, an amendment to the Education for all Handicapped Children Act, indicates that interdisciplinary services provided to infants and toddlers with disabilities must be family directed and, to the maximum extent appropriate, those services be provided in the child's natural environment (Rantala, Uotinen, & McWilliam, 2009; Howard, Williams, Port, & Lepper, 2001). Research demonstrated the effectiveness of intervening early for young children with disabilities; it also showed that significant brain development occurred in the first 3 years of life. The focus on the family as the primary teacher of their children was one of the underlying foundations of Part C of Public Law 99–457. Congress found that it was important "to maximize the potential for individuals with disabilities to live independently in society; to enhance the capacity of families to meet the special needs of their infants and toddlers with disabilities . . ." (U.S. Department of Education, 2004).

This legislation created a system of services in each state. Services were provided for children from birth to age 3 with an Individualized Family Service Plan (IFSP). This document, created by a team that included the parents, describes what supports will be provided to the infant and the child's family. This family-directed support approach is the hallmark of Part C services. Supporting the family to best meet their child's needs is a major component of the IFSP.

The National Early Intervention Longitudinal Study (NEILS) of Part C services demonstrated that the program has been successful in supporting young children and their families. Children receive Part C services in three categories: those with diagnosed delays (as measured by assessment), those who are at a high risk for delay due to a condition that will most likely lead to a delay (for example, Down syndrome or cerebral palsy), and those children in states that had the option to serve children at risk. The NEILS study was completed over a 10-year period based on a random sample of children less than 3 years of age at the beginning of the study.

Congress expected that supporting children and families early would lead to savings in later costs of education. The study found that, overall, intervening early was effective; 37% of those in the study did not receive preschool special education services and 42% did not receive special education services in kindergarten. For families, most reported at 36 months and again at kindergarten that they knew how to help their child and felt optimistic about how their child was fairing (SRI International, 2007).

For children up to age 9, IDEA allows students to be categorized as developmentally delayed. Each state has developed its own criteria for developmental delay. This category serves two important functions: (1) it allows children to be served without being labeled with a disability that may carry a stigma; and (2) it allows children to be served under developmental delay even if they do not qualify for a specific label, as long as they demonstrate the state-required delay. Thirty-six percent of students are served as developmental delay. For 3- to 5-year-olds, the highest category served (47% of children) is that of speech and language impairments. Children with autism make up another 6% of those served. Other categories over 1% include other health impairments (2.55%), intellectual disabilities (1.75%), hearing impairments (1.2%), and multiple disabilities (1.1%).

IDEA also addressed the concept of least restrictive environment. This legal term is used to define the right of children with disabilities to be educated in settings that are not segregated from children without disabilities (Howard et al., 2001). There is a preference for including children with disabilities in regular classrooms along with their specialized services. Inclusion is a continuum of services that depends on the child's needs, the preferences of parents, the need for related services, and the level of progress in the regular setting (Howard et al., 2001).

How a child performs in one setting rarely constitutes a complete picture of how that given child performs in all settings. It is for this and other reasons that professionals should readily provide the family ample opportunity to share their perspectives regarding their child (Salisbury, 1992; Turnbull, Turnbull, Shank, & Leal, 2010). Parental input has definite value in that it may furnish the professional(s) with critical information not easily obtained during the course of clinical observation or the teaching regimen. Also, such input reminds the professional that the child is a unique individual with various needs that are met in different settings by many providers.

In summary, many significant pieces of legislation have provided a tremendous increase in new educational programs and opportunities for all infants, toddlers, preschoolers, school-aged children, youth, and young adults with disabilities. The importance of family involvement in the collaborative educational pursuit of their children's opportunities is central to much of this legislation. It is for this reason that professionals must continue to learn how to work more effectively within the family system.

$\mathcal{R}$*eflection...*

Given the history of special education, what would be the ideal preschool or elementary classroom? How would children with special needs fit into those classes?

Family Systems

This section is based on the premise that families of children with disabilities, like families of all other children, want their offspring to have meaningful, enjoyable, and successful lives. Furthermore, it recognizes that in order for this to be possible professionals must respect and appreciate each family's unique position as they strive toward this end. The overall family dynamics that are affected by the presence of a child with a disability are first presented. Second, the reader is introduced to fathers and siblings and their perspectives, which are often neglected in literature that has traditionally emphasized the mother's role within the family system. Finally, parental viewpoints and opinions regarding community inclusion for their children with disabilities are discussed.

Adjustments: Dealing with the Disability

Reactions.   When a family is first told their long awaited "bundle of joy" has a disability, it is not easy to predict how each family member will react (Powers, 1993). Most families first receive this information from medical professionals while they are dealing with the hospitalization of their infant or toddler (Long, Artis, & Dobbins, 1993; Pearl, 1993). Receiving information pertaining to the birth (or diagnosis) of such a child is indeed overwhelming (Buck, 1950; Long et al., 1993; Meyer, 1986b).

Each family member's reaction stems from intense feelings and draining emotions, often leaving them confused, bewildered, and full of questions. Of course, a major key to working effectively with such families is to respect their right to express this intense and constantly varying range of emotions (Fewell, 1986; Gibbs, 1993).

> Over the years I have often heard that parents must learn to accept the fact that their child has disabilities. I know no parent who hasn't accepted their child's disabilities. When you get up in the morning and force your child's legs

into braces, put them in a wheelchair, feed them breakfast, give their antiseizure medication, you have accepted and are dealing with your child's disability. (Statum, 1995, p. 68)

Professionals naturally may make generalizations regarding how parents might react and respond to their child with a disability. This is usually in hope of working more effectively with the families. Often, however, parental feelings, emotions, and behaviors are unpredictable. After all, few families are prepared to face the complex issues confronting them (Singer & Powers, 1993).

Emotional Impact.   Parental expectations regarding their child's disability can be strongly influenced by the different types and severity of the disability (Fewell, 1986; Kroth & Edge, 1997). Parents have long anticipated the birth of their child and their anticipation is full of hopes and dreams. Parental grief and reactions to the birth of their child with a disability is a result of the loss of their "normal" child (Murray & Cornell, 1981).

Thus the birth of a child with a disability is frequently a stressful event for families due to the variety of feelings, reactions, and responses felt by the various family members (Dunst, Trivette, & Jordy, 1997; Featherstone, 1980; Murray & Cornell, 1981; Turnbull, Brotherson, & Summers, 1985). Farber (1975) indicated several adaptations that families develop when having a child with a disability. Murray (1980) indicated that families frequently go through a series of reactions and responses. Kirk, Gallagher, and Anastasiow (2005) and Kübler-Ross (1969) found that some parents and other family members, including siblings, grandparents, and other extended family members, are faced with a variety of feelings, reactions, and responses at the birth of a child with a disability. These feelings, reactions, and responses may change as life goes on, especially as the internal and external resources increase (Kroth & Edge, 1997).

Even though family members report additional stress from a child with a disability, they also experience positive outcomes. A study by Taunt and Hastings (2002) interviewed 47 parents of children with developmental disabilities. The findings revealed that there were several positive outcomes of having a child with a disability: the parents focused on the positive aspects of their child; they experienced a changed perspective on life; there were opportunities to learn about children, themselves, and others; it improved the family dynamics; there were opportunities to meet and share with other parents of children with disabilities; and they were able to influence policy.

Professionals have become more aware of how family members are affected by the presence of a child with a disability. Professionals also need to take into consideration the roles and needs of each family member (Goldenberg & Goldenberg, 1980; Turnbull et al., 1985). The framework developed by Turnbull and Turnbull (2001) for understanding the emotions, dynamics, and elements of family systems has allowed professionals to work more effectively with these families. The four elements of this framework are (1) family resources, (2) daily interactions among family members, (3) different individual family needs, and (4) changes that occur over time that affect family members (Turnbull & Turnbull, 2001).

Accommodations: Getting On with Life

Adaptiveness.   Families are remarkably adaptive to the needs of their child (Seed, 1988; Lobato, 1990; Pearl, 1993). Moreover, the role of each family member assumes varying dimensions depending on the respective attitudes and behavior displayed regarding the child's disability (Meyer, 1986b; Nixon, 1993; Seed, 1988).

A broad range of emotion is experienced while attempting to reconcile those feelings regarding the family's child with a disability (Hawkins, Singer, & Nixon, 1993; Meyer, 1993; Seed, 1988). The anguish and stress are often tremendous, yet somehow each family member learns to cope with a mechanism that is frequently quite efficient in carrying other family members through the substantial turmoil. In other words, the family often draws closer as they depend on one another.

Balanced Lifestyle.   A family's daily routine typically focuses around the child with the disability. Thus, their attempt to find a balance in a family routine is an arduous task at best, given that they often are having to juggle appointments dealing with various medical specialists, therapists (physical, occupational, speech and language), and early interventionist home visits. Clearly, it is time consuming to visit a multitude of professional offices while trying to find answers to questions regarding the diagnosis or treatment of a child with a disability. Also, it is an exhausting pursuit for families to find the best services and newest information regarding their child's condition. Again, the family's attempt to find a requisite balance and perceived normalcy is an issue with which they frequently wrestle.

Child–Peer Relations.   Parents are constantly seeking opportunities for children with disabilities to actively engage in typical early childhood experiences with their peers (Boswell & Schuffner, 1990; McLean & Hanline, 1990; Ruder, 1993; Statum, 1995). Also, critical to these children's development is the growth they continually experience from interactions as members of their own families (Frey, Fewell, Vadasy, & Greenberg, 1989; Pearl, 1993; Statum, 1995). Thus, an additional difficulty is the family's effort to continually locate positive peer interactions so their exceptional child has an opportunity to enhance his or her learning experiences (Bailey & Bricker, 1984; Guralnick, 1990; McLean & Hanline, 1990; Ruder, 1993).

Child Care.   Finding an appropriate child-care program for any family often is a trying event and even more stressful to families attempting to locate a program that will accept a child with a disability (DeVore & Bowers, 2006). Quite frankly, child-care providers are not customarily informed on how to work with young children with disabilities and thus are reluctant to accept responsibility for such children. They are, however, increasingly being asked to care for these children.

Seeking Services.   Families seek the best services to provide for their child. Consequently, their homes are often like New York's Grand Central Station in trying to schedule various needed services. Furthermore, opening one's home to the numerous specialists arriving to provide services to their child and family is an intrusion on family privacy with which other families do not have to contend (Hanson, Lynch, & Wayman, 1990; Pearl, 1993). Nevertheless, these families are frequently required to carry out the programs prescribed for their child if they want to ensure their child's progress.

Early childhood special education interventionists attempt to work with families and their children with disabilities in a caring, sensitive, and supportive manner (Fewell, 1986; Pearl, 1993). Obviously, the services provided must be flexible and responsive to the diversity of family needs and resources (DeGangi, Wietlisbach, Possison, Stein, & Royeen, 1994; Hanson et al., 1990).

In addition to handling everyday life stressors, families learn how best to provide for the various needs of their child. Therefore, early intervention services must strive to be family friendly, family focused, and family centered. Moreover, services need to be provided to families in the various settings that each family requires, such as home, child care, or community.

Values.   Cultural and religious values heavily influence a family's structure as well as their views of disabilities (DeGangi et al., 1994; Hanson et al., 1990; Howard et al., 2001). Families will differ by cultural, economic, and religious influences, as well as by membership and structure of the family itself (Hanson et al., 1990; Howard et al., 2001). Such values can impact the effectiveness of the family's acceptance and willingness to implement intervention strategies. Therefore, professionals must be respectful of families' value systems and their services flexible enough to be in accordance with differing family value systems and cultures (DeGangi et al., 1994; Hanson et al., 1990; Linan-Thompson & Jean, 1997).

Extended Family.   Another important factor is the extended family, which is often a wonderful resource for providing that additional assistance needed in dealing with their child. An extended family can include grandparents, aunts, uncles, cousins, neighbors, and close friends who have joined the family circle. These members frequently provide the continual encouragement, respite relief, moral support, comfort, and unconditional understanding needed by the parents and other family members (Fewell, 1986; Gallagher, Cross, & Scharfman, 1981; Long et al., 1993; Pearl, 1993).

Support Groups.   Parents of children with disabilities often need additional support other than that provided by professionals (Long et al., 1993; Meyer, 1993). Consequently, there is a growing network of parent support groups across the nation. Networking is a process linking parents interested in talking to other parents who have coped with similar situations—felt anguish, needed relief, and paved the road for tomorrow (Frey et al., 1989; Gibbs, 1993; Grossman, 1972). These networks of extended support allow family members to grow through personal shared experiences.

Friends.   We all rely on friends for a variety of activities, be they colleagues at work, social acquaintances, casual friends, or those we rely on as confidants. When a child is born with a disability, often family and friends do not know how to respond. Families often find that the people they associate with change dramatically after the birth of their child. The social network they were accustomed to is now different, and they find themselves building new or modified social networks.

Case Study

Ms. Lawrence is in her second year of teaching at Roosevelt Elementary School. In her class of 22 third graders, she has a delightful little boy named Matthew. Matthew and his family moved to town during the summer. His father works for a computer company and his mother teaches piano.

Since the beginning of the school year, Ms. Lawrence has had increasing concerns about Matthew's reading. Matthew knows the names of all of the letters and a few sight words, but cannot read text more difficult than mid-first-grade level. Even though Ms. Lawrence has tried numerous strategies to help Matthew with his reading, he continues to struggle.

Parent–teacher conferences are 2 weeks away and Ms. Lawrence would like to talk to his parents about referring Matthew for testing to see whether he has a reading disability.

Questions and Considerations

1. Are there other steps that you would take before suggesting a referral for testing?
2. If you were Ms. Lawrence, how would you present your concerns to Matthew's parents?
3. Would you present your concerns at the parent–teacher conference? Why or why not?
4. Are there other professionals that should be involved in the meeting with Matthew's parents?

Perspectives of Family Members

Fathers. Traditionally, professionals have focused on mothers' perspectives regarding parental concerns of families and their children with disabilities. Interestingly, however, these mothers have long recognized the need to facilitate the father's involvement with their child's intervention program (Gallagher et al., 1981). In response, professionals have begun to address the significant needs of fathers and their active involvement in their child's intervention program (Lamb & Meyer, 1991; Young & Roopnarnine, 1994).

"A man's pride in his child's abilities influences his perspective of his parenting abilities, which increases his pride in his abilities as a parent" (Meyer, 1993, p. 83). A father's attitude toward his child's disability frequently influences the attitude of the family as a whole (Frey et al., 1989; Lamb & Meyer, 1991).

Typically, when a man becomes a father he evaluates his future in respect to his ability to provide and influence the development of his child. He assesses his accomplishments, career satisfaction, family, and marriage. The diagnosis of a disability can directly influence how a man assesses his family life (Meyer, 1986b), which in turn can directly influence the overall family unit's perception.

As a result of their recognized importance, there are now support programs specifically designed to meet the individual needs of fathers (Meyer, 1986a; Young & Roopnarine, 1994). One example provides an opportunity for fathers to participate in discussions regarding how their views of accomplishment and family have changed in the wake of the child's diagnosis (Meyer, 1993). Fathers bring their children to the program and are given the opportunity to be primary caregivers, thus increasing their feelings of "expertise" regarding their child's disability. Father-focused support groups assist the family in handling everyday life stressors while attending to the various needs of their child.

> When people speak of acceptance, they imply that parents must learn that their child's disability prevents them from having all the things normal people have, that these children can't be a real part of our society. They must be separate even though it is bad and painful. But it isn't the job of a parent of a child with disabilities to accept things the way they are. It is our job to do anything we possibly can do to change things. (Statum, 1995, p. 68)

Siblings.   Professionals, while providing services to the child with a disability, have also unintentionally overlooked siblings. The literature suggests that siblings of children with disabilities experience feelings of isolation, guilt, resentment, perceived pressure to achieve, increased care-giving demands, and uncertainty about their future role in life regarding their sibling (Harland & Cuskelly, 2000; Hannah, 1999). Fortunately, professionals now have begun to address the significant need of siblings, and their sincere interest to be involved in the intervention program.

Siblings are curious about their brother's or sister's disability and genuinely want to increase their knowledge and understanding of their sibling's condition. Also, according to Meyer (1993), "Nondisabled siblings frequently complain about people who view their sibling *as* the disability" (p. 85). Thus, siblings need more information as well as the skill to share with others what they have learned.

Several sibling programs have been established to provide brothers and sisters opportunities to meet others who share the experience of having a sibling with a disability (Meyer, Vadasay, & Fewell, 1985; Powell & Ogle, 1985). Through these programs, "participants share strategies to address common sibling concerns, such as what to do when classmates make insensitive comments about people with disabilities or when siblings embarrass them in public" (Meyer, 1993, p. 84).

In spite of the challenges due to their brother's or sister's disability, there are unanticipated benefits that contribute to their lives (Gibbs, 1993; Meyer, 1993). Some of the reported sibling benefits of these shared experiences include increased understanding of other people, more tolerance and compassion, and greater appreciation of their own good health and intelligence (Grossman, 1972). After acquiring these (and other) benefits, "brothers and sisters frequently express pride in their siblings' accomplishments and view their siblings in terms of what they can do" (Meyer, 1993, p. 85).

Mothers.   Mothers, like fathers and siblings, are individuals and respond accordingly. But there are also some experiences that are common to many mothers. It is not uncommon for some mothers to feel a personal responsibility for their child's condition. They blame themselves for not having been more careful during pregnancy. They wonder if it is something they did or perhaps something they didn't do. Thoughts such as these often result in feelings of self-recrimination and condemnation (Buscaglia, 1975).

Mothers often find their lives dramatically changed after the birth of a child with a disability. The woman who had been actively involved in the community, with personal interests, employment, and so forth, may find that her world becomes very small. Because of the demands of time, energy, and emotion, the mother may find that her whole life is changed, leaving little time for her own interests and needs. Burnout is often a consequence of this change in life circumstances (Berger, 2007).

As with the other family members, the mother will need to grieve her loss—the loss of the dream of the "perfect child." This may be complicated by the fact that mothers often feel they are responsible for helping other family members deal with their grief and neglect their own need to grieve, thus prolonging it.

Diverse Background Families.   Consider the importance of significant people with whom the child and the family interacts. The child's family members, peers, friends, and church members influence the child. A family's cultural background has a major impact and influences the behaviors of each family member (Nieto, 2008; O'Shea, O'Shea, Algozzine, & Hammitte, 2001). The family's culture has a set of values and beliefs that guides the members' diversity and dynamics (Shimoni & Baxter, 2001). Thus, understanding the child's cultural and ethnic background will influence the understanding of the family's customs and traditions (O'Shea et al., 2001; Hager-Olsen, 2001). Acceptance of diversity and effective communication increase the opportunities to value diversity, including a disability. This can be shared by the family and will influence the decisions being made on the behalf of the child and family (Kroth & Edge, 1997; Shimoni & Baxter, 1996).

Reflection...

If a child with special needs is from a diverse ethnic background, how does that ethnic group view the child and family (American Indian, black, Latino/Hispanic, Asian American or refugee family such as those from Bosnia, Nigeria, Cambodia, and El Salvador)?

Extended Families.   Some extended families include relatives or close friends who reside in the same house permanently (Shimoni & Baxter, 1996). Other extended families include relatives or close friends who do not reside in the house but have significant roles or responsibilities for the family. Extended families provide support for both the child with a disability and for the other family members (Shimoni & Baxter, 1996). Understanding family structure and how it affects the family dynamics is crucial in providing effective services for the family.

Blended Families.   Blended families are becoming more common. Nearly one out of three individuals is a member of a stepfamily (Larson, 1992). Complex family situations frequently arise because various family traditions and values are blending together. The quality of family functioning is increasingly important as the family members bond. Family members build effective links of communication, together-ness, and trust, which enable them to better cope with and manage family situations.

Community

> Full inclusion affords children with disabilities an opportunity given to other peo-ple: to live a meaningful life. I know that every day Anna spends in an integrated environment is a meaningful day. Every transaction she has with another child counts for something. Every day she is teaching lessons that no one else can teach. She is bringing out the best in others who bring out the best in her. She deserves that opportunity, and so do they. (Statum, 1995, p. 68)

As expected, parents and families are concerned with providing supportive and nurturing environments for their children with disabilities (Rainforth, York, & Macdonald, 1997). IDEA legislation (PL 102-119) specifically ensures that profession-als will address the issue of transition from early intervention programs for infants and toddlers to preschool programs. The smooth and successful transition of these children (and their families) from early intervention programs to community-based programs should be a primary concern of all individuals involved (Seed, 1988; Singer et al., 1993).

Parents and families are often concerned that children with disabilities will ex-perience isolation from their peers. The fact is that all children can and do learn through shared experiences with their peers. In return, peers without disabilities also benefit and begin to recognize that these new friends are a part of their neighbor-hood. Several studies have shown that in integrated settings, nondisabled children develop at the expected rate, and children with disabilities make progress (McLean & Hanline, 1990; Odom & Strain, 1984). An important lesson is that children are cruel only because such experiences are lacking (Seed, 1988).

> I withdrew her from the special center she had attended for several years and enrolled her in a Head Start program. Anna was the only child in her class in a wheelchair, the only one who couldn't speak. The teacher had never taught a child with severe disabilities before. That first morning when we came rolling into that room full of noisy, active 4-year-olds, the teacher said to me, "Go home and don't worry; everything will be fine." And it was. Whatever problems we had, we worked out together. By year's end, Anna was beginning to speak. And I learned that it doesn't take a special person to teach children with disabilities. It simply takes a special person to be a good teacher. (Statum, 1995, p. 66)

Early childhood professionals should remember as they work with families the concept of choice. Bronfenbrenner (1979) provides a model for looking at not just the child but what he terms the mesosystem—the system that includes the family, extended family, their friends, and the community (support groups, schools, churches, etc.) in which they live. By recognizing the support systems that can di-rectly affect them, families can use these systems to alleviate some of the stressors that have an impact on their daily lives.

All families, not just those with disabilities, dream of their child's future. What will they be when they grow up? The dreams of that young family who celebrated the "joyous birth" of a child did not disappear because the child has a disability.

They did, however, change. Refocusing the dreams is a process that evolves as the child grows.

Early childhood professionals must help families to work through these changes so that they can readjust as needed for the new challenges. Educators must work with families to help children be as independent as possible. Professionals must help families to make good choices. Good choices require good information. The role of the professional is to supply the information to help families make those informed choices. With each choice, the dream becomes clearer.

Summary

The general perspectives held by professionals, communities, and families of children with disabilities have matured. No longer is the birth of a child with a disability viewed as a burden. As families and parents are empowered through their experiences (e.g., coping, adapting, seeking support), they have become active leading members in their child's learning opportunities. Families have also learned to effectively implement strategies and techniques that best fit their families' goals and objectives.

All families, including families of children with disabilities, have hopes, dreams, and desires for their children. For families with children with disabilities these expectations are more difficult to attain. To pursue their goals, families and professionals must learn to work in a collaborative partnership. Together, professionals and parents must in turn learn how to be more respectful and genuinely sensitive in their collaborative partnership efforts. There is always an undying hope and belief that, as a result of their efforts, the community will accept their children with dignity and respect (Santelli, Turnbull, Lerner, & Marquis, 1993; Seed, 1988).

> There is a hitherto unacknowledged place in the world for our children and we need to claim it. The current movement toward full inclusion gives us a hope that no other generation of parents of children with disabilities has had; the hope that when our children are grown they will be accepted as full members of the human community. We are luckier than we thought. (Statum, 1995, p. 68)

Recommended Activities

1. Interview a teacher and find out the strengths children with special needs bring to the classroom. What are some of the challenges teachers have with children with special needs?

2. Interview a special education director to determine the types of special needs in that school district.

3. How do you support parents and help them accept their child's diagnosis as having special needs?

4. Identify special support services within a community for families with children of various disabilities.

5. Identify the referral process within a school system. How are families informed and involved in this process?

6. Research the support of children with special needs in public, private, and charter schools.

Children's Books

The following children's books are suggested as a way of helping your students consider issues in this chapter.

Autism

Andy and His Yellow Frisbee
Mary Thompson
Woodbine House (1996)

Down Syndrome and Cerebral Palsy

Be Quiet, Marina!
Kristen DeBear, Laura Dwight (Photographer)
Star Bright Books (2001)

Physical

Don't Call Me Special
Pat Thomas, Lesley Harker (Illustrator)
Barron's Educational Series (2002)

Susan Laughs
Jeanne Willis, Tony Ross (Illustrator)
Henry Holt and Company (2000)

We Go in a Circle
Peggy Perry Anderson
Houghton Mifflin/Walter Lorraine Books (2004)

Different Disabilities

Friends at School (2nd ed.)
Rochelle Bunnett, Matt Brown (Photographer)
Star Bright Books (1995)

Blindness and Hard of Hearing

Listen for the Bus: David's Story
Patricia McMahon, John Godt (Photographer)
Boyds Mills Press (1995)

Down Syndrome

My Friend Isabelle
Joan Fassler, Joe Lasker (Illustrator)
Woodbine House (2003)

The Best Worst Brother
Stephanie Stuve-Bodeen, Charlotte Fremaux
   (Illustrator)
Woodbine House (2005)

A Very Special Critter
Gina Mayer & Mercer Mayer
Golden Books (1993)

Physical and Cognitive

Special People, Special Ways
Arlene Maguire
Future Horizons, Inc. (2000)

ADHD

The Girls Guide to AD/HD
Beth Walker
Woodbine House (2004)

A comprehensive list of additional children's book titles about disabilities may be obtained at http://ericec.org/fact/kidbooks.html

Additional Resources

Families of Children with Disabilities

Books

Batshaw, M. (2000). *When your child has a disability: The complete sourcebook of daily and medical care* (rev. ed.). Baltimore: Paul H. Brookes.

A parent's guide that offers detailed information about the daily and long-term care requirements of specific disabilities, including mental retardation, Down syndrome and other genetic syndromes, spina bifida, epilepsy, cerebral palsy, hearing loss, communication disorders, visual impairment, autism spectrum disorders, ADHD, and learning disabilities. Some of the topics covered in this book include child development, behavior, nutrition and feeding, medications, therapies, education and early intervention, legal rights and benefits, and genetic counseling.

Bowe, F. G. (2007). *Early childhood special education: Birth to age eight* (4th ed.). Albany, NY: Delmar Publishers.

This book provides an introduction to early childhood special education from birth to 8 years of age. This foundation book offers information on IDEA, on issues and trends in early childhood special education, and on a variety of disabilities within the context of child development.

Burnett, F. H. (1911). *The Secret Garden*. New York: Harper Collins Publishers.

This book has passed the test of time due to its theme: the healing power inherent in living things. The story is about a girl who is sent to live with her uncle in England. She discovers the secret garden her deceased aunt had developed. She becomes friends with a wheelchair-bound child and they explore the garden together.

Curran, D. (1989). *Working with parents*. Circle Pines, MN: American Guidance Service.

Topics covered in this book for professionals working in the parent education field include conducting groups that empower parents, reexamining traditional assumptions about parents, and listening to identify parents' needs.

Dettmer, P., Thurston, L., & Dyck, N. (2005). *Consultation, collaboration, and teamwork for students with special needs*. Boston: Allyn & Bacon.

This book is a comprehensive guide for preparing general and special educators to work collaboratively in educating students with special learning needs. Topics include the team process; educational roles and opportunities; processes for teaching, learning, and interacting; and improving educational partnerships to serve special needs of students.

Falvey, M. (2005). *Believe in my child with special needs! Helping children achieve their potential in school*. Baltimore: Paul H. Brookes.

Drawing on her experiences as a parent of a child with a disability and as an educator, the author helps parents understand their child's rights, pursue an inclusive education, collaborate with other IEP team members, promote their child's access to the general education curriculum, encourage educators to use appropriate modifications and assessment strategies, support their child's social skills, and develop transition plans.

Featherstone, H. (1980). *A difference in the family: Living with a disabled child*. New York: Penguin Books.

A woman shares her own personal story regarding the impact a disability has on the family as a whole as well as on each individual family member. She shares the family dynamics and frank discussion of their decisions regarding the child with a disability.

Gallagher, P. A., Powell, T. H., & Rhodes, C. A. (2006). *Brothers and sisters: A special part of exceptional families* (3rd ed.). Baltimore: Paul H. Brookes.

This book contains personal stories shared by brothers and sisters of exceptional siblings. Topics include sibling adjustment, effective listening, and innovative teaching programs.

Gill, B. (1997). *Changed by a child: Companion notes for parents of a child with a disability*. New York: Broadway Books.

This book has numerous accounts of parents who share their inner feelings and thoughts about raising a child who has a disability.

Harry, B. (1992). *Cultural diversity, families, and the special education system: Communication and empowerment*. New York: Teachers College Press.

This thought-provoking book explores the quadruple disadvantage faced by the parents of poor and minority children with disabilities whose first language is not that of the school they attend.

Howard, V. F., Williams, B. F., Port, P. D., & Lepper, C. (2005). *Very young children with special needs: A formative approach for the 21st century* (2nd ed.). Upper Saddle River, NJ: Merrill/Prentice Hall.

This book provides an introduction to early childhood and early childhood special education professionals who provide child and family services as well as intervention to very young children with disabilities. This foundation book offers the philosophy, history, family impact, legal issues, and medical concerns that are important to early intervention and early childhood services to very young children with disabilities and their families.

Jorgenson, C., Schuh, M., & Nisbet, J. (2005). *The inclusion facilitator's guide.* Baltimore: Paul H. Brookes.

This book addresses the role of inclusion facilitators who are educators that advocate for change in schools and communities. This guidebook prepares staff for the challenges of facilitating full inclusion. Topics covered in this book include promising practices for supporting 10 key elements of inclusion, functioning effectively as a collaborative team leader and a source of information and support, learning strategies for supporting students to be full participants and learners within the general education curriculum and classroom, and advance organizational changes in specific areas such as scheduling and technology.

Kalyanpur, M., & Harry, B. (1999). *Culture in special education: Building reciprocal family--professional relationships.* Baltimore: Paul H. Brookes.

This book helps educators understand the importance of developing education plans that will enhance children's learning and respect their cultural beliefs. Filled with personal anecdotes, case examples, and detailed theoretical discussions, this book brings to light the potential impact of cultural assumptions on parent–professional interactions in special education.

Keller, H. (1905). *The story of my life.* New York: Grossett & Dunlap.

This is a time-honored story about one of the early individuals in American history who deals with her disabilities. Helen Keller was born deaf and blind.

Klein, S., & Schive, K. (Eds.). (2001). *You will dream new dreams: Inspiring personal stories by parents of children with disabilities.* New York: Kensington Publishing.

Parents of children with disabilities share their personal experiences about the journey of having a child who has special needs.

Kroth, R. L., & Edge, D. (2007). *Strategies for communicating with parents of exceptional children* (4th ed.). Denver, CO: Love.

A book of techniques based on the premise that all parents have strengths from which to contribute to their child's education as well as needs to be met. It is aimed at teachers who would like to improve their skills in working with parents.

Marsh, J. (Ed.). (1995). *From the heart: On being a mother of a child with special needs.* Bethesda, MD: Woodbine House.

Nine mothers share their personal experiences of raising children with special needs. They discuss topics such as relationships with professionals, family life, and school issues.

Martin, N. (2005). *A guide to collaboration for IEP teams.* Baltimore: Paul H. Brookes.

Developed for administrators, teachers, resource professionals, and parents, this skills-based book will help members of the IEP team design, review, and modify IEPs for children with special education needs.

McHugh, M. (2002). *Special siblings: Growing up with someone with a disability* (rev. ed.). Baltimore: Paul H. Brookes.

In this book, the author shares her experience across the lifespan as the sister of a man with cerebral palsy and mental retardation. Interviews with others who have a sibling with a disability are shared regarding the issues that may arise in childhood, adolescence, and adulthood.

Meyer, D. (Ed.). (1995). *Uncommon fathers: Reflections on raising a child with a disability.* Bethesda, MD: Woodbine House.

Nineteen fathers share their experiences and perspectives concerning raising a child with special needs.

Meyer, D. J., & Vadasy, P. F. (1994). *Sibshops: Workshops for siblings of children with special needs.* Baltimore: Paul H. Brookes.

The easy-to-use Sibshop is a practical resource that brings together 8- to 13-year-olds to express their feelings about brothers and sisters with disabilities.

Naseef, R. (2001). *Special children, challenged parents: The struggles of raising a child with a disability* (rev. ed.). Baltimore: Paul H. Brookes.

Written from a father's perspective, the author describes the grieving process and his experiences living with his own child who has autism. He shares how to work effectively with medical and educational professionals.

O'Shea, D., Bateman, D., Algozzine, B., & O'Shea, L. (2004). *The special education due process handbook*. Longmont, CO: Sopris West.

Developed for parents, administrators, special education teachers, and general education teachers, this guidebook offers information about special education due process.

Rainforth, B., & York-Barr, J. (1997). *Collaborative teams for students with severe disabilities: Integrating therapy and educational services* (2nd ed.). Baltimore: Paul H. Brookes.

A text on how to establish effective transdisciplinary teaming with professionals and parents. Various models of effective collaboration in educational settings are discussed. Detailed case studies illustrate how to integrate therapy into educational programming.

Snow, K. (2005). *Disability is natural: Revolutionary common sense for raising successful children with disabilities* (2nd ed.). Woodland Park, CO: BraveHeart Press.

The author shares her journey with her son, Benjamin, who was born 7 weeks prematurely. As a result of the premature birth, Benjamin and his family were thrown into "Disability World" filled with therapies, specialists, and special education. The author shares her ideas about the importance of using people-first language and that disability is a natural part of the human experience.

Videos/DVDs
A New IDEA for Special Education

This video or DVD guides the viewer step-by-step through the process of identifying students with special needs, starting with a referral (by parents, teachers, or a physician), evaluation through setting up of Individual Education Plan (IEP) meetings, and placement in either inclusive or self-contained settings. 2005. (55 minutes)

Brookes Publishing
Phone: 800-638-3775
www.brookespublishing.com

Disability Is Natural

This video/DVD poses provocative questions about how we view disabilities in our society.

BraveHeart Press
Phone: 866-948-2222
www.disabilityisnatural.com/

Growing Up with Autism

This 20-minute video features Taylor Crowe, a young man diagnosed at an early age with autism. Featuring home movie footage shot throughout Taylor's life, viewers see Taylor as a typical infant and toddler, and then watch the emergence of the language and social characteristics over the preschool years that culminated in the diagnosis of autism. Interviews with Taylor's speech therapist and with his father add depth, while the most powerful moments of the video are those of Taylor himself speaking about his life and his autism. 2003.

Council for Exceptional Children
Phone: 888-232-7733
www.cec.sped.org

Raising Kids with Special Needs

This 21-minute video provides an intimate look into the lives of parents of elementary school age children, each with a very different disability. Tristan is deaf, Olivia has a visual impairment, and Emily lost a leg in a farm accident. Interviews with the parents of these three children focus on key issues such as safety concerns, dealing with anger and grief, and the importance of a support network.

Child Development Media, Inc.
Phone: 800-405-8942
http://childdevelopmentmedia.com/
    family-perspectives/50215a.html

Mothers of Courage

The story of how one mother advocates for her daughter, Bethany, who has multiple physical and developmental disabilities. (48 minutes)

Fanlight Productions
Phone: 800-876-1710
www.fanlight.com/orderinfo.html

When Parents Can't Fix It–Living with a Child's Disability

Five families share their experiences raising children with disabilities. The parents discuss the problems that arise and how they have learned to cope with the day-to-day stressors and responsibilities. (58 minutes)

> Fanlight Productions
> Phone: 800-876-1710
> www.fanlight.com/orderinfo.html

Websites

> Circle of Inclusion
> www.circleofinclusion.org

> Clearinghouse on Disability Information
> www.ed.gov/about/offices/list/osers/codi.html

The Council for Exceptional Children
www.cec.sped.org

Family Village: A Global Community of Disability Related Resources
www.familyvillage.wisc.edu/index.htmlx

Inclusion.com
www.inclusion.com

National Dissemination Center for Children with Disabilities
www.nichcy.org

National Resources for Parents of Children and Youth with Disabilities
www.washington.edu/doit/Brochures/Parents/naparent.html

References

Bailey, E., & Bricker, D. (1984). The efficacy of early intervention for severely handicapped infants and young children. *Topics in Early Childhood Special Education, 4*(3), 30–51.

Berger, E. (2007). *Parents as partners in education: Families and schools working together* (6th ed.). New York: Merrill.

Boswell, B., & Schuffner, C. (1990). Families support inclusive schooling. In W. Stainback & S. Stainback (Eds.), *Support networks for inclusive schooling: Interdependent integrated education* (pp. 219–230). Baltimore: Paul H. Brookes.

Bronfenbrenner, U. (1979). *The ecology of human development: Experiments by nature and design.* Cambridge, MA: Harvard University Press.

Brown, C. (1990). *My left foot.* London: Martin Secker & Warburg, Ltd.

Buck, P. (1950). *The child who never grew.* New York: John Day.

Buscaglia, L. (1975). *The disabled and their parents.* Thorofare, NJ: Charles B. Slack.

DeGangi, G., Wietlisbach, S., Possion, S., Stein, E., & Royeen, C. (1994). The impact of culture and socioeconomic status on family–professional collaboration: Challenges and solutions. *Topics in Early Childhood Special Education, 14*(4), 503–520.

DeVore, S., & Bowers, B. (2006). Childcare for children with disabilities: Families search for specialized care and cooperative childcare partnerships. *Infants & Young Children: An Interdisciplinary Journal of Special Care Practices, 19*(3), 203–212. Retrieved from Education Research Complete database.

Dunst, C. J., Trivette, C. M., & Jordy, W. (1997). Influences of social support of children with disabilities and their families. In M. J. Guralnick (Ed.), *The effectiveness of early intervention* (pp. 499–522). Baltimore: Paul H. Brooks.

Farber, B. (1975). Family adaptations to severely mentally retarded children. In M. J. Begab & S. A. Richardson (Eds.), *The mentally retarded and society: A social science perspective* (pp. 247–266). Baltimore: University Park Press.

Featherstone, H. (1980). *A difference in the family: Living with a disabled child.* New York: Penguin Books.

Fewell, R. (1986). A handicapped child in the family. In R. Fewell & P. Vadasy (Eds.), *Families of* handicapped children: Needs and supports across the life span (pp. 87–104). Austin, TX: PRO-ED.

Frey, K. S., Fewell, R. R., Vadasy, P. F., & Greenberg, M. T. (1989). Parental adjustment and changes in child outcome among families of young handicapped children. *Topics in Early Childhood Special Education, 8*(2), 38–57.

Gallagher, J., Cross, A., & Scharfman, W. (1981). Parental adaptation to a young handicapped child: The father's role. *Journal of the Division of Early Childhood, 3,* 3–4.

Gibbs, B. (1993). Providing support to sisters and brothers of children with disabilities. In G. Singer & L. Powers (Eds.), *Families, disability, and empowerment: Active coping skills and strategies for family interventions* (pp. 27–66). Baltimore: Paul H. Brookes.

Goldenberg, I., & Goldenberg, H. (1980). *Family therapy: An overview.* Monterey, CA: Brooks/Cole.

Grossman, F. K. (1972). *Brothers and sisters of the retarded children: An exploratory study.* Syracuse, NY: Syracuse University Press.

Guralnick, M. (1990). Major accomplishments and future directions in early childhood mainstreaming. *Topics in Early Childhood Special Education, 10*(2), 1–17.

Hager-Olsen, B. (2001). Increasing parent involvement of Hispanic families, with or without children with special needs, in early childhood settings. Unpublished master's thesis. University of North Dakota.

Hannah, M. (1999). Competence and adjustment of siblings of children with mental retardation. *American Journal on Mental Retardation, 104,* 22–37.

Hanson, M. J., Lynch, E. W., & Wayman, K. I. (1990). Honoring the cultural diversity of families when gathering data. *Topics in Early Childhood Special Education, 10*(1), 112–131.

Harland, P., & Cuskelly, M. (2000). The responsibilities of adult siblings with dual sensory impairments. *International Journal of Disability, Development and Education, 47*(3), 293–307.

Hawkins, N., Singer, G., & Nixon, C. (1993). Short-term behavioral counseling for families of persons with disabilities. In G. Singer & L. Powers (Eds.), *Families, disability, and empowerment: Active coping skills and strategies for family interventions* (pp. 317–341). Baltimore: Paul H. Brookes.

Howard, V. F., Williams, B. F., Port, P. D., & Lepper, C. (2001). *Very young children with special needs: A formative approach for the 21st century* (2nd ed.). Upper Saddle River, NJ: Merrill/Prentice Hall.

Kirk, S. A., Gallagher, J. J. & Anastasiow, N. J. (2005). *Educating exceptional children* (11th ed.). Boston: Houghton Mifflin.

Kroth, R. L., & Edge, D. (2007). *Strategies for communicating with parents of exceptional children* (4th ed.). Denver, CO: Love.

Kübler-Ross, E. (1969). *Death and dying.* New York: Macmillan.

Lamb, M. E., & Meyer, D. J. (1991). Fathers of children with special needs. In M. Seligman (Ed.), *The family with a handicapped child* (pp. 151–179). Boston: Allyn & Bacon.

Larson, J. (1992). Understanding stepfamilies. *American Demographics, 14,* 360.

Linan-Thompson, S., & Jean, R. E. (1997). Completing the parent participation puzzle: Accepting diversity. *Teaching Exceptional Children, 30*(2), 46–50.

Lobato, D. J. (1990). *Brothers, sisters, and special needs: Information and activities for helping young siblings of children with chronic illness and developmental disabilities.* Baltimore: Paul H. Brookes.

Long, C., Artis, N., & Dobbins, N. (1993). The hospital: An important site for family-centered early intervention. *Topics in Early Childhood Special Education, 13*(1), 106–199.

McLean, M., & Hanline, M. (1990). Providing early intervention services in integrated environments: Challenges and opportunities for the future. *Topics in Early Childhood Special Education, 10*(2), 62–77.

Meyer, D. J. (1986a). Fathers of children with special needs. In M. E. Lamb (Ed.), *The father's role: Applied perspectives* (pp. 227–254). New York: Wiley.

Meyer, D. J. (1986b). Fathers of handicapped children. In R. Fewell & P. Vadasy (Eds.), *Families of handicapped children* (pp. 35–73). Austin, TX: PRO-ED.

Meyer, D. J. (1993). Lessons learned: Cognitive coping strategies of overlooked family members. In A. Turnbull et al. (Eds.), *Cognitive coping, families and disability* (pp. 81–92). Baltimore: Paul H. Brookes.

Meyer, D. J., Vadasy, P. F., & Fewell, R. R. (1985). *Sibshops: A handbook for implementing workshops for siblings of children with special needs.* Seattle: University of Washington Press.

Murray, J. N. (1980). *Developing assessment programs for the multi-handicapped child.* Springfield, IL: Charles C Thomas.

Murray, J. N., & Cornell, C. J. (1981). Parentalplegia. *Psychology in the Schools, 18,* 201–207.

Nieto, S. (2008). *Affirming diversity: The sociopolitical context of multicultural education* (5th ed.). New York: Longman.

Nixon, C. (1993). Reducing self-blame and guilt in parents of children with severe disability. In G. Singer & L. Powers, *Families, disability, and empowerment: Active coping skills and strategies for family interventions* (pp. 175–201). Baltimore: Paul H. Brookes.

Odom, S., & Strain, P. (1984). Classroom-based social skills instruction for severely handicapped preschool children. *Topics in Early Childhood Special Education, 4*(3), 97–116.

O'Shea, D. J., O'Shea, L. J., Algozzine, R., & Hammitte, D. J. (2001). *Families and teachers of individuals with disabilities: Collaborative orientations and responsive practices.* Boston: Allyn & Bacon.

Pearl, L. (1993). Providing family-centered early intervention. In W. Brown, S. Thurman, & L. Pearl (Eds.), *Family-centered early intervention with infants and toddlers: Innovative cross-disciplinary approaches* (pp. 81–101). Baltimore: Paul H. Brookes.

Powell, T., & Ogle, P. (1985). *Brothers and sisters: A special part of exceptional families.* Baltimore: Paul H. Brookes.

Powers, L. (1993). Disability and grief: From tragedy to challenge. In G. Singer & L. Powers (Eds.), *Families, disability, and empowerment: Active coping skills and strategies for family interventions* (pp. 119–149). Baltimore: Paul H. Brookes.

Rainforth, B., York, J., & Macdonald, C. (1997). *Collaborative teams for students with severe disabilities: Integrating therapy and educational services* (2nd ed.). Baltimore: Paul H. Brookes.

Rantala, A., Uotinen, S., & McWilliam, R. (2009). Providing early intervention within natural environments: A cross-cultural comparison. *Infants & Young Children: An Interdisciplinary Journal of Special Care Practices, 22*(2), 119–131. Retrieved from Education Research Complete database.

Ruder, M. (1993). The provision of early intervention and early childhood special education within community early childhood programs: Characteristics of effective service delivery. *Topics in Early Childhood Special Education, 13*(1), 19–37.

Salisbury, C. (1992). Parents as team members: Inclusive teams, collaborative outcomes. In B. Rainforth, J. York, & C. Macdonald (Eds.), *Collaborative teams for students with severe disabilities: Integrating therapy and educational services* (pp. 37–56). Baltimore: Paul H. Brookes.

Santelli, B., Turnbull, A., Lerner, J., & Marquis, J. (1993). Parent to parent programs: A unique form of mutual support for families of persons with disabilities. In G. Singer & L. Powers (Eds.), *Families, disability, and empowerment: Active coping skills and strategies for family interventions* (pp. 27–66). Baltimore: Paul H. Brookes.

Seed, P. (1988). *Children with profound handicaps: Parents' views and integration.* Philadelphia: Falmer Press.

Shimoni, R., & Baxter, J. (2001). *Working with families: Perspectives for early childhood professionals* (2nd ed.). Reading, MA: Addison-Wesley.

Singer, G., Irvin, L., Irvin, B., Hawkins, N., Hegreness, H., & Jackson, R. (1993). Helping families adapt positively to disability: Overcoming demoralization through community supports. In G. Singer & L. Powers (Eds.), *Families, disability, and empowerment: Active coping skills and strategies for family interventions* (pp. 67–83). Baltimore: Paul H. Brookes.

Singer, G., & Powers, L. (1993). *Families, disability, and empowerment: Active coping skills and strategies for family interventions.* Baltimore: Paul H. Brookes.

SRI International. (2007, January). *Early intervention for infants and toddlers with disabilities and their families: Participants, services, and outcomes.* Final Report of the National Early

Intervention Longitudinal Study (NEILS). Washington, DC: U.S. Department of Education, Office of Special Education Programs. www.sri.com/neils/reports.html

Statum, S. (1995). Inclusion: One parent's story. In P. Browning (Ed.), *Transition IV in Alabama: Profile of commitment.* State Conference Proceedings, January 1995 (pp. 65–68). Auburn, AL: Auburn University.

Taunt, H. M., & Hastings, R. P. (2002). Positive impact of children with developmental disabilities on their families: A preliminary study. *Education and Training in Mental Retardation and Developmental Disabilities, 37,* 410–420.

Turnbull, A. P., Brotherson, M. J., & Summers, J. A. (1985). The impact of deinstitutionalization on families: A family systems approach. In R. H. Bruininks (Ed.), *Living and learning in the least restrictive environment* (pp. 115–152). Baltimore: Paul H. Brookes.

Turnbull, A. P., & Turnbull, H. R. (2001). *Families, professionals, and exceptionality: A special partnership* (4th ed.). Upper Saddle River, NJ: Merrill/Prentice Hall.

Turnbull, H. R., Turnbull, A. P., Shank, M., & Leal, D. (2010). *Exceptional lives: Special education in today's schools* (6th ed.). Upper Saddle River, NJ: Pearson.

Chapter Nine

Family Involvement Models

In this chapter, three writers identify different models of family and parent involvement in the schools. The models cover programs that serve children from infancy to 15 years of age. The authors will identify national models or identify a model that can be used at any middle or secondary level. Please keep in mind that these are only representatives of many models that are available for discussion. This chapter helps you to:

▶ Identify various parent/family-involvement models at the preschool, elementary, middle, and special education level

▶ Compare and contrast models in and between levels

▶ Recognize the components of successful parent- and family-involvement models

▶ Comprehend why one model may work at one level and not at another level

Family Involvement in Special Education

Margaret (Peggy) Shaeffer
James Madison University

Inclusion has made all children the concern of the "regular" classroom teacher. Unfortunately, most classroom teachers are not prepared to work with the parents of children with special needs. The special education segment of this chapter shares successful parent involvement models and other information that will be most helpful to educators.

Models of family involvement in special education have been strongly influenced by the legal system established by federal law, which regulates the education of students with disabilities. Chapter 10 provides you with information on special education law and parental rights, which are ensured through the law. The Individuals with Disabilities Education Improvement Act (IDEIA), formerly known as the Education of All Handicapped Children Act, is the law that has had the greatest impact on the involvement of parents in the education of their children with disabilities. The reauthorization of this law in 1975 (PL 94-142) established the rights of students with disabilities to a free and appropriate public education. Prior to PL 94-142, parents were frequently turned away from public school programs that did not provide educational services for children with disabilities. As described in Chapter 10, this law also established procedural safeguards for parents, such as the right to access their children's educational records (and the right to limit access by others), the requirement of parental consent prior to initial evaluation and initial placement of a child in special education, and the right to written notice in the event that the school proposes to change or refuses to change services. Furthermore, in cases in which a disagreement occurs between parents and the school in relation to children's educational programs, the right to due process of law is ensured. The most recent reauthorization of the bill, the Individuals with Disabilities Education Improvement Act (2004), imposes significant new responsibilities on the families, expecting them to not only be active participants and advocates for their children, but also hold extensive knowledge and understanding of special education law, in some respects expecting them to be experts on the interpretation and application of the law (Turnbull et al., 2010).

This is no easy task, even for service providers who work within the parameters of the law on a daily basis. If we are to expect that families can be successful in taking on the added responsibilities, we must ensure that we are providing programs to support their full understanding and participation in the process.

The requirements of the law clearly have a significant impact on the relationship between parents of children with disabilities and school personnel, and, to a great degree, these requirements structure the interactions that occur. Parent education has played a major role in providing support to families throughout the law's tenure. Parent education typically refers to "systematic activities implemented by professionals to assist parents in accomplishing specific goals or outcomes with their children" (Mahoney et al., 1999). There are many forms of parent education that can lead to family involvement, including one-on-one coaching, group activities, or self-directed materials (Mahoney et al., 1999; McIntyre & Phaneuf, 2008; Zaidman-Zait & Jamieson, 2007). The type, format, and context for parent education are highly dependent on the strengths, challenges, and values of the family.

This type of family involvement is far different from the early days in which parent education was viewed from a deficit perspective. Families with children who had disabilities were seen as needing training to improve the quality of the home situation and create a better environment so as to ensure the success of the interventions (Mahoney et al., 1999). The professional was viewed as the expert, providing the training to the family based on the assessment of the service delivery team. As the field of special education continued to evolve, it became increasingly clear that the most effective programs were those that provided services that were not only individualized to meet the needs of the child but also individualized to meet the needs of the family. This perspective views the planning, implementation, and evaluation of services as a complex system of providing support in which the family is central to the process. Programs see their role as one of providing support as the family undertakes activities necessary for family functioning, including the activities necessary to provide for the child with a disability. The entire context of the family constellation and factors that mitigate their understanding and interpretation of their own personal situation are taken into consideration. Such programs incorporate a *family-centered* philosophy.

A Family Systems Conceptual Framework

During the late 1970s and early 1980s, family systems theory emerged as a foundation for intervention in the helping professions. Family systems theory views the family as a social system wherein all members have an impact on each other. Built on the ecological theory proposed by Bronfenbrenner (1979), the context in which the family operates is viewed as a system of interdependent and linked experiences, providing a network of supports, often referred to as complementary learning (Weiss, Caspe, & Lopez, 2006). The impact on the family system and individuals within the family as a result of activity in any one of the microsystems (school, community, church, workplace, etc.) is significant. Experiences within the contexts inform families in their decision-making process. When applied to special education, this theory emphasizes the idea that intervention with one family member will affect all members. In other words, professionals should recognize that the provision of special education services to a child not only affects the child, but also affects family functioning in a manner that may be beneficial or detrimental.

Turnbull and Turnbull (2001) presented a family systems conceptual framework that incorporates information from family systems theory and the special education literature to provide a framework for evaluating the impact of special education services on family functioning. Applying this framework to the provision of educational services to children with disabilities leads the educator to consider the impact of educational activities on the family and to attempt to see the world from the family's perspective. The framework requires us to consider input variables, characteristics of family interactions, and lifecycle changes. It becomes apparent that each family is unique and complex; there will be considerable diversity among families in beliefs and values, in resources, in the challenges they face, and in the coping and interaction patterns of the family members. Furthermore, educational intervention will have an impact on the entire family system and will not be confined to the member with a disability. Families also change over time. Intervention systems will need to be able to accommodate changes in the family system, which will have an impact on the child with a disability (Kaczmarek, Goldstein, Florey, Carter, & Cannon, 2004; Murray, Christensen, Umbarger, Rade, Aldridge, & Niemeyer, 2007).

Reflection ...

Family systems theory or a family-centered philosophy seems to be such an important part of the models in this section. Why do you think this is the case? Has this theory or philosophy been evident in other parts of the text? Or is this just author bias?

Family-Centered Intervention

As educators have become more aware of how families function and the impact of the family on the success of intervention efforts, a philosophy of intervention has emerged, known as family-centered intervention. Family-centered philosophy moves intervention efforts from an agency-oriented approach to a family-oriented approach. It is eloquently described by the following passage from Turnbull, Brown, and Turnbull (2004):

> Copernicus came along and made a startling reversal—he put the sun in the center of the universe rather than the Earth. His declaration caused profound shock. The earth was not the epitome of creation; it was a planet like all other planets. The successful challenge to the entire system of ancient authority required a complete change in philosophical conception of the universe. This is rightly termed the "Copernican Revolution." Let's pause to consider what would happen if we had a Copernican Revolution in the field of disability. Visualize the concept: the family is the center of the universe and the service delivery system is one of the many planets revolving around it. Now visualize the service delivery system at the center and the family in orbit around it. Do you recognize the revolutionary change in perspective? We would move from an emphasis on parent involvement (i.e., parents participating in the program) to family support (i.e., programs providing a range of support services for families). This is not a semantic exercise—such a revolution leads us to a new set of assumptions and a new vista of options for service. (p. 64)

Over time, the philosophy and practices of family-centered intervention have been revisited and modified to meet the changing needs of children and their families. The changing demographics of our country have led us to new understandings of working with families from diverse cultural and ethnic backgrounds. Families' values and beliefs must be considered as we traverse the collaboration network. Socioeconomic impacts on the workings of families affect the development and implementation of services. In addition, as the body of knowledge has increased, so has our understanding and skill sets in working with specific disabilities, and we are continually researching for evidence-based practices to inform our policies and practices. The components and interplay of the critical features of these philosophies have evolved over time. Dunst (2000) examined multiple ways of identifying and operationalizing key components of the family systems approach to intervention that considers the complex factors of family, environment, and planned and unplanned events. This generation of a family-centered model is taking us deeper into the arena of maximizing the child's and family's natural environments for supporting development. The context of the family is expanded to include not only the home but also the school and the community at large (Bruder & Dunst, 2001). Regardless of the terminology or the exact way in which the philosophy is implemented, the common idea held by all is that intervention should be provided in collaboration with family members, in a manner that facilitates the family's decision-making role, and in a manner that is in line with the family's priorities. To incorporate a family-centered philosophy, a paradigm shift must occur. Intervention must move away from being child focused and agency directed to being family focused and, to a large extent, also family directed.

Family directed refers not only to the active engagement of families in the education of their children but also to the roles families play in the development, delivery, and implementation of programs for other families of children with disabilities. When families are viewed from a strength perspective, they take on a powerful role of informing and supporting not only other families, but also school and health agencies, policy makers, and other professionals (Gallagher, Rhodes, & Darling, 2004). Recruiting the talents of parents who have experienced the challenges of working within the social, educational, and health systems with a child with a disability adds a perspective and strength to our service provision. There are several models that have been implemented. The following three programs exemplify a family-centered philosophy by drawing from the strengths of parents who have lived the experience and employing them as experts.

Family-Centered Preschool Model

Services to infants and toddlers are typically provided in the home setting. The result is that the family has regular and often intense relationships with the service provided. One-on-one services, regularly scheduled visits, and the personal relationships that are established contribute to the development of strong partnerships between families and service providers. As the context for the delivery changes (i.e., when the child moves from home-based to center-based delivery systems), the dynamics of the relationship between the family and service providers might change.

Interactions between the family and the related services personnel might be limited, and certainly will not be as personal as the home-based interactions. Recognizing the need to ensure that families would receive support of the quality and nature required for them to continue to be informed advocates for their children, the Family-Centered Preschool Model was developed (Kaczmarek, Goldstein, Florey, Carter, & Cannon, 2004). At the heart of the model are family consultants (FCs), parents of children with disabilities who serve as support staff for the classroom-based programs and liaisons between the families and the school. The roles of the FCs evolved over time with a range of activities such as providing transition support, attending IEP meetings, facilitating group meetings, and being a resource for community resources and information. Perhaps most importantly, the FCs provided emotional support for the families, facilitating parent-to-parent networking and hands-on support in negotiating the special education service bureaucracy. A key to the success of the FCs was the ongoing training, support, and mentoring.

Evaluation of the program testifies to the positive impact the FCs had on the engagement of the families. Three major themes emerged from the data: information, support, and contributions to improved parenting. In fact, one of the most significant changes occurred in the parent's perceptions of themselves as parents and as advocates for their children. The implications of promoting self-determination in parents are significant when one considers that the well-being of the family and hope for the future has such a powerful positive impact on the children (Lee, Palmer, Turnbull, & Wehmeyer, 2006). `

The developers of the program offer encouragement and advice for others who would consider implementing the model. Of paramount importance is the selection and training of the FCs. The FCs are viewed as critical members of the team, adding richness to the variety of personnel to meeting the needs of the family. Their entry-level skills are recognized and the expertise they bring to the team is highly valued and utilized. The roles of the FCs are flexible, and change over time as the needs of the families and the programs change. Staff members' understanding and appreciation of the expertise of the FCs and their willingness to "release" some of their work to the FCs is also critical for the full implementation of the model. Only when viewed in this collaborative manner will the concept of parents as professionals and full members of the team be fully realized.

The Family-Centered Preschool Model demonstrates the potential of establishing strong family relationships within the context of a classroom-based model. It lays the foundation for enhanced communication between teachers and families, while drawing on the expertise of parents.

Parent Educator Model

A second model of supporting the active engagement of families in the education of their children is the Parent Educator Model, a statewide program that employs parents as professionals in one state's early intervention (EI) system. Working through a consortium of six universities in Georgia, this statewide program was initiated in 1995 to promote Babies Can't Wait (BCW), the state's Part C program. A component of Project SCEIs (Skilled Credentialed Early Interventionists), the program has a rich history of partnering with parents as trainers of early interventionists, developing materials for professional development of service providers, and as supporters for other families of children with disabilities (Gallagher, Rhodes, & Darling, 2004).

The roles of the BCW parent educators are varied, ranging from working directly with families to providing support for the professional development of service providers to serving on policy-making boards at the local and state levels. They are viewed as experts who are able to translate for families the complexity of the health and educational system and also to provide insights to other professionals from the parent perspective.

As in the Family-Centered Preschool Model, the BCW parent educators are supported in their work through numerous professional development and training activities. In addition to orientation training and participating in the SCEI training modules, specialized workshops are held on at least an annual basis.

After over 10 years, the evaluation of the program suggests that the impact of the parent educators is far reaching. Service providers consistently report that the parent educators are providing a valuable addition to their programs by serving as a liaison to the families and an information source to the programs. Families also voice their satisfaction and appreciation for the parent educators' help in obtaining information and for providing support.

The impact on the parent educators themselves is also noteworthy. They see themselves not only as providing a critical service to other families of children with disabilities, but also as being a valuable member of the team, as a professional who can make a difference.

Parent to Parent Model

The Parent to Parent Model was established in 1971 as the foundation for the Pilot Parents Program in Omaha, Nebraska. At its foundation is the belief that parents of individuals with disabilities can serve as resources to other parents of individuals with disabilities as well as to professionals (Turnbull, 1999). In 2010, the program continues to have a strong presence in the arena of family involvement in special education, with affiliations in 34 states. Basically, it serves as a matching program between "veteran" parents of an individual with a disability to parents who are just beginning the journey of meeting the challenges of a disability within the family. It was reported that nearly 650,000 families were receiving services through approximately 600 local and statewide Parent to Parent programs (Turnbull, Turnbull, Shank, & Leal, 2001). More than one third of the programs are funded through Part C (Santelli, Turnbull, Marquis, & Lerner, 2000).

The organization of Parent to Parent programs varies across the states. Some have very centralized models; others are run more at the local level. The Parent to Parent programs are run by volunteer parents and range in size from perhaps two or three parents to statewide networks of programs supported by volunteer and professional staffs (Santelli et al., 2000). Referrals to the program come from a variety of sources, from medical, educational, and social service agencies to personal contacts through family and friends. Once a family has been contacted, care is taken to determine the best family match considering such multiple dimensions as location, disability, family structure and lifestyle, and cultural influences. The new families' strengths and concerns also dictate the method and type of interactions that occur between the matched families. For example, in some instances the contacts might be minimal in terms of telephone interactions with occasional conversations; in other instances there might be more intensive support provided such as problem-solving sessions, identification of community resources, and training in advocacy skills.

The efficacy of using parents as providers of education to parents and professionals is documented. As Turnbull (1999) reports, parents who use the Parent to Parent services are better able to cope with the challenges of living with a disability in the family. In addition, the participating families are living the experiences with families who are like them, and that feeling of sameness is beneficial. The parents also provide a support system for developing coping skills and serve as a resource for gathering necessary skills and information.

Summary

These three models are not the only models that are being implemented to involve families of children with disabilities in education. As the field of special education continues to evolve, as we learn more and more about families, and as we research and explore evidence-based practices, we will develop new models. Families as central to the process, however, should guide our explorations and inform our practice.

Family Involvement Models in Elementary Education

Pamela Beck
University of North Dakota

> *Schools with strong partnership programs are more likely to have greater parent involvement at school.* (Sheldon, 2005, p. 182)

Educators have long known that involving parents in the education of children can provide benefits such as higher achievement, better attitudes, and a more supportive school climate. In fact, the power of partnerships is considered to be so important that the No Child Left Behind Act requires that schools develop formal programs to increase family involvement. The No Child Left Behind Act of 2001 reauthorized the Elementary and Secondary Education Act of 1965 (ESEA) to include policies encouraging families, educators, and communities to work together to improve teaching, learning, and student achievement (No Child Left Behind, 2004). According to the U.S. Department of Education (2005), Part A, Section 1118, "A local educational agency may receive funds under this part only if such agency implements programs, activities, and procedures for the involvement of parents in programs assisted under this part consistent with this section. Such programs, activities, and procedures shall be planned and implemented with meaningful consultation with parents of participating children."

Federal, state, and local legislators, educators, and parents across the nation value the importance of parent involvement in student performance and achievement. Parents *want* the best education for their children; they *want* to be more involved in the school, and likewise, teachers *want* parents to be more actively involved in their students' learning, but oftentimes, neither stakeholder knows how to integrate such a partnership effectively. Hoover-Dempsey and colleagues (2005) encourage the school systems to guide and support parent involvement toward educational success, stating: "Overall, when schools take steps to motivate parental involvement, they support parents' effectiveness in helping their children learn" (p. 124). The research is clear; school practice that encourages parents to participate is the most important factor in whether or not parents will become actively involved with their children's education. However, the question for many still remains, What can schools do to create a school culture of active parent involvement?

Although it may be easy to research one program and to try to fully develop it within a school district, it is important to look at a variety of programs for family involvement. No one model is a best fit for all schools; each has its strengths to be examined and utilized as necessary. The following examples illustrate a continuum of models for family involvement beginning with a teacher-centered approach and moving toward whole family involvement in school decision making.

Teachers Involve Parents in Schoolwork (TIPS)

The Teachers Involve Parents in Schoolwork (TIPS) process highlights and utilizes the critical bond between teachers, parents, and students in a child's education at the elementary, middle, or high school level. One classroom teacher, an entire school, or an entire district can implement the program. To incorporate TIPS into practice, teachers design assignments that promote interactions between the child and a family partner (e.g., parent, grandparent, sibling, or other) who is willing to explore a particular curricular concept previously taught in the classroom.

According to Van Voorhis (2004), there are four critical components to each TIPS assignment: "(a) a brief letter to the family partner outlining the objectives of the assignment, (b) clear directions for students regarding how to involve a family partner in conversations and activities, (c) a section for home-to-school communication, and (d) a two-page limit" (p. 209). All correspondence sent home explaining the assignment goals and objectives must be written in nontechnical language, and the roles of participants must be clearly established. Discussions with students regarding their role in their own learning must be clear as well. As Van Voorhis (2004) states, "Interactive assignments are the responsibility of the student and should not require parents to teach school skills. The activities offer students an opportunity to share what they are learning in class with a parent or family" (pp. 209–210). In addition, teachers must give students and family partners sufficient time to complete the assignment together, so careful and realistic planning is critical. Assignments can take as little as 10 minutes or as long as 1 hour to complete, but research suggests a "family friendly schedule" including one interactive assignment each week or every other week (Van Voorhis, 2004). After assignment completion, the student and family partner supply written feedback using the TIPS home-to-school communication form created by the teacher. The teacher then uses the student work and feedback as a vehicle to assess conceptual understanding and plan further instruction.

Adoption of the TIPS program "may have the dual benefit of increasing parent–student interactions related to schoolwork and increasing parent opportunities to see what students are learning in school" (Hoover-Dempsey, Walker, & Sandler, 2005, p. 51) and can ultimately enhance parent–teacher communications. TIPS is an easily managed program for classroom teachers and gives a message to the students that both the classroom teacher and family partners care about the work they do in school.

MegaSkills

The MegaSkills Program, developed in 1972 by Dr. Dorothy Rich, is a recognized program with an established academic and character development track record and has been adopted by over 4,000 schools across the nation for over 20 years. The program aims to strengthen the bond between home and school, and through participation in workshops families learn new ways to support their children's education and become more involved in school activities. The MegaSkills Program focuses on helping students develop study skills, academic interests, and overall self-discipline. It involves families in activities that complement the work of school and aims to prevent at-risk behaviors in children. The training illustrates how academics and character development are part of everyday life. The goal is to set a pattern for parents of new educational strategies that they can continue to use to support their children's education long after they have completed the workshop program. Although the "megaskills" needed to become a lifelong learner are reinforced in a classroom setting, their real power comes from being taught, modeled, and encouraged in the home. Over 100,000 families, including African American, Hispanic, American Indian, and at-risk families, have successfully participated in MegaSkills workshops (MegaSkills Education Center, 2010a).

The MegaSkills Center Home and School Institute published results from a 10-year study of MegaSkills parent workshops conducted by the Warwick, RI, Public Schools' Title I Program (MegaSkills Education Center, 2010b). These findings indicated that a strong majority of parents were more confident in helping their child, possessed a greater ability to structure both their own and their child's use of time, had a better understanding of their child's strengths and needs, demonstrated more effective communication with teachers, had higher educational aspirations for their child, and were more involved in other school activities. The parents also reported that their children had become more organized and self-reliant, were more confident and able to express themselves, developed better relations with family members and other children, were more interested in school, had better behavior, and had stronger academic performance as reported by teachers.

National Network of Partnership Schools (NNPS)

The National Network of Partnership Schools (NNPS) was established in 1996 at Johns Hopkins University to help education leaders promote research-based school improvement strategies to develop and sustain comprehensive programs of school, family, and community partnerships. When the program began, there were 28 initial sites across the United States. Currently, every state in the union has established a parent information resource center designed to increase family involvement in education.

All schools in the NNPS are expected to establish an Action Team for Partnerships (ATP) to organize and sustain a program of school, family, and community partnerships where teachers, administrators, parents, community members, and others can work together to connect family and community involvement with specific school improvement goals and student outcomes (Sheldon, 2005). ATPs are responsible for writing yearly action plans linked to selected school improvement goals, deliberately including family and community involvement into the plan. They recruit teachers, parents, and other community members to participate in, organize, and coordinate involvement activities; monitor the strengths and needs of the plan; document results; and resolve problems (National Network of Partnership Schools, 2009).

Parents Plus

Although the Parents Plus operates nationwide, let's look at Wisconsin as an example. As a member of the National Network of Partnership Schools, Parents Plus of Wisconsin focuses on family, school, community partnerships, family resource centers, and home visits to increase family involvement in children's education. In the area of partnerships, they specifically use Epstein's six types of family, school, and community involvement to train participants to work together to build effective partnerships. The six types of involvement are parenting, communicating, volunteering, learning at home, decision making, and collaborating with the community (Epstein, 1995). These six types of involvement were addressed in more depth in Chapter 7.

Schools form an Action Team for Partnerships (ATP) consisting of at least three parents of children in varying grade levels, three teachers of different grade levels, an administrator, community members, and, at the middle and high school levels, students. They receive training in the six types of involvement, after which they work together to determine the goals that will best meet the needs of their population. The action team is then responsible for devising partnership activities that will help them achieve these goals.

Along with training teachers, parents, and administrators in partnerships, Parents Plus of Wisconsin also utilizes family resource centers to help parents stay involved in their children's education. The resource centers provide parents with information regarding parenting and education, as well as links to other available resources within the community. For first-time parents who are interested, staff members from family resource centers also provide home visits. Although these specific services do not directly affect the school system, their benefits are noteworthy. Through a combination of direct and indirect services, over one million people in Wisconsin were served through this project (Rodriguez, personal communication, August 11, 2010).

Parental Information Resource Center (PIRC)

In pursuit of the objectives of the No Child Left Behind Act, the Parental Information Resource Center (PIRC) awards grants to help schools "implement successful and effective parental involvement policies, programs, and activities that lead to improvements in student academic achievement and that strengthen partnerships among parents, teachers, principals, administrators, and other school personnel in meeting the education needs of children" (U.S. Department of Education, 2010).

School-based and school-linked parental information and resources centers such as the above-mentioned Parents Plus of Wisconsin is one of the few agencies to receive continued PIRC funding for its statewide program implementation. In collaboration with the Wisconsin State Department of Public Instruction and a state advisory board, and with support from PIRC funds, Parents Plus of Wisconsin "puts action teams wherever they are wanted or needed" (Rodriguez, 2010) by offering training to school districts statewide. The agency offers the ATP model training as a free service to all potential team members, including parent leadership training to any parent who serves on a school action team. For example, the Milwaukee, Wisconsin, school district was identified as a failing district, and at the time of this writing, is in year five of its improvement process. The school district has been working to establish an Action Team for Partnerships (ATP) in every school. To date, it has trained 160 schools in the ATP model with the help of PIRC funding. Rodriguez (2010) values the ATP model stating, "With ATP, everybody is represented."

Comprehensive School Model (CSR)

The Comprehensive School Reform (CSR) program also grew from the work of the National Network of Partnership Schools (NNPS) and encourages school and student improvement outcomes. Participating schools receive 3 years of federal funding for participating in the process. In the CSR approach, schools assemble action comprised of teachers, administrators, parents, and community members to organize a plan for school improvement connected to the specific goals of student achievement and an established climate of partnership.

Epstein (2005) conducted a study of an urban elementary school district in Connecticut, serving a diverse student population where 51% of students received free or reduced lunches and 40% of families spoke English as their second language. The school district participated in the CSR model to improve school, family, and community partnerships linked to student achievement in reading, writing, math, behavior, and climate of partnership. The district adopted the CSR model based on the theory and research-generated framework of the six types of involvement (see Chapter 7), an Action Team for Partnerships (ATP) structure, and tools for planning and evaluation. Action teams were established for each goal area for a total of five teams. Each team wrote plans, organized activities, and invited participation from all members of the school community (including parents and community partners). Each team held monthly meetings to write and review the plans and to evaluate the effectiveness of the program.

Some of the activities implemented included parent nights focused on specific academic areas, Teachers Involve Parents in Schoolwork (TIPS) interactive homework at all grade levels, staff development for improved instruction, schoolwide partnerships in character education program implementations, parent and community volunteers, collaborations with community organizers to purchase materials, and many opportunities for families and community efforts such as school picnics, frequent newsletters, holiday photo night, to name a few. Translators were available for all events. Data from this study provided evidence that "the school's scores on state achievement tests in math, reading, and writing improved over 3 years at the CSR site more than at comparison schools. The CSR school began to close the gap in test scores between its students and the district as a whole. School data also indicated that student behavior improved" (Epstein, 2005, pp. 164–165).

Comer School Development Program (SDP)

"First introduced in two low-achieving schools in 1968, over the years the School Development Program has been implemented in hundreds of schools in more than 20 states, the District of Columbia, Trinidad and Tobago, South Africa, England, and Ireland" (Yale School of Medicine Child Study Center, 2010). James Comer founded the School Development Program (SDP) in 1968 at Yale University's Child Study Center to promote the development and learning of children by building supportive bonds between children, parents, and school (Comer, 1988). Comer (2001) believes a good education should help students become responsible problem solvers who are "motivated, contributing members of a democratic society" (p. 1). To accomplish this, schools need to be places where students feel comfortable, valued, and secure and are enabled to form positive emotional bonds with their parents and school staff. This bonding then leads to positive attitudes toward school and promotes the overall development and academic learning of students (Comer, 1993).

The SDP accomplishes this task by implementing a program based on staff collaboration and parent involvement. Although each school implements the program based on its own specific needs, each has three governance teams in place: the School Planning and Management Team, the Mental Health Team, and the Parents' Group.

Together, these three teams create comprehensive school plans that include identification of specific goals, periodic assessment and modification of these goals, and staff development to achieve the goals. Each team, however, is charged with a specific task.

The first team, the School Planning and Management Team, is composed of parents, teachers, administrators, and support staff. They identify target goals for social and academic programs and devise and monitor program activities. For example, some teams have designed a Discover Room where students who have lost interest in learning work to regain that interest.

The second team, the Mental Health Team, meets to discuss social and behavioral patterns within the school setting and determines solutions for recurring problems. Members of this team work with individual children who may exhibit behavior problems, but members also look at school conditions that aggravate the problems and advocate for positive changes (Comer, 1993). Its members consist of teachers, administrators, psychologists, social workers, and nurses.

The third governance team is the Parents' Group. The mission of this team is to involve parents in all aspects of school, ranging from volunteering in classrooms to school governance.

Summary

Family involvement in a child's education can have lasting effects both academically and emotionally. "When parents and schools focus on building the student's cognitive, social, and emotional skills essential to effective learning, schools, families, teachers, and students benefit" (Hoover-Dempsey, Walker, & Sandler, 2005, p. 52). By providing parents with a variety of opportunities through which they can become involved, schools strengthen the bond between home and school.

Family Involvement Models in Early Childhood Education

Soo-Yin Lim
University of Minnesota

Early childhood educators have for a long time recognized the need for parents to be actively involved in influencing their children's development and learning at an early age. Early childhood education is also based on the beliefs that parents are their children's first teachers, know their children best, and have valuable insights and information to share with teachers. Teachers have the background knowledge in child development and experiences with young children that become a valuable resource for parents (Balaban, 1985). Together, teachers and parents share a common perspective and interest—the children's optimal growth and development to reach their fullest potential as learners.

The following section describes seven current program models that are national and state initiatives to facilitate family and school involvement.

Head Start

Head Start, established in 1965, is the nation's most extensive investment in the education of preschool children from low-income families. The program has many years of developing and refining strategies to involve families in the program (Zigler & Freedman, 1987). Head Start provides holistic, comprehensive services for children ages 3 to 5 and their families. Head Start's services include four components: health and nutrition, education, social services, and parent involvement. The program's services are designed to respond appropriately to each child's developmental level as well as each family's cultural, ethnic, and linguistic milieu. Head Start presently serves over one million children and is administered by the Head Start Bureau, the Administration on Children, Youth and Families (ACYF), the Department of Health and Human Services (DHHS), and the Administration for Children and Families (ACF). Head Start funding comes from two sources: 80% of the funds come from federal monies through the DHHS and the remaining 20% must come from sources at the community level of each individual program.

The overall mission of Head Start is to increase school readiness and foster the healthy development of young children in low-income families. In most communities, Head Start programs incorporate both center- and home-based services. Children typically attend half-day preschool classes and receive periodic home visits from teachers and parent and family service coordinators. Head Start classes generally follow the schedule of local public school systems, but some programs include full-day and full-year child-care services. A child who is enrolled in Head Start will generally receive a comprehensive screening before the start of preschool classes. This includes assessment of the child's developmental areas, language and speech, hearing, vision, nutrition, physical health and development, and immunizations. The results of the screening are shared with the child's parents. Children's growth and development are assessed on an ongoing basis throughout the year.

Parent Involvement Practices

In Head Start, parent involvement is viewed as essential, and parents are supported as the most important educators, nurturers, and advocates for their children. According to the Head Start Parent Involvement handbook, parent participation should lead to positive effects in five outcome areas: effective parenting, self-esteem and confidence, family life, education (of the parent), and employment. The Head Start Policy Manual mandates performance standards for four areas of parent involvement:

1. Provide opportunities for parents to have direct involvement in the area of decision making on program planning and operations.
2. Provide opportunities for parents to work with their own children in cooperation with Head Start teachers and staff.
3. Provide opportunities for parents to participate in the classroom as volunteers and with the possibility of becoming paid employees.
4. Provide opportunities for parents to plan and implement parent activities.

Parents are not only encouraged but expected to work with Head Start staff members to set goals for their children and their families and to participate in the program as much as possible. They are encouraged to visit their children's classrooms, to serve as volunteers or aides to teachers and staff, and to contribute their talents and services for the good of the program. Parents have opportunities to share their opinions and ideas when planning curriculum and evaluate Head Start curriculum and services. All parents of enrolled children are members of Head Start Parent Committees. The committee meets on a regular basis and discusses issues relating to curriculum, services, and policies. The Parent Committees elect representatives to the Head Start Policy Council, which is the governing body of the program. These parents can also be elected to serve as officers on local, state, and national Policy Councils.

Classes and workshops concerning families and parenting are offered for parents on a regular basis. These classes cover a wide variety of topics, which are chosen by parents through the use of an interest survey. Head Start programs are often linked to adult learning and job placement programs within a community. Parents are supported in their efforts to reach educational and career goals.

Classroom teachers typically carry out individual home visits to meet with families and children at the beginning and the end of the school year. During the teacher's initial home visit, teachers review curriculum with parents and complete a planning form on which parents have the opportunity to include ideas and suggestions. The year-end home visit comprises assisting children and parents in planning for the child's transition to kindergarten. Parents are provided with information on helping their children to make the transition, as well as on local kindergarten registrations. Additional home visits by parent and family service coordinators are scheduled throughout the year. At least two parent–teacher conferences are scheduled for parents during the year.

Early Head Start

Early Head Start was created as an extension of the Head Start program to serve low-income families with infants and toddlers, as well as pregnant women. In 1994, the U.S. Congress passed a reauthorization of the Head Start Act, which mandated the Head Start Bureau to initiate a new program to provide comprehensive early intervention for these families. The Early Head Start was established in 1995 and has grown from the original 68 programs to 650 community-based programs nationwide, serving 90,415 children (U.S. Department of Health and Human Services, 2010). Grants for Early Head Start programs are administered by the Administration for Children and Families (ACF).

The mission of Early Head Start is "to promote healthy prenatal outcomes for pregnant women, enhance the development of very young children, and promote healthy family functioning" (U.S. Department of Health and Human Services, 2009). The program goals include enhancing the physical, cognitive, social, and emotional development of children; helping parents learn how to best care for and teach their children; and assisting parents in moving toward economic independence. Early Head Start programs work closely with community agencies including child-care providers in meeting the needs of children and families.

Children are eligible for Early Head Start until age 3 and are later transitioned into a regular Head Start program. This fosters continuity of care, relationships, and services in the community. Services are provided through home-based, center-based, and combination options as a response to the individual needs of families and specific community needs. Home-based programs include weekly home visits and bimonthly group socialization events. Center-based programs include periodic home visits by the child's teacher and other center staff. Certified family child care is also an option designed to serve families and children.

Parent Involvement Practices

Early Head Start mandates parent involvement similar to the performance standards of Head Start programs discussed earlier. The programs have governing systems such as parent committee and policy councils through which parents can participate in the process of planning curriculum, policy making, and decision making. Along with Early Head Start staff, parents participate in developing and updating an individualized plan for their own children's growth and development and an individualized family partnership agreement. This helps to ensure that services are responding to the goals and needs of families. Prenatal education and health care is provided to pregnant women, and programs must establish procedures to record and follow the provision of health care services to families. Parents with very young children are provided with opportunities to increase their knowledge and understanding of child development, parenting skills, and their children's education needs. Family support and intervention programs play a crucial role in the lives of the very young children and families in the child welfare system. Families are provided with health and mental health services as needed (National Head Start Association, 2010; U.S. Department of Health and Human Services, 2009).

Title I/Even Start

Even Start is a family-centered education program authorized as part of Chapter 1 or Title I of PL 100-297, which provides funds to local educational agencies to improve the educational opportunities for the nation's children (ages 1 through 7) and adults by integrating early childhood education and adult education for parents into a unified family-centered program (Gestwicki, 2009; U.S. Department of Education, 2009). At present, there are approximately 800 sites across the nation that serve approximately one million parents and children. Home-based programs are one of the outreach mechanisms; they promote (1) adult literacy, including basic skills, GED certificate, and workforce skills; (2) preparation of parents to support their children's education and growth; (3) helping parents understand their roles in influencing their children's education; and (4) preparation of children for school success.

National Association for the Education of Young Children (NAEYC)

The National Association for the Education of Young Children (NAEYC) has developed standards of professional practice and serves as a guide for accrediting high-quality early childhood programs. One of the 10 components used to accredit high-quality programs includes relationships among teachers and families. The rationale for parental involvement is that "young children are integrally connected to their families. Programs cannot adequately meet the needs of children unless they also recognize the importance of the child's family and develop strategies to work effectively with families. All communication between centers and families should be based on the concept that parents are and should be the principal influence in children's lives" (NAEYC, 2007).

There are 11 specific areas of staff–parent interaction that should be included in the accredited early childhood program's parental involvement plan:

1. Provide information to parents on the program's philosophy and operating policies and procedures.
2. Provide orientation for new children and families.
3. Maintain regular, ongoing communication with families to build trust and mutual understanding.
4. Welcome parents into the program at all times and encourage them to get involved in various ways.
5. Establish verbal and written systems to allow sharing of day-to-day happenings that may affect children.
6. Encourage joint decision making on how best to support children's development and learning.
7. Provide information to parents on program activities in a variety of ways.
8. Provide and communicate transition plans to parents to ensure smooth transition from one program to another.
9. Show acceptance of and respect for various family structures and cultural perspectives.
10. Become familiar with community services and resources and connect families with needed services and resources.
11. Establish policies and techniques on ways of negotiating difficulties and differences.

Minnesota Early Childhood Family Education (ECFE)

The Early Childhood and Family Education (ECFE) program was founded in Minnesota in 1974 and is the oldest state-funded effort. The development of ECFE progressed from 1974 to 1983, through a series of pilot programs that were coordinated by the Minnesota Council on Quality Education and funded by Minnesota legislature. In 1984, the legislature ruled that any school district with a community education program could establish an ECFE program. These programs are now funded through a combination of local levies, state aid, registration fees, and funds from other sources.

The mission of ECFE is to strengthen families and help parents create an environment that will encourage the healthy growth and development of their children. The program is available to all families with a child or children between birth and 5 years of age, regardless of family structure, income, or special needs. ECFE also works with education, health, and human service agencies to connect families and children to needed services.

Classes are designed to provide learning experiences for children, interaction time for parents and children, and parent group discussion time. Classes may be offered for specific age groups or for children of mixed ages and typically run for 2 or 2.5 hours a week throughout the school year. Field trips and special events are often scheduled outside of regular class times. Other activities and services include home visits and lending libraries of books, toys, and learning materials.

Parent Involvement Practices

The ECFE program recognizes parents as children's first and most important teachers. An underlying premise of ECFE parent involvement practices is that, during the early years of a child's life, parents are often most receptive to information and support. Classes and events are specifically designed for parents to participate in activities with their children. These experiences are to help parents become aware of and understand their children's interests and abilities. A licensed parent educator leads parent group discussions, and his or her role is to provide information and facilitate discussion on a variety of topics related to parenting. While parents are meeting, children are engaged in activities with a certified early childhood education teacher. Support and encouragement from other parents is also an important component of parent group discussion time. Individual ECFE programs are required to have an advisory council in which parents make up a majority of the membership. The advisory councils assist program staff in planning, developing, and monitoring the ECFE programs.

AVANCE

The AVANCE Family Support and Education Program is a private, nonprofit organization located in San Antonio, Texas. Gloria G. Rodriguez established the program in 1973 with funding from the Zale Foundation to provide comprehensive, community-based, family support programs targeted for at-risk and Hispanic populations. *AVANCE* is a Spanish word meaning "to advance" or "to progress." At present, there are 100 AVANCE sites located throughout Texas, California, and New Mexico and supported by a funding consortium consisting of the Carnegie Corporation of New York and various other foundations. AVANCE is open to all families with children under age 4 residing within the designated boundaries of each program.

The mission of AVANCE is to "strengthen families in at-risk Hispanic communities through the most effective parent education and support program" (AVANCE, 2010). The program provides services that will "strengthen the family unit, enhance parenting skills, promote educational success, and foster the personal and economic success of parents" (AVANCE, 2010). AVANCE offers parent education, social support, adult education, early childhood education, youth programs, personal development, and community empowerment (AVANCE, 2010; Gestwicki, 2009; Hyslop, 2000).

Parent Involvement Practices

AVANCE parent education is a 9-month center-based program that families attend once a week for three 1-hour segments. The classes are offered in English and Spanish, and typically the first hour focuses on toy making, followed by an hour on child development and parenting topics, and ends with information on the availability and accessibility of community resources and services. While parents are attending the parenting classes, the children participate in early childhood education. Other services include home visits that are made monthly for observing parent–child interactions, special programs for fathers, and literacy training. AVANCE established a public policy center to address policy issues that are pertinent to Hispanic children and families, encourages families and individuals to participate in the policy-making process, and works on representing and supporting the voices of the families. AVANCE also operates a national training center that disseminates information to over 40 states and other parts of the world. Curriculum resources are sold in 15 states, and training for individuals has reached 24 states (AVANCE, 2010; Hyslop, 2000).

Parent and Child Education (PACE)

Kentucky's Parent and Child Education (PACE) program was established in 1986 and became the first government-sponsored family literacy program. Currently known as PACE for Family Independence, the program is funded through the school districts and administered by the Department for Adult Education and Literacy (DAEL) in the Workforce Development Cabinet. The program also served as a model for the federally funded Even Start program and other state programs.

The mission of PACE is to improve the educational future for undereducated parents, and at the same time to provide quality early childhood education for their children. The rationale is based on the premise that illiteracy and academic failure tend to repeat themselves in generations to come. The eligibility requirement is that parents have not obtained a high school diploma or have high school diplomas but function at a very low literacy level and have a child or children ages 0 to 8.

Parents and children who have not yet enrolled in public schools attend classes 3 days a week. The program consists of four components: adult basic skill education, early childhood education, parent education and support, and regular opportunities for parent–child interaction. A typical PACE class has parents and children arriving at school in buses provided by PACE. Adult education classes consist of preparation for the GED and basic skills. The early childhood education program promotes and enhances the developmental needs of young children and adopts the HighScope Preschool Curriculum. Parent education provides parents with support groups and discussion of parenting topics that meet the needs of the families (Gestwicki, 2009; National Center for Family Literacy, 2009).

Summary

The seven models discussed in this early childhood education section represent programs that encourage active parent participation in early childhood education settings. Early childhood education supports the basic fundamental beliefs that (1) parents are their children's first and most influential teachers at a very young age, (2) parents have valuable insights and information to share with program staff and other parents, and (3) parents and children are a family unit and cannot be seen as a separate entity. Creating an environment in which parents and children can interact together is one of the crucial components in parent involvement.

Recommended Activities

1. Pick three models, and compare and contrast the models.
2. Identify models in your community. Speak with the director or coordinator of one of the models to determine the components of the family involvement model.
3. Ask your parents whether they participated in any of these models. Ask them to describe the family interaction.
4. What challenges can you identify in the different family involvement models?
5. Explain whether the family involvement models will work with all ethnic groups, such as African American, Asian, Hispanic, Native American, and Caucasians.
6. Do all these models work effectively with single-parent, grandparent-headed, dual-parent, and same-sex families?
7. Although the chapter focuses on preschool and elementary school age children, what do you think the difference would be with families of middle school children or high school children?

Additional Resources

Websites

AVANCE
www.avance.org

Center for the Improvement of Child Caring (CICC)
Phone: 800-325-CICC
www.ciccparenting.org

Center on School, Family, and Community Partnership
Phone: 401-332-4575
www.csos.jhu.edu/p2000/center.htm

Comer School Development Program (SDP)
Phone: 203-737-1020
info.med.yale.edu/comer

Early Childhood Family Education (ECFE)
http://ecfe.mpls.k12.mn.us

National Head Start Association
Phone: 703-739-0875 Fax: 703-739-0878
www.nhsa.org

MegaSkills Online Education Center
Phone: 202-466-3633
www.megaskillshsi.org

Minnesota Early Childhood Family Education
Phone: 651-582-8200
http://education.state.mn.us/mde/

National Association for the Education of Young Children (NAEYC)
Phone: 800-424-2460
www.naeyc.org

National Black Child Development Institute
Phone: 202-833-2220
www.nbcdi.org

National Coalition for Parent Involvement in Education (NCPIE)
Phone: 703-359-8973
www.ncpie.org

National Middle School Association (NMSA)
Phone: 614-895-4730
www.nmsa.org

National Network of Partnership Schools
Phone: 410-516-8800
www.csos.jhu.edu/p2000

National PTA
www.pta.org

Parent and Child Education (PACE)
Phone: 502-564-5114; Fax: 502-564-5436
www.education.ky.gov

Parent to Parent (P2P) National Center
www.p2pusa.org/

Parents as Teachers National Center
Phone: 314-432-4330; Fax: 314-432-8963
www.patnc.org

The Search Institute
Phone: 612-376-8955
www.search-institute.org

Zero to Three: National Center for Infants,
    Toddlers and Families
202-638-1144
www.zerotothree.org

References

AVANCE. (2010). *AVANCE*. Retrieved August 4, 2010, from www.avance.org

Balaban, N. (1985). *Starting school: From separation to independence*. New York: Teachers College Press.

Bronfenbrenner, U. (1979) *The ecology of human development: Experiences by nature and design*. Cambridge, MA: Harvard University Press.

Bruder, M., & Dunst, C. (2001). Expanding learning opportunities for infants and toddlers in natural environments: A chance to reconceptualize early intervention. *Zero to Three (20)*3, 34–36.

Comer, J. P. (1988). Educating poor minority children. *Scientific American, 259*(5), 42–48.

Comer, J. P. (1993). *James P. Comer, M.D., on the school development program: Making a difference for children* (ERIC Document Reproduction Service No. ED 358 959). New York: Columbia University, National Center for Restructuring Education, Schools, and Teaching.

Comer, J. P. (2001). Schools that develop children. *The American Prospect, 12*. Retrieved April 30, 2001, from www.prospect.org/print/v12/7/comer-j.html

Dunst, C. (2000). Revisit, rethinking early intervention. *Topics in Early Childhood Special Education, 20*(2), 95–104.

Epstein, J. (2005). A case study of the partnership schools comprehensive school reform (CSR) model. *The Elementary School Journal,* (2), 151–170.

Gallagher, P. A., Rhodes, C. A., & Darling, S. M. (2004). Parents as professionals in early intervention: A parent educator model. *Topics in Early Childhood Special Education 24*(1), 5–13.

Gestwicki, C. (2009). *Home, school, and community relations* (7th ed.). New York: Delmar Cengage Learning.

Hoover-Dempsey, K., Walker, J., & Sandler, H. (2005). Parents' motivations for involvement in their children's education. In E. Patrikakou &

R. Weissberg (Eds.), *School–family partnerships for children's success* (pp. 40–56). New York: Teachers College Press.

Hoover-Dempsey, K., Walker, J., Sandler, H., Whetsel, D., Green, C., Wilkins, A., & Closson, K. (2005). Why do parents become involved? Research findings and implications. *The Elementary School Journal, 106*(2), 105–130.

Hyslop, N. (2000). *Hispanic parental involvement in home literacy* (ERIC Document Reproduction Service No. ED 446 340). Indianapolis, IN: Clearinghouse on Reading, English, and Communication.

Kaczmarek, L. A., Goldstein, H., Florey, J. D., Carter, A., & Cannon, S. (2004). Supporting families: A preschool model. *Topics in Early Childhood Special Education 24*(4), 213–226.

Lee, S-H., Palmer, S. B., Turnbull, A., Wehmeyer, M. L. (2006). A model for parent-teacher collaboration to promote self-determination in young children with disabilities. *Exceptional Children 38*(3), 36–41.

Mahoney, G., Kaiser, A., Girolametto, L., MacDonald, J., Robinson, C., Safford, P., & Spiker, D. (1999). Parent education in early intervention: A call for a renewed focus. *Topics in Early Childhood Special Education 19*(3), 131–140.

McIntyre, L. L., & Phaneuf, L. K. (2008). A three-tier model of parent education in early childhood: Applying a problem-solving model. *Topics in Early Childhood Special Education 27*(4), 214–222.

MegaSkills Education Center. (2010a). *Introduction to MegaSkills*. Retrieved August 8, 2010, from www.megaskillshsi.org/introduction.html

MegaSkills Education Center. (2010b). *Research on MegaSkills program effectiveness*. Retrieved August 8, 2010, from www.megaskillshsi.org/impactResults.html

Murray, M. M., Christensen, K. A., Umbarger, G. T., Rade, K. C., Aldridge, K., & Niemeyer,

J. A. (2007). Supporting family choice. *Early Childhood Education Journal 35*(2), 111–117.

National Association for the Education of Young Children. (2007). *NAEYC early childhood program standards and accreditation criteria: The mark of quality in early childhood education.* Washington DC: Author.

National Center for Family Literacy. (2009). *Creating a literate nation by leveraging the power of the family.* Retrieved August 2, 2010, from www.famlit.org/ncfl-and-family-literacy

National Head Start Association. (2010). *National Head Start Association.* Retrieved August 4, 2010, from www.headstartinfo.org

National Network of Partnership Schools. (2009). Retrieved August 11, 2010, from www.csos.jhu.edu/p2000/nnps_model/school.htm

No Child Left Behind. (2004). *Parental involvement: Title I, Part A, Non-regulatory guidance. Retrieved August 12, 2010,* from www2.ed.gov/programs/titleiparta/parentinvguid.doc

Sandell, E. (1998). Family involvement models in early childhood education. In M. Fuller & G. Olsen (Eds.), *Home–school relations* (pp. 177–184). Boston: Allyn & Bacon.

Santelli B., Turnbull, A., Marquis, J., & Lerner, E. (2000). Statewide parent to parent programs: Partners in early intervention. *Infants and Young Children 13*(1), 74–88.

Sheldon, S. (2005). Testing a structural equation model of partnership program implementation and parent involvement. *The Elementary School Journal 106*(2), 171–187.

Turnbull, A. (1999). From parent education to partnership education: A call for a transformed focus. *Topics in Early Special Education, 19*(3), 164–171.

Turnbull, A., Brown, I., & Turnbull, III, H. R. (Eds.). (2004). *Families and persons with mental retardation and quality of life: International perspectives.* Washington, DC: American Association on Mental Retardation.

Turnbull, A. P., & Turnbull, H. R. (2001). *Families, professionals, and exceptionality: A special partnership* (4th ed.). Upper Saddle River, NJ: Merrill/Prentice Hall.

Turnbull, R., Turnbull, A., Shank, S., & Leal, D. (2001). *Exceptional lives: Special education in today's schools* (3rd ed.). Upper Saddle River, NJ: Merrill/Prentice Hall.

Turnbull, A., Zuna, N., Hong, J. Y., Hu, X., Kyzar, K., Obremski, S., Summers, J. A., Turnbull, R., & Stowe, R. (2010). Knowledge-to-action guides: Preparing families to be partners in making educational decisions. *Teaching Exceptional Children 42*(3), 42–53.

U.S. Department of Education. (2005). *Part A, Section 1118 Parent Involvement.* Retrieved August 11, 2010, from www2.ed.gov/policy/elsec/leg/esea02/pg2.html

U.S. Department of Education. (2009). *Even Start.* Retrieved August 4, 2010, from www2.ed.gov/programs/evenstartformula/index.html

U.S. Department of Education. (2010). *Parental Information and Resource Centers.* Retrieved August 11, 2010, from www2.ed.gov/programs/pirc/index.html

U.S. Department of Health and Human Services. (2009). *Early Head Start. The Early Head Start National Resource Center.* Retrieved August 4, 2010, from www.ehsnrc.org

U.S. Department of Health and Human Services. (2010). *Fiscal year 2009: Head Start program fact sheet.* Retrieved August 2, 2010, from www.acf.hhs.gov/programs/ohs/about/fy2010.html

Van Voorhis, F. (2004). Reflecting on the homework ritual: Assignments and designs. *Theory Into Practice 43*(3), 205–212.

Weiss, H. B., Caspe, M., & Lopez, M. E. (2006, Spring). *Family involvement in early childhood education.* Retrieved from www.hfrp.org/

Yale School of Medicine Child Study Center. (2010). *Comer school development program.* Retrieved August 16, 2010, from http://medicine.yale.edu/childstudy/comer

Zaidman-Zait, A., & Jamieson, J. R. (2007). Providing web-based support for families with infants and young children with established disabilities. *Infants and Young Children 20*(1), 11–25.

Zigler, E., & Freedman, J. (1987). Head Start: A pioneer of family support. In S. L. Kagan, D. R. Powell, B. Weissbourd, & E. F. Ziegler (Eds.), *America's family support programs: Perspectives and prospects* (pp. 57–76). New Haven, CT: Yale University Press.

Chapter Ten

Education Law and Parental Rights

Gloria Jean Thomas
Idaho State University

This chapter presents information on the legal rights and responsibilities of parents and schools. It describes the history of the legislation related to the home and the school and cites court cases as they relate to the issues of compulsory attendance, school fees, curriculum, special education, students' rights, student safety, liability, and discrimination and harassment.

This chapter helps you to:

▶ Discuss the history of the legal relationship between parents and schools.

▶ Identify the origins of local taxes for schools, compulsory attendance laws, and academic standards for schools.

▶ Understand how the issue of religion has been a constant source of tension between parents and schools.

▶ Understand the significance for all students, parents, and school personnel of the Individuals with Disabilities Education Act (IDEA).

▶ Recognize the significance of sexual harassment lawsuits in the K–12 school system today.

▶ Comprehend the significance of *Brown* v. *Board of Education of Topeka, Kansas* (1954) in relation to school and parents, then and now.

▶ Distinguish between school rights and student rights.

▶ Understand the role of schools and parents in the safety of students at school.

▶ Identify the significance of the No Child Left Behind Act of 2001 on the relationship between schools and parents.

Parents have always been a child's first teachers. Only in recent history have governments assumed responsibility for a child's formal education. Even when schools are established, parents retain their rights to influence and guide a child's upbringing. This chapter discusses the legal rights and responsibilities of parents and schools in today's litigious society. The history of the legal relationship between parents and schools is first explained, followed by a discussion of the legal role of the states in the education of their citizens. Court cases are used to demonstrate the role of the federal and state courts in resolving disputes between parents and schools.

History of the Legal Relationship Between Parents and Schools

In 1642 the colonial legislature of Massachusetts Bay became concerned that parents were so busy eking out survival in the harsh New World that they were shirking their duty to educate their children. Children who were not taught to read the Bible were sure to fall prey to "ye olde deluder Satan." Therefore, the legislature passed a statute charging all parents to see to the education of their children. In 1647 the legislature required towns of 50 households to appoint a teacher and towns of 100 households to build a school. Taxes could be levied to support these schools, which were not only to ensure that children could read the scriptures but to facilitate a literate society for the good of the colony. Thus, these laws became the first compulsory education laws, the first school funding laws, and the first official recognition of a legal relationship between schools and parents.

However, the legal rights of parents for the education of their children predate any written law. From the beginning of time, parents have been a child's first teachers, assuming responsibility for instructing the child in survival skills and tribal or community mores to enable society to exist and perpetuate itself. Because the right of parents to guide the upbringing and education of their children is recognized as natural and inherent, that right is regarded as fundamental for citizens of the United States.

Fundamental rights are those that citizens of this country take for granted because they have always existed in a free society. Other fundamental rights include the right to marry whomever one chooses (or not to marry), the right to have children (or not to have children), and the right to choose one's job, career, or profession. These rights are not written down in any federal or state constitution or statute. Yet, they are protected as if written in the U.S. Constitution, the Supreme Law of the Land (Article VI). Therefore, the right of parents to guide the upbringing and education of their children is a protected right.

The legal status of children as minors means that children under the age of majority (age 18 for most purposes in the United States) are not expected to have adult judgment to determine what is best for their own welfare. Because minors are not considered capable under the law of exercising responsibility for their own decisions, laws prohibit them from signing binding contracts, from buying harmful substances (such as alcohol and tobacco products), and from being held to the criminal and civil codes of law as adults. Children are under the protection of their parents, who are charged with ensuring the safety and welfare, including the education, of their minor children.

Because parents have the ultimate legal authority for the education of children, the role of schools is *in loco parentis* (in place of the parent). The concept of *in loco parentis* dates back to old English law that allowed schoolmasters to have power over pupil conduct. However, the schoolmaster had only that portion of parental powers necessary for the conduct of the school. Parents could never give up all authority over their child because of the "natural relation of parent and child . . . the tenderness which the parent feels for his offspring, an affection ever on the alert, and acting rather by instinct than reasoning" (*Lander* v. *Seaver*, 1859).

Therefore, when children go to school, the school as an entity and teachers as individuals are *in loco parentis* to those children. School personnel are responsible for the safety, welfare, and education of the child in place of the parents. However, parents do not abdicate their ultimate authority over the upbringing of their children simply because they comply with state compulsory attendance laws by sending their children to school.

The issue becomes one of finding the balance between the school's right and responsibility (delegated to it by the state) to prepare children to be knowledgeable, productive citizens of a democratic society and the parents' right and responsibility (inherent because of their being parents) to guide the upbringing of their children. All legal issues involving parents and schools are based on the tension between these two sets of rights and responsibilities.

Reflection...

Should the rights of parents or the rights of schools weigh more heavily when a dispute reaches the courts? What else needs to be considered?

State Constitutions and Education

Education is not mentioned in the U.S. Constitution, perhaps by conscious design, but probably because the writers of the Constitution had themselves been educated in private schools, by tutors, and by self-learning. The idea of public schools, even though in existence since the Massachusetts Bay Colony, had not become universally accepted. In the 1700s, a few pauper schools existed for the children of the poor, orphans, and other wards of the states, but education was generally a private concern of parents.

However, interpretation of the Tenth Amendment gradually resulted in education becoming the responsibility of the states. The Reserved Powers Clause of the Tenth Amendment meant that education would come under the authority of the states:

The powers not delegated to the United States by the Constitution, nor prohibited by it to the States, are reserved to the States respectively, or to the people.

Over time, the states recognized the importance of education for all children if the experiment in democracy were to succeed. Colonial legislatures wrote education clauses into their state constitutions. Later, territorial legislatures were required to include provisions for education in their constitutions prior to applying for statehood. Most territorial authorities followed the lead of older states, resulting in the education clauses in many state constitutions being worded very similarly. The North Dakota Constitution, written in 1889, is similar to that of many states admitted to the Union after the Civil War. Article VIII, with variations, could be found in the constitutions of many states:

Section 1. A high degree of intelligence, patriotism, integrity and morality on the part of every voter in a government by the people being necessary in order to insure the continuance of that government and the prosperity and happiness of the people, the legislative assembly shall make provision for the establishment and maintenance of a system of public schools which shall be open to all children of the state of North Dakota and free from sectarian control. This legislative requirement shall be irrevocable without the consent of the United States and the people of North Dakota.

Section 2. The legislative assembly shall provide for a uniform system of free public schools throughout the state, beginning with the primary and extending through all grades up to and including schools of higher education, except that the legislative assembly may authorize tuition, fees and service charges to assist in the financing of public schools of higher education.

After writing lofty ideals into their constitutions, most states did not get involved in the local control of schools for many years. Frontier villages were so isolated that parents were the only teachers, fundraisers, architects, builders, administrators, and evaluators for tiny one-room schoolhouses. As communities grew and state governments became more organized and stable, the role of the states, as defined in state constitutions, became important.

Reflection...

What does your state constitution say about education?

State Legislatures and Education

From the days of the Massachusetts Bay Colony, state legislatures assumed limited responsibility for the schools. As populations of cities grew, the problems of low educational standards, inadequate curricula, minimal training for teachers, inconsistent school funding, and lack of school governance structure became apparent. Relying on state constitutions that indicated state responsibility for schools, state legislatures slowly became involved in schools.

In the 1800s, reformers such as Horace Mann and Charles Barnard took their causes to state legislatures and encouraged laws to be passed to improve the physical facilities of schools, to mandate compulsory attendance of children, to require local tax support for schools, to require state credentialing of teachers, and to establish minimal academic standards for schools. Other state legislatures followed the lead of Massachusetts, Connecticut, and other progressive states of the 19th century.

As the nation's population grew, school districts were formed with school boards elected from the citizenry of the district in accordance with state laws. School board members were officers of the state, charged with implementing state statutes in the local schools. As schools became more complex, state legislatures became more involved in the day-to-day operation of the schools, passing laws regulating teacher qualifications, the curriculum, teacher evaluation, high school graduation requirements, the school calendar, extracurricular activities, school consolidation, bond elections, personnel records, student records, disciplinary procedures, fees, bus service, textbooks, vaccinations, religious exercises, and testing. To enforce the myriad of laws being passed, state departments of education evolved from advisory to regulatory bodies and assumed responsibility for enforcement of state statutes.

As education became accepted as one of the primary responsibilities of the state, responsibility for the funding of schools shifted from the local community to the state. Prior to this shift, funding for schools had depended on the goodwill of local tax assessors and city councils because the school tax was usually a tax on local property.

In the 21st century, state responsibility for schools is an accepted fact. As the responsibility for the funding of schools shifted from the local community to the state, the control of decision making for the schools also shifted from the local community to state education agencies. The result has been a loss of control and sense of responsibility for schools at the local level for all persons involved in the school, but especially parents. Where once they hired, evaluated, and fired the teachers; chose the textbooks and the curriculum; held box lunch auctions, passed the hat at school concerts, and donated land to finance equipment, supplies, books, furniture, and teachers' salaries; and designed and built school buildings, parents now pay state taxes and are asked to adhere to their elected state legislators' decisions about their schools. The legal distance between parents and schools has increased as the state has exercised its legal authority over the educational system.

Reflection...

Why are school boards comprised of laypersons, not professional educators? What are the advantages and disadvantages of this system of governance?

State and Federal Courts and Education

Although most disputes between parents and the schools never go beyond discussions with school administrators or before local school boards, the courts have long been involved when disputes cannot be resolved easily. Because education is a state responsibility, most disputes arise over state laws or policies passed by school boards acting as agents of the state. Therefore, the majority of court cases involving schools are brought in state courts. Only when the dispute involves the federal Constitution or a federal law can a case be heard in federal court. Involvement of the federal courts to any great extent did not arise until the 1950s when conflicts over desegregation of the schools became a national concern.

When a dispute arises between parents and the schools, generally the courts are asked to balance the fundamental rights of the parents to guide the upbringing of their children against the delegated rights of the school to educate productive citizens for the democratic state. The question of whose rights weigh more heavily, those of the parent or those of the state, has been the subject of court cases that have been appealed all the way to the U.S. Supreme Court. This fundamental right of parents to guide the upbringing of their children was the core issue of a very early case brought before the U.S. Supreme Court in 1925. In *Pierce* v. *Society of Sisters* (1925), an Oregon law requiring all parents to send their children between the ages of 8 and 16 years to only public schools was challenged successfully. This Supreme Court decision allowed parents the right to send their children to parochial or other types of private schools.

> [W]e think it entirely plain that the Act of 1922 unreasonably interferes with the liberty of parents and guardians to direct the upbringing and education of children under their control. . . . The child is not the mere creature of the state; those who nurture him and direct his destiny have the right, coupled with the high duty, to recognize and prepare him for additional obligations. (*Pierce* v. *Society of Sisters*, 1925)

In resolving disputes between parents and schools, the courts almost always must interpret state laws or school board policies. Fundamental rights of parents will weigh very heavily in these cases, but reasonable laws and policies of the school will be upheld if parents' fundamental rights are not in jeopardy.

Court Involvement Before 1954

For several reasons, very few court cases against the schools were brought by parents before the 1950s. Before World War II, local communities were still in control of their schools, with parents feeling that they knew the school personnel and the activities going on at the school. People did not leave their small towns, and the teachers, administrators, and board members were their next-door neighbors. The curriculum had not changed drastically since parents had been in school. Radio brought the world closer to the hometown, but national and international news concerned places that had little to do with the local community. Therefore, parents rarely used the courts to make changes in their local schools.

The federal courts were almost never involved in the schools prior to the desegregation cases of the 1950s. Therefore, court cases prior to the 1950s were almost all heard in state courts because usually state laws or school board policies were the subject of disputes. Prior to 1954, the courts heard a few cases dealing with issues such as vaccinations and religion.

In spite of the fundamental rights of parents to guide the upbringing of their children, the courts do not always honor parental requests. When parental desires or requests endanger the health, safety, or welfare of their child or others, the courts rule against the rights of parents. In an era before medical science stopped deadly diseases from causing epidemics in communities, schools were often closed when smallpox, tuberculosis, diphtheria, influenza, and other contagious diseases struck. When vaccinations were developed against some of these diseases, schools often required students to be immunized before they were allowed to go to school. However, some parents were against vaccinations, often citing religious reasons. Courts have ruled against parents even when formerly deadly diseases like smallpox were declining, stating, "A local board of education need not await an epidemic, or even a single sickness or death, before it decides to protect the public. To hold otherwise would be to destroy prevention as a means of combating the spread of disease" (*Board of Education of Mountain Lakes* v. *Maas,* 1959). Changes in medical sciences beginning in the 1950s would ease the terror brought by formerly fatal diseases and result in the courts amending earlier decisions related to vaccinations.

When disputes about the school curriculum involve religion, the federal courts have long been involved because these disputes always center on the First Amendment of the U.S. Constitution. Questions related to the relationship between church and state, as defined by the First Amendment, can be brought before the federal courts. The two religion clauses of the First Amendment are the Establishment and Free Exercise Clauses:

> Congress shall make no law respecting an establishment of religion, or prohibiting the free exercise thereof.

In 1943 the Supreme Court handed down the first of its many controversial decisions dealing with religious exercises in the schools. A West Virginia school board had adopted a resolution ordering that the salute to the flag become a regular part of the curriculum of the schools. The children of parents who were Jehovah's Witnesses refused to participate because the flag salute is against the tenets of their religion. Jehovah's Witnesses literally interpret the second of the Ten Commandments from the Holy Bible:

> Thou shalt not make unto thee any graven image, or any likeness of anything that is in heaven above or that is in the earth beneath, or that is in the water under the earth; thou shalt not bow down thyself to them nor serve them. (Exodus 20:4-5)

The parents brought suit in U.S. District Court, asking for an injunction to stop enforcement of the policy. In ruling for the parents, the U.S. Supreme Court noted that "the refusal of these persons to participate in the ceremony does not interfere with or deny rights of others to do so" (*West Virginia State Board of Education* v. *Barnette*, 1943).

The flag salute case was brought in the patriotic heat of World War II, and the conclusion of that war brought a cry for a return to values of the past. Attempts were made by parents and religious organizations to bring religious instruction into the schools. In Illinois, parents and clergy of Jewish, Roman Catholic, and a few Protestant faiths formed an association and obtained permission from the school board to offer religious instruction in school. The classes were voluntary in that parents signed cards requesting that their children be permitted to attend the religion classes. However, those students who did not enroll had no other class option but merely were sent to another room to study. Parents and others who believed that bringing in rabbis, priests, and ministers to teach religion classes was a violation of the Establishment Clause brought suit. The U.S. Supreme Court agreed that these classes fell "squarely under the ban of the First Amendment" (*McCollum* v. *Board of Education*, 1948).

However, in 1952, the Supreme Court upheld a released-time program in which students were released by their parents from school to attend religion classes held at nearby churches. The court ruled that schools may accommodate religion because there is "no constitutional requirement which makes it necessary for government to be hostile to religion" (*Zorach* v. *Clauson*, 1952). Thus, the stage was set for the battle over the separation of church and state to be waged in the public schools.

These early cases set precedents for the many cases that would soon follow as society became more complex. With the end of World War II, the nation grew rapidly, not only in numbers but in diversity and complexity. Immigrants were no longer from primarily Judeo-Christian, European countries, and they brought their own cultural and religious beliefs, plus memories of traumatic experiences during the war. Farming became mechanized, forcing small farmers out of business and requiring fewer farmers' children to remain on the farm. Immigrants, farmers, and others looking for a better life flooded the cities, multiplying urban problems. People became mobile, not staying in one place long enough to know their neighbors. Communication systems improved, and people became aware of changes and trends in other states and cities across the country. Compulsory attendance laws began to be enforced by the states, and parents realized that the only way their children could get jobs and improve their lives was by staying in school through high school. The United States took center stage in world affairs, and the schools were pressured to revise and expand the curriculum to ensure that the nation was the best in everything from military armaments to space travel to industrial output. The casual, informal, neighborly relationship between parents and the schools changed to a formal, legal relationship because of the changing world.

Reflection...

What changes did the end of World War II bring to your community, including the schools?

Court Involvement After 1954

The year 1954 is often used as the watershed year for school law and the relationship of parents and schools. In the 1950s, the National Association for the Advancement of Colored People (NAACP), along with other organizations and individuals, began a campaign to end segregation of the schools on the grounds that separation of the races forever branded minority people as second-class citizens. In Topeka, Kansas, the case of Linda Brown and several other black children who were forced by Kansas state law to attend all-black schools provided an appropriate test case. With Thurgood Marshall as the attorney for the plaintiffs, *Brown* v. *Board of Education of Topeka, Kansas* (1954) became the most important school law case ever brought before the courts. Declaring that the doctrine of "separate but equal" has no place in public education, the U.S. Supreme Court changed forever the relationship between the schools and the federal government and, hence, the relationship between parents and the schools. The *Brown* case officially desegregated the schools, but it also brought the federal court system into the schools to a degree never before known. Because of continual resistance to desegregation, the federal courts took on the role of overseers of some school districts, imposing mandates on hiring of teachers and administrators, enrollment systems, district boundaries, busing, and school board elections. The 9–0 vote of the Supreme Court in *Brown* signaled to the nation that the time had come for society to change, for the civil rights of all people to be recognized and protected, and for the schools to provide an education for all children. That decision also indicated that the courts would be used to enforce mandated changes when society refused to make the changes voluntarily.

Reflection...

Why is *Brown* v. *Board of Education* often considered by many to be the most important school law case ever heard by the U.S. Supreme Court? Did the case have any effect on your local school district?

Parents were often the ones reluctant to accept court mandates for change. The images of adults screaming at black children walking to school under the protection of federal marshals have been imprinted on the national conscience. As one group's rights came to the forefront in the media, other minority groups began seeking their children's rights. Individual rights became important to persons who had previously given little or no thought to their fundamental or constitutional rights. As society became more complex, as awareness of rights grew, as disenchantment with the public schools increased, and as local communities lost control of their schools, parents turned to the courts to resolve their problems and to reclaim their right to guide the upbringing of their children. Educators felt threatened when parents wanted to become more involved in schools than school personnel desired, and an adversarial relationship sometimes developed. Controversies led to court cases dealing with compulsory attendance, school fees, the curriculum, special education, student rights, student safety, liability, and discrimination and harassment. All of these issues raise questions that are still debated by school personnel and parents today.

Compulsory Attendance. Although some southern states attempted to circumvent desegregation orders by repealing their compulsory attendance laws, all states had such laws in place by the 1970s and started enforcing the laws even for groups that had previously been exempt. In Wisconsin, the Amish had traditionally allowed their children to attend public schools through only the eighth grade. Fearing a threat to their lifestyle and their religion if their children were exposed to worldly values, several Amish parents did not enroll their children in high school and were convicted of violating the state compulsory attendance law. The U.S. Supreme Court in *Wisconsin* v. *Yoder* (1972) once again upheld the fundamental right of parents to guide the upbringing of their children:

> Thus, a State's interest in universal education, however highly we rank it, is not totally free from a balancing process when it impinges on fundamental rights and interests, such as those specifically protected by the Free Exercise Clause of the First Amendment, and the traditional interest of parents with respect to the religious upbringing of their children. . . . The primary role of the parents in the upbringing of their children is now established beyond debate as an enduring American tradition. (*Wisconsin* v. *Yoder,* 1972)

The U.S. Supreme Court carefully stated that the *Yoder* decision applied only to the Amish or other religious groups with a similar history. However, other religious sects, private schools, and home schools have attempted, usually unsuccessfully, to use the "Amish exception" in the *Yoder* decision as a basis for challenging compulsory attendance laws.

Compulsory attendance laws continue to be challenged by parents who do not wish to comply with vaccination rules. Although many contagious diseases have been eradicated or at least controlled in the United States, the courts still uphold reasonable requirements for vaccinations for such diseases as smallpox, polio, and tuberculosis. When the argument is forwarded that vaccinations are against the parents' religion, the courts often respond with statements such as the following made by the Arkansas Supreme Court:

> Anyone has the right to worship God in the manner of his own choice, but it does not mean that he can engage in religious practices inconsistent with the peace, safety and health of the inhabitants of the State, and it does not mean that parents, on religious grounds, have the right to deny their children an education. . . . A person's right to exhibit religious freedom ceases where it overlaps and transgresses the rights of others. (*Cude* v. *Arkansas*, 1964)

As contagious diseases proliferate without cures (AIDS and Ebola), previously controlled diseases emerge with new deadly strains (hepatitis, meningitis, tuberculosis, and avian flu), and the threat of biological terrorism looms, debates over vaccination (if available), quarantine, and school attendance by stricken children will arise as parents feel their children's lives are threatened. Although many persons in this nation may feel that deadly diseases no longer threaten lives in the United States, the courts are likely going to be asked to continue to weigh the rights of parents to exercise their personal and religious beliefs about disease and vaccination against the right of schools to protect the health and welfare of all children and personnel.

As sexually transmitted diseases increase among students, the issue of sex education in the curriculum remains a topic of debate. Until the 1970s, some teachers handled topics related to human sexuality in health classes, but when those topics were labeled "sex education," many parents became concerned about the content of such courses. They claimed that their rights to guide the upbringing of their children certainly included the right to teach them about sex and intimacy according to family or religious values. However, sex education was purported to be a solution to the explosion in the number of teen pregnancies. Recognizing the susceptibility of the teenage population to the still dangerous effects of HIV and the harmful, disfiguring effects of other sexually transmitted diseases, some schools argue that sex education must be compulsory because all students are at risk and parents may not have the knowledge to teach their children about the new dangers that accompany sexual behavior. The courts are divided in their rulings about sex education courses, upholding those that include an excusal system (see *Medeiros* v. *Kiyosaki*, 1970; *Smith* v. *Ricci*, 1982) as well as those that mandate the course for all students (see *Cornwell* v. *State Board of Education*, 1969). Recognizing the state's interest in the health curriculum, the United States Court of Appeals, Second Circuit, ruled against a father who wanted his seventh-grade son excused from attending mandatory health education classes. The school permitted parents to excuse their children from the six classes related to family life instruction and AIDS education, but this father wanted his son excused from all health education for religious reasons. In rejecting the father's claim, the court denied "the existence of a fundamental right of every parent to tell a public school what his or her child will and will not be taught" (*Leebaert* v. *Harrington,* 2003).

As parents become disillusioned with public schools, more challenges to compulsory attendance laws are anticipated. Where once there were only two school systems—the public schools and the Catholic parochial schools—alternative educational systems are proliferating in every state. Many religions are establishing their own schools. Entrepreneurs are setting up for-profit schools. States are passing legislation allowing the establishment of charter schools of various types, some funded by the state and some funded by private entities. More parents are home schooling their children, although some states continue to attempt to ensure that children are, indeed, receiving an education and not just being kept home (see *In re Interest of Rebekah T.,* 2002). With advances in technology, virtual online schools cross school district and even state boundaries. Voucher systems that provide funds for parents to send their children to any public or private school are being proposed and upheld by some courts, including the U.S. Supreme Court (see *Zelman* v. *Simmons-Harris,* 2002) and struck down by other courts (see *Owens* v. *Colorado Congress of Parents, Teachers and Students,* 2004). Some states are attempting to regulate these new alternative schools, but advocates of these schools claim that state guidelines merely perpetuate the problems that new schools are attempting to combat.

Parents are not alone in becoming disillusioned with public schools. Ever since the publishing of *A Nation at Risk* in 1983, the federal government has taken increasing interest in the nation's schools. In the No Child Left Behind Act of 2001, the federal government mandated that states establish standards that every child must meet prior to graduating from high school. Although some states and school districts are challenging various provisions of NCLB (see *School District of the City of Pontiac* v. *Secretary (Spellings) of the United States Department of Education,* 2008), the law currently states that parents may remove their child from a school that fails to meet adequate yearly progress as defined by the state and enroll the child in another school where academic success may be achieved. Old compulsory attendance laws that define where and when a child is to attend school are becoming obsolete.

When parents feel that the schools are failing in their responsibility to prepare students for productive lives, then parents will challenge the validity of compulsory attendance laws. When the federal and state governments feel that the schools are failing in their responsibility to educate students, then those schools face sanctions, loss of funding, and loss of students. The courts will continue to be faced with the task of balancing the rights of parents to guide the upbringing of their children with the right of states to require school attendance and the meeting of state standards. Teachers and administrators will need to be prepared to defend the role of public schools in society and how the standards-based curriculum will prepare a child for the future.

Reflection...

Should children be compelled to attend school? Why? What types of schools exist in your community? What policies govern who attends these schools? What impact has the No Child Left Behind Act had on the schools in your community?

School Fees.   Public school education in the United States has always been free; that is, no tuition is charged when a student enrolls in the school. However, the charging of fees has a long history, dating back to when every student took a turn bringing a bucket of coal for the pot-bellied stove. In today's more sophisticated world, fees are charged for everything from the school yearbook to towels for physical education classes to anticipated breakage in laboratory classes to participation in extracurricular activities to textbook rental. When a state constitution guarantees a free public education for every child in the state but then fees are assessed, some parents have challenged the legality of such fees. Courts are then faced with having to interpret what the state constitution writers meant when they included the word "free" in the description of public schools.

A North Dakota school district's authority to charge rental fees for textbooks was challenged by a group of parents in 1978. The state supreme court ruled in favor of the parents:

> The term "free public schools" without any other modification must necessarily mean and include those items which are essential to education. It is difficult to envision a meaningful educational system without textbooks. No education of any value is possible without school books. (*Cardiff* v. *Bismarck Public School District,* 1978)

However, other state courts have ruled that "free" applies only to the lack of tuition and that charging for essentials like textbooks is legally tenable.

Other fees have been challenged in other states. In California, for example, the charging of fees for extracurricular activities was ruled unconstitutional under its state law that requires the legislature to "provide for a system of common schools by which a free school shall be kept up and supported in each district" (*Hartzell* v. *Connell,* 1984). Extracurricular activities were shown to be a vital part of public schooling in California, and fees were not allowed. The outcome in some states has been the elimination of extracurricular programs because of lack of funding.

Court challenges by parents against school fees will likely continue as the resources of school districts diminish, costs of educating students increase, and parents are called upon to bear more of the cost of their children's "free" education. Teachers will have to be careful not to waste any of the district's resources or expect parents to provide too many expensive items, such as elaborate treats, costumes, or supplies, to replace what the school was once expected to provide. School administrators may want to consider including parents as members of committees that develop fee levels and structures and that determine which academic and extracurricular activities and programs may have to be dropped in the face of rising costs.

Reflection...

With two children in high school, Kathy and Robert are faced with having to pay substantial school fees. Amy and Steve want to play basketball, and Amy wants to play soccer and volleyball as well as audition for the school play. The school charges a fee for each extracurricular activity plus towel fees for each sport and for the required physical education classes. In addition, there are fees for a card to get admitted to school activities (games, plays, concerts, etc.), for the school newspaper, for the yearbook, for having one's picture taken for the yearbook, and for class expendables (workbooks, paper, etc.). Kathy and Robert do not see how they can afford the fees; yet, they understand the value of their children participating in and attending school activities.

▶ What legal questions should Kathy and Robert ask of the school district? Of the building principal? Of the coaches or advisers?

▶ What do your state constitution, statutes, and case law say about school fees?

Curriculum.   The curriculum has long been considered the prerogative of professional educators, and those who challenge the curriculum have been considered troublemakers. Yet, parents have a right to know what their children are learning and should have a voice in determining the curriculum. Too often, school personnel forget that parents can be the best allies of the school in assisting children to learn. The curriculum is becoming too complex for parents to be left out of the teaching–learning process. Today's parents have a difficult time cooperating with schools in guiding the upbringing of their children if they have no idea what the schools are teaching their children, especially in the light of new state and federal mandates.

As stipulated in the No Child Left Behind Act, states are developing standards for what is to be taught in schools. States are also instituting high-stakes tests, including tests at various grade levels and final tests that must be passed before a child is allowed to graduate from high school. School personnel are working diligently to align their curricula with state standards; getting trained in instructional delivery methods that will assist students to achieve at the required competency levels; and implementing remedial, tutorial, and other aids to ensure that all children meet the standards and pass the tests. Teachers, administrators, students, and parents are feeling the stress that accompanies new curricula, new standards, and new testing requirements. Inviting parents to participate in the curriculum alignment process and communicating with parents about new standards and testing requirements and processes, especially new high school graduation requirements, will ensure that parents are willing and able to help their children succeed in school.

Challenges to the curriculum are made for many reasons but are usually settled at the local school board level. The majority of those cases that reach the courts are brought on the basis of religious arguments. These cases are often brought by parents who believe that the schools are fostering secular humanism (usually defined as a belief in the supremacy of humans instead of supernatural beings) instead of a belief in God or teaching values antithetical to family values. On the other hand, our national history as a haven for persons of all religious creeds has led to an increasing number of diverse religious backgrounds and beliefs being represented in the schools. Schools have been called the battleground for the struggle to define the separation of church and state. The conflict becomes especially difficult when the two religion clauses of the First Amendment become pitted against each other, as happens when the school claims that allowing a religious practice to occur on school property would be a violation of the Establishment Clause, and parents claim that not allowing that religious practice to occur on school property would be a violation of the Free Exercise Clause.

In 1963 the U.S. Supreme Court unleashed a furor when it ruled in *Abington School District* v. *Schemmp* that vocal prayers in school violate the Establishment Clause of the First Amendment. Many accused the Supreme Court of being atheist when the ruling went in favor of arguments made by the "professed atheist," Madeline Murray, on behalf of her son in the companion case, *Murray* v. *Curlett* (1963). Church–state cases comprise the school-related issue on which the U.S. Supreme Court has made the second greatest number of rulings (the first being desegregation).

In 1985 a Mobile, Alabama, attorney named Ishmael Jaffree sued the state of Alabama (represented in the title of the court case by its governor, George Wallace) in an attempt to get two state statutes declared unconstitutional on grounds of violation of the Establishment Clause. One state statute authorized a one-minute period of silence for meditation or voluntary prayer, and the second authorized teachers to lead "willing students in a prescribed prayer to Almighty God . . . the Creator and Supreme Judge of the world." The federal district court ruled that the two statutes were constitutional because "Alabama has the power to establish a state religion if it chooses to do so." However, the United States Court of Appeals, Eleventh Circuit, held the two statutes to be unconstitutional, and the U.S. Supreme Court agreed, stating that "the individual freedom of conscience protected by the First Amendment embraces the right to select any religious faith or none at all" (*Wallace* v. *Jaffree*, 1985).

Thus, vocal prayers in the classroom as well as moments of silence for the specified purpose of prayer have been ruled unconstitutional. The focus then turned to prayers and other religious exercises at school-related activities. In the early 1990s, the issue of prayer at public school graduation ceremonies arose when Daniel Weisman went to court to get a permanent injunction to prevent prayers at his daughter Deborah's middle-school graduation. The court did not act quickly enough to stop the school from inviting a rabbi to offer a prayer that was to be in accordance with guidelines in a school pamphlet. Eventually, the U.S. Supreme Court in *Lee* v.

Weisman (1992) ruled that clergy-led prayers at public school graduation ceremonies do violate the Establishment Clause of the First Amendment even though attendance at graduation is voluntary and even though the prayers are short and nonsectarian.

Religion will continue to be a divisive issue for schools. Prayers before athletic contests or graduation, students reading the Bible, students or teachers wearing religious jewelry, students depicting religious topics in artwork, and school music or drama programs with religious themes have all been challenged in lower courts. In 2000, the U.S. Supreme Court ruled in *Good News Club* v. *Milford Central School* that allowing religious organizations to meet on school grounds was not a violation of the Establishment Clause nor did it interfere with a parent's right to guide a child's upbringing. Even the phrase "under God" in the Pledge of Allegiance was challenged on the grounds that it violates the Establishment Clause. In 2004 the U.S. Supreme Court determined that the noncustodial father in *Elk Grove Unified School District* v. *Newdow* (2004) did not have standing to bring the case, thus allowing the Ninth Circuit Court of Appeals ruling that banned the phrase to stand. Future cases will be brought to court that will address the real issue in this controversy. As our nation becomes more diverse, the number of challenges to the curriculum and extracurricular activities based on religious arguments will increase.

Reflection...

Your school has always had a Christmas concert with choruses, orchestras, and bands performing songs of the season, including some traditional Christmas carols. A Muslim family has recently moved in and has requested that no Christian music be performed in the school. One of their children is in the orchestra. What is your response? Other families join the dispute, citing tradition and community values as reasons to continue the concert. How will you handle this issue?

Another First Amendment issue that has involved parents, schools, and the courts is book censorship. The Free Speech Clause of the First Amendment of the U.S. Constitution generally rules against any type of book banning. In the 1980s, the number of challenges to textbooks and curriculum materials soared as several organizations began sponsoring conferences about and publishing lists of books that the organizers claimed should not be found in schools. A New York school board took action to remove several of these books from the school library, and a group of students, parents, and teachers went to court, claiming censorship. Asserting that "the State may not, consistent with the spirit of the First Amendment, contract the spectrum of available knowledge," the U.S. Supreme Court in *Board of Education, Island Trees Union Free School District* v. *Pico* (1982) settled the question about school library books by stating that once books are on the shelf, they may not be removed.

Two cases related to textbook censorship were heard in 1987 by federal circuit courts of appeal. A Tennessee case involved several parents who argued that the required Holt, Rinehart and Winston reading series contained stories that contradicted the religious beliefs of the parents in violation of their Free Exercise rights. In an Alabama case, parents wanted 44 textbooks banned because of their secular humanism teachings. In both cases, the parents prevailed at the federal district court level. However, the United States Courts of Appeal, Sixth and Eleventh Circuits, overturned the lower court decisions. The Sixth Circuit Court decision noted that the parents "testified that reading the Holt series 'could' or 'might' lead the students to come to conclusions that were contrary to teachings of their and their parents' religious beliefs. This is not sufficient to establish an unconstitutional burden . . ." (*Mozert* v. *Hawkins County Board of Education*, 1987). The Eleventh Circuit Court stated:

> There simply is nothing in this record to indicate that omission of certain facts regarding religion from these textbooks of itself constituted an advancement of secular humanism or an active hostility towards theistic religion prohibited by the establishment clause. (*Smith* v. *Board of School Commissioners of Mobile County*, 1987)

School personnel must have policies in place to deal with requests for banning books. Every year school boards, teachers, administrators, and librarians face community organizations that want such books as *Huckleberry Finn, Lord of the Flies,* or *Canterbury Tales* banned. In 2003, the U.S. District Court, Western District, of Arkansas heard a case involving the popular *Harry Potter* books. In a 3–2 vote, a school board had voted to restrict access to the *Harry Potter* books in the school library based on "(a) their concern that the books might promote disobedience and disrespect for authority and (b) the fact that the books deal with 'witchcraft' and 'the occult'" (*Counts* v. *Cedarville School District*, 2003). The federal district court ruled that requiring students to have parental permission to check out any of the *Harry Potter* books from the school library was a violation of students' First Amendment rights. Therefore, anticipating these requests and having policies in place will usually defuse an emotional outburst, community conflict, or confrontation with parents.

Reflection...

What are your school policies for handling requests to remove a book from a reading list, a course curriculum, or a library?

Other curricular areas that incite much debate are biology and earth sciences. Dating back to the Scopes "Monkey Trial" of 1925, religious views of the origin of humans have conflicted with scientific views. In 1965 Susan Epperson was a biology teacher in Arkansas and found herself in a dilemma. The prescribed textbook contained a chapter on evolution, but the state of Arkansas had adopted an "anti-evolution" statute in 1928. In *Epperson* v. *State of Arkansas* (1968), the U.S. Supreme Court reversed the Arkansas Supreme Court, declaring that the statute forbidding the teaching of evolution was unconstitutional. Nearly 20 years later, Louisiana attempted to "balance" the teaching of evolution with the teaching of creationism, as espoused in the Book of Genesis of the Bible. Again, the U.S. Supreme Court ruled against the state:

> The Louisiana Creationism Act advances a religious doctrine by requiring either the banishment of the theory of evolution from public school classrooms or the presentation of a religious viewpoint that rejects evolution in its entirety. The Act violates the Establishment Clause of the First Amendment because it seeks to employ the symbolic and financial support of government to achieve a religious purpose. (*Edwards* v. *Aguillard,* 1987)

A more recent national movement promotes the teaching of "intelligent design" in science classrooms. Parents and religious organizations have lobbied school districts, advocating a theory of the origin of humans that differs from the theory of evolution. In 2005 a Pennsylvania federal district court heard the issue, ruling against the parents (*Kitzmiller* v. *Dover Area School District*, 2005). To prepare to meet such challenges, school personnel and parents need to cooperate in establishing a science curriculum that meets state standards and prepares students for the future.

Parents are going to continue to challenge the school curriculum. Instead of such challenges becoming a threat to the autonomy of the schools or the academic freedom of teachers, parents should be welcomed as members of textbook selection and curriculum improvement and evaluation committees. Their suggestions and criticisms should be taken seriously, but school administrators must ensure that representatives of all segments of the community are heard, not just the loudest, most organized, or most articulate. Parental input must be balanced against the professional expertise of teachers and administrators. Schools should have a coherent curriculum revision process to ensure that all textbooks, classroom activities, and instructional methods are meeting educational objectives and standards. Teachers must be sure that their textbooks, supplemental materials, lessons, and activities are based on sound educational principles and are meeting district and state educational objectives and standards. Processes for handling challenges to textbooks, methods, and materials should be developed and followed. Reasonable exceptions should be allowed, but policies defining exceptions to the standards-based required curriculum should be established before the first request is made. Welcoming parents as partners in the teaching–learning process, even in the building of the curriculum, may encourage parents to view the schools as their allies in guiding the upbringing of their children.

Reflection...

The Bradshaws are becoming concerned about how African Americans are portrayed in the literature taught in their children's English classes. They know that *Huckleberry Finn* and *Gone with the Wind are* required reading, but they also know that students are not required to read anything that portrays African Americans in other than slave roles nor are they required to read anything written by African American authors. The Bradshaws do not want any books removed from the curriculum, but they would like to request that books such as *The Autobiography of Malcolm X* and *I Know Why the Caged Bird Sings* be added to the required reading list.

▶ What legal questions should the Bradshaws ask of their children's English teachers? Of the school district?

▶ What do your school board policies, state laws, and case law state about textbook selection?

▶ Who selects textbooks and makes curriculum decisions in your school district?

Special Education.   When the writers of state constitutions provided for systems of public schools that were to be open to all children, they did not consider children with disabilities. Most children with disabilities were not in public schools at the time state constitutions were written, and few persons would have thought that they ever would be. The history of most states in regard to the education of children with mental and physical disabilities is shameful. Either the children were excluded from any type of education at all or were in settings where they received few, if any, educational benefits. Many states felt they had met the needs of children with disabilities by providing residential state schools for the deaf, blind, and "trainable," and quasi-hospital settings for those with severe or multiple mental and physical disabilities.

By the early 1970s, advocacy groups for disabled Vietnam War veterans and other persons with disabilities organized their efforts to secure the civil rights of a formerly silent minority group—the disabled. The result was legislation at the federal level that banned discrimination on the basis of disability (the Rehabilitation Act of 1973) and that awarded funding to schools that provided an individualized, free, appropriate public education in the least restrictive environment for children with disabilities (the Education for All Handicapped Children Act of 1975 or PL 94-142). Amended as the Individuals with Disabilities Education Act (IDEA) in 1991 and again in 2004 as the Individuals with Disabilities Education Improvement Act (IDEIA), this special education law affected the rights of parents in relation to the schools as no previous legislation, at either the state or national level, had done. Because children with disabilities are the least able to serve as their own advocates, the rights of parents as advocates for the rights of their children are safeguarded in this law. In fact, parents are required to be involved in their child's education as they must be active members of the child's Individualized Education Plan (IEP) team. The

IEP team is the group that determines the special education and related services the child will receive during the school year.

IDEIA is a very complex law, but major parental rights that are defined in the law and that affect the relationship between parents and the school include the following:

- The right to be informed of parental rights under IDEIA
- The right to be informed in the parents' native language or other appropriate means
- The right to be informed prior to assessment being done if placement in special education may be the outcome of the assessment
- The right to be informed of outside evaluators and no- or low-cost legal services
- The right to be involved in determining educational goals, services, placement, and transition plans through membership on the IEP team
- The right to be informed prior to any change in placement or services
- The right to see the child's records
- The right to initiate a due process hearing
- The right to receive a transcript of the hearing and the decision
- The right to appeal through the court system

Much case law has resulted from IDEIA and its predecessor laws. In fact, special education has become the subject of most school-related litigation in state courts. The number of children who qualify for special education is increasing each year as medical science improves the survival rate of at-risk babies and accident victims, as assessment measures become more sophisticated and better able to identify children with special needs earlier, and as more physical and mental conditions are categorized as qualifying for some type of special education service. Advocacy groups for children with disabilities are very powerful, and both parents and school personnel need to become more aware of the legal rights of these once forgotten children and work together to facilitate their special education. Otherwise, lawsuits will proliferate.

Reflection...

Can all children be educated? Should all children be educated at public expense?

The first special education case that reached the U.S. Supreme Court involved a hearing-impaired child whose parents wanted the school to provide a full-time sign language interpreter in the classroom. Noting that "this very case demonstrates [that] parents and guardians will not lack ardor in seeking to ensure that handicapped children receive all of the benefits to which they are entitled by the Act," the Supreme Court, nevertheless, ruled against the parents in *Board of Education of Hendrick Hudson Central School District Board of Education* v.

Rowley (1982) because of the efforts the school had made to assist Amy Rowley to benefit from her education. The court said that a school district does not have to "maximize the potential of each handicapped child commensurate with the opportunity provided nonhandicapped children." Amy was advancing at grade level academically and socially, and even the sign language interpreter testified that her services were superfluous.

In 1984 the U.S. Supreme Court was asked to determine the definition of "related services" as provided in the law. Amber Tatro needed clean intermittent catheterization (CIC) every 3 or 4 hours, which the school argued was a medical service that should not be required of school personnel. The parents argued that the service was merely a procedure that would enable Amber to benefit from special education and could be performed by a layperson with minimal training. In ruling in favor of the parents in *Irving Independent School District* v. *Tatro* (1984), the Supreme Court affected the relationship between parents and the school by requiring school personnel to provide services once provided only by parents or nurses.

In 1989 a New Hampshire school district attempted to get the courts to rule that some children with very severe disabilities could not benefit from any type of education and so would be excluded from coverage by the law. Timothy W. was multiply and profoundly mentally and physically disabled, but the United States Court of Appeals, First Circuit, ruled that a child does not have to demonstrate the ability to benefit from education in order to qualify for services, no matter how minimal:

> The law explicitly recognizes that education for the severely handicapped is to be broadly defined, to include not only traditional academic skills, but also basic functional life skills, and that educational methodologies in these areas are not static, but are constantly evolving and improving. It is the school district's responsibility to avail itself of these new approaches in providing an education program geared to each child's individual needs. The only question for the school district to determine, in conjunction with the child's parents, is what constitutes an appropriate individualized education program (IEP) for the handicapped child. We emphasize that the phrase "appropriate individual education program" cannot be interpreted, as the school district has done, to mean "no educational program." (*Timothy W.* v. *Rochester, New Hampshire School District*, 1989)

The *Timothy W.* decision meant that all children with disabilities are to be served by special education, no matter how severe their disabilities. The U.S. Supreme Court merely confirmed this decision without comment, and so it is used as precedent for lower court cases.

Placement of students with disabilities is probably the most controversial topic dividing parents and the schools. Unfortunately, IDEIA and all earlier special education laws have never been fully funded by Congress, leaving states and local districts with much of the cost of compliance. When parents and school personnel disagree over the services or placement of a child with a disability, the issue almost always involves the cost. The parents are interested in getting the best services possible for their child, and the school personnel are interested in containing costs. The result is a growing number of special education lawsuits.

A case that involved the cost of placement was *Florence County School District Four* v. *Carter* (1993). This case resulted from a dispute between a school district and parents over services for a child with learning disabilities. Frustrated by the school district's lack of attention to their requests, the parents removed their daughter Shannon from the public school and placed her in a private school that specialized in services for children with learning disabilities. After Shannon completed her schooling, the parents sued the school district for reimbursement of the tuition charged by the private school. Ruling in favor of the parents, the U.S. Supreme Court commented on the cost argument of the school district:

> There is no doubt that Congress has imposed a significant financial burden on States and school districts that participate in IDEA. Yet public educational authorities who want to avoid reimbursing parents for the private education of a disabled child can do one of two things: give the child a free appropriate public education in a public setting, or place the child in an appropriate private setting of the State's choice. This is IDEA's mandate, and school officials who conform to it need not worry about reimbursement claims. (*Florence County School District Four* v. *Carter*, 1993)

A conflict between parents and school personnel over the least restrictive environment for the education of a child with severe disabilities was heard by the United States Court of Appeals, Seventh Circuit, in 2002. Beth B. had Rett syndrome, a serious neurological disorder that results in severe cognitive and physical disabilities. Her mental capability was difficult to assess due to her extreme communicative and motor impairments but may have been that of a 12- to 18-month-old child. Under the "stay-put" requirement of IDEA, Beth had been educated in regular classrooms at her neighborhood public school for 7 years while the dispute between her parents and school personnel continued. The school recommended that Beth be placed in an Educational Life Skills (ELS) program housed in a neighboring public school and designed for students with mild, moderate, and severe disabilities. The parents disagreed with the ELS placement, and eventually the case went to court. The Seventh Circuit Court ruled that the school's recommended placement of Beth in the ELS program did not violate the least restrictive environment provision of IDEA (*Beth* v. *Van Clay*, 2002).

Placement will continue to be a major source of conflict between parents of special education students and school personnel. In 2007 the United States Court of Appeals, Fourth Circuit, ruled that the IEP must identify the school where educational services are provided, not just that the services are provided somewhere in the district, so that parents are able to evaluate the public school services offered as opposed to private school placement (*A.K.* v. *Alexandria City School Board*, 2007)

A three-factor test commonly used to determine whether or not placement in a regular classroom (mainstreaming or full inclusion) or a special education classroom is appropriate was derived from the United States Court of Appeals, Third

Circuit, in *Oberti v. Board of Education of Clementon School District* (1993). The three factors are (1) reasonable efforts to accommodate the child in a regular classroom; (2) comparison of benefits in a regular classroom with supplementary aids and services to benefits in a special education classroom; and (3) possible negative effects of inclusion with other students in the regular class. These factors are considered by many courts when the placement of a child with a disability is contested.

Which party bears the burden of proof became an issue in a 2005 case. Up to that time, the burden of proof had always been on the school district to show that the disputed decision was the correct one, regardless of whether the parent or the school district brought the case. The U.S. Supreme Court ruled in *Schaffer v. Weast* (2005) that the burden of proof in administrative hearings carried out under the provisions of IDEA lies with the party bringing the dispute to hearing, whether that party is the parent or the school. Because generally the party dissatisfied with a decision involving a special education child is the parent, this decision assured school personnel that when disputes arise with parents, school personnel will not automatically have to show that the decision was the correct one but that parents will first have to show that the decision was the incorrect one.

Reasonable attorney fees are allowed for the winning party in a dispute involving due process issues under IDEA. However, the U.S. Supreme Court ruled that the fees of experts who are not attorneys are not reimbursable to parents (*Arlington Central School District v. Murphy*, 2006).

As parents recognize the advantages of individualized education plans, some demand those services for their child, regardless of the child's disability status. In 2007, the United States Court of Appeals, Fifth Circuit, ruled that a child with behavioral problems that were not related to a legally recognized disability did not qualify for services under IDEIA (*Alvin Independent School District v. A.D.*, 2007).

Attempting to stay abreast of case law plus the continually changing regulations in Section 504 of the Rehabilitation Act, the Individuals with Disabilities Education Improvement Act, and the Americans with Disabilities Act will be a challenge for parents of children with disabilities and the schools that must provide special education and related services. All teachers, not just special education teachers, will have an opportunity to work with children with disabilities. Teachers must learn about special needs and how to meet them through classroom and curriculum modifications and accommodations. Because of the involvement of parents in the education of their children with disabilities, many parents are becoming more involved in the education of all children to a degree not known by the schools previously. Some parents question why every child's education cannot be individualized and why more services are not available for all children. For school personnel, the increased interest of parents in their children's education can be an opportunity to set a tone of cooperation and partnership in striving to meet the needs of all children. Parents can become the greatest advocates for schools if they know schools are working to assist their child in gaining an education. Then the adversarial relationship between parents and the schools will not exist, and costly, time-consuming lawsuits can be avoided.

Reflection...

Joyce has been notified that her daughter, Angie, is going to be assessed for a possible learning disability. Joyce is to sign a card, indicating her approval for the tests, and return it to the school. Because she had no idea that Angie was having any difficulty in school, Joyce is upset and does not want to sign the card.

▶ What legal questions should Joyce ask? What are her rights as a parent?

▶ What do your state law and federal laws say about assessment and parents' rights?

▶ What questions should Joyce ask of the school district? Of the classroom teacher or the special education teacher?

Student Rights.   With all the emphasis on special education, sometimes the rights of students in general seem to take second place. Actually, the rights of students with disabilities were recognized only because of the *Brown* (1954) case, which led to the conclusion that all children have a right to an equal education, and because of an historic student rights case in 1969. In *Tinker* v. *Des Moines Independent Community School District* (1969), the United States Supreme Court declared that "it can hardly be argued that . . . students . . . shed their constitutional rights to freedom of speech or expression at the schoolhouse gate." Thus, the constitutional rights of students were legally recognized for the first time, and the relationship between the school and parents and their students subtly changed. Although *in loco parentis* still governs that relationship, *Tinker* and successive court decisions determined that students have a legal right to an education. That right cannot be denied without due process. When that right to an education is in jeopardy, parents become involved in working with the school's disciplinary procedures, sometimes taking their child's case to court. In most court cases involving student rights, whether the issue is expulsion of a student because of fighting or a student being sent home to change a T-shirt with a vulgar message, the parents are the plaintiffs in the lawsuits because of the legal status of almost all students as minors.

The question often arises of "what process is due" when a student claims that his or her rights have been violated. Unless school officials know about due process, often a student's claim will prevail because the school official will back off in fear of violating a student's rights. Then the rights of other students and school personnel to an orderly educational atmosphere may be jeopardized. Generally, as long as rules allow a student to tell his or her side of the story, are fairly and consistently enforced, and provide for fair and consistent sanctions, due process is satisfied (see *Williams* v. *Cambridge Board of Education*, 2004, and *Wofford* v. *Evans*, 2004). Students and teachers must know what the rules are. The role of student handbooks in due process is to serve as notice to students and parents of the rules and the applicable punishments. The more serious the infraction, the more serious the sanction should be.

More student rights cases are going to court for resolution because of the awareness of individual rights by students and their parents and because many school personnel are not sure of the status of student claims to rights. When school personnel fail to follow due process as outlined in the student handbook or, worse, fail to have a process established, a student's rights may be jeopardized and the courts may be willing to hear the student's case. Generally, the courts do not desire to become involved in the disciplinary procedures of the schools; they prefer leaving those decisions to the educational experts. However, when a student's constitutional rights are violated, the courts will step in.

Reflection...

What rights are included in your school's student handbook? Are rules and sanctions for violation of rules clearly stated? How are parents informed of the school rules and disciplinary sanctions?

One of the areas of student and parent rights that has a long history of violation prior to the passage of a federal law is student records. Before the Family Education Rights and Privacy Act (FERPA) was passed in 1974, school records policies were generally nonexistent. Parents had little or no access to their child's records; yet, third parties (college recruiters, military recruiters, police officers) had only to make a request and a student's file was made available. Few processes were in place to ensure accuracy of records, and the result was blatant violation of the privacy of a student and often the family. FERPA specifies that only parents and educators (who have a need to know) should have access to a student's educational file. That file should contain only official transcripts and other official school documents, not anecdotal notes. The parents have the right to question the information in the file and to write responses to what they perceive as inaccurate data. Requests to see files, to get copies, and to get test scores interpreted do not have to be met on demand; the school cannot be expected to produce records, especially archival records, without notice. Only parents can give permission for third parties to see a student's records. Schools cannot keep secondary or secret files that are used for any decision making about the student's education. Teachers should be aware of records policies and follow them, realizing that parents have rights to see the records of their child but not those of other children. Only one official educational file should exist for each student; a teacher's personal notes are not official records so do not have to be shown to parents. However, those notes should not be used for informing decisions about the child nor kept in any permanent file. In 2002 the U.S. Supreme Court ruled that the practice of students grading each other's papers and then calling out the scores as the teacher posts them in a grade book does not violate FERPA because the classroom assignments are not educational records, as defined by the law (*Owasso Independent School District* v. *Falvo*, 2002). The school can facilitate good relations with parents by informing them of their rights under FERPA, having good records policies in place, and following them.

A new issue to come before the courts deals with the use of the Internet and cell phones in schools. The rapid proliferation of technological devices makes it difficult for courts to keep up, and, to date, the *Tinker* case has been used to determine whether a student's free speech rights have been violated by the use of the Internet and various personal communication devices. In an early case, *Beussink v. Woodland R-IV School District* (1998), a Missouri federal district court used *Tinker* to rule that a homepage created at home by a student was protected speech even though the homepage criticized the school in "crude and vulgar language." However, the United States Court of Appeals, Second Circuit, used *Tinker* to uphold the suspension of a student who used the Internet at home to send out a drawing of a named teacher being shot because the image disrupted the school environment (*Wisniewski v. Board of Education of the Weedsport Central School District*, 2007). Two other federal district courts have also ruled in favor of schools' disciplinary sanctions against students whose use of the Internet to distribute derogatory pictures of school personnel was deemed disruptive (see *Layshock v. Hermitage School District*, 2006, and *Requa v. Kent School District No. 415*, 2007).

In a case involving cell phone use at school, parents claimed that a school policy prohibiting possession of cell phones violated their fundamental right to communicate with their children. The New York Superior Court ruled against the parents (*Price v. New York City Board of Education*, 2007). Therefore, parents' claims that off-school behavior should not result in school disciplinary sanctions and that cell phones are a constitutional right are not being upheld because of the blurring of the line between in-school and off-school actions. However, the higher courts, including the U.S. Supreme Court, have not ruled, yet, on Internet, cell phone, and other communications technology use by students. Instead of waiting for court actions, school personnel should be proactive in developing policies regarding the use of technology before problems arise and then ensure that students and parents are aware of the policies.

Encouraging good relations between parents and the school should be the goal of all teachers and administrators. Parents who feel comfortable coming to the school, calling teachers, or visiting with administrators over school-related issues will be less likely to take their child's side without checking the school's side of the story. Communication channels with parents should be open so that parents know of the school rules and expectations; then they will be less likely to argue when their child breaks the rules. Students and their parents have constitutional rights that cannot be arbitrarily or capriciously violated by the schools, as may have happened in the days prior to *Tinker*. Teachers must be prepared to know the rules, enforce the rules fairly and consistently, and follow the due process outlined in handbooks. Focusing on the student's education and the partnership with parents that can enhance that education may preclude legal resolution to problems that may arise over a student's claim to individual rights.

Student Safety.   With school violence constantly in the media, parents are right to be concerned about their child's safety at school. Although Columbine High School events are shocking, they are rare. Yet, several research studies have reported that many students feel threatened at school, whether physically by bullies or emotionally by cyberbullies. As has been shown in the media, parents of violent students often are unaware of their children's mental or physical capabilities until it is too late.

Therefore, school officials have to take every threat seriously; include sanctions for bullying, fighting, threatening violence, and other antisocial behaviors in student handbooks; and work with law enforcement to ensure the safety of the majority of students at school.

There have always been school bullies and schoolyard fights. However, the escalation of violence in society has led to deadly violence at schools, requiring school officials to determine whether a threat is real. A federal district court in Pennsylvania defined a "true threat" as "statements where the speaker means to communicate a serious expression of an intent to commit an act of unlawful violence to a particular individual or group of individuals." The court went on to list five points to consider in establishing whether a "true threat" has occurred: (1) the speaker's intent, (2) how the intended victim reacted to the alleged threat, (3) whether the threat was communicated directly to its victim, (4) whether the threat was conditional, and (5) whether the victim had reason to believe that the maker of the threat had a propensity to engage in violence. The court in *Latour* v. *Riverside Beaver School District* (2005) used these criteria in overturning the expulsion of a student for composing four rap songs. Although a middle school girl's name was mentioned in one rap song, the court concluded that rap songs, even if they contained violent language, were merely rhymes and metaphors that did not constitute a true threat.

However, a federal district court in New York upheld the 30-day suspension of a 12-year-old student who wrote a story and read it to other students about a boy who went on a killing spree of named students. The court upheld the common judiciary stance that student discipline is a matter for school officials, not for the courts (*D.F.* v. *Board of Education of Syosset Central School District*, 2005).

Teachers and administrators may be the only safety net for students who feel threatened by violence at home, on the streets, and even at school. Schools cannot be sanctuaries for bullies or violent juveniles. Therefore, school officials must protect the rights of all students to a safe educational atmosphere. Most parents want their children to be protected at school and are willing to work with school personnel to ensure that safe school environment.

Reflection...

In light of school violence, including the use of weapons, what rights do school personnel have? What constitutes a weapon? Is it the same for the kindergarten as the high school? What rights do victims of violence in the schools have?

Liability.   This is a litigious age in the United States, and *tort law* is where much of the litigation is occurring. When a suit is brought under tort law, the plaintiff is looking for monetary awards for damages. Anyone can sue anybody for almost anything under tort law. Schools in states that no longer have the policy of governmental immunity (*governmental immunity* means one cannot sue the government) can be held liable for injuries to anyone in the school or at school-related activities if the injuries are shown to have been caused by intent to injure or by negligence. More and more people are willing to sue government entities such as schools because they believe that nobody is really being hurt by a damage award. However, the cost of litigation is very high, regardless of the outcome. Time spent preparing for the case, emotional energy expended on attempting to settle the issue amicably, and actual money damages or increase in insurance premiums are some of the indirect and direct costs associated with every lawsuit filed against a school. School personnel must take all reasonable precautions to prevent students, employees, and guests from being injured while at school, recognizing that lawsuits claiming negligence are all too frequent.

Parents believe that their children will be safe at school and are becoming more willing to sue for damages when a child is injured. Yet, most injuries are the result of accidents, not willful, malicious, or negligent actions by teachers, administrators, or other students. Schools are held to a very high standard of care for students, and when that standard of care is breached, the courts will award damages. Every teacher and administrator must remember that the standard of behavior the courts will use is the ordinary, reasonable, prudent person standard but adapted to allow for the professional training and experience of educators. If a teacher does not do what the ordinary, reasonable, prudent teacher would have done when in the same situation and a student is injured, negligence may have been the cause of the injury and the teacher and school district may be found liable for damages (see *James v. Jackson*, 2005). Similarly, if a teacher or administrator knew or should have known about a potential injury-causing event, structure, or person and an injury occurs, claims of negligence may be upheld. Threats made by students against the safety of others or themselves must be taken seriously and actions must be taken to deter injury. Such threats cannot be ignored, passed off as "kids wanting attention," or "kids just joking or playing around" if liability for injury is to be avoided.

Injuries will happen at school, but parents should be immediately informed and every reasonable action taken to care for the child. Guidelines for all school activities should include provisions for preventing injuries and procedures to follow should injuries occur. All educators should know and follow such guidelines in order to prevent claims of negligence or intent to injure. However, school rules and guidelines should not substitute for common sense and should be written so that teachers and administrators have some flexibility in applying the rule. A band director in Iowa followed his school's zero tolerance policy in regard to student use of tobacco, alcohol, or other drugs when on school trips and sent a ninth grader home alone on a 1,100-mile bus trip. The father sued, claiming the school district and the band director breached their duty of care for the boy's safety (*Ette ex rel. Ette v. Linn-Mar Community School District*, 2002). School personnel must realize that they will be held to a high standard when student safety is jeopardized.

In the legal relationship between parents and the school, liability can become an issue when parents are in the school as visitors, but a related issue is the parent who is working in the school or at school-related activities as a volunteer or paraprofessional. Teachers and staff are generally covered by liability policies of the school when they are acting in the course of their employment. However, insurance policies may or may not cover persons acting under the supervision of an employee, and school personnel should check their district liability policies before asking parents to drive students to activities, to chaperon field trips or other off-campus activities, to supervise classroom activities such as reading groups or art projects, to work as volunteer coaches, to supervise playgrounds or lunchrooms, or to perform any of the dozens of tasks that many parents welcome as opportunities to become involved in their child's school. Everything goes smoothly when parents are involved in the school's activities until either a parent or a student under the parent's supervision is injured. Then lawsuits may arise if malice, intent, or negligence can be shown.

Teachers and administrators cannot delegate their responsibility, which means that if a child or a parent is injured when the teacher or administrator is the person in the supervisory role, the ultimate responsibility for the injury will rest with the employee, not with the volunteer. Therefore, it becomes essential for teachers and administrators to train parent volunteers adequately for their roles, whatever they may be. The professional teaching certificate indicates that the teacher or administrator is experienced in the supervision of large numbers of children and should be able to foretell what types of behavior may occur. The parent volunteer may have no such experience in the school setting and cannot be held liable for being unable to foretell that an action may lead to an injury. Schools should develop guidelines for the use of parent volunteers and follow the guidelines in the selection, training, and supervision of such volunteers. There is some irony in the fact that just at a time when the schools need all the help they can get and want to encourage involvement of parents in the schools, the threat of litigation might deter involving parents. The standard to use always is to do what the reasonable, prudent teacher or administrator would do in similar circumstances.

Reflection...

Susan has begun volunteering at her daughter Jenny's school one afternoon per week. She helps with reading groups, assists the classroom teacher with supervising the playground during afternoon recess, and tutors individual children with spelling, writing, and reading. During one afternoon recess, the classroom teacher was called to the office for an emergency phone call, leaving Susan as the only adult on the playground. The teacher had been gone only a couple of minutes when a small girl fell out of a swing and broke her arm. When running over to the swing set, Susan tripped over a rolling basketball and fell, spraining her ankle badly. Angry at the teacher for leaving her alone, Susan is also worried because she is not sure her health insurance will cover her injury.

▶ What legal questions should Susan ask of the building principal? School district?

▶ Generally, do school insurance policies cover volunteers and children?

One of the areas of liability in which the relationship between parents and schools can become most strained is in the reporting of suspected child abuse. The role of educators in reporting suspected child abuse is mandated by law; teachers and administrators must report abuse to the state social services agency or other designated authority. Schools should have guidelines in place about identifying child abuse, verifying reports of abuse, and the actual reporting process. Failure to report can lead to civil or possibly criminal recriminations against the teacher or administrator.

Reporting a parent for suspected child abuse sets up the potential for a very bad relationship with the parents, but the welfare of the child must be the top priority in all cases. *In loco parentis* is probably most critical here; the school is acting in place of the parent when the parent has abdicated his or her rights by violating the rights of the child. State laws always provide a good faith clause so that teachers who follow the mandate to report suspected abuse are protected should the report turn out to be false but was made in good faith.

One of the worst situations that may arise to destroy good school–parent relationships is when a school employee is suspected of sexually molesting or abusing students and parents learn that other school personnel knew and did nothing about the actions of the abuser. In *Franklin* v. *Gwinnett County Public Schools* (1992), parents reported to school officials that a teacher was having sexual contact with their daughter, and the school officials did not take the report seriously. Only a minimal investigation was conducted, and nothing was done to stop the abuse or remove the teacher from the school. The U.S. Supreme Court ruled that Title IX could be applied to this case, setting the stage for federal court involvement in the violation of student civil rights in these cases when educators, in their official role as government employees, are guilty of abusing students and administrators reasonably knew or should have known the abuse was occurring and did nothing to stop it.

In 2005, the United States Court of Appeals, Eleventh Circuit, ruled that school officials in a Georgia school had conducted an adequate investigation into allegations (that turned out to be true) of a sexual relationship between a female teacher and a high school male student and so had not been "deliberately indifferent," the standard that must be met for a successful Title IX claim (*Sauls* v. *Pierce County School District*, 2005). Therefore, school officials must conduct an investigation into any allegations of improper relationships between students and teachers or staff members in order to protect the student from abuse—both physical and emotional—and the school district of claims of deliberate indifference and potential damage awards under Title IX.

Schools are liable for injuries that occur on the school grounds, whether those injuries are physical or emotional. Developing good relationships with parents so that school personnel and parents can work together when injuries to students occur can prevent the bitterness that sometimes leads to punitive lawsuits. Schools must work to prevent injuries to students and parents when they are on school property or at school-sponsored events. Teachers must realize how vulnerable they are to being held liable for student injuries and take every precaution to prevent injuries. Even though parents cannot sign away their own or their child's rights, permission slips (not waiver slips) for out-of-school activities are necessary to give parents notice about an event and an opportunity to give or deny permission for their child to participate. No one can prevent a lawsuit from being filed, but doing what the reasonable, prudent educator would do in similar circumstances may prevent a lawsuit from going to trial or large damage awards being made.

Discrimination and Harassment. With our nation becoming more diverse, claims of discrimination by members of various minority groups are on the rise as well as claims of reverse discrimination by members of majority groups. Not all claims are valid because not all minority groups are protected under federal and state laws. Discrimination against protected classes of people is illegal. Members of religious minority groups are protected by the First Amendment. Members of racial and ethnic minority groups are protected by the Fourteenth Amendment and such federal civil rights laws as Title VI and Title VII of the Civil Rights Act of 1964. Women (and sometimes men, depending on which gender has historically been the majority group in a setting) are protected by various federal laws, including Title IX of the Education Amendments of 1978. Persons with disabilities are protected by the Rehabilitation Act of 1973 and the Americans with Disabilities Act of 1991. The claims of these and other groups also may be protected by state or municipal laws. In addition, all children are to receive an equal opportunity for an education under federal and state statutes.

For educators, students, and parents, these antidiscrimination laws mean that all children are entitled to an equal opportunity for an education in the nation's public schools. Policies separating students because of race, color, ethnicity, religion, gender, and disability are almost impossible to justify. School districts that are found to discriminate on the basis of these generally unchangeable characteristics risk losing their federal funding.

One area related to discrimination that has received much publicity is athletics. Title IX is very definite in specifying equal opportunity for girls and boys in athletics, and school districts found not to be in compliance with Title IX risk losing all their federal funding, not just funding for athletics. However, Title IX applies much more broadly than just to athletics. School districts must provide equal opportunities for girls and boys in all areas, including curriculum, extracurricular activities, and facilities.

Official discrimination by school districts or school employees is usually brought to public notice quickly and handled through formal channels. More difficult to handle are claims of harassment, which has been defined by the courts as a form of discrimination. Claims of sexual and racial harassment are increasing, whether because of awareness of the problem, media attention to the problem, or intolerant attitudes toward growing diversity in our population. Harassment is difficult to define because every person's tolerance for jokes, comments, teasing, touching, graffiti, and threats differs. However, the relative position of the perpetrator and the victim often determines whether harassment has occurred. Persons in higher positions (employers, supervisors, administrators, teachers) should be very careful that persons in subordinate positions (employees, trainees, students) will not be able to interpret the superordinate's words or actions as harassment.

Teachers and other school personnel must never be involved in any type of harassment of students and should not allow students under their supervision to harass or bully other students. One of the latest issues to come before the courts involves sexual and racial harassment of students by students. In several leading Minnesota cases, parents informed school officials that their children were being harassed by other children, and the school officials did little, if anything, to stop the harassment. When the courts have become involved in harassment cases, whether teacher-to-student or student-to-student, generally the rulings have been in favor of the victims and their parents, especially when documentation exists that the parents complained to the school officials but the harassment or bullying continued.

Reflection...

Connie and Bob are becoming very concerned about stories Allison and Jason are bringing home from school. On the playground at noon, several boys in the fifth grade have started "picking on" some of the younger boys in the first and second grades. The older boys taunt the younger ones, steal their Frisbees, balls, and other toys, and sometimes even pull down the jeans of the younger boys. Jason has become afraid to go outside at noon, but the school rules allow students to stay inside only during bad weather.

▶ What legal questions should Connie and Bob ask of the principal? School district?
▶ What does your state law and case precedent state about harassment?

As our nation's complex diversity increases, so will the potential for discrimination and harassment. Schools will help solve this national problem when discrimination and harassment are not tolerated in schools and students are educated about tolerance for persons who are not like them in every way. Most parents will protect their children from the mental and physical harm of discrimination and harassment, even if they have to go to court. Therefore, teachers and administrators must do all they can to stop discrimination, harassment, and bullying in schools.

Summary

The legal relationship between parents and the schools is becoming more complex every day as more federal and state laws are passed and more court decisions are handed down. Yet, the courts do not want to become involved in school issues; they would prefer that parents and school personnel work out their differences outside the courtroom. School personnel set the tone for parental involvement in schools. If schools refuse to recognize the fundamental right of parents to guide the upbringing of their children, the relationships between parents and the schools may become adversarial. If school personnel fear lawsuits and are always looking for an attorney behind the parent who wants to be involved in his or her child's education, they probably will find one because they will always be on the defensive. If teachers fail to respect the rights of students and parents and fail to maintain an orderly educational atmosphere in their classrooms, all students suffer and parents will be disillusioned about the value of public schools. If schools genuinely welcome parents' involvement in their child's education because it will further the teaching and learning process, then schools and parents can become partners in educating children, not parties to lawsuits where no one wins.

Case Study

The Johnson family is moving to Twin Lakes during the summer because Jack Johnson, the father, has found employment at one of the industrial plants there. Besides Jack (45), the family includes Barbara (44), the mother, and children Jerry (16), David (13), and Julia (9). The Johnsons are a middle-class family who want the best for their children and so are very interested in finding out as much as they can about the Twin Lakes School District before they decide where to look for a house to buy.

Jerry will be a junior in high school and wants to continue playing soccer and baseball. He is also interested in taking as many AP classes as are available because he wants to attend an Ivy League college. David will be an eighth grader, and he struggled last year in a middle school where he was the target of some bullies. Not a natural athlete like Jerry, David might want to try out for track but is more interested in playing his trumpet in a jazz band and writing for the school newspaper. Julia has Down syndrome and attended the fourth grade last year, spending most of her time in a special education classroom where she met her IEP goals for academic and social skills.

Devout Christians, the Johnson family has considered home schooling their children. In their former hometown, Jack and Barbara belonged to an organization that promoted the study of intelligent design in the schools. One of the reasons they are enthusiastic about moving to Twin Lakes is that it is a larger community that should offer greater educational opportunities for their children.

Twin Lakes (population 40,000) is a Midwest city with roots that predate the Civil War. Formerly a blue-collar industrial city, Twin Lakes is becoming home to more professionals as the community college expands its academic curricula and several technology companies relocate to Twin Lakes. Its school district has two high schools, four middle schools, and six elementary schools. Last year a charter school that promotes independent study through an online curriculum was established after its charter was accepted by both local and state school boards.

Questions and Considerations

1. What legal issues may have an impact on the Johnsons as they move to Twin Lakes?
2. What legal questions should the Johnsons ask of school district personnel?
3. To whom should the Johnsons talk to find out about the educational situation in Twin Lakes?
4. What advice would you give the Johnsons if you were an administrator in the Twin Lakes School District?

Recommended Activities

1. Read the sections in your state constitution that deal with education. How are they similar to or different from the example education clause in the North Dakota Constitution?

2. After the next legislative session in your state, get a copy of all the new laws dealing with schools. How will these laws affect your local schools? The parents in your district?

3. How do the schools in your district "accommodate" religion? Do you agree or disagree with these practices?

4. How would you answer parents' arguments that sex education is a family or religious issue that has no place in schools?

5. What student fees are charged in your school district? Why are fees charged? Where do the fees go?

6. What are the standards for the school curricula in your state? What types of standardized high-stakes tests are mandated in your state or local district? Interview some administrators, teachers, and parents about their views of the standards and high-stakes tests.

7. Discuss classroom modifications needed by students in special education with special educators and regular classroom teachers.

8. Visit a local elementary, middle, and high school and watch for signs of student-to-student bullying or harassment in the halls, lunchroom, playgrounds, and other common areas.

9. What do regular education teachers need to know about special education? What related services are provided students with disabilities in your school district? Why has special education become such a litigious issue in many schools?

10. How can school personnel control drugs, alcohol, gangs, and weapons in the schools and not violate student rights?

11. What textbooks or other education materials have been challenged in your school district? By whom? For what reasons?

12. Interview some students about their feelings about safety at their school. Do they feel safe? Do they know of weapons being brought to school? Would they feel safe reporting incidents of bullying, cyberbullying, inappropriate cell phone use, drug use or dealing, or other activities that are generally against school rules to a teacher or principal? Why or why not?

13. What do you think will be the role of the courts in parent–school conflicts in the future?

Children's Books

The following children's books are suggested as a way of helping your students consider issues in this chapter.

Our Living Constitution Then and Now
J. Aten
Reading Level: Ages 3–6
Good Apple (1987)

Supreme Court Book
P. J. Deegan
Abdo & Daughters (1992)

Everything You Need to Know about Your Legal Rights
K. Fox
Rosen Publishing (1992)

The Congress
C. R. Green & W. R. Sanford
Rourke Publishing (1990)

The Presidency
C. R. Green & W. R. Sanford
Rourke Publishing (1990)

The Constitution
G. K. Jenkins
Rourke Publishing (1990)

Separation of Church and State
I. C. Kleeberg
Franklin Watts (1986)

The Bill of Rights and Landmark Cases
E. Lindop
Franklin Watts (1989)

*We the People: The Constitution of the United
   States of America*
P. Spier
Doubleday (1987)

The United States Constitution
J. K. Williams
Compass Point Books (2004)

Additional Resources

Educational Law and Parental Rights

Websites

American Bar Association
www.abalawinfo.org
American Civil Liberties Union
www.aclu.org

Children's Defense Fund
www.childrensdefense.org

Children Now
www.childrennow.org

FindLaw
http://public.findlaw.com

References

A.K. v. Alexandria City School Board, 484 F. 3d 672 (4th Cir. 2007).

Abington School District v. Schemmp and Murray v. Curlett, 374 U.S. 203, 83 S. Ct. 1560 (1963).

Alvin Independent School District v. A.D., 503 F. 3d 378 (5th Cir. 2007).

Arlington Central School District v. Murphy, 126 S. Ct. 2455 (2006).

Beth v. Van Clay, 282 F. 3d 493 (7th Cir. 2002).

Beussink v. Woodland R-IV School District, 30 F. Supp. 2d 1175 (E.D. Mo. 1998).

Board of Education, Island Trees Union Free School District No. 26 v. Pico, 457 U.S. 853, 102 S. Ct. 2799 (1982).

Board of Education of Hendrick Hudson Central School District Board of Education v. Rowley, 458 U.S. 176, 102 S. Ct. 3034 (1982).

Board of Education of Mountain Lakes v. Maas, 152 A. 2d 394 (App. Div. 1959).

Brown v. Board of Education of Topeka, Kansas, 347 U.S. 483, 74 S. Ct. 686 (1954).

Cardiff v. Bismarck Public School District, 263 N.W. 2d 105 (ND 1978).

Cornwell v. State Board of Education, 314 F. Supp. 340 (D. Md. 1969), affirmed 428 F. 2d 417 (4th Cir. 1970), cert. denied 400 U.S. 942, 91 S. Ct. 240 (1970).

Counts v. Cedarville School District, 295 F. Supp. 2d 996 (W.D. Ark. 2003).

Cude v. Arkansas, 377 S.W. 2d 816 (Ark. 1964).

D.F. v. Board of Education of Syosset Central School District, 396 F. Supp. 2d 119 (2005).

Edwards v. Aguillard, 482 U.S. 578, 107 S. Ct. 2573 (1987).

Elk Grove Unified School District v. Newdow, 542 U.S. 1 (2004).

Epperson v. State of Arkansas, 393 U.S. 97, 89 S. Ct. 266 (1968).

Ette *ex rel.* Ette v. Linn-Mar Community School District, 656 N.W. 2d 62 (Iowa 2002).

Florence County School District Four v. Carter, 114 S. Ct. 361 (1993).

Franklin v. Gwinnett County Public Schools, 112 S. Ct. 1028 (1992).

Good News Club v. Milford Central School, 121 S. Ct. 2093 (2000).

Hartzell v. Connell, 679 P. 2d 35 (Cal. 1984).

In re Interest of Rebekah T., 654 N.W. 2d 744 (Neb. Court of Appeals 2002).

Irving Independent School District v. Tatro, 468 U.S. 883, 104 S. Ct. 3371 (1984).

James v. Jackson, 898 So. 2d 596 (La. App. 4th Cir. 2005).

Kitzmiller v. Dover Area School District, 400 F. Supp. 2d 707 (W.D. Pa. 2005).

Lander v. Seaver, 32 Vt. 114 (Vermont 1859).

Latour v. Riverside Beaver School District, 2005 WL 2106562 (W.D. Pa. 2005).

Layshock v. Hermitage School District, 412 F. Supp. 2d 502 (W.D. Pa. 2006).

Lee v. Weisman, 112 S. Ct. 2649 (1992).

Leebaert v. Harrington, 332 F. 3d 134 (2nd Cir. 2003).

Medeiros v. Kiyosaki, 478 P. 2d 314 (1970).

Mozert v. Hawkins County Board of Education, 827 F. 2d 1058 (6th Cir. 1987).

Oberti *ex rel.* Oberti v. Board of Education of Clementon School District, 995 F. 2d 1204 (3rd Cir. 1993).

Owasso Independent School District v. Falvo, 534 U.S. 426, 122 S. Ct. 934 (2002).

Owens v. Colorado Congress of Parents, Teachers and Students, 92 P. 3d 933 (Col. 2004).

People of State of Illinois ex rel. McCollum v. Board of Education of School District No. 71, Champaign County, Illinois, 333 U.S. 203, 68 S. Ct. 461 (1948).

Pierce v. Society of the Sisters of the Holy Names of Jesus and Mary, 268 U.S. 510, 45 S. Ct. 571 (1925).

Price v. New York City Board of Education, 387 N.Y.S. 2d 507 (N.Y. Sup. 2007).

Requa v. Kent School District No. 415, 492 F. Supp. 2d 502 (2007).

Sauls v. Pierce County School District, 399 F. 3d 1279 (11th Cir. 2005).

Schaffer v. Weast, 546 U.S. 49, 126 S. Ct. 528 (2005).

School District of the City of Pontiac v. Secretary (Spellings) of the United States Department of Education, 512 F. 3d 252 (6th Cir. 2008).

Smith v. Board of School Commissioners of Mobile County, 827 F. 2d 684 (11th Cir. 1987).

Smith v. Ricci, 446 A. 2d 501 (1982).

Timothy W. v. Rochester, New Hampshire School District, 875 F. 2d 954 (1st Cir. 1989).

Tinker v. Des Moines Independent Community School District, 393 U.S. 503, 89 S. Ct. 733 (1969).

Wallace v. Jaffree, 472 U.S. 38, 105 S. Ct. 2479 (1985).

West Virginia State Board of Education v. Barnette, 319 U.S. 624, 63 S. Ct. 1178 (1943).

Williams v. Cambridge Board of Education, 370 F. 3d 630 (6th Cir. 2004).

Wisconsin v. Yoder, 406 U.S. 205, 92 S. Ct. 1526 (1972).

Wisniewski v. Board of Education of the Weedsport Central School District, 494 F. 3d 34 (2nd Cir. 2007).

Wofford v. Evans, 390 F. 3d 318 (4th Cir. 2004).

Zelman v. Simmons-Harris, 536 U.S. 639, 122 S. Ct. 2460 (2002).

Zorach v. Clauson, 343 U.S. 306 (1952).

Chapter Eleven

Family Violence: The Effect on Teachers, Parents, and Children

Tara Lea Muhlhauser
Director of Children and Family Services Division, North Dakota Department of Human Services

Douglas D. Knowlton
Dakota State University

To understand the impact of family violence it is important to be aware of the dynamics of child maltreatment (abuse and neglect) and domestic violence. This chapter prepares teachers by providing general information about the characteristics of child victims, working with parents regarding the care and nurture of their children, and the impact on children of violence between adults and other children in the home. Specific recommendations for action and decision making are found throughout the chapter. This chapter helps you:

▶ Understand the educational and developmental implications of child abuse, child neglect, and domestic violence.

▶ Grasp the severity and prevalence of family violence and the impact on children.

▶ Gain applicable skills for communicating with children and parents when high-risk indicators for violence and abuse are present.

▶ Understand the role of teachers in reporting and identifying high-risk situations and in working with parents in these situations.

▶ Have access to information on resources available at the county, state, and national level.

▶ Understand the family dynamics of, and nexus between, child abuse and domestic violence.

▶ Understand the impact of the dynamics of violence on every family member, including others in the household.

Every teacher envisions a classroom of energetic, enthusiastic, and responsive students—students who come to school nurtured, nourished, and without worries that might intrude on their ability to actively engage in the learning process. This vision is now tempered by our growing realization of the fact that "it is not always happy at our house." Many students are instead coming to school encumbered by the anxieties, fears, and diminished self-esteem typical of children who have been victims of abusive and neglectful situations (Becker et al., 1995; Cohen & Perel, 2004; Miller-Perrin & Perrin, 1999; Sousa et al., 2010). The following statistics regarding these children alert us to the magnitude of this problem:

- In 2008, there were an estimated 772,000 child victims of maltreatment in this country; 71% were neglected, 16% physically abused, 9% sexually abused, and 7% emotionally maltreated.
- Nationwide approximately 3.3 million children were referred for preventative services because of a protective service or safety concern in 2008.
- An estimated 1,740 children died as a result of abuse or neglect in 2008.
- More than half of all reports of maltreatment came from professionals. Educators were the single largest professional category of reporters (17%). Other professionals included law enforcement officials, medical professionals, and child-care providers.
- One in four women will experience domestic violence in her lifetime.
- Research has shown that child abuse occurs in up to 70% of families that experience domestic violence, and 40% to 60% of men who batter woman also batter their children.

Although these data on children as direct victims of violence are sobering, it is clear that just being in the presence of one family member perpetrating violence against another member, such as spouse abuse, may have a significant negative impact. In the past, domestic abuse and child abuse had traditionally been treated as separate issues with interventions offered by different agencies in the community. More recently, agency personnel recognize the need for collaboration to effectively and efficiently address the multiplicity of issues presented by violent families (Schechter & Edleson, 1999). As the research clearly points out, violence between partners frequently occurs in the same homes where violence is perpetrated against children (Bancroft, 2007; Carter, Weithorn, & Behrman, 1999).

Children who are living in a home situation that is threatening or assaultive will expend energy coping with that probability. Whether it is devising plans for avoiding the threat or obsessively thinking about what might happen after school, these students may not have their full resources available for functioning in the classroom. They may experience developmental delays and face a myriad of difficulties gaining social competence (Herrenkohl et al., 2008; Cohen & Perel, 2004; Gerwitz & Edleson, 2004).

Studies estimate that anywhere from 45% to 50% of men who batter their female partners also abuse children in the home. In an early study, Stark and Flitcraft (1988) found that as many as two-thirds of abused children had mothers who were being beaten. Other studies, including more recent research, have confirmed this premise (Carter et al., 1999). This abuse might be from direct physical aggression or by being in the wrong place at the wrong time; for example, the children might try to protect the parent or they simply get in the way. Given that these child witnesses may also be victims due to the exposure to violence, it becomes important to have an appreciation of the level of domestic violence occurring in our homes. It is estimated that 4 million women are battered every year—one every 9 seconds. Two million are beaten severely, and the FBI estimates that between 1,400 and 1,500 women are murdered every year by former husbands or boyfriends. The U.S. Department of Justice estimates that 95% of assaults on spouses/partners or ex-partners are committed by men against women.

In addition, we cannot overlook our national concern about the increase of violent and antisocial behaviors on the part of our children. If we are to understand the root causes of this antisocial behavior, including the daily reminders of the increase in adolescents' school and community violence, the need for information regarding possible explanations becomes a high priority. Over the span of two decades a significant body of information has pointed to child maltreatment as a causative factor for this aggression (Renner et al., 2006; Hoffman-Plotkin & Twentyman, 1984; Wodarski, Kurtz, Gaudin, & Howing, 1990). Although our national attention has been focused on this aggressive behavior, other important developmental consequences for children have also been found: increased anxiety (Wolfe & Mosk, 1983), depression (Kaufman & Cicchetti, 1989), attachment and social interaction deficits (Crittenden, 1992), academic difficulties (Salinger, Kaplan, Pelcovitz, Samet, & Kreiger, 1984), and decreased self-esteem (Fantuzzo, 1990). Any one of these consequences has implications for a child's school performance, and all of them have been tied to school success or failure.

From this data we know that children are arriving for their busy school day having experienced traumas that clearly influence their responsiveness in the classroom. If we are to serve these children well, we need to understand some of the theories about family violence, as well as the characteristics of children who are victims, the characteristics of parents who are victims, and the characteristics of parents who may engage in this violent behavior. In addition, there are societal issues that have frequently been cited as environmental factors contributing to child maltreatment. Economic factors such as high unemployment and poverty are associated with increased incidents of abuse. More recently we have seen an increase in homeless families, and the children in these families are vulnerable to a variety of maltreatment issues. One prominent researcher has recently begun to link child abuse and domestic violence with animal abuse (Linzey, 2009).

- How have some of the named environmental factors contributed to a society in which children are routinely maltreated?
- What attitudes, values, and beliefs do we hold that might support maltreatments?
- When does "appropriate" discipline become abuse?

All of these questions are relevant to the relationships between families and teachers because the answers may have an impact on a child's capacity to learn. Once we understand some of these dynamics and can recognize their impact on our students, we then need to know what we can do to support and, if necessary, intervene with these families. It is clear that children who are physically and emotionally maltreated are going to present significant challenges for our schools and communities. Although some educators might find it tempting to try to ignore this problem or perceive it as just a "family" issue, our students' needs and their cries for help will continue to push us toward a more proactive approach.

Reporting Child Abuse and Neglect

Child abuse and neglect is a widespread social phenomenon. The dynamics of abuse and neglect can be found in all settings within the community. Income, race, gender, and family structure aside, the dynamics of adult-to-child violence and the effects of such violence cut across many strata in our classrooms. Although the risk factors may be more obvious with certain groups of children, all children remain at risk from abuse and neglect in every home represented in our classrooms.

Child abuse is widely defined as an act of power and control over a child by use of corporal punishment, exploitation (sexual and physical), or emotional or psychological maltreatment. Abuse is often categorized as physical, emotional, or sexual maltreatment (Tower, 1999). *Neglect* is often defined as the deprivation of the child's needs that in turn leaves the child vulnerable to a variety of conditions, harm, or emotional strain. Neglect is categorized as physical, emotional, or medical neglect and includes "lack of supervision" (Dubowitz, 1999; Tower, 1999). Psychological maltreatment is often found within other forms of abuse and neglect and is a devastating byproduct of abuse and neglect (Tower, 1999).

Although defining the terms is not difficult, identifying individual acts or situations as abusive or neglectful can be challenging. Many times the categorization or identification of an act as abusive or neglectful depends on factors such as severity, frequency, and pervasiveness of the action as well as the age and vulnerability of the child.

Generally we hold those in caretaking positions responsible for meeting the child's needs and protecting the child from exploitation; those caretakers may not always be the child's parents. A diverse group of adult caretakers (e.g., child-care providers, relatives, live-in partners, grandparents) and the abusive or neglectful caretakers' access to the child can complicate the child abuse and neglect dimension.

Characterizing the home life of abused and neglected children requires the examination of three separate areas: the caretakers, the child, and the environment where abuse and neglect is found. The dynamics are often described as either *conduct*—what the parent/caretaker does (e.g., striking the child), or *conditions*—the issues a parent/caretaker may be faced with (e.g., mental illness, drug, or alcohol addiction).

Parental Factors in Child Abuse and Neglect

Caretakers who resort to violence in their interactions with children frequently are described as making poor decisions in a time of stress, that is, using corporal punishment out of anger to exert control over a difficult situation. Their reaction is often intensified by the lingering presence of drugs or alcohol (or the effects of an addiction), the effects of mental illness, the presence of physical illness or depression, or unhappiness about their life situation. All of these factors can trigger a stress response. In addition, research has identified two other important variables in predicting the risk of child maltreatment: caretakers for whom violence is a learned response (often because of violent family histories and relationships) and caretakers who lack basic parenting skills. In this latter group, the lack of skills can mean a deficit in understanding a child's developmental needs and vulnerabilities as well as a lack of skills to respond to a child's perceived misbehavior (e.g., an infant who cries a lot).

Reflection...

Corporal punishment in schools and spanking as a form of discipline are much debated issues. The Swedish government has banned all spanking. Should the U.S. government take similar steps to ban spanking or corporal punishment? Should there be specific limitations on types of physical discipline? Are there social supports of use of physical discipline in our communities? For more information on corporal punishment, see S. Hart (Ed.), *Eliminating Corporal Punishment: The Way Forward to Constructive Child Discipline* (2005).

For example, an underskilled and stressed parent may resort to shaking a baby because the parent is frustrated and thinks the act will provide a signal to the baby that it is time to quit crying and resume sleep. In doing so, the parent exposes the infant to a developmental vulnerability (head injury by shaking the baby) and misjudges the child's developmental readiness to understand both act and consequence. Frequently, abusive parents simply don't understand how damaging certain attempts to discipline or punish younger children can be. Lack of skills also plays a part in the abuse of older children. With younger children, parents frequently reach a threshold of frustration and strike out. These parents think that the child will then heed their request or understand and learn their point of view.

Children who are sexually exploited by family members (often called intrafamilial child sexual abuse) also have caretakers who fall into the above dynamic, but in a slightly different way. In these families it is common to see a blur of boundaries among the generations (for example, between parent and child). The expectations of family members follow that pattern, and the children are expected to step into the shoes of an adult member for some of the family functions (i.e., sexual partner). This creates great chaos and confusion in the family, which compounds the secret being kept between the adult and child in regard to the intimate relationship (Faller, 1990; Miller-Perrin & Perrin, 1999).

The caretaker's available cognitive and emotional skills have a significant impact on the choices they make, particularly when stressed. The lack of such skills or compromised skills can contribute to a condition that makes children in their care more vulnerable to abuse.

Many of the same characteristics are seen in neglectful situations. Neglect dynamics are also inextricably bound to environmental characteristics. These conditions frequently set the stage for a situation of child neglect to occur. Often the scenario of a child's life includes both neglect and abuse.

Chronic neglect can be one of the most difficult situations to work with in the classroom. It is not uncommon to find conditions of physical neglect creating a dynamic of emotional neglect for a child in class. For example, a child who has poor hygiene creates a social situation that affects his or her ability to build or sustain peer relationships. Even with intervention, sometimes the parental condition and conduct are so pervasive and deeply ingrained in the family structure and history that successes are small and take time. In these situations, it is important not to underestimate the impact a positive school relationship can have on a child. We may be meeting, or have an opportunity to meet, some basic self-esteem, emotional, and developmental needs that are not being met in the home.

As we work to build relationships with parents or caretakers who may arouse our concerns, remember that they often are isolated physically, emotionally, or psychologically from the needs of their children because they are frequently overwhelmed with other issues in life. Isolation, in combination with a lack of parenting or social/emotional skills and any conditioning factors (such as alcohol abuse or mental illness), can be difficult to work with. You may benefit from working with others as a team to build and maintain personal relationships with these parents. Teachers play a crucial role in identifying children's needs and in assessing how children respond to various stimuli. Therefore, in a teaching role, they are important in helping parents "learn" how to help their children learn. Providing this mentoring can be significant in helping parents develop skills and strengths that will have a positive impact on the parents' relationship with the child(ren). As a result, teachers are working with parents in the "teamwork" relationship to develop stronger parent–child bonds, thus increasing the "protective factors" that have a positive impact on child safety.

Environmental Factors in Abuse and Neglect

Although child abuse and neglect are widespread in all communities, we must be aware of the important environmental indicators of risk. Poverty and the surrounding conditions (unemployment, poor housing and diet, etc.), social isolation, and the stress of single parenting, or a combination of these factors, are widely accepted as environmental risk factors. Certainly the lack of income contributes in direct and indirect ways to the child abuse and neglect dimension (Tower, 1999). For instance, a parent may not have the ability to afford after-school child care; this places the child in an unsupervised situation every day for several hours. This may not be a true reflection of the parent's decision-making capability; it may instead reflect the financial reality the parent faces and how the parent may have to balance and weigh risk factors (e.g., a job that will bring in money versus supervising their 8-year-old child after school). Parents who are not socially isolated in this scenario may have the ability to leverage available resources to provide care for their child in the form of a neighbor or a play/recreation group with revolving parental supervision. If the parents are socially isolated, their choices and alternatives narrow and this may create undue stress on the parent–child relationship, leaving the child more vulnerable to risk. This can be a significant factor of stress for new American families or those with limited English-language capacities.

This scenario creates a good opportunity for home–school partnerships with an emphasis on a win-win outcome. If the school or community provides alternatives for working parents in these situations, the child stays in a safe after-school environment where he or she is supervised. In this setting, the child is given the chance to build peer relationships or enhance a variety of skills. The parent can then complete a full day of work with assurance that his or her child is safe. This can provide that layer of support that can make a tremendous difference in the parent–child relationship.

Characteristics of Child Victims

All of us will at some time be involved with a child who has been a victim of physical or emotional abuse, sexual abuse, and/or neglect or who has been a witness to family violence. Therefore, it is important that we are familiar with the characteristics and behaviors of these children. Although each child is an individual and will have a different configuration of symptoms or classroom problems, there are some commonalities to their psychological and behavioral status. Sometimes children will give us simple clues that indicate they are uncomfortable in certain situations or appear to be different than other children in the classroom. At other times, they may be hostile and angry and may tend to alienate other children as well as teachers or other adults in the school setting. Perhaps one of the most striking symptoms is a dramatic change in a child's demeanor or personality. These changes are often sudden; for example, a child who has been outgoing and involved with other children may suddenly become isolated and avoidant. These changes are often reflected in a student's performance, grades, or social situations. A sudden drop in responsiveness or accomplishment in the classroom can be a cue that something significant is going on in the child's life. Below are some of the typical distressful emotions that a child victim may experience and explanations of how they might affect children at different developmental points.

Anxiety.   One of the child's early developmental needs is for security and safety. A young child who does not feel safe may have significantly elevated anxiety. This might show up in simple nervous behaviors (habits such as twirling hair or biting nails) or actually be seen in the development of phobias, panic disorders, obsessive-compulsive disorders, and so forth. At times this anxiety may be associated with a particular person or environment, or it may be more generalized with the child constantly feeling on edge or irritable. Young children often use avoidance to cope with this kind of anxiety or develop other symptoms such as nightmares, bed-wetting, or physiological symptoms such as headaches or stomach distress.

As the child gets older, the anxiety may take on other behavioral manifestations. In adolescence these young people may cope with their anxieties by becoming aggressive or resorting to the use of alcohol and drugs to numb some of the agitation or irritability they may experience.

Depression. Depression can be seen in children through classical symptoms (e.g., change in appetite, change in sleep patterns, overall mood problems). It is important to note that in young people, depression can also look like an agitated state with increased activity and inattention. There have even been children diagnosed with attention deficit disorder (ADD) or attention deficit hyperactivity disorder (ADHD) who may have been depressed, but their activity levels were significantly increased due to agitation. Although the diagnosis of depression is not often made for very young children, these symptoms could clearly be manifestations of a child who is in an abusive situation.

In the area of adolescent development, depression may take on a more serious note, particularly as it is paired with an increase in adolescent impulsive behavior. This impulsiveness can add to the potential for drug and alcohol abuse and the risk of adolescent suicide.

Anger. When expressed by young children, anger may simply be increased irritability or uncontrollable behavior; it may be a result of their difficulty understanding and/or expressing feelings of anger. Sometimes this anger can become self-directed and contributes to depression or high-risk behavior. At other times, these children may display behavioral difficulties and become more aggressive, particularly toward other children. This behavior is often difficult to manage in the classroom, and if we don't see this behavior as a cry for help, we may take a destructive or punitive approach with the child. Anger expressed by adolescents tends to be more hostile and can be seen in aggressive behaviors with the increased possibility of sexually aggressive behavior.

Self-Concept. It is becoming increasingly clear that a child's sense of self can be negatively affected by involvement in any abusive situation. Levels of self-esteem (a child's positive view of him- or herself) and appropriate self-concept (a child's realistic view of his or her capabilities) are crucial to the ongoing psychological development and well-being of children. An assault on this self-esteem can negatively affect the child's developmental progress. When children have an impaired sense of self or a reduced sense of self-esteem, they are often unable to control their own emotions. They may not be able to calm or soothe themselves when they are in a situation in which there is a lot of stress. This can also have an impact when children need to separate or become independent from others; a diagnosis of separation anxiety disorder may be associated with these particular times. Later in the child's development, there may be difficulties defining one's own boundaries or appreciating the needs and desires of others in their environment. In addition, there are reports of increased suggestibility or gullibility, inadequate self-protectiveness, and a greater likelihood of being victimized or exploited by others.

Posttraumatic Stress Disorder (PTSD).   Highly distressing or threatening environmental situations can cause a reaction that has been called posttraumatic stress and diagnosed as posttraumatic stress disorder (PTSD). This disorder is evidenced by (a) a numbing of emotions or responsiveness to events; (b) frequent reexperiencing of events sometimes through intrusive thoughts or nightmares; and (c) increased irritability, sleep disturbance, and poor concentration. Children who have been abused tend to exhibit more posttraumatic fear, concentration problems, and anxiety than do children who have not been abused.

Although these symptoms are most common in children who have been exposed to high levels of violent or abusive behavior, there are other symptoms that are sometimes problematic and indicative of this type of exposure. These include the potential for suicide, high-risk sexual behavior, and a higher incidence of suicidal thinking and behavior in children. Some children, particularly adolescents, might engage in indiscriminant sexual behavior as an expression of the need for acceptance and self-worth. It is also not uncommon to see eating disorders such as anorexia or bulimia. Bulimia is evidenced primarily by binging and purging behaviors, and these symptoms have been associated with higher incidents of abuse, particularly sexual abuse.

One of the most obvious characteristics of these children is their difficulty negotiating within their personal relationships. A sudden change in the child's relationship with other children can be a clue that there is a source of additional stress in his or her life. These children may engage in avoidance behaviors (withdrawal, isolation), which create problems with their interpersonal activities. These children may actually perceive themselves as less worthy of appropriate relationships. In general, abused children have been found to be socially less competent, more aggressive, and more withdrawn than their nonabused counterparts. In later life, it becomes difficult for these children to develop intimate relationships, and if they do develop, the relationships often center on some type of ambivalence or fear about becoming vulnerable.

Reflection...

Consider the characteristics of abused children and how each would appear in a classroom environment. How will you be able to recognize these behaviors? How will you address the undesirable behaviors? Would the characteristics differ for neglected children?

Intervention and Treatment

Obviously, the intervention and treatment process cannot begin until the children and families at risk of further abuse and neglect have been identified. That is why it is so crucial for us to identify and report abusive and neglectful situations and incidents to the local child protection agency. Once identified, an assessment process is conducted by social workers to determine the safety of the child in his or her present environment, to identify risks, and to recommend a treatment service. Usually this process will include some determination, by the child protection services agency or multidisciplinary child protection team, of whether the reported act or situation is recognized as abusive or neglectful.

If the child is in need of immediate protection from further abuse or harm, the child protection agency will seek the authority of the court to remove the child from this harmful environment. Taking temporary or emergency custody of a child generally means that the child will be placed with a nurturing relative or in a foster home or facility until the agency personnel and court determine it is safe for the child to return home. If it is found that the abuse or neglect did occur, the court will usually mandate parents/caretakers to participate in some kind of recommended treatment before the child will be returned home. In child sexual abuse cases, the child protection agency may require that the abusive adult leave the home and cease to have contact with the child. In this situation, sometimes the child can remain at home with the supervision of a supportive parent while the abusive adult is monitored and allowed to return home after completing a sex offender treatment program or is released from a secured facility.

Treatment recommended by the child protection agency is generally part of a plan for the child and/or family. Many different treatment options are available and can vary greatly depending on the resources available in each community. Often the family is involved in some educational process to assist the parents/caretakers with developing or enhancing parenting skills. Support groups, individual therapy, family therapy, and in-home, family-based services (with a specific set of goals and a caseworker in the home) are used. If there are conditions such as mental illness or alcoholism, the parent/caretaker is referred to the appropriate treatment facility or agency prior to participating in the aforementioned treatment services. Also, social workers frequently work with families to provide or suggest resources in the community to assist with financial issues, feelings of isolation, and domestic violence. In some cases, we may be asked to be involved in a team process to monitor, recommend, and assist agency treatment providers with assessment, development, or implementation of a treatment plan for a child and/or family.

Long-Term Effects of Abuse on Children

Significant research and pages of popular media have been devoted to the long-term effects of abuse and neglect on children. There are so many possible effects that it is difficult to predict an outcome. Some individuals even claim to gain a sense of strength from the early maltreatment. Much of the current research on resiliency indicates that positive forces in a child's life may be able to mitigate some or most of the harm of abuse and neglect, although nothing will completely obliterate the abuse or neglect harm from a child victim's life or memory (Cohen & Perel, 2004; Wolin & Wolin, 1993). The maltreatment clearly has a diminishing effect on a child's abilities, although which abilities and to what degree seem to vary on a case-by-case basis.

Research has documented neurological, cognitive, behavioral, psychological, emotional, and intellectual effects. Educationally, the effects of child abuse and neglect have been linked to academic outcomes and lower test scores, indicating that maltreatment may diminish a child's ability to fully participate and advance (Herrenkohl et al., 2008; Cohen & Perel, 2004; Tower, 1992).

Domestic Violence

Domestic violence is defined as a pattern of assaultive and controlling behaviors in the context of an intimate adult relationship. Although domestic violence is often referred to as spouse abuse, that term is not inclusive enough to apply to the violence that happens between adult intimates outside of marriage or in the context of a familial environment. The pattern of assaults and control frequently takes the form of coercion, terrorism, degradation, exploitation, and actual violence in the form of physical assault (Peled, Jaffe, & Edelson, 1995; Renzetti, Edelson, & Bergen, 2001). One author (Ganley, 1993) describes domestic violence as "hands-on" (meaning the physical assaults) and "hands-off" (meaning the psychological pattern of terrorism that leaves no visible scars). According to the FBI in its 1990 Uniform Crime Report, battering is the establishment of control and fear in a relationship through violence and other forms of abuse. The batterer uses acts of violence and a series of behaviors, including intimidation, threats, psychological abuse, isolation, and privilege, to coerce and control the other person. The violence may not happen often, but it remains as a hidden (and constant) terrorizing factor.

When research tells us that 30% of all women will suffer from some form of abuse in an adult relationship (Peled et al., 1995), it is clear that the effects of domestic violence are far reaching in any community setting, including the classroom. The pattern of adult violence usually has ebbs and flows; there are periods of chaos and immediate fear interrupted by periods of controlled calm, apology, and remorse. The violence often escalates with each new onset and in the later stages often involves weapons. As domestic violence survivors will tell you, they must spend tremendous energy "keeping a lid" on everything so that an episode of violence does not erupt. A frequent question is why they stay in such situations. Aside from the obvious issue of parenting, there are financial concerns, family issues, and practical issues of where to live (many battered women who leave abusive relationships find themselves and their children homeless), how to provide for children if one leaves a relationship, and danger (LaViolette & Barnett, 2000). Also, research confirms that women who leave their batterers are at a 75% greater risk of being killed by the batterer than those who stay (Hart, 1990). Casey Gwin, a prominent prosecutor who led legal reform in this area through his work with the City of San Diego, reminds us that the better question to ask is "Why does he hit her?"

Characteristics of Violent Households

Although the great majority of reported incidents of battering involve male batterers, there is a small percentage of reported battering by women. Because domestic violence is a crime, the report of an incident can be a difficult time for a family and a confusing time for the children. Many once thought that the effects on children living in a violent home were minimal, but research is strongly confirming that the effects are clearly damaging, both because children are caught, literally, in the crossfire and because they are passive witnesses to violent and abusive acts (Holden, Geffner, & Jouriles, 1998; Jaffe, Wolfe, & Wilson, 1990; Peled et al., 1995; Roy, 1988).

Reflection...

Isn't it difficult to understand why someone who is being battered or exploited doesn't leave the relationship? Why might it be difficult or dangerous for someone to leave a violent relationship? What are the risks of leaving? What are the risks of staying? What might be some of the early characteristics or signals in our own relationships that could include the potential for violent interactions?

Often we hear of violent incidents that children disclose in the classroom long before the incidents are reported to any authority. As classroom teachers, we must be prepared to listen to the children and let them talk about what they have observed and heard at home and give them an opportunity to talk about what they are feeling. How, and if, you then approach the issue with a parent will be a crucial decision. Consideration must be given to issues of safety, shame, and guilt of the victim; the stigma of being battered; and fear on the part of both the child and the battered parent. The pattern of control in violent families is so pervasive that it may take a battered parent years before she is ready to take the risk of leaving the violent relationship—or even acknowledge the violence in the relationship.

Violent interaction between intimate partners creates the same kind of recurring crisis and chaos that we see in families where there is abuse and neglect. Although conditions such as alcohol use and abuse and mental illness may aggravate the pattern of power and control in a family, the use of power and control to dominate family members is a learned behavior, not a result of the use or misuse of chemical substances, biological factors, or a chemical imbalance. According to researchers and therapists in the field, men who batter minimize or deny the seriousness of their behavior; externalize responsibility for the violence to other situations and people; have a need to control and dominate people, most specifically their partners; and isolate their victims to keep the abuse inside the family (Cardarelli, 1997; Stordeur & Stille, 1989).

From the other perspective, battered women can be so compromised by fear that their ability to respond to a situation of violence can be diminished. Psychologically, research shows that battered women can be characterized by the following:

> learned helplessness (i.e., the belief that their best efforts to be effective will produce random results); a diminished perception of alternatives (to the violence, especially); a heightened tolerance for ideas that do not belong together (e.g., I love him and I fear him); and knowledge of the abuser's potential for violence and the range of violent acts which they can perform. (Blackman, 1996)

These characteristics can also diminish these women's ability to nurture children and provide the necessary encouragement and support for their children's emotional growth and development and sense of security. Susan Schechter, an expert in the field of domestic violence, was frequently quoted as saying "the best way to protect the children is to protect their mother." Because of the battered woman's response to the violence, she may not be able to fully protect her children while they continue to live in a violent environment (Roy, 1988). However, we shouldn't assume that a mother who is in a violent relationship is automatically unable to meet her child's needs.

Intervention and Treatment

Because domestic violence is a crime, intervention is available through law enforcement agencies. Most states have a protocol used for domestic violence cases that determines how arrests will be made and how the case will proceed in the criminal justice system. Arrest has been shown to be an effective intervention in domestic violence situations. It is important for the intervention process to include a comprehensive treatment component to assist batterers with "unlearning" the learned behavior. During treatment, the batterer learns new skills and ideas to help replace old behavior with acceptable and appropriate ways of expressing anger and managing power and control in relationships. Many treatment programs are available in community settings; the best programs combine elements of education, therapy, self-awareness, and crisis management in a group therapy setting. Most comprehensive programs include weekly sessions for at least 24 weeks.

Battered women are provided treatment consisting of support through formal support group sessions and individual therapy, generally available through a community domestic violence agency. Many programs also provide treatment services for children by using a support group/education process or play therapy to help the child identify, express, and understand feelings.

Many communities currently have efforts of ongoing collaboration to provide a team approach for delivery of services and to enhance the array of services and intervention available to assist families and children living in violence (Shepard & Pence, 1999). Because the effects of violence are so far reaching in our communities, it is important for us to be involved with collaborative efforts and understand the issues from the perspectives of domestic violence advocates, child abuse and neglect agencies, and law enforcement (Klein, Campbell, Soler, & Ghez, 1997). Involvement at this level can also assist us in building confidence in how we can respond when one of our students discloses a violent incident at home, when a colleague discloses a violent incident, or when a parent confides in us about a situation. The potential for lethality in these incidents is great, and we must be prepared to use community resources in assisting families and children in finding a safe haven and a way out of the cycle of violence.

Long-Term Effects of Domestic Violence on Family Members

The effects of domestic violence on children, as stated earlier, correlates with the child's developmental stage and the severity and frequency of the abuse. The effects must always be assessed on a case-by-case basis—some children may experience a traumatic result from witnessing or being exposed to only one act. Other children possess amazing resiliency. Generally, research shows that boys who witness violence are three times more likely to grow up to use violence in their intimate relationships than those boys not exposed to family violence (Stark & Flitcraft, 1996). This same research shows that violence is quite a legacy; sons of violent fathers have an estimated rate of woman abuse 1,000 times higher than the sons of nonviolent fathers. Conversely, girls who witness their mothers being abused may have a greater rate of tolerance for abuse in a relationship (Hotaling & Sugarman, 1986). The body of research on the connection between violence and short- and long-term effects continues to grow. Several of the experts in the area recently noted that almost 100 studies report associations between exposure to adult domestic violence and current child or later adult problems (with the current child population studied for both direct and secondary impact) (Gerwitz & Edleson, 2004).

According to Jaffe in some early research in the field, one-third of the children witnessing violence show behavioral and emotional disruptions, anxiety, sleep disruption, and school problems. Approximately 20% to 40% of the families of chronically violent delinquent adolescents had family histories of domestic violence (Jaffe et al., 1990). Other research indicates that depression and reduced verbal, cognitive, and motor abilities are predictable results of witnessing adult violence (Holden et al., 1998; Carter et al., 1999; Schechter & Edleson, 1999). Significant volumes of research consistently show that witnessing violence as a youth promotes the use of violence in adulthood as a means of solving problems and gaining control. Research on the long-term effects on adults show that depression, low self-esteem, emotional trauma and posttraumatic stress, and revictimization are often experienced by survivors of violence (Bolton & Bolton, 1987). All of these factors must be considered before examining a specific situation and creating a plan or opportunity to work on building a relationship with a parent who is living with violence.

The Link Between Child Abuse and Domestic Violence

As educators we have been sensitized to the issues of child abuse. We have been given information on the reporting procedures to employ when we suspect abuse, but few of us have been aware of the significant problems caused when children witness or are exposed to adult violent behavior in their homes. There is a growing awareness of the link between domestic violence and child abuse in children's lives. The American Humane Association (AHA) was one of the first national organizations to highlight this link in its publication *Protecting Children* (1995).

One of the articles in the AHA publication, written by Schechter and Edleson (1995), cited studies that indicate the link among patterns of response between children who are witnesses and those who are actually abused themselves. Many other authors and researchers (see references in previous sections) continue to reconfirm this link in the area of family violence. Increased aggression and antisocial behaviors, lowered social competence, higher anxiety and depression, and lowered verbal, cognitive, and motor abilities were found to exist when children are exposed to the range of family violence (Holden et al., 1998). The cognitive and emotional implication for the educational setting is obvious. If we, as teachers, are to promote and facilitate learning, we must be aware of the negative impact family violence has on our students.

Because the impact of family violence may affect the child differently at different ages and developmental phases, it is important for educators and child-care providers to understand its impact from the age and developmental perspectives of their students (Schechter & Knitzer, 2004). Recent research shows that the development of risk and resiliency frameworks for better understanding the child's behavioral and developmental response to the violence is an essential tool for educators. This will assist the educator and child-care provider to understand and give a context for creating an environment that will help the child move forward (Cohen & Perel, 2004; Gerwitz & Edleson, 2004).

Because of the interrelatedness of child abuse and domestic violence, there has been some tension between the Child Protective Services and those services directed at helping victims of domestic violence. For example, child protection social workers might determine that if a woman is not able to protect herself, then she might not be able to protect her children. The domestic violence advocates feel that the battered woman is the best person to judge the level of safety and fear. If she continues to stay in the situation, they respect her decision and provide support. These different perspectives can lead to differences in the recommended intervention. Thus, cross-agency collaboration is crucial in arriving at a resolution that will protect both mother and child(ren).

Another interesting factor that has recently received the attention of researchers and policy makers is the connection between family violence and animal abuse (Arkow, 2003; Flynn, 2000; Ascione, Weber, & Wood, 1999). The co-occurrence of animal abuse and family violence was first "discovered" by domestic violence advocates as they heard the stories of women and children who came into shelters for protection across the country. Those women and children would not only recount the horrors of the treatment they received, but also express concern for their pets, who often had to be left behind as they fled the violent home. Research has documented that 88% of homes with abused and neglected children also have abused or neglected pets (Boat, 2002; Ascione, Weber, & Wood, 1997).

Our vision of a classroom of children who are completely free from violence in their homes may not be realistic. However, the first step in creating change in our communities is to recognize, identify, and acknowledge the presence of family violence. For an interesting call to action on how to end child abuse and neglect, see Victor I. Vieth, *Unto the Third Generation: A Call to End Child Abuse in the United States within 120 Years* (2004). The problem can be overwhelming and lead to a feeling that nothing can be done to protect our students. The information presented in this chapter is best used as a knowledge base to increase our confidence and empower us to make a difference in our students' lives. The following recommendations provide positive and proactive courses of action.

Recommendations for Action

Be Alert to Behavioral Cues

By educating ourselves we can be aware of the kinds of behavioral manifestations that we may see in our classrooms. These are most clearly seen in academic and social clues, with the primary indicator being sudden changes in academic performance, social isolation, or aggression. There may also be indications in achievement test score problems, truancies, suspensions, and infractions of disciplinary codes.

Emotional and psychological cues are also evident and may include the change from one particular demeanor to another—for example, a child who has been cooperative becoming more hostile, angry, and alienating.

Be Alert to the Cues That Parents May Provide

Your contacts with family members, such as conversations with parents during parent conference time or other contacts may provide some clues as to what may be going on in the family. Be especially alert for the following parental behaviors that may be an indication of potential problems:

- Blames or belittles child
- Sees the child as different from his or her siblings (in a negative way)
- Sees the child as bad, evil, or a "monster"
- Finds nothing good or attractive in the child
- Seems unconcerned about the child
- Fails to keep appointments or refuses to discuss problems the child may be having in school
- Misuses alcohol or drugs
- Behaves in bizarre or irrational ways

By being in contact with the family, we may be able to tell whether there are situations arising that are potentially dangerous to both the child and the family members.

And, because of the special relationship teachers enjoy with parents, teachers are in a perfect position to recognize cues and work to build stronger parent–child interactions and relationships, thus increasing the protective factors that will work to keep children safer in their home.

Interacting with the Child

When having a conversation with a child in which issues arise that lead to concern, there are some guidelines that can be helpful in responding to the child. Remember that there is no benefit in conducting an investigation yourself—that is the role of the child protective services staff. When it is necessary to talk to the child about a situation, remember that the child may be fearful, apprehensive, or actually in pain. It is, therefore, important to make the child as comfortable as possible. The person who talks with the child should be someone whom the child trusts and with whom he or she feels safe. There may be an individual in the school who has been trained and is more capable of performing these interviews, such as the school social worker or psychologist. Remember to conduct these kinds of conversations in a private and nonthreatening place to reinforce to the child that he or she has not done anything wrong. The following suggestions will prove helpful in the interviewing process:

- Children need to be assured and reassured that they are not in trouble and they have not done anything wrong. Children in these situations often feel responsible and blame themselves for the abuse, neglect, or family dynamics, and there is some potential that a conversation about these issues could increase those feelings. Children need to know clearly and directly that they are *not* at fault.
- It is important to assure the child that information he or she provides will not be shared with other teachers or classmates, but may have to be shared with a social worker or law enforcement officer.
- If we feel that we will have to report the information, we should inform the child while continuing to let the child know that we will be his or her support and that the child can come to us at any time.
- When talking with a child, make sure the language used is at an appropriate developmental level. If the child says something that is confusing or not understandable, ask for clarification.
- Do not press for answers or details if a child seems unwilling to give them. Again, this should not be an investigation; the child needs to feel protected if he or she provides information. Initial and repeated interviews in cases like this have sometimes led to the dismissal of criminal charges because of legal problems with the interview process.
- Don't ever insist on seeing a child's injuries; if the child wants to show the injuries, don't hesitate to let him or her do so using good professional judgment. Be sure pieces of clothing are never removed; if for some reason we must remove clothing to view an injury, we must be sure a school nurse or an appropriate school official is present.

Guidelines for Talking with Parents

Sometimes a conversation during a parent conference leads to concerns about abuse or violent behavior. A decision should be made as to whether the teacher is the most appropriate person to meet with the parent or whether a principal or some other staff member would be in a better position to speak with the parent. Often, parents will be apprehensive and may be angry when first confronted about the existence of violent behavior. It is important to make the parents feel as comfortable as possible. Again, conversations should be in private and parents should be informed immediately as to what action might be taken. Try to be empathetic and do not display any kind of anger, repugnance, or shock. It is usually best not to give advice but to allow the parent to make some determination of his or her own course of action. This is particularly true for cases in which there has been some domestic violence and the mother has disclosed information; it will be up to her to make some decisions regarding future action. To force her into some kind of position or to give strong advice may be disempowering to her and create more problems for the family.

Reporting Child Abuse and Neglect

Educators are mandated, by both state laws and federal standards and regulations, to report concerns or suspicions about child abuse and neglect and sometimes about domestic violence. These regulations often tell us what is required and expected of us. Many state statutes specifically name educators as mandated reporters; other statutes indicate that any citizen must report. It is necessary for teachers to have copies of their state's guidelines, laws, and local regulations regarding this reporting and to be prepared by reviewing this information. When reporting incidents or suspicions, most states will require some basic information. This may include:

1. Child's name, age, and address; parent's name and address
2. Nature and extent of the injury or condition observed
3. Prior injuries and when they were observed
4. Reporter's name and location (sometimes this is not required but it is often helpful to child protective services staff)

The National Education Association offers a publication entitled *How Schools Can Help Combat Child Abuse and Neglect*. As cited in Tower (1992), it provides an outline to aid schools in preparing appropriate school policy. Such a policy should include answers to the following questions:

1. At what point should the teacher report child abuse? Suspicion? Reasonable cause to believe? (This may be based on not only school policy but also state law.)
2. Who does the teacher notify? Nurse? Principal? School social worker?
3. What specific information does the teacher need to know to report?
4. What other school personnel should be involved?
5. Who makes the report to the appropriate authorities? How?
6. What information should be included in the report? (This may be dictated by state law and protective service agency protocol.)

7. What followup is expected on reported cases?
8. What role will the school play in possible community/child protection teams?
9. What commitment does the school have to in-service training or community programs? (pp. 36–37)

Reporting is often a difficult and anxiety-provoking process for us. Often personal feelings about parents or a particular child may have an impact on our decisions. It is difficult for people to make decisions that cause others to become angry. Because of this, we sometimes fear for our own safety. At times, we may also feel that we are not appropriately supported by administrators or other school officials, and this may have some impact on our decisions. In other cases, previous difficulties or bad experiences with child protective services or law enforcement may make us hesitant about reporting. This hesitancy may involve thoughts that "nothing can be done." Often we feel left out of the "information loop" with regard to what happens to the child after child protective services has become involved. State confidentiality laws and policies at times reduce the ability to share information with all individuals involved with the child and family. However, some state laws often allow a release of information from child protective services to other professionals when the individual is the member of a multidisciplinary team. This is another area in which you must read your state law and policy to discover what role and what information you will be allowed in the case.

Awareness of Community, State, and National Resources

It is important for us to be aware of the various programs in our community that offer services to children and families, particularly those intervening in and providing treatment for violent families. Locate your child protection agency for more information regarding child abuse and neglect issues in your community and contact either the domestic violence program or a law enforcement agency for more information on domestic violence issues. These programs can provide a profile of the needs of families in the community as well as educational resources to assist you and your students, colleagues, and parents in learning more about the issues and available services.

Several national resources provide information on family violence. The National Resource Center on Domestic Violence (www.nrcdv.org) is an excellent resource that has many fine materials available at no cost. The Child Welfare Information Gateway (www.childwelfare.org) also has excellent materials. There may be similar state entities or affiliates that provide information specific to your state or community. The local child welfare or domestic violence programs will be able to provide you with local resources.

Our Role as Educators

The most important role we can play in family violence situations is to identify and recognize the presence of violence. If the violence involves or affects a child, we need to report and support the child and parent in the best possible way. This is the first step in breaking the cycle of family violence.

Case Study

Geenha is a 31-year-old working mother of two children: Sarty, who is 7 and in school, and Bim, who is 16 months old. Geenha is new to the Dorchester community. She has lived there about 6 months and resides in an apartment with her kids. Geenha works as an administrative assistant for a small insurance company. She is separated from Bill, Bim's father, and he currently lives in another state.

Geenha and Bill are not married and resided together for the past 4 years, with the exception of the past 6 months when she relocated. They have not had a prior history of violence or threats of violence in their relationship, although they've had a "stormy" relationship. Neither Geenha nor Bill have had any contact with protective service agencies in the past regarding the children in their household.

Recently, Bill came to Dorchester to visit the children. Geenha and Bill got into a violent argument and Bill beat Geenha badly. He got scared and left; she called 911. The argument happened when Sarty was at school; Bim was at home sleeping in another room. Before the ambulance came, Geenha made arrangements with her neighbor who was her regular child-care provider to pick up Sarty at school and to take care of Bim; she called and the neighbor came over. Geenha then went to the hospital where she was treated for a broken arm, internal bleeding, and a concussion. They admitted her to the hospital. Several hours later the neighbor called to tell Geenha the police arrived and took the children into custody. They stated that the children would be placed into foster care because "they couldn't be in the custody of a stranger." Geenha was upset and

called her cousin (who lived across the border in a neighboring state) to go to the precinct office and get the children. The cousin attempted and the police refused to disclose where the children were. They refused to place the children with this cousin. Geenha was then served with papers to appear in court where she as charged with child neglect for "engaging in domestic violence."

In the child protective agency in Dorchester, the policy was to remove and place any children who were exposed to adult domestic violence in foster care as it was determined to be maltreatment of a child.

Questions and Considerations

1. Should witnessing domestic violence automatically be considered child maltreatment?
2. If so, what are the implications from the perspective of the child, the adult victim, and the adult offender? What are the public policy implications of this action and agency policy?
3. If not, what are some other factors you might consider in determining whether witnessing abuse is child maltreatment?
4. If a child tells you about the fights the adults in his or her home are having, would you as an educator or child-care professional report this as child abuse and neglect?

(*Note:* This was an actual case taken from a recent landmark court case in New York: *Nicholson v. Williams*, 203 F. Supp. 2d 153. You can find more information on this case and the decision the court(s) made on the websites listed.)

Summary

Preservice teachers and even some beginning teachers often say that they just want to "teach." However, as this chapter has shown, the idea of just "teaching" is not true anymore. Children bring many different issues to school that interfere with their ability to learn. One of the major issues is family violence. Teachers need to understand the dynamics and symptoms of family violence in order to help the child or refer the child to other professionals for help. This chapter helped you understand the educational and developmental implications of child abuse, neglect, and domestic violence. Whereas the focus in the past was just on child abuse and neglect, educators and others realize that domestic violence has a tremendous impact on the child in your classroom. Teachers need to have the resources available and know the high-risk indicators for violence in order to help the child and family deal with the violence and even escape the violence by moving to safer environments. The child, in that situation, needs to know that his or her classroom is part of that safe environment.

Recommended Activities

1. Invite child protective services or domestic violence staff to provide a staff development in-service on reporting and identifying high-risk situations.

2. Participate in child abuse and neglect prevention activities such as wearing a blue ribbon during the month of April to bring attention to the issues.

3. Investigate whether a specific curriculum has been adopted by your school to address family violence or child abuse and neglect issues.

4. Have students design a poster and theme for the class on child abuse/neglect or domestic violence to speak to children living with daily violence in their home.

5. Gather and distribute a list of community resources of agencies/groups that respond to and help families who are violent.

6. Role-play a parent conference in which you suspect your student has witnessed significant violence in the home. Identify your feelings as you struggle with the idea of reporting or identifying the violence.

7. Get involved as a community or agency volunteer in a "safe shelter" or domestic violence prevention agency.

Children's Books

The following children's books are suggested as a way of helping your students consider issues in this chapter.

Child Abuse
Gail Stewart
Reading Level: Ages 8–10
Thomson Gale (2002)

Child Abuse
William A. Check, Dale C. Garell, Solomon
   H. Snyder, Robert W. Blum, Charles
   E. Irwin (Eds.)
Reading Level: Young Adult
Chelsea House (1991)

Whispers Down the Lane
Beverly Lewis
Reading Level: Ages 12 & up
Bethany House (1991)

*Something Happened and I'm Scared to Tell: A
    Book for Young Victims of Abuse*
Patricia Kehoe, Carol Deach (Illustrator)
Reading Level: Ages 5–7
Parenting Press (1986)

Family Violence
Kate Havelin
Reading Level: Ages 9–11
Capstone Press (1999)

No More Secrets for Me
Oralee Wachter, Jane Aaron (Illustrator)
Reading Level: Ages 6–10
Little, Brown & Company (2002)

*A Place for Starr: A Story of Hope for Children
    Experiencing Family Violence*
Howard Schor, Mary Kilpatrick (Illustrator)
Reading Level: Ages 9–12
Kidsrights (2002)

My Body Is Private
Linda Walvoord Girard, Linda W. Girard, Kathleen
    Tucker (Eds.), Rodney Pate (Illustrator)
Reading Level: Ages 5–8
Albert Whitman (1992)

What Jamie Saw (A Newbery Honor Book)
Carolyn Coman
Reading Level: Ages 9–12
Front Street (1984)

*I Don't Want to Go to Justin's House
    Anymore*
Heather Klassen
Reading Level: Ages 9–12
CWLA Press (1999)

What Is Up When You Are Down?
David Marx
Reading Level: Ages 4–8
Children's Press (2000)

Mommy and Daddy Are Fighting
Susan Paris
Reading Level: Ages 4–8
Seal Press (1986)

*Home Is Where We Live: Life at a Shelter
    Through a Young Girl's Eyes*
Jane Hertensten
Reading Level: Ages K–3
Cornerstone Press (1995)

A Safe Place
Maxine Trottier
Reading Level: Ages 4–8
Albert Whitman & Co. (1997)

Additional Resources

Monographs and Fact Sheets

Bragg, H. (2003). *Child protection in families experiencing domestic violence.* U.S. Department of Health and Human Services, Administration on Children and Families.

Excellent publication available from the National Clearinghouse on Child Abuse and Neglect Information, website is listed in Website resources.

Children and Domestic Violence Facts—National Coalition Against Domestic Violence. Listed under Websites; on the website, go to "resources."

Schechter, S. (Ed.). (2004). *Early childhood, domestic violence, and poverty: Helping young children and their families.* Packard Foundation.

This is a series of six papers, with an introductory paper, that looks at the varying impacts and responses to children who witness and are impacted by domestic violence. Highly recommended for educators and child-care providers. [*Note:* This is an excellent resource that you can download at: http://www.uiowa.edu/~socialwk/Community Resources.shtml

Child Abuse and Neglect, Domestic Violence, and Family Violence

Books

Cardelli, A. (1997). *Violence between intimate partners: Patterns, causes, and effects.* Boston: Allyn & Bacon.

Dubowitz, H. (Ed.). (1999). *Neglected children: Research, practice, and policy.* Thousand Oaks, CA: Sage.

Jasinski, J., & Williams, L. (Eds.). (1998). *Partner violence: A comprehensive review of 20 years of research.* Thousand Oaks, CA: Sage.

Kantor, G., & Jasinski, J. (Eds.). (1997). *Out of the darkness: Contemporary perspectives on family violence.* Thousand Oaks, CA: Sage.

Myers, J., Berliner, L., Briere, J., Hendrix, C., Jenny, C., & Redi, T. (Eds.). (2001). *The APSAC handbook on child maltreatment* (2nd ed.). Thousand Oaks, CA: Sage.

Nelson, M., & Clark, K. (Eds.). (1986). *The educator's guide to preventing child sexual abuse.*

This may be the best single source on the topic of child sexual abuse. It is an important part of every educator's professional library.

Tower, C. (1999). *Understanding child abuse and neglect* (4th ed.). Boston: Allyn & Bacon.

Videos

Child Abuse

This video deals with the subject of physical and emotional abuse. It identifies common characteristics of the offender, examines therapy for young victims of physical and sexual abuse, and offers tips in selecting child-care settings for young children. (19 minutes, color)

Films for the Humanities & Sciences
Phone: 800-257-5126

Websites

American Humane Association
www.americanhumane.org

American Professional Society on the Abuse of Children (APSAC)
http://www.apsac.org/

Child Abuse and Prevention Network
www.child-abuse.com

Child Welfare Information Gateway
www.childwelfare.gov

Domestic Violence
www.domesticviolence.org

End Abuse
www.endabuse.org

Minnesota Center Against Violence and Abuse
www.mincava.umn.edu

National Clearinghouse on Child Abuse and Neglect Information
http://www.happinessonline.org/LoveAndHelp Children/p7.htm

National Coalition Against Domestic Violence
www.ncadv.org

National Domestic Violence Hotline
www.ndvh.org

National Council on Child Abuse and Family Violence
www.nccafv.org

National Institute of Mental Health (NIMH)
www.nimh.nih.gov

National Resource Center on Domestic Violence
www.nrcdv.org

Prevent Child Abuse America
www.preventchildabuse.org

Stop Family Violence
www.stopfamilyviolence.org

References

Arkow, P. (2003). Breaking the cycles of violence: A guide to multi-disciplinary interventions. *The Latham Foundation for the Promotion of Humane Education,* 8–9.

Ascione, F., Weber, C., & Wood, D. (1999). The abuse of animals and domestic violence: A national survey of shelters for women who are battered. *Society and Animals, 5*(3), 205–218.

Bancroft. L. (2007). *When Dad hurts Mom: Helping your children heal the wounds of witnessing abuse* . NY: Berkley Publishing Group.

Becker, J., Alpert, J., Subia Big Foot, D., Bonner, B., Geddie, L., Henggeler, S., Kaufman, K., & Walker, C. (1995). Empirical research on child abuse treatment: Report by the child abuse and neglect treatment working group, American Psychological Association. *Journal of Clinical Child Psychology, 24,* 23–46.

Blackman, J. (1996). "Battered women": What does this phrase really mean? *Domestic Violence Report, 1*(2), 5, 11.

Boat, B. (2002). Links among animal abuse, child abuse, and domestic violence. *Social Work and the Law.* Binghamton, NY: Haworth.

Bolton, F. G., & Bolton, S. R. (1987). *Working with violent families: A guide for clinical and legal practitioners.* Newbury Park, CA: Sage.

Cardarelli, A. (Ed.). (1997). *Violence between intimate partners.* Boston: Allyn & Bacon.

Carter, L. S., Weithorn, L. A., & Behrman, R. E. (1999). Domestic violence and children: Analysis and recommendations. *Domestic Violence and Children, 9*(3), 4–20.

Cohen, J .A ., & Perel, J. M. (2004). Treating child abuse-related posttraumatic stress and comorbid substance abuse in adolescents. *Child Abuse & Neglect 27,* 1345–1365.

Crittenden, P. (1992). Children's strategies for coping with adverse home environments: An interpretation using attachment theory. *Child Abuse and Neglect, 16,* 329–343.

Dubowitz, H. (Ed.). (1999). *Neglected children: Research, practice, and policy.* Thousand Oaks, CA: Sage.

Faller, K. C. (1990). *Understanding child sexual maltreatment.* Newbury Park, CA: Sage.

Fantuzzo, J. (1990). Behavioral treatment of the victims of child abuse and neglect. *Behavior Modification, 14,* 316–339.

Federal Bureau of Investigation. (1990). *Uniform crime report.* Washington, DC: U.S. Government Printing Office.

Flynn, C. (2000). Why family professionals can no longer ignore violence toward animals. *Family Relations, 49*(1), 87–95.

Ganley, A. L. (1993). Workshop Notes, "Domestic violence in civil cases," North Dakota Judicial Conference, Bismarck, ND, November, 22, 1993.

Gerwitz, A., & Edleson, J. (2004). Young children's exposure to adult domestic violence: Toward a developmental risk and resiliency framework for research and intervention. *Early Childhood, Domestic Violence, and Poverty: Helping Young Children and Their Families, 6.*

Hart, B. (1990). Gentle jeopardy: The further endangerment of battered women and children in custody mediation. *Mediation Quarterly, 7,* 317–330.

Hart, S. (Ed.). (2005). *Eliminating corporal punishment: The way forward to constructive child discipline.* Paris, France: UNESCO.

Herrenkohl, T. I., Aisenberg, E., & Herrenkohl, R. C. (2008). *Trauma, violence, and abuse.* Retrieved January 11, 2011 from www .herrenkohlconsulting.com/avresources.asp

Hoffman-Plotkin, D., & Twentyman, C. (1984). A multimodel assessment of behavioral and cognitive deficits in abused and neglected preschoolers. *Child Development, 55,* 794–802.

Holden, G., Geffner, R., & Jouriles, E. (Eds.). (1998). *Children exposed to marital violence.* Washington, DC: American Psychological Association.

Hotaling, G. T., & Sugarman, D. B. (1986). An analysis of risk markers in husband and wife violence: The current state of knowledge. *Violence and Victims, 1*(2), 101–124.

Jaffe, P., Wolfe, D., & Wilson, S. (1990). *Children of battered women.* Newbury Park, CA: Sage.

Kaufman, J., & Cicchetti, D. (1989). Effects of maltreatment on school age children's socioemotional development: Assessment in a day camp setting. *Developmental Psychology, 25,* 516–524.

Klein, E., Campbell, J., Soler, E., & Ghez, M. (1997). *Ending domestic violence: Changing public perceptions/Halting the epidemic.* Thousand Oaks, CA: Sage.

LaViolette, A., & Barnett, O. (2000). *It could happen to anyone: Why battered women stay.* Thousand Oaks, CA: Sage.

Miller-Perrin, C. L., & Perrin, R. (1999). *Child maltreatment: An introduction.* Thousand Oaks, CA: Sage.

Peled, G., Jaffe, P. G., & Edleson, J. L. (1995). *Ending the cycle of violence.* Newbury Park, CA: Sage.

Renner, L. M., & Slack, K. S. (2006). Intimate partner violence and child maltreatment: Understanding intra- and intergenerational connections. *Child Abuse & Neglect, 30*(6), 599–617.

Renzetti, C., Edelson, J., & Bergen, R. (2001). *Sourcebook on violence against women.* Thousand Oaks, CA: Sage.

Roy, M. (1988). *Children in the crossfire.* Deerfield Beach, FL: Health Communications.

Salinger, S., Kaplan, S., Pelcovitz, D., Samit, C., & Kreiger, R. (1984). Parent and teacher assessment of children's behavior in child maltreating families. *Journal of the American Academy of Child Psychiatry, 23,* 458–464.

Schechter, S., & Edleson, J. (1995). In the best interest of women and children: A call for collaboration between child welfare and domestic violence constituencies. *Protecting Children, 11*(3), 6–11.

Schechter, S., & Edleson, J. L. (1999). *Effective intervention in domestic violence and child maltreatment cases: Guidelines for policy and practice.* Reno, NV: National Council of Juvenile and Family Court Judges.

Schechter, S., & Knitzer, J. (Eds.). (2004). *Early childhood, domestic violence, and poverty: Helping young children and their families.* Packard Foundation and University of Iowa-Social Work. (Series of 6 papers).

Shepard, M., & Pence, E. (Eds.). (1999). *Coordinating community responses to domestic violence.* Thousand Oaks, CA: Sage.

Stark, E., & Flitcraft, A. (1988). Women and children: A feminist perspective on child abuse. *International Journal of Health Services, 18,* 97–118.

Stark, E., & Flitcraft, A. (1996). *Women at risk: Domestic violence and women's health.* Thousand Oaks, CA: Sage.

Stordeur, R. A., & Stille, R. (1989). *Ending men's violence against their partners: One road to peace.* Newbury Park, CA: Sage.

Tower, C. (1992). *The role of educators in the protection and treatment of child abuse and neglect.* U.S. Department of Health and Human Services. DHHS Publication No. (ACF) 92-30172.

Tower, C. (1999). *Understanding child abuse and neglect* (4th ed.). Boston: Allyn & Bacon.

Vieth, V. (2004). Unto the third generation: A call to end child abuse in the United States within 120 years. *Journal of Aggression, Maltreatment & Trauma, 12*(3/4).

Wodarski, J., Kurtz, P., Gaudin, J., & Howing, P. (1990). Maltreatment and the school age child: Major academic, socioemotional, and adaptive outcomes. *Social Work, 35,* 506–513.

Wolfe, D., & Mosk, M. (1983). Behavioral comparison of children from abusive and distressed families. *Journal of Consulting and Clinical Psychology, 51,* 702–708.

Wolin, S. J., & Wolin, S. (1993). *The resilient self: How survivors of troubled families rise above adversity.* New York: Villard Books.

Chapter Twelve

Poverty: The Enemy of Children and Families

Mary Lou Fuller
University of North Dakota

The number of children in poverty is growing, and educators must understand the complexities of poverty in the lives of these children and their families. Schools have traditionally been designed for middle-class Euro-American students, so teachers must do things to make classrooms a positive learning environment for children in poverty. This chapter helps you to:

▶ Understand the demographics of poverty.

▶ Examine some of the myths about poverty.

▶ Understand the effects of poverty on the lives of children and their families.

▶ Explore the school's relationship with these children and their families.

▶ Examine the effects of homelessness on children.

The true measure of a nation's standing is how well it attends to its children—their health and safety, their material security, their education and socialization, and their sense of being loved, valued, and included in the families and societies into which they are born. (UNICEF, 2010)

There are obvious differences between the families of those who have financial resources to live as they'd like and those who do not. And there are more subtle differences between these two groups, differences that are both damaging to families in poverty generally and their children specifically. This means that, if, as educators, we are to engage in effective partnerships with lower-income families, we must understand the dynamics and the effects of both kinds of differences on families. We need, in other words, to understand poverty's impacts on families.

As an educator, you must understand the structures of families living in poverty and how those families function. It is equally important that you understand how the lack of financial resources affects the ways families function, recognizing that the consequences of limited financial resources can be obvious as well as subtle.

Children living in poverty often lack adequate diet, sufficient health care, adequate housing, and child care. But poverty also affects the less obvious needs that influence a child's ability to do well academically. In addition, and as schoolchildren get older, clothes become more important for peer acceptance—whether this means designer clothes or simply wearing new clothing with a particular label.

What Is Poverty?

The government officially defines what constitutes poverty, the standards varying with the size of the family, total family income, and an annual adjustment for inflation (reflecting the rising cost of rent, food, utilities, clothing, transportation, etc.). For example, the current poverty level for a family of two is $12,490, a family of three is $15,670, and four is $18,850 (U.S. Census Bureau, 2010)—which does not mean that a family of four can provide for all family members' basic needs with this sum. Rather, the figure represents that amount on which a family can marginally exist; it doesn't even mean basic medical and dental care—much less "extras" such as orthodontist visits, trips to Disneyland, special lessons, or sports. Parents in poverty, in other words, lack options commonly seen in other families.

Reflection...

Consider the ways in which the life of a child living in poverty is different from the life of a middle-class child. Consider not only the major areas (such as nutrition), but also the small pleasures and other experiences of childhood. What are some of your favorite childhood memories? Do children of poverty have access to these experiences?

The U.S. Department of Agriculture predicts that the cost of rearing a child to the age of 18 for a middle-income family is $291,570, and this doesn't include postsecondary education. Compare this with the $184,000 low-income families are projected to spend, and you can begin to understand the inequality in the experiences of middle-class children and those of children in poverty. Compare the resources of middle-income and low-income families and you can begin to understand the inequality of the experiences of children of poverty compared to their middle-class counterparts. Conclusion? Middle-class families simply have more choices as to how they'll raise their children, whereas families living in poverty are less able to purchase goods and services allowing them to share in a way of life that is characteristically American. What's more discouraging is that the gap between the haves and the have-nots is widening (Reuters, 2009).

Interestingly, there is a difference between being "broke" and living in poverty. Being broke is a temporary state, whereas people living in poverty usually see their situation as a hopeless, permanent condition. Many educators can recall being broke as college students, barely surviving from month to month, but knowing that their financial situations would improve when they "get out" and started working. People in poverty generally don't see themselves "getting out."

A sizeable number of families live just above the poverty line and also struggle to meet the basic needs of their children. Called the "working poor," information on this group is harder to come by, and so it is easier to discuss people living in poverty. When considering the working poor, recall that poverty means enough money to just scrape by, and so people just at or slightly above the poverty line still have the problems associated with poverty. The observations in this chapter, in other words, are also pertinent to this very large population.

Who Lives in Poverty and Why?

In 2008, 14 million (19%) children under the age of 18 lived in poverty (Feeding America, 2010). Although the United States is the wealthiest country in the world, it nevertheless ranks 20th out of the 21 most industrialized countries in terms of the percentage of children living in poverty. Sweden, Norway, and Finland have the fewest number of such children (UNICEF, 2007).

When the 21% of children in the families of the working poor are added in, a startling 40% of our students live in families lacking the resources required to meet kids' needs and provide the advantages enjoyed by middle-class children (Douglas-Hall & Koball, 2004). In other words, these kids are apt to lack the experiences and resources that support academic success. Who are these families? Many of them are headed by a single parent—usually the mother. Mother-only families are at high risk for poverty due to the absence of a second adult wage earner and the historically lower earning power of women.

There are recent additions to families of the working poor and those in poverty. These are former working-class and middle-class families whose adult members have lost their jobs and/or homes and now live in poverty. These lost jobs can be attributed to the current economy—a cause especially affecting new workers and those with less than a college education, though college degrees do not guarantee employment as they have in the past.

The 2008 guidelines defining poverty were not written to provide enough money to support a family; they only assist families struggling to survival. This means that families living below the poverty line must sacrifice, and these sacrifices are often in the area of necessities—medical care, adequate food and housing, and so on (U.S. Census Bureau, 2010).

What Do You Know About Poverty?

To allow you to consider your level of knowledge about poverty, take the test in Table 12.1. Cover the answers before you start.

Reflection...

Make a list of the costs for a middle-class family of four. Include the obvious (e.g., food, shelter, utilities, clothing, medical care, recreation, transportation) as well as those less obvious items (e.g., a car and expenses, health insurance, life insurance, funds for emergencies, the dentist/orthodontist, lessons, computer, vacations). Add up these costs and note (1) the discrepancy between what's needed for the family and how much is available to families in poverty, and (2) the difference in income between middle-class families and those living in poverty.

Poverty dims the future and creates stress and anxiety in the present. It limits opportunities and prospects. Although poor children can and often do succeed despite their poverty, researchers have documented a host of ways in which basic economic security helps children and poverty hurts them.

Money Buys Good Food

Sufficient money buys good food, and good food results in healthy children. Conversely, lack of good food may result in iron deficiency, hunger, stunted growth, clinical malnutrition, and an increased rate of high-risk pregnancies and premature births among low-income pregnant women.

Money Buys Safe and Decent Shelter

With poverty comes a lack of safe and decent shelter, homelessness, inadequate housing, and frequent moves from house to house and consequently from school to school. This housing situation also includes problems such as heating and electricity difficulties, utility shutoffs, cold and dampness, mold and allergies, cockroaches and rats, peeling paint and falling plaster, lead poisoning, crowded housing, and fire-prone homes.

TABLE 12.1 What's Your Knowledge About Poverty?

Statement About Poverty	Response	Answer Key
1. One in six Americans does not have access to enough food.	True or False	True. Not having access to enough food to sustain a healthy life is a reality to one in six Americans, including children and seniors.
2. Most individuals struggling with hunger are homeless and out of work.	True or False	False. Hunger is not an issue just for the people who struggle with poverty and homelessness. Only 12% of the clients are homeless and 36% of individuals served by the Feeding America network have at least one working adult in the family.
3. Very few children struggle with hunger because there are programs to take care of them.	True or False	False. According to the USDA, more than 14 million children are living in food-insecure households. School lunch programs do help, but they don't solve the whole problem.
4. Most people in low-income households would be fine if they just worked harder.	True or False	False. Thirty-six percent of households served by the Feeding America network include at least one adult who works.
5. Even college-educated people struggle with issues of hunger in this country.	True or False	True. Twenty-six percent of the adults interviewed during the Hunger Study have attended college or a technical school. Education is extremely important, but sometimes it's just not enough.
6. The lack of adequate nutrition only affects children's physical growth.	True or False	False. The lack of adequate nutrition affects the cognitive and behavioral development of children.
7. In school, children from food-insecure households perform just as well as children who have enough nutrition daily.	True or False	False. Children from food-insecure, low-income households are more likely to experience irritability, fatigue, and difficulty concentrating compared with other children. This can make performing in school very difficult.
8. More than 2 million rural households experience food insecurity.	True or False	True. More than 2 million rural households experience food insecurity—that means they don't have dependable access to enough food to sustain a healthy life.
9. Urban counties have the highest poverty rates in the United States.	True or False	False. Counties with disproportionately high rates of persistent poverty are often rural, where it can be more difficult for food banks and food emergency assistance to support them effectively.
10. More than 49 million Americans don't have dependable, consistent access to enough food due to limited money and resources.	True or False	True. According to the USDA, limited resources prevent more than 49 million Americans from getting enough food.

Money Buys Opportunities to Learn

Growing up in a family in poverty means children are more likely to attend an inferior school with inadequate supplies and equipment. These schools are also often unable to retain the most skilled teachers and administrators. Poor children also have fewer educational materials at home (including computers) and fewer stimulating activities (such as trips, lessons, museums, concerts). In contrast, children from more affluent families often enter school with a strong educational background and degree of familiarity with computers. Children in poverty also have greater home responsibilities that compete with school and schoolwork.

Money Reduces Family Stress and Conflict

Low incomes have an effect on mental health both for the parent and for the child. As the availability of money decreases, people's lives become unpredictable and parents' stress levels and depression go up as economic hardships increase. Often, conflict emerges among adults over how best to use the limited available resources with children feeling shame, fear, and anger. And as this stress increases, the chances of child abuse and neglect go up.

Money Buys a Decent Neighborhood

The lack of resources increases the chance that children will live in crime-ridden neighborhoods that also pose a threat from environmental stressors such as noise and pollution. The neighborhood is also less likely to have libraries, organized recreational opportunities, and parks.

Money Buys Health Care, Health Supplies, and Safety Devices

Poor families have trouble affording supplies and services associated with health and safety. The dollars available, for example, often do not stretch far enough to cover basic health-care supplies (such as vitamins, sterile bandages, and antiseptics) and safety devices (such as safety locks for doors and windows, smoke detectors, child car-safety seats). And even with Medicaid, medical care—including prevention such as immunization and dental care—must compete for resources with food and housing. The result is that poor people are less likely to seek care early in a disease's history and so they're more likely to delay until the illness is so bad that care must be sought immediately from an emergency room—a very expensive way to get health care. These problems are compounded by the fact that because poor people are often ill-educated, they do not understand issues associated with health and illness or safety and prevention, so conversations they have with people who might help them such as doctors and nurses range from nonproductive to difficult and stressful with the result that medical advice is not understood or is ignored.

Money Buys Healthy Recreation

Even though children from low-income families will benefit from extracurricular activities and community recreational facilities, their families are less able to afford the sports equipment, fees, and uniforms required, and recreational facilities such as swimming pools usually charge a fee. The result is that kids may be exposed to things (such as drugs) and groups (such as gangs) that both put them at risk and would be of lesser importance if their families had the resources available to others.

Money Buys Transportation, Communication, and Economic Opportunity

One form of these resources is transportation. People in poverty lack cars, and if there is public transportation, it may be too expensive (the cost of a Sunday family outing to a city park may be prohibitive) or bus and train routes may not coincide with the family's needs. More generally, the lack of transportation may limit access to child care, health services, recreation, jobs, job-training programs, postsecondary education, and low-cost stores (grocery stores in an inner city are often more expensive than in other neighborhoods).

Many poor homes lack a telephone. This limits access to opportunities, emergency services, and contact with the school. In addition, an inability to be in regular contact with important people in their lives may produce the feeling of isolation.

Having read the above list you can now begin to comprehend the effects of poverty on the lives of these families. And the children lacking these things and facing these privations are our students and their families. Though their lives are different from children with greater resources, their needs are not, and without knowledge of, and concern for, the limitations imposed by poverty, educators will be unable to understand these families and how they function. Lacking those understandings and the skills to address the needs the understandings describe, we will be less effective as educators; we're hampered in our abilities to teach these kids what they need to be successful children and then adults.

Schools and Families of Poverty

Poverty is a serious issue, both because the children it touches risk unsatisfied biological, safety, social, and esteem needs (Maslow's hierarchy) and because public schools are not designed to serve impoverished children. Rephrased, this means children of poverty bring their needs to school with them, and teachers must understand and be able to deal with poverty and its consequences if they're to help their students address those needs. Toward that end, the following information provides insights into how teachers can understand poverty and how they relate successfully to children of poverty and their families. These insights are presented in the hope that they will help prepare preservice teachers to understand and teach children of poverty because, with all their problems, these children have impressive potential and must not be underestimated.

Children

Unlike their middle-class peers, children in poverty often experience discontinuities between schooling and other areas of their lives. Studies focusing on the relationship between socioeconomic status and academic success show that schools (1) expect students to have middle-class experiences and opportunities, and (2) evaluate children's behavior and scholastic outcomes with middle-class standards. This includes middle-class social and language behaviors. Middle-class children generally acquire these behaviors prior to entering school, whereas students with limited resources commonly lack these advantages and, consequently, enter schools that were designed for someone else.

Because substantial numbers of parents of children of poverty dropped out of school before completing high school, and because many children of poverty have parents who did not attend school in the United States, their parents are unprepared to help them at school. Indeed, the home environment is often cited as the reason for lack of academic achievement among low-income students.

These parents, for example, are apt to be criticized for not being sufficiently involved at school. They're criticized for not working with their kids at home, not attending parent–teacher conferences, and so on. These criticisms are offered without consideration of how survival issues (e.g., earning money for food, clothing, affordable housing, and adequate health care) command low-income parents' time, leaving them so tired that they often are incorrectly described as too distracted to attend to their children's educational needs.

Parents

As stated, low-income parents are often thought to have little interest in the education of their children. The limited school involvement of low-income parents can be attributed, in part, to their lack of trust in school personnel, as well as a lack of understanding of the ways schools function. Often, differences in economic backgrounds between teachers and parents lead to discomfort on the part of parents when interacting with schools. This psychosocial distance between parents and teachers also leads to a lack of understanding among teachers of the dynamics operating within low-income families. Haberman (2005), in his book *Star Teachers*, discusses the difference between "star" teachers' perceptions of parents of poverty and those of other teachers.

Most teachers define "support from home" as parents helping children with assigned homework or supporting some action of school discipline. Star teachers, on the other hand, described parental support in terms of parents showing interest in what their children do in school and providing them with basics such as privacy, safety, sleep, nutrition, and health (Haberman, 2005).

Parents in poverty, like parents of all other socioeconomic groups, love their children, but, for reasons already described, may feel uncomfortable in their children's schools. They frequently feel helpless in their relationships with schools and teachers, and, in some cases, may feel denigrated by the way that schools and teachers

Case Study

Nathan and Justin, both age 8, are in the third grade in Denver. They both enjoy playing sports and watching television, and each has a younger brother and sister. Although they have a lot in common, their lives are actually dramatically different.

Nathan

Nathan lives in a single-family residence in an upper-middle-class neighborhood. He has his own room with a variety of toys, a bookcase full of books, his own computer, and a well-lit desk where he does his homework.

Nathan also enjoys family vacations. This last summer they went to the Grand Canyon and to Disneyland. He also looks forward to several skiing trips during the winter. He has become an excellent snowboarder and is anxious for their next ski weekend so that he can improve his skills. He also takes piano lessons (though not gladly) and is the goalie on his hockey team (which he does do gladly).

Justin

Justin lives in a two-bedroom apartment in public housing. Although his father has a 40-hour-a-week minimum wage job, they live below the poverty line and lack health insurance and other benefits. This is a problem for Justin who has asthma aggravated by the pollution from factories in their locale.

Justin is a good student who likes to read. He has few books of his own, however, and the public library is some distance from his apartment. The school library has a limited number of books and to ensure that all students have equal access to them, the librarian allows the students to take only one book every 2 weeks.

Transportation is also a problem for Justin's family. Their car is in poor repair, which is problematic because Justin's father needs it to get to work. They try not to use it for anything other than for work though they do use it when Justin's asthma requires them to take him to the emergency room. Occasionally, they take public transportation for a family outing, but the fare for two adults and three children makes a dent in their budget.

Questions and Considerations

1. How do Justin and Nathan's lives differ?
2. Consider your childhood. With whom do you most closely identify, Justin or Nathan?
3. What would you predict Justin's and Nathan's futures will be like? Why?
4. Pretend that one boy brought a note home saying ". . . he did well with addition and subtraction, but he is having trouble with his multiplication tables. We're currently working on the tables of 3 and 4, and it would be good if you'd help him with them. . . ." Which boy is most likely to be taking this note home? Why do you think your answer is reasonable?
5. Pretend the boy is Nathan. How do you expect his parents will interpret the note? And how will they respond to the request that they help him with the tables of 3 and 4?
6. Pretend the boy is Justin. How will his parents interpret the note? And how will they respond to the request they help him with the tables of 3 and 4?
7. Pretend the principal suggests to Nathan's and Justin's teacher that the boys are so alike in their interests that a friendship between them would broaden each boy's horizons. What issues must the teacher consider in planning how to facilitate such a friendship?

communicate with them. Haberman observes that star teachers do not blame parents even though they may learn a lot about the child or the family. The teachers use this information to help the children (Haberman, 2005).

Poverty wears people down and defeats them, leaving little energy to deal with family problems outside of fulfilling basic daily needs. Low-income parents feel inadequate to participate in their children's learning, and their experience has been that the school assumes and retains the responsibility to educate kids; they just don't know they have an important role to play that complements what schools do, that without their contribution, their kids won't do as well. And they likely do not have the skills to help and support their children's education at home. Lack of information, skill, time, and transportation all serve to further isolate parents from the schools.

Working with Low-Income Families

In establishing a working partnership with low-income parents, you must remember that parents' lack of resources doesn't indicate a lack of love or dreams for their children. Furthermore, although they may not be pedagogical experts, they are experts on their children, and we need their expertise.

There are disparities in the life experiences of middle-class teachers and students who are children of poverty. Because of these disparities, it takes a conscious effort on a teacher's part to gain the perspectives needed to understand these student's experiences and the ways in which those experiences influence their lives. The story that follows is an actual event and is presented to demonstrate the way a gifted teacher of children of poverty approached an incident in her classroom.

> Jeanette B. is a wonderful first-grade teacher in a low-income rural area in Kansas. I visited her classroom the day a little boy surprised her with a gift. Jeanette could tell both that the 6-year-old had wrapped it himself in a brown paper sack and that his inability to stand still was evidence of how excited he was to see her open his wonderful gift. He knew she would love the gift, and love it she did. It was a can of cream-style corn, which they both agreed was their very favorite.
>
> That evening at dinner, Jeanette's third-grade daughter announced that she needed a package of colored macaroni for a class art project. Jeanette smiled, said they would get it after dinner, and then dismissed herself from the table, as she needed a moment to think.
>
> Jeanette was struck by the contrast of food as a special gift and food as art supplies. To her student, food was a precious commodity and something very special, whereas, to her daughter, it was commonplace and the girl had no difficulty using it as art supplies. How, she wondered, did these two children come to such divergent perspectives? In the boy's case, poverty led him to see food as a scarce commodity to be husbanded carefully and used on special occasions, whereas to her daughter, a middle-class pantry meant food had value beyond its nutritional importance. "How," Jeanette wondered, "would the little boy feel about doing something to food other than eating it? And what would her daughter think about receiving a can of corn as a present?"

Teachers from middle- and lower-middle-class families have been enculturated into a middle-class world. Unless educators have had exposure to poverty and an understanding of the dynamics of poverty, they will subconsciously take their middle-class expectations of parent–school relationships into their classrooms with them—and this is perfect when they teach at middle-class or lower-middle-class schools. These expectations handicap both teachers and students, however, when the children they teach live in poverty.

Not only are many teachers ill-informed about the poverty of their students, their students are correspondingly unfamiliar with the culture of their middle-class teachers. For example, during the school day Jeanette, the teacher mentioned before, noticed that she had a flat tire and called an auto service for assistance. A few minutes after school was dismissed a student returned to the classroom yelling, "Mrs. J. come quick! Your car is being repossessed!" We interpret events by the experiences we have lived.

The prolonged burdens and pressures of low-income families are considerable and not normally within the experience of most educators. Consequently, it is important to be well informed and sensitive when working with low-income families. The educator and the parent(s) have a strong common bond—all want the best for the child—and this should be the basis for good working relationships.

Suggestions for Working with Low-Income Parents

Check Your Attitude

I observed a young teacher in her classroom a few years after she'd taken a course in multicultural education from me as part of her preservice training. When I interviewed her afterwards about what she'd done in class, and I asked her about a student who was clearly a child of poverty (e.g., he qualified for free breakfast and lunch), she told me about his parents. "If they just tried harder," she said, "they could significantly improve their financial situation."

When I spoke with her principal later on, he offered a different perspective. The parents, he noted, both worked at minimum wage jobs, cared for their children, and were able to do so only by scrimping. "Did they have time to get their GEDs and train for better paying jobs?" I asked. He shook his head sadly saying, "No. It is all they can do to keep a roof over their heads, keep food on the table, and keep their kids clothed. They're one crisis away from being destitute."

Was there a problem here? Indeed there was, and it belonged to the young teacher. Until she reached the point where she understood her student's situation, her expectations would be at odds with those of the child and the child's family with the result that her efforts to teach him and his efforts to learn were much less successful than they could be. She was, in effect, wasting her time (which is sad) and his (which is unprofessional).

What did she need to do? She needed to learn more about her student and his family so she could better attune her teaching activities to his expectations because, failing that, she'd be expecting him to have her middle-class experiences and expectations when, in fact, they were not his. And this meant that she had difficulty addressing his needs.

How can a teacher know whether she (or he) entertains inappropriate expectations for children in poverty? If you find yourself thinking "If they can afford to have a television and VCR, they can't be doing too badly" without learning how and why they came to have the electronics, at best you're premature; at worst you're wasting your time.

Do you feel that people of poverty are intellectually inferior to those of the middle class? For example, do you find yourself thinking "If they were more intelligent, they wouldn't be poor," you might want to visit with your students' parents and ask them about how they see their children's schooling in relation to other things (such as owning the TV and VCR).

Educators are sensitive people who want the best for their students, but they still may have some unexamined attitudes toward poverty. How did you formulate your attitudes toward poverty? Have you checked to see whether your attitudes are shared by others? By the parents of your students, for example, or with other teachers in your school who are well regarded by their students and their students' families?

Know the Environment in Which Your Low-Income Children Live

If your students come from an urban/suburban area or a small town, walk around their neighborhood. See where your students play and investigate the quality and quantity of the recreational facilities that are available to them. Where do families shop for groceries? Walk through the stores and observe the selections available and the cost. In many such stores in these settings, the items are more expensive and the choices more limited than those in some middle-class neighborhoods. Is there a library in the neighborhood? Are there churches? A disproportionate number of bars? What is the cultural makeup of the area? If you feel that this is not a safe environment to explore (although this is not usually the case), ask someone to join you in this adventure.

If your students live in a more rural environment, drive around the area until you know it well. Again, familiarize yourself with the stores in the area and identify the churches, recreational facilities, bars, and so on. Who lives where? Ride the school bus on each of the routes your students ride and see where they get off. How long a ride do they have to and from school? How long is their walk from the bus stop to their home? What is the nature of the housing in that area? It is important to remember not to criticize your low-income students' physical environment. The area is a part of the child, and, as a result, they will feel demeaned by negative comments. After exploring your low-income students' environment, identify the strengths and weaknesses of the area and determine how these will affect your teaching strategies.

Gathering Basic Information About Low-Income Families

The school office is a good place to start becoming acquainted with families. There you will find a record that can act as an introduction, and you will discover information that will help you understand some of the dynamics of the family. How many children are there in the household? What are their ages? Are any preschool age? How many parents are in the home? Do one or both work? Is the place of employment listed? What is the address of the family? Do they have a telephone? Is there a work number listed?

Communicate with the Low-Income Parents and Children

The best communication model is two-way communication—parents and educators talking and listening to one another, and this should be every teacher's ultimate communication goal. Unfortunately, this is not always possible; some parents are unable, unwilling, or uncomfortable communicating with the schools. Nevertheless, it is important to actively endeavor to inform parents. Contacting parents about positive matters will make it easier and more productive if you need to work with them on a problem at a later date. Writing notes to parents about their child's positive behaviors and academic successes will demonstrate that you care about their child and that you appreciate their child. Remember that not all parents can read notes written in English. Usually there are people in the school who can translate your note into the language of the community.

If there is a phone in the home, calls can be particularly helpful in establishing positive parent–teacher communication. Also, brief calls to make a positive comment about a student encourages parents to become more actively involved in communicating with the school; after all, if a parent starts to believe, "That teacher likes my child," parental enthusiasm in school matters is more likely to result. Unfortunately, not all low-income families have phones, which means a letter or visit may be necessary.

Getting Low-Income Families Actively Involved: Creating a Partnership

The view of parent involvement has changed over the last 25 years. In the past, high-profile, low-participation situations were the norm. This involvement often took the form of large meetings held in the evenings where parents listened to what educators had to say. The schedules of contemporary families no longer make this a viable activity for most families. More important, these meetings no longer fit the contemporary goals of parental involvement—they were monologues rather than conversations. The nature of parent involvement has changed, and true parent involvement is now seen as a partnership between the school and the home.

Low-income families have many demands on their time, as mentioned earlier in the chapter, and lack the economic resources necessary to reduce the stresses caused by these demands. In addition, some low-income parents may have had negative school experiences and do not feel comfortable in the school environment. Flexibility, practicality, and creativity can help you mitigate some of these problems. For example, meetings with parents needn't always be held in the classroom. You can meet for a cup of coffee, make a home visit, and so forth.

Partnerships are based on respect, and it is imperative that parents are shown the same respect we show our colleagues. Also, in partnerships with low-income parents, it is important to remember that the stresses of life may be such that there will be times when parents do not have the emotional or physical energy to be full partners. A single parent who has a minimum wage job, a sick child, no child care, and is being evicted may have to expend his energies elsewhere.

Become Involved in the Community

To understand families, you must understand them as a part of a community as well as individual units. The following recommendations are suggestions for becoming involved in a community.

Although teachers are busy people who work hard emotionally, intellectually, and physically, and need time to rejuvenate at the end of the school day or week, the opportunities to learn about students and families continue beyond the classroom. You may not be able to participate in all of the suggested activities, but select those that interest you most. In addition, your friends or family might want to join you in some of these activities.

If there is a community celebration, such as street fairs, ethnic holidays, and events such as pow-wows, attend. Accept as many invitations as you can: Bas- or Bar-Mitzvahs, confirmations, first communions, quinceañeras, and so forth. If you have a student singing a solo with a church choir, playing in the little league finals, or being honored for their talents in any way, attend.

Be Sensitive to the Financial Limitations of Low-Income Families

Low-income families may find it very difficult to send money for field trips, school projects, or special materials. Even requests for cookies for a party may be beyond some families. Also, some children are not able to participate in school sports due to the cost of the registration fee, equipment, or clothing. Imagine how demeaning and disappointing these situations are to children and their parents.

Homelessness

The first three editions of this textbook did not include information about the homeless. However, there has recently been a marked increase in the number of homeless families, which means that educators are more apt to have homeless children in their classes and must be knowledgeable about the needs of these children.

It is difficult to know just how many families are homeless. Some homeless people are more apparent than others as they may live on the streets or in shelters and are consequently more easily identified.

Recently, many American families have experienced diminished financial resources, and consequently the number of homeless families has increased significantly. These families defy the stereotype of the homeless person as a derelict who lives on the street, begs for money, and is apt to be an alcoholic, a drug addict, or mentally disturbed—which is itself a stereotype.

What Is Homelessness?

Different definitions of homelessness apply in different contexts. Generally, though, homeless families lack a fixed, regular, and adequate night-time residence. Thus you don't have to be living on the streets to be homeless; a homeless family may live in a shelter, move temporarily from one friend's/family's house to another, or live in a car (regardless of whether the car runs).

There are also homeless families who live in tents, tent cities, and campgrounds. Regardless of whether we know the kids are homeless, they are young and frightened, and their parents and families are frustrated and desperate.

What Does It Mean to Be Homeless?

Educators often not only have little understanding of homelessness but also have a difficult time recognizing it in the classroom. Homeless children and their families often try to hide their living conditions from the school. Although the reasons families are homeless vary, common reasons they hide their homelessness include the fear that child protective services might be notified and the children will go into foster care, the very human emotion of pride, and the expectation that the school will see them negatively.

Homelessness for any given family is caused by a combination of factors, often including the effects of a lack of affordable housing, extreme poverty, decreasing government support, changing demographics of the family, the challenges of single parenthood, domestic violence, and fractured social supports. The gap between housing costs and income continues to widen until eviction or foreclosure occurs for extremely poor families and those with vulnerabilities (e.g., a family member suffers from a serious illness) or minimal to no safety net (e.g., no extended family to help) so that even an otherwise minor event can trigger a catastrophe that propels a family onto the streets (National Center on Family Homelessness, 2010).

What Are Some of the Characteristics of Homeless Families?

Homeless families are like all families in that they are diverse in nature, so it is important not to stereotype them. The generalizations below are meant to help the reader consider some issues that may affect the lives of children from homeless families.

- The mother is in her late twenties and has two children.
- Adults in many homeless families work. When this happens, it is common that others in the workplace are unaware of their coworker's homeless status.
- Forty-two percent of children in homeless families are under age 6. This is a significant issue because the period from birth to 6 years of age is a time of critical development.

- Eighty-four percent of families experiencing homelessness are female-headed.
- More than half of all homeless mothers do not have a high school diploma. This means that these women are disadvantaged when it comes to finding jobs paying a living wage (National Center on Family Homelessness, 2010).

Effects of Homelessness on Children

Recess is over and Adam sits in your classroom looking much like the other children. He is a little disheveled but the dust, messy hair, etc., come from the playground and not from "home." He looked as neat and clean as the other boys when he arrived this morning; he is just a "typical" kid. But he is not typical because he is homeless. Adam, his mother, and his sister have spent the last 2 weeks with a family friend, but because the friend is a single mother like Adam's mother, and has four children of her own, the friend's apartment was only a temporary refuge, and Adam and his mom and sister are now sleeping in their car.

The family used to live in an apartment near the school but was evicted when Adam's mother was ill, lost her job, and could not pay the rent. Before the illness, she was working for less than minimum wage and had no benefits; the little money they had went for medical bills. She has a part-time job, and she's trying to save enough for another apartment: The first and last months' rent, deposits for utilities, and a security deposit.

Things may appear normal in the classroom, but they're not. One has to look at the dangers Adam faces to understand the seriousness of his situation.

- Homelessness places families at greater risk of additional traumatic experiences such as assault, witnessing violence, or abrupt separation.
- The stresses associated with homelessness can exacerbate other trauma-related difficulties and interfere with insufficient resources available to allow recovery. And homeless people (especially children) need no reminders of the challenges they face. Simply put, children bear the brunt of homelessness.
- Homeless children are sick twice as often as other children. They suffer twice as many ear infections, have four times the rate of asthma, and have five times more diarrhea and stomach problems.
- Homeless children go hungry twice as often as other kids.
- More than one-fifth of homeless preschoolers have emotional problems serious enough to require professional care, but less than one-third of them receive treatment.
- Homeless children are twice as likely to repeat a grade compared with other children.
- Homeless children have twice the rate of learning disabilities and three times the rate of emotional and behavioral problems of other children.

And adding to the burden of the above list, half of school-age homeless children experience anxiety, depression, or withdrawal from educational, community, and social activities (National Child Traumatic Stress Network, 2010).

What Can You as an Educator Do?

Five Principles for Educators

We have a responsibility as professionals to contribute to the well-being of our students, and we can fulfill this responsibility when we:

- *Do not stigmatize children in homeless situations.* Do not think of them as homeless children, but rather as children temporarily without a home due to circumstances beyond their control and often, their understanding. They need sensitivity, understanding, and the recognition of their individual strengths and needs. Having high expectations for their success tells them you value them as people.
- *Make schools safe havens.* The family and community life of these children can be so unstable that schools must provide a sense of belonging and security. In the midst of chaos, a teacher and a school can be a positive support in the form of a source of hope and encouragement.
- *Think of the needs of the whole child.* Work with school and community resources to improve the child's physical health, mental health, and nutritional needs. Helping meet their basic needs puts them in a position to learn and achieve since it's hard to learn when you're hungry or tired.
- *Work with parents or guardians to develop concrete goals and plans to address those goals.* Parents who are homeless have goals for their kids as do other parents. Understand, too, that adults in homeless families may be stretched thin, balancing many demands on them with fewer resources to address them. The result is that their time may be even more limited than adults in other families.
- *Reach out to the community.* Building a collaborative school and community network is critical to mounting a comprehensive effort to helping children who are homeless (Kennedy, 2004).

Summary

As educators, we have a wonderful opportunity and a responsibility to help children of poverty specifically and their families generally. These parents deserve respect for a variety of reasons including their perseverance, hard work, and, of course, strong desire for success and a good life for their children. That said, the stigma of poverty is a powerful force that manipulates teacher behavior in ways educators themselves often don't recognize: It can, for example, lower a teacher's expectations for a child, which initiates a self-fulfilling prophecy of failure. Well-informed teachers should not be influenced by the stereotypes of poor children.

Finally, educators who are knowledgeable and skillful can add to the quality of life for these children and their families as well as grow professionally themselves.

Recommended Activities

1. View the movies *Freedom Riders* and/or *Stand and Deliver* and note what these two gifted teachers did to encourage their low-income students. Both of these movies are based on true stories and are inspiring examples of exceptional teachers of children of poverty.

2. Volunteer at a homeless shelter and keep a journal of your experiences.

3. Interview a social worker about the lives of children and families living in poverty.

4. Volunteer in a thrift shop. Write a description of three of the regular customers.

5. Ask a social worker, Head Start teacher, and nutritionist from WIC to speak to your class about the problems of children and families in poverty, either individually or as part of a panel.

6. Volunteer in a Head Start classroom and keep a journal of your experience.

7. Collect demographics about the resources of the poor as opposed to the middle class. Then use those figures to predict the kind of childhood experience kids from each group will have.

8. Determine the income and expenses of a single parent making minimum wage and raising three children. Use your community to determine expenses: housing, food, transportation, health care, and so forth.

Children's Books

The following books are suggested as a way of helping your students consider issues in this chapter.

Books About the Homeless

A Shelter in Our Car
Monica Gunning, Elaine Pedlar (Illustrator)
Reading Level: Ages 4–8
Children's Book Press (2004)

Fly Away Home
Eve Bunting, Ronald Himler
Reading Level: Ages 4–8
Clarion Books (1993)

The Lady in the Box
Ann McGovern, Marni Backer (Illustrator)
Reading Level: Ages 4–8
Turtle Books (1999)

Uncle Willie and the Soup Kitchen (Reading Rainbow Book)
Dyanne Disalvo-Ryan (Illustrator)
Reading Level: Ages 4–8
Harper-Trophy; Reprint edition (1997)

Books About Poverty

A Day's Work
Eve Bunting, Ronald Himler

Reading Level: Ages 4–8
Clarion Books (1997)

Tight Times (Picture Puffins)
Barbara Shook Hazen, Trina Schart Hyman
   (Illustrator)
Reading Level: Ages 4–8
Puffin Books (1983)

An Angel for Solomon Singer
Cynthia Rylant, Peter Catalanotto
Scholastic (1996)

The Table Where Rich People Sit
Byrd Baylor, Peter Parnell
Reading Level: Ages 4–8
Aladdin; Reprint edition (1998)

Someplace to Go
Maria Testa, Karen Ritz (Illustrator)
Reading Level: Ages 4–8
Albert Whitman & Company (1996)

*Home Is Where We Live: Life at a Shelter
   Through a Young Girl's Eyes*
Jane Hertensten (Ed.), B. L. Groth
   (Photographer)
Reading Level: Ages 4–8
Cornerstone Press Chicago (1995)

Additional Resources

Books

Haberman, M. (2005). *Star teachers of children in poverty*. Houston, TX: Haberman Educational Foundation.

Haberman is recognized as an expert in teacher education for urban schools—primarily schools that serve children of poverty. In this book, he describes how those who have been recognized as "star" teachers work with children of poverty. It is practical and yet sensitive and makes specific suggestions.

Payne, R. K. (2005). *A framework for understanding poverty*. Highlands, TX: aha! Process.

People in poverty face challenges virtually unknown to those in middle class or wealth—challenges from both obvious and hidden sources. The reality of being poor brings out a survival mentality, and turns attention away from opportunities taken for granted by everyone else. If you work with people from poverty, some understanding of how different their world is from yours will be invaluable. This book gives you practical, real-world support and guidance to improve your effectiveness in working with people from all socioeconomic backgrounds. Since 1995 *A Framework for Understanding Poverty* has guided hundreds of thousands of educators and other professionals through the pitfalls and barriers faced by all classes, especially the poor. Carefully researched and packed with charts, tables, and questionnaires, *Framework* not only documents the facts of poverty, it provides practical yet compassionate strategies for addressing its impact on people's lives.

Videos

America's Children: Poorest in a Land of Plenty

A narration by Maya Angelou of the tragic neglect of children in the United States and a call for change.

NTC Resource Center
Phone: 972-490-3438
Fax: 972-490-7216
E-mail: sgordon@ntcumc.org

Faces of Poverty

A correction of a number of misconceptions about the poor and reveals them not as objects of compassion, but as our neighbors.

NTC Resource Center
Phone: 972-490-3438
Fax: 972-490-7216
E-mail: sgordon@ntcumc.org

The Homeless Home Movie

Produced in collaboration with homeless people and shown on PBS. This thought-provoking homeless video is recommended by the National Coalition for the Homeless. The video is widely considered to be the best and most broadly applicable case study available on the scope and diversity of homelessness in America.

Media Visions, Inc.
www.2.bitstream.net/~mvisions/purchase.htm

Organizations

National Association for the Education of Homeless Children and Youth
Phone: 202-364-7392
www.naehcy.org

National Coalition for the Homeless
Phone: 202-462-4822 x. 19
E-mail: info@nationalhomeless.org
www.nationalhomeless.org

Websites

Child Welfare Home Page
www.childwelfare.com

Child Welfare Library
www.childwelfare.com/kids/library.htm

Institute for Children and Poverty
www.opendoor.com/hfh/icp.html

Institute for Research on Poverty
www.ssc.wisc.edu/irp

National Center for Children in Poverty
www.cait.cpmc.columbia/edu/dept/nccp

Politics of Poverty
www.americanradioworks.org/features/
14_million

References

Douglas-Hall, A., & Koball, H. (2004). *Low-income children in the United States*. Retrieved January 11, 2011 from http://NCCP.org

Feeding America. (2010). *Hunger and poverty statistics*. Retrieved January 12, 2011 from www.feedingamerica.org/faces-of-hunger/hunger-101/hunger-and-poverty-statistics.aspx

Haberman, M. (2005). *Star teachers of children in poverty*. Houston, TX: Haberman Educational Foundation.

Kennedy, M. (2004). *Educating homeless children*. Retrieved January 12, 2011 from www.edc.org/newsroom/articles/educating_homeless_children

National Center on Family Homelessness. (2010). The characteristics and needs of families experiencing homelessness. Retrieved January 12, 2011 from www.familyhomelessness.org/q=node/4/

National Child Traumatic Stress Network. (2010). Factions on trauma and homeless children.

Retrieved January 12, 2011 from www.NCTSNet.org

Reuters. (2009). *Special report: The haves, the have-nots and the dreamless dead*. Washington, DC: U.S. Department of Health & Human Services.

UNICEF. (2007). *An overview of child well-being in rich countries*. Retrieved from www.unicef.org/media/files/ChildPovertyReport.pdf

UNICEF. (2010). Report card 7: Child poverty in perspective. Florence: Innocenti Research Centre. Retrieved January 11, 2011 from www.unicef.org/media/files/ChildPovertyReport.pdf

U.S. Census Bureau. (2010). 2008 poverty guidelines. Retrieved from www.workworld.org/wwwebhelp/external/pov08combo.pdf

U.S. Department of Agriculture. (2009). *Annual study: What is the average cost to raise a child?* Release No. 0365.09. Retrieved January 12, 2011 from www.usda.gov/wps/portal/usda/usdahome?contentidonly=true&contentid=2009/08/0365.xml

Fathering, Schools, and Schooling: What Fathers Contribute and Why It Is Important

Charles B. Hennon
Miami University

Glen Palm
St. Cloud State University

Glenn Olsen
University of North Dakota

This chapter enables the reader to recognize the role of the father in a child's life in the context of family, school, and society. The father's role in schools and schooling is discussed, and change relating to that role is presented. This chapter helps you to:

▶ Describe the culture and practice of fatherhood.

▶ Recognize fathering in the context of family and other systems.

▶ State the relationships between fathering conduct and the school achievement of children.

▶ Understand the importance of family, especially father, involvement in schools and schooling to foster children's academic achievement.

▶ Recognize ways of involving fathers in schools and the schooling of their children.

In recent years there has been increased interest in the roles and functions of fathers. "The importance of fathering that focuses on loving and supporting children has been judged by some to be the most pressing social concern in contemporary American family life" (Brotherson, Dollahite, & Hawkins, 2005, p. 2). At the same time, it seems that there is a scarcity of good social scientific evidence about fatherhood in general, father–child relationships more particularly, and how fathers influence the academic achievement of their children (Coakley, 2006; DeBell, 2008; Duchesne & Larose, 2007; Featherstone, 2009; Goldberg, Tan, & Thorsen, 2009; Hennon & Wilson, 2008; Junttila, Vauras, & Laakkonen, 2007; Lu et al., 2010; Stuchell & Barrett, n.d.). How fathering differs by socioeconomic or other contexts also requires further investigation (Adamsons, O'Brien, & Pasley, 2007; Beckert, Strom, Strom, & Yang, 2006; Braithewaite & Baxter, 2006; Brown, Copeland, Costello, Erkanli, & Worthman, 2009; Coakley, 2006; Hennon, Hildenbrand, & Schedle, 2008; Hennon & Wilson, 2008; Lu et al., 2010; National Center on Fathers and Families, n.d.a; Newsome, Bush, Hennon, Peterson, & Wilson, 2008; Peterson & Hennon, 2007; Radina, Wilson, & Hennon, 2008; Tasker, 2010; Taylor & Behnke, 2005; Terrel, 2005).

The advantages of families being more in partnership with schools are recognized by educators (Darling, 2008; Domina, 2005; Epstein et al., 2009; Ferguson, 2008; Henderson & Mapp, 2002; Hill & Tyson, 2009; Hutchins, Maushard, Colosino, Greenfeld, & Thomas, 2009; Lee, n.d.; National Network of Partnership Schools, 2010; Seitsinger, Felner, Brand, & Burns, 2008; Souto-Manning & Swick, 2006). Schools, students, families, and communities benefit and techniques for building such partnerships are being disseminated (e.g., Epstein et al., 2009; Harvard Family Research Project, 2010; Kuhmann, 2004; Michigan Department of Education, n.d.). One aspect commonly overlooked is the role fathers play in forming these partnerships as well as fathers' roles in the academic achievement of their children. The examination of fathers' roles is imperative to the understanding of family dynamics and how they influence children, including academic success.

Good fathering does matter—over clock time, over family time, over lifetime, over generations (Conway & Hutson, 2008; Cook, Jones, Dick, & Singh, 2005; Martin, Ryan, & Brooks-Gunn, 2010; Morman & Floyd, 2006; National Center on Fathers and Families, n.d.b; Oren & Oren, 2009). Although some fathers stay involved with their children, it is widely believed that divorce and fatherless homes have dire consequences for school achievement and other child outcomes (Aulette, 2010; Dudley & Stone, 2001; Featherstone, 2009; Garasky & Stewart, 2007; Hawkins, Amato, & King, 2007; Lamb, 2010; Lu et al., 2010; Menning, 2006a; Menning & Stewart, 2008; Potter, 2010; Steinberg, 2007). Perhaps less recognized is the influence of fathers in all types of family systems on school attendance, schoolwork, and academic and personal success (Aulette, 2010; Featherstone, 2009; Hawkins, Amato, & King, 2006; Hennon & Wilson, 2008; Kalil & Ziol-Guest, 2007; Lamb, 2010; Lee, n.d.; Lu et al., 2010; Miller, Murry, & Brody, 2005; Parke, 2004; Stuchell & Barrett, n.d.; Terrel, 2005; Williams & Kelly, 2005). These influences are explored in this chapter.

In some people's view, the role of gender in parenting is swinging from the clearly defined difference in roles and complement of functions of the 1950s to an ideal of parenting in which gender differences grow smaller if socialization changes (cf., Biblarz & Stacey, 2010; Coakley, 2006; Crowl, Ahn, & Baker, 2008; Culbertson, 2010; Featherstone, 2009; Pleck, 2010). There have even been questions raised about fathers as essential. We believe that fathers are *important* and can contribute in novel ways to the upbringing of children (Pleck, 2010). Fathering should be considered in its own context; it is not just an adjunct to mothering. Although "research has not identified any gender-exclusive parenting abilities (with the partial exception of lactation)," on becoming parents, men and women tend to engage in different activities for and with their children and relate to them in different ways (Biblarz & Stacey, 2010, p. 16). It is thus imperative to understand the complexity motivating the experiences of fathers and how men and women have both similar and unique parental experience (Adamsons, 2006; Aulette, 2010; Brotherson et al., 2005; Featherstone, 2009; Kim, Cain, & McCubbin, 2006; Lu et al., 2010; Martin et al., 2010; McBride, Schoppe-Sullivan, & Ho, 2005; Tan & Goldberg, 2009; Oren & Oren, 2009). Gender as a concept is mired in a complex of social and political issues and often is discussed in emotionally charged atmospheres (Culbertson, 2010; White & Kline, 2008). Some writers express ambivalence about delineating parenting roles based on gender while understanding that the changing roles of fathers represent both threats to the status quo and opportunities (Brotherson et al., 2005; Coakley, 2006; Featherstone, 2009; Parke, 2004).

Stuchell and Barrett (n.d.) implored:

> Be careful not to compare fathers to mothers as this may induce an "idealized motherhood template," with motherhood always being framed as the dominant, privileged, and preferred model for parenting, and which may contribute to a "cult of motherhood." Be wary of mother-privileged assessments of effective parenting and advocate a perspective that values both fathering and mothering for their similar and unique contributions to family life. (p. 2)

"Interacting with one's children represents an essential component of contemporary fatherhood. Fathers are taking an active role in the lives of their children in a variety of ways including teaching, providing emotional support, playing, and just sharing time, even in 'prosaic behavior' consisting of ordinary activities" (Pehlke, Hennon, Radina, & Kuvalanka, 2009, p. 136). Fathers reaffirm commitment to their children by demonstrating behavior that shows interest in the children and their activities. The authors of this chapter are advocating for more father involvement in all aspects of children's lives. Society in general, and families and schools in particular, benefit from supporting men in their roles as fathers. We believe that, on average, fathering is qualitatively different from mothering and that although some men and women desire less gender-specific parenting practices, others support more traditionally gendered approaches to parenting.

Here we highlight some of the advantages of quality father involvement while articulating differences and strengths that fathers bring to parenting. We respect individual values and approaches to fathering and cultural differences in conceptions of fatherhood and fathering behavior.

Our approach is not value free. We believe that more involvement by fathers with their children is valuable for the child, the father, the mother, the schools, and the society. We believe that fathers can be involved in positive ways regardless of their marital status and living arrangement relative to the child. Recognizing diversity in family forms and functioning, we believe that certain principles and practices can be more universally applied, whereas in other cases more selected interventions may be appropriate to foster parental capacity. For example, married fathers living with their children, divorced fathers living elsewhere, remarried fathers living with stepchildren while their own children are living with stepfathers, fathers in prison, recent immigrant and migrant fathers, and fathers in intimate same-sex relationships who are living with their children, all face unique issues and may benefit from different resources, supports, and services (Hennon, Hildenbrand, & Schedle, 2008; Hennon, Peterson, Hildenbrand, & Wilson, 2008; Lamb, 2010; Oren & Oren, 2009; Meek, 2007; Sweeney, 2010; Tasker, 2010). It is important to remember that there are not only differences between fathers and mothers but also great diversity among fathers.

As we explore fatherhood and father involvement, especially investment with education and schooling, we first examine how the culture of fatherhood both pressures and reinforces fathers. Secondly, we discuss the conduct of fathering. Next, we discuss how family systems influence fathering and thus how interventions must be sensitive to systemic rather than merely individualistic characteristics. Finally, we turn to a discussion on involving fathers in schools and schooling.

Basic Premises

Six premises underlie the focus on the unique characteristics of men as parents. These underline the importance of fathers and fathering and are the guiding principles and rationale for making specific efforts to increase and support father involvement in families, schooling, and schools. (*Note:* In this chapter *father* is typically the term employed but it should be read as also including others—e.g., uncles, grandfathers, stepfathers, same-sex partners as co-fathers, mother's current partner—who fulfill the role and conduct the functions characteristically associated with the biological father.)

- *Worldwide, parents have three universal goals for children.* Parents want their children to survive, be healthy, and reproduce; to have the requisite human and social capital to be successful in economic activities and thus maintain themselves; and to develop in many areas (e.g., morality, religion, intellectual capacity, personal satisfaction, self-realization) so as to contribute to society and cultural values (Oates, 2010). Ideas and strategies as to how these goals are to be achieved can differ between fathers and mothers, and from culture to culture (Hennon & Wilson, 2008).
- *Fathers and mothers are different.* Not as clear-cut as they used to be, gender boundaries for individuals have been stretched so that men can be nurturers and women providers. Individual differences aside, there are generic gender differences

based on the interaction of biology and gender socialization (Coakley, 2006; Featherstone, 2009; Lamb, 2010; Parke, 2004; Paquette, 2004; Stuchell & Barrett, n.d.). Men and women tend to approach parenting with different goals, values, and styles, differences more subtle than the instrumental and expressive functions described by Parsons (1955). Scholarship on the competency of fathers in caring for children shows that fathers are often capable and sensitive, responsive, and emotionally connected to children. The current trends of careful investigation and rigorous theorizing allow for better appreciation of the variety and complexity of fathering experiences (Biblarz & Stacey, 2010; Brotherson et al., 2005; Crowl et al., 2008; Lamb, 2010; Pleck, 2010).

- *Fathers are important and not easily replaceable.* Although lone-mothers and lesbian couples often do a quality job of child rearing, children benefit from the style and investment of male energy in their upbringing (Brotherson et al., 2005; Coakley, 2006; Featherstone, 2009; Lamb, 2010; Parke, 2004; Paquette, 2004; Pleck, 2010; Tasker, 2010; however, see Biblarz & Stacey, 2010, for a discussion of how lesbian two-mother families might be better for children, and two-parent families of any type might be best for children). The real importance of fathers may hinge more on their being different from mothers than being a clone of a good mother. Meeting the developmental and other needs of children is a leading validation for promoting quality fathering.

- *Standards for fatherhood must be revised to reflect a higher common ground.* Fatherhood standards have changed, perhaps eroded, as family diversity and self-gratification have been accepted as predominant values, changing the focus from clear expectations to fuzzy criteria for good fathering. It seems critical to articulate a set of high standards that respects diversity of family forms and cultural practices. Being a good father means meeting one's needs without diluting the commitment to children. Engagement, accessibility, and responsibility are areas where standards need to be emphasized. The world could use more responsible, generative fathering.

- *Fathers and mothers often contribute different human, financial, and social capital resources.* Children's development is related to the quality and quantity of resources provided by parents (Parcel, Dufur, & Cornell, 2010). Human capital is the skills, knowledge, and traits that promote achievement. Numeric and verbal ability, effective work habits, and knowledge of correct forms of dress and speech are among the human capital resources that parents can possess. Parents with high levels of human capital can foster their children's cognitive and scholastic abilities through providing stimulating home environments, modeling behavior, and encouraging high academic and occupational aspirations. Financial capital includes income as well as the goods and experiences purchased. Parents with adequate financial capital can provide children good food and shelter, safe environments, access to high-quality schools, support for attending college, and commodities facilitating academic success such as computers, Internet access, books, tutoring, and travel (Davis-Kean, 2005). Social capital is a resource related to the relationships among people. Social capital, or social networks, is a resource that can be tapped to foster children's experiences and opportunities

beyond the immediate family circle benefiting the cognitive and social development of children (Pong, Hao, & Gardner, 2005).

■ *Differences between mothers and fathers should be reframed from deficits to
strengths.* Previously, research seemed to be based on the assumption that some
fathers are "good," and are enlightened, contributing, loving, full and equal parent participants performing duties with skill, care, and concern. Other fathers
are "bad," being bumbling, reluctant, absent, dysfunctional, or violent men failing in or rejecting the duties of fathering (Stuchell & Barrett, n.d.). Although
sometimes having been portrayed as the family's weak link or having role inad-
equacy, men have characteristics based on their socialization that can be beneficial to the parent role. Problem solving, sense of humor, playfulness, risk taking,
and a more physical style of play are just some examples (Lamb, 2010; Parke,
2004; Paquette, 2004; Stuchell & Barrett, n.d.). How men interact with their
children forces youth to "stretch" both emotionally and physically. Fathers push
children to deal with the world outside the mother–child bond. Children, consequently, develop a complex set of interactive and emotional communications skills.
Fathers also encourage differentiation from the family and help adolescents, in particular, develop individual autonomy. Men can benefit from learning more about
empathy and expressing feelings and sensitivity, but they are more likely to focus
on these when feeling respected for some of the strengths they bring to parenting
(Doherty, Kouneski, & Erickson, 1998). Men also gain personally from being involved fathers, developing a somewhat flexible sense of "fatherness," "parenting
possible selves," or "paternal self-confidence" over time as children age and new
situations are encountered and meanings established (Meek, 2007; Oren & Oren,
2009). Parenting is not a one-way influence, of father to child; rather fathers and
children influence each other and thus innovate changes in values and behaviors
(Ashbourne, 2009; Peterson, Hennon, & Knox, 2010).

Differences must be acknowledged by schools to better involve more men in the
education process and to support their unique contributions to children as learners
as well as to schools as institutions. Educators can use the premises identified to develop a clearer understanding of how to facilitate fathers encouraging children to
achieve their best, take risks, and solve problems.

Reflection...

What are the differences, from your experience and reading, between fathers and mothers? Do you think
the differences are based on biology or gender socialization? Because there are differences, how do we
as a society deal with the differences? Do we desire to change men, change women, or change society?
Do we want androgynous humans? What other factors besides gender socialization and biology influence
parenting attitudes and behavior?

Fatherhood in Context

Culture of Fatherhood

A popular culture of fatherhood exists in the United States, and "the 'culture of fatherhood' is alive and well in academic journals" (Goldberg et al., 2009, p. 159). This fatherhood culture is fueled by the mass media and academic research, supported by many parenting experts and social movements, and can influence how fathers parent. Consumers of this culture are those attentive to the mass media's presentations about the fathering role and how fathers ought to parent. This popular culture includes ideals about the appropriate amount and type of father–child interactions, responsibilities of fathers, and such things as how fathers ought to be involved in their children's schooling. This popular culture exalts new, modern, generative, and responsible fatherhood, and researchers are increasingly focusing on the roles of fathers and their perhaps unique contributions to child development and children's academic success.

Some media, educators, and social scientists are portraying and advocating more nurturing, responsible, or generative fathering. Men should place less emphasis on being a distant and stern father who is a good provider, it is argued, and place more emphasis on playing, talking, caring, and nurturing.

The promotion of responsible fathering is a moral position. It advocates an "ought to do and be like" stance with desired norms for judging fathers' behavior and conveys moral meanings of right and wrong as it suggests that some fathers can be considered irresponsible. Such responsible fathering consists of a man behaving responsibly toward his child by waiting to have a child until he is financially and emotionally prepared to support his child; establishing his legal paternity when fathering a child; and sharing in an active manner with the child's mother in the physical and emotional care as well as the financial support of their child from pregnancy onward (Doherty et al., 1998). The term *generative fathering* is used to describe a process of responding "readily and consistently" to a child's changing developmental needs (Brotherson et al., 2005, p. 2). This perspective is a nondeficit one rooted in the ethical obligation to meet the needs of the next generation and focuses on the strengths of fathers. This perspective might describe reality, but mainly purports to suggest what is desirable and possible.

Four factors influence fathers' involvement with their children: motivation, skills, social support, and institutional practices. Optimal father involvement is forthcoming "when a father is highly motivated, has adequate parenting skills, receives social support for his parenting, and is not undermined by work and other institutional settings" (Doherty et al., 1998, p. 283). Dimensions of paternal parenting are often considered to be *engagement* (direct play, leisure, and caregiving), *accessibility* (availability to the child), and *responsibility* (knowing the child's needs and making responsive decisions) (Lamb, 2010). Given the changes in both the culture and conduct of fathering, the roles of fathers likely are becoming more complex and confused. Traditional measures for being a good father may no longer prevail (Lamb, 2010; Oren & Oren, 2009). This focus on new fatherhood is not confined to the United

States. Similar questioning of fathers' roles is found in many societies (Bernard van Leer Foundation, 2003; Hennon & Wilson, 2008; Lamb, 2010).

Reading about, or other media portrayal of, parenting is not likely to have a great influence on a father's behavior if there are other, more pressing desires and needs (Pehlke et al., 2009). These other desires and needs might include worries about unemployment, job security, career advancement, perpetual overworking, and so on. Attention to social and economic achievement and providing for one's family appears to be a major focus of men (Doherty et al., 1998; Oren & Oren, 2009; Hennon & Wilson, 2008). This is apparent even in the face of data suggesting that "family comes first," or that men are now more involved with and attuned to their families.

The change observed in the conduct of fathering might be illusional. LaRossa (1988) argued there has been more change in the culture of fatherhood than there has been in the conduct of fathering, but some change is occurring and discussing fatherhood is a positive sign. Discourse is an important preliminary step and may lead to action. It can also be seen as more pressure on men to change and be something else, perhaps something they do not want to be. Whereas some men relish involved fatherhood and appreciate information on and support for better nurturing and involvement, others do not. Some do not because fathering is a private affair, and some do not because they are already fulfilling the role in the way they think is best. It is their mode of fathering, perhaps the same as their fathers, and it works. "Best" may or may not include a lot of direct caregiving and responsibility.

Modern Father

Given the popular parental culture and the sense of egalitarianism prevailing today in many segments of U.S. and other societies, it is likely that fathering will continue to evolve (Avenilla, Rosenthal, & Tice, 2006; Brotherson et al., 2005; Featherstone, 2009; Lamb, 2010; Oren & Oren, 2009; Parke, 2004; Peterson et al., 2010). This is especially likely in the white middle class. The middle class is the driving force behind the changes, at least attitudinally, in the culture of fatherhood.[1] Thus men socialized to be fathers in a more conventional mode might feel pressure and tension to accept and change to a more modern mode.

Some modern fathers may be feeling pressured by more traditional wives to change their fathering activities. Research points to certain women protecting their turf and monitoring and evaluating men's household and child-care activities in ways men find uncomfortable (Aulette, 2010; Brotherson et al., 2005; Cook et al., 2005; Lu et al., 2010; Pew Research Center, 2007; Wood & Repetti, 2004). Or at least some women do not expect men to be very involved.[2] Men and women tend to develop parenting and household management strategies along lines of believed competencies. Both parents assess their own abilities and preferences relative to those of the partner and their expectations of their partners. Likely, each then assumes responsibility for tasks within the areas where they hold competencies and expertise (Anderson & Sabatelli, 2010).

Both parents can learn and master many tasks. However, earlier socialization, cultural, and reference group expectations influence the perceptions of competencies as well as "what ought to be." Fathers tend to become involved when their wives and others (e.g., maternal grandmothers of the child in single-parent homes; Lu et al., 2010) expect them to be highly engaged in household management and child care, usually when the wife spends many hours in employment and when there is a greater number of children. A father's willingness to engage as an equal partner in family life, child care, and child socialization sways the extent of involvement. This in turn is influenced by cultural norms as well as individual factors such as motivation, and family factors such as the mother's desires. Nevertheless, the distribution of household and child-care tasks may be more a function of power and its use than strict cultural norms about parenting. Women continue to do most of the housework; fathers have less involvement with children than do mothers; and other "fathers may be unsupportive, behaving in ways that alienate children and create a lost of respect" (Aulette, 2010; Hennon & Wilson, 2008; Pehlke et al., 2009, p. 135).

Reflection...

Who did most of the household and child-care tasks in your home when you were growing up? Will it be the same in your household? Does relative power influence decisions about household tasks, or is it more about values?

Radoslav and Maria

Radoslav and Maria Popescu emigrated as children 25 years ago from eastern Europe and are living in an ethnic neighborhood in a large midwestern city. They grew up in a cultural context emphasizing more formal but loving relationships between fathers and children, especially sons. Fathers were stern and worked to care for and protect their families. In fact, Radoslav and Maria's fathers worked hard to get their families to the United States where they could experience a better life. In the United States, the families wanted to acculturate and be like the rest. Radoslav and Maria grew up speaking English, listening to rock music, watching portrayals of family life on television and in movies, and made friends with American kids in their schools. In their neighborhood, some things remained more traditional and yet there was pressure to "be American."

After high school, Radoslav (Rad as he is called) got work with a construction firm owned by his uncle. Maria pursued a nursing degree part-time at a community college, while working part-time. Being in love, they got married and soon had two children. Now, the older child is in fifth grade and the younger one is in third. Maria is back in school part-time, attending day classes so she can be home evenings with her family. A problem is arising with the older child. In school, she seems distracted and is falling behind the other students. The school psychologist wants to meet with the parents. A question thus arises: Does Radoslav take time off work to go?

The macrocultures (society) of the United States and that of the original home-land may be in conflict in this case. Perhaps Rad goes only if there is a behavioral problem and he needs to "straighten his daughter out," or perhaps if he perceives the school is at fault and he wants to straighten out the school. He remembers that his dad wanted him to do well in school, but Rad's father always respected and deferred to the school as the authority. His mother attended meetings; his dad never set foot inside a U.S. school. Rad's work buddies and the uncle who owns the company depend on him. Taking time off work would be a problem, and he would have to explain this to his uncle and workmates. Besides, even though Rad supports and loves his daughter, this is "women stuff," not an issue for men (at least accord-ing to his friends).

But the mesoculture (community) may also offer some different and conflicting norms. Some neighbors seem to be involved in PTO, field trips, parent–teacher conferences, and the like. Some fathers help their children with homework. And the microculture (family) also influences thinking about what is right. Maria is working and going to school, and she is "modern." She expects and even demands that Rad get involved with his children, reminding him of how much he disliked the distant relationship he had with his dad. She would have to miss either work or class to go to the meeting. She thinks, "Why should I be the one to always make the sacrifices?" Besides, she remembers how Rad used to be so considerate in helping with house-work and watching the children. What has happened? Why do their expectations about Rad's role as father seem to be at odds, and why is this creating conflict in their marriage?

Conduct of Fathering

On Time Activities

Although some research indicates that today there is more male involvement in household management and child-rearing activities, it is not clear exactly how widespread this change in family organization might be (Anderson & Sabatelli, 2010; Coltrane, 2000; Doherty et al., 1998; Gordon & Conger, 2007; Lamb, 2010; Marsiglio, Amato, Day, & Lamb, 2000; Pew Research Center, 2007; Wical & Doherty, 2005). Although in the 1990s women reduced their time contributed to housework, and men slightly increased, women still did at least twice as much routine housework as did men (Coltrane, 2000). When both paid and unpaid work is considered, men and women average about 60 hours per week, men with more paid employment and women unpaid housework. A commonly cited statistic is that men in dual-earner households do about 30% of the housework. In some studies, child care is included in housework.[3]

Empirical data are confusing and inconsistent concerning the amount of father involvement with their children and how much change, if any, there has been in this involvement. Although earlier research indicated that many people reported being at least somewhat dissatisfied with contemporary fathering, a recent study has found that the role of fathers, as perceived by mothers, is relatively positive (Pew Research Center, 2007; Pehlke et al., 2009). Over 55% of women surveyed reported that they think today's dads are raising their kids as well as or better than fathers did a generation ago. Married working (at least part time) mothers were even more positive: over 75% assessed the performance of fathers today as doing as good as or better than fathers a generation ago in terms of raising children.

Earlier research found that men were moving closer to child-care parity with women, especially in households with mothers employed full-time outside the home. Fathers in dual-career households spend twice the time (5.3 hours per day) as fathers in single-career households (2.1 hours) in solo child care. Although levels of fathers' engagement and accessibility remained significantly lower than those for mothers, research documents, since the 1970s, a slow increase in the level of father involvement in two-parent households, in proportionate and absolute terms (Hennon, Olsen, & Palm, 2008). Doherty and colleagues (1998) reported that in the late 1990s, fathers' engagement relative to mothers' engagement was about 40%, and accessibility was about 67% compared to mothers (other sources reported that the engagement by fathers was between 55% and 70%). These proportions are higher than those reported for the 1970s and 1980s. This compares to global studies indicating that in Sweden, men do 45% of child care; Aka Pygmies are on average within an arms' reach of infants 47% of the time and might hold their infants close for about 2 hours each day; and British fathers average about 33% of child care. Worldwide, fathers do between 25% and 33% as much child care as do women. Of 156 cultures investigated, about 20% promote a father's close relationship with infants and about 5% with young children (Bernard van Leer Foundation, 2003; Hennon, Olsen, & Palm, 2008; see also Hennon & Wilson, 2008). In some cases, father supportiveness matters most when mother's (due to depression and so on) supportiveness is low (Martin et al., 2010). Fathers can also play a mediating role in their children's school achievement, supplementing lack of neighborhood and family resources, beyond that accounted for by mothers' involvement (McBride et al., 2005).

Fathers' participation in child care appears to be explained by mothers' work hours, other responsibilities such as employment, the quality of the marriage, residing with the child (compared to nonresidency such as not marrying the mother or after divorce), cultural norms and ethnicity, personal expectations about being involved, the father's and mother's gender role ideology and adherence to traditional gender roles, and being in same-sex relationships (Cook et al., 2005; Doherty et al., 1998; Henley & Pasley, 2005; Lamb, 2010; Lu et al., 2010; Marsiglio et al., 2000; Peterson et al., 2010; Raikes, Summers, & Roggman, 2005; Tasker, 2010; Taylor & Behnke, 2005; Terrel, 2005; Wical & Doherty, 2005). Men, in general, often participate in child care because of necessity. Women and girls execute more than their fair share of housework, and overall mothers, rather than fathers, are responsible for children (Hennon, Olsen, & Palm, 2008). U.S. society is experiencing an evolution, not a revolution, concerning fathers' involvement in the full range of child-related chores. It is important to remember that the fathers' contributions are important, even if not on parity with women (Paquette, 2004; Lamb, 2010). "Good fathering is one of many factors promoting good child outcomes, having positive consequences independent of other influences such as good mothering, and having these consequences in ways not necessarily linked to fathers' masculinity. Though being one of many sources of positive development rather than being all-determinative, good fathering is no less important on that account" (Pleck, 2010, pp. 27–28).

Research indicates that fathers are less likely than mothers to provide most of the continuous care for children and are less likely to sacrifice their own time to do so. Fathers are less involved in providing care; attending to, responding to, holding, soothing, comforting their children; and performing other child-care tasks (Hennon, Olsen, & Palm, 2008). Even fathers completing specially designed parent education programs are not especially invested in parent–child interaction. This is possibly due to work responsibilities, social obligations, and other factors.

There are contradictions in the evidence about fathering. Although doing less "on time" activities with their children than mothers, men report parenting to be an important role (Bernard van Leer Foundation, 2003; Brotherson et al., 2005; Lamb, 2010); several studies suggest that fathers consider their primary responsibility as being a good provider (Doherty et al., 1998; Hennon & Wilson, 2008). Many studies report increased involvement in parenting, especially among younger men in dual-earner families. However, statements such as "men appear to be more conscientious parents than some might expect" (Canary, Emmers-Sommer, & Faulkner, 1997, p. 110) and "men's greater involvement . . . in parenting likely is the hallmark of the 1990s" (Gilbert, 1993, p. 43) can be contrasted with "although people are moving toward the idea that fathers should be more involved with children, demographic and social changes have resulted in fathers being less involved with children than perhaps at anytime in U.S. history" (Amato & Booth, 1997, p. 228).

In a 1992 National Center for Fathering Gallup Poll, 96% agreed that fathers needed to be more involved in their children's education, 54% agreed that fathers spent *less* time with their children than their fathers did with them, and only 42% agreed that most fathers knew what was going on in their children's lives (U.S. Department of Education, 2000). A 2007 survey reported that about 40% of fathers believed they were doing as well as or better than their fathers, and 55% believed they were doing worse (Pew Research Center, 2007). Given the available data, the involved father may be more apparent than real.

Although the concern about fatherless families drove much of the debate about fatherhood during the 1990s, understanding of the contributions of nonresidential fathers has also increased (Dudley & Stone, 2001; Henley & Pasley, 2005; Potter, 2010). The focus on the social pathology related to absent fathers and fatherless homes (and the comparisons of nonresident fathers to resident fathers in two-parent homes) has detracted from gaining knowledge about and appreciating the contributions made by nonresident fathers. This group is composed of divorced fathers who do not have or share custody of their children, and fathers who are unmarried and might have cohabited for a period of time. Many of these fathers are young and their families are sometimes described as fragile (Lamb, 2010). Another group of "fatherless children" could be those being raised by lesbian mothers or having gay fathers not residing with them (Lamb, 2010; Oren & Oren, 2009; Tasker, 2010.) A growing number of fathers are absent through incarceration (Cooper, Sabol, & West, 2009; Meek, 2007). Nonresident fathers are not a homogeneous group of deadbeat, absent fathers. The paths to nonresident fatherhood are diverse and such fathers have varying levels of commitment and involvement. A study of unmarried fathers found that they had the same amount of involvement with their children at the age of 4 as they did when they were 1 year old. However, the degree of involvement that can be sustained over the first 18 years of life is unknown (Hennon, Olsen, & Palm, 2008). Nonresident fathers can be involved with their adolescent offspring (Hawkins et al., 2007). In general, it appears that nonresident fathers have less involvement, especially in day-to-day activities, and face barriers sometimes resulting from ongoing conflict with the ex-spouse or partner, or the gatekeeping activities of grandparents, to increasing or maintaining their involvement.

In the real lives of men, fathers may not perceive the necessity or appropriateness of being involved with their children in other than playful or providing ways. Those wishing to negotiate a change in this social reality could find more profit from working directly with men and their families. These agents of change may want to pay special attention to what fathers say is important about what they do and what they see as shortcomings. Learning the meanings that real men attach to parenting and to how they might wish to change may be more constructive in negotiating social change. It will also be important to construct policy, services, and resources such as family-life and parent education programs that are culturally specific and sensitive; attentive to the needs of men, women, and children; and adapted to the diverse family settings that have evolved for nonresident fathers (Featherstone, 2009; Hennon, Peterson, Polzin, & Radina, 2007; Hennon, Wilson, & Radina, in press; Lu et al., 2010; Radina, Wilson, & Hennon, 2008; Oren & Oren, 2009; Peterson et al., 2010).

Conceptual Framework

A commonly used conceptualization for considering father involvement discriminates among *engagement* (time spent in one-on-one interaction with a child, in nurturing, playing, or disciplining), *accessibility* (less intense interaction, in which the father is engaged in another task but is available to respond to the child if needed), and *responsibility* (being accountable for the child's welfare and care, such as making and tracking appointments and being sure the child's needs are being met) (Brotherson et al., 2005; Lamb, 2010). Being responsible does not always require direct interaction with the child. A father can be anxious, worried, satisfied, or planning for contingencies while otherwise engaged (such as in driving a car, in employment, or in playing soccer). This typology indicates the wide range of possibilities, some of which could include quality interactions, whereas others might include being accessible when necessary and taking responsibility either directly or indirectly for the welfare of his children. This typology articulates with a culturally specific and diverse clarification of father involvement as cultural, ethnic, and religious minorities can have varied views of what it means to be a good father. Puerto Rican fathers might place more emphasis on disciplining children and less on direct caregiving. Asian American fathers might place their greatest emphasis on being economic providers. At the same time, these fathers can reinforce academic achievement, emotional maturity, self-control, and social courtesies. Hispanic American families tend to emphasize a close mother–child relationship, with fathers helping instill values of interpersonal responsiveness including understanding the importance of interacting and relating to others with respect and dignity. Mormon American fathers might have less frequent individual contact with each child due to larger family size, thus helping less with homework, for example, while still influencing positive social values (Anderson & Sabatelli, 2010; Aulette, 2010; Beckert et al., 2006; Coakley, 2006; Kim et al., 2006; Morman & Floyd, 2006; Oren & Oren, 2009; Pong et al., 2005; Radina et al., 2008). Whatever the differences, these fathers can be considered good fathers who are engaged, accessible, and responsible within the parameters of particular cultural contexts.

The relative distribution of their saliency and the time and energy directed to the engagement, accessibility, and responsibility components of fathering can vary widely (1) across cultural and socioeconomic groups, (2) by phase of the life cycle, (3) from family to family, (4) from child to child within a family, and (5) from day to day, not to mention from minute to minute. However, we argue here that each family establishes rules about the relative distribution of the various but interrelated components of parenting among the members of the parenting subsystem. These parenting strategies reflect each family's themes and thus exhibit some stability. However, these rules and strategies can be renegotiated and can change over time given different circumstances and needs (Anderson & Sabatelli, 2010). An important aspect of good parenting is a coparental relationship in which parents present a unified authority structure. Such structures, even if parents are divorced, show children that there is agreement on rules and discipline, that parents support each other's decisions, and that parental authority is not arbitrary. Such hierarchical authority learned in the family helps youth adjust to other institutions so organized, such as schools. Supportive coparenting also influences the parent–child relationship, as mothers become more effective and fathers improve the quality of their parenting.

One reflection of family system dynamics and themes is the *traditionalization of gender roles* (LaRossa, 1988). Regardless of how egalitarian their marriages are before the arrival of children, men often do less household work after, relative to the increased total workload. On becoming parents, fathers and mothers experience a growing separation of roles (Cook et al., 2005). There is thus regression to more familiar cultural expectations. Men appear to often maintain "role distance" from parenting, whereas women embrace the parenting role (Adamsons, 2006; Aulette, 2010; Stuchell & Barrett, n.d.). Women often engage parenting in ways distinctive from how men connect with parenting practices. However, there are neglectful and/or abusive mothers, and loving, nurturing fathers.

One explanation for the traditionalization phenomenon suggests that spouses have biographic and socialization experiences giving them competencies in what are considered traditional domains. Gender socialization, cultural values, and expectations appear to play a part in how and how much fathers parent. Families can negotiate more or less equivalent divisions of child care and other labor.

Understanding Fathering

Sometimes fathering might be perplexing, confusing, or frustrating for men. Sometimes it is forgotten or not in one's immediate stream of consciousness. But often fathering is joyful, engaging, easy, unquestioned, and taken for granted. In the United States there is a *folk psychology* about fathering. It is distilled from living in and experiencing the culture. This folk psychology includes the readily understood, experiential meaning of being a father, without attention to issues of race, ethnicity, and so on. It is what fathering is. This folk psychology is one of the taken-for-granted, generally unquestioned aspects of the natural world. It is the way things are. Although being a father is complex and not easily understood, it is perhaps even harder for outsiders to grasp in a scientific way than it is for insiders who are experiencing it and understanding it in their natural, taken-for-granted way. Outsiders, that is, researchers and other professional experts, may also create and use "fictions" (e.g., concepts and theories unrecognizable by fathers in their own lived experiences) to describe parenting that are not real to the lived experiences of fathers. That is, as fathers perceive how they are socially situated and act in their families, jobs, friendship groups, communities, and society in general (Hennon, Olsen, & Palm, 2008; Marsiglio, Roy, & Fox, 2005). Fathers have an important role in "appropriating or discarding cultural and contextual messages, in formulating a fathering identity and developing fathering skills with their own children, in working out their feelings about their own fathers, and in dealing collaboratively with their children's mother" (Doherty et al., 1998, p. 289). Fathers hold a pivotal role in the social construction of fatherhood as an evolving creation.

To better understand fathering, one must include in the consideration the *ethnoculture* (or stock of knowledge) of fathers (in contrast to either the popular parental culture or culture as known to the social scientist or educator). This ethnoculture consists of the values, norms, beliefs, attitudes, and material objects as known to specific fathers. This stock of knowledge is the reality within which individual fathers operate. It is their reference world, with images of "who I am as a father" based at least partially on expectations held by significant others and reference groups. It is the personal meaning of fatherhood. Fathers' transactions with this lived culture (or lifeworld as it is also known), as they understand and attend to it, influence their cognitive and behavioral actions. Other men, as well as children and women, help in shaping a father's lifeworld and stock of knowledge. Aspects of the popular parental culture as well as other media sources may be a part of this lived culture (Pehlke et al., 2009). Although it might be assumed that the predominant culture is hegemonic, in the contemporary United States, with all its diversity, one cannot assume that it is prevalent and directive everywhere and for everyone. That is, while there is some general, society wide (macro) sharing of values and basic understandings concerning fatherhood, ethnic and other subculture enclaves (meso) can provide stronger context for behavior. And within these subtexts, idiosyncratic individual and family systems (micro) behavior will be found.

To reiterate, although there is more hegemonic macrocultural context for fathering in the United States, there are also important distinctions of a more meso- and microcultural level, such as the environmental context differences that might be found within an Indian reservation in Wisconsin versus suburban Connecticut, or between a Jewish enclave in New York City and African American Mennonites in North Carolina, or a divorced architect with one child both living in New Mexico and a married father of nine children all living in southern Idaho. To understand fathering in these various contexts, and to design better ways of increasing and enhancing investment in schooling, it is important to (1) recognize difference, (2) be open to cultural definitions varying from one's own, (3) appreciate cultural context and how even though culture is not deterministic in an absolute manner, it can shape behavior depending on how closely one identifies with a culture, (4) accept that a carefully constructed program may be culturally abrasive, (5) understand family system influences, and (6) consider fathering as part of the larger tapestry of men's lives.

Fathering and School Achievement

Some research indicates that fathers experience the same parental joys, worries, and frustrations as mothers (Lamb, 2010; Peterson et al., 2010). There are, however, qualitative differences between mothers and fathers in how parenting is commonly conducted. There are, as well, differences within groups of fathers. Fathers bring certain strengths to parenting. In some cases, fathers would like to change the way they father, becoming more involved, nurturing, skillful, emotionally close, and so forth. Some fathers want involvement in their children's schooling whereas others do not know how, feel alienated from school systems in general (especially if their own school experiences were not positive), or do not feel comfortable within a particular school setting. Some fathers perhaps do not realize that active school involvement is appropriate or useful.

Irrespective of other factors such as social class, family structure, or developmental characteristics and stage of the child, positive outcomes for children appear to be related to certain parenting styles (Davis-Kean, 2005). Various publications report positive developmental outcomes for children associated with parenting styles characterized by logical reasoning, clear communication, appropriate monitoring, support, involvement with the children, and love (Anderson & Sabatelli, 2010; Dwairy, 2008; Gordon & Conger, 2007; Peterson et al., 2010). Children raised with this style of parenting are observed to be successful in school, altruistic, cooperative, trusting, having good self-esteem, and better able to enter into and maintain intimate relationships. Likewise, a style characterized by being sensitive to the children's developmental needs, nurturing without being overly restricting, acting responsive without being overly controlling, and stimulating without being overly directive is related to positive academic and other outcomes for children (Gordon & Conger, 2007; Marsiglio et al., 2000; Peterson et al., 2010; Steinberg, 2007). This is a style referred to as authoritative parenting, and research indicates that it is this style that best predicts more desirable outcomes among children, including academic success.

Research on school attendance, achievement, and adjustment indicates that various aspects of family and household environments appear to influence educational outcomes of youth.[4] Some characteristics identified include socioeconomic status (SES), parents' employment status and educational backgrounds, family structure, and the role of the father (Davis-Kean, 2005; Kalil & Ziol-Guest, 2007; Marsiglio et al., 2000; National Institute of Child Health, 2008). For example, several studies, even when controlling for SES, demonstrate a relationship between father absence and poor academic performance and dropping out of school (Henley & Pasley, 2005; Lamb, 2010; Lee, n.d.; Steinberg, 2007). Father absence is associated with poor academic attainment and school dropout, perhaps more so than the effect of poverty alone, but poverty or socioeconomic status can have a significant influence on other problems such as delinquency. One important aspect of father absence is the payment or nonpayment of child support. The amount of child support is positively associated with children's school grades and fewer behavioral problems at school. Reading and math scores and years of school attainment are also positively associated with the amount of child support paid. These associations do not appear to differ by the gender or race of the child.

Among teens, nonresidential fathers are less likely than are resident fathers to be the primary source for discussions about school and careers (Dudley & Stone, 2001). Teens also describe their dads as being more distant than their mothers. Daughters particularly often describe their fathers as uninvolved. Possibly, fathers more often show intimacy toward their teenage children through sharing an activity or helping out in some way, such as fixing something. That is, "doing" rather than verbally expressing their love and concern.

Given the relationship between school adjustment and aspects of the family environment, including fathers' support, it would appear that a better understanding of fathering and fathers' involvement with schools might provide better foundations for enhancing children's school adjustment and success. Factors such as the quantity and quality of contact between parents and the child's school could be consequential for academic outcomes. Although we realize that promoting this idea can create more pressure and higher expectations for father involvement, we believe that fathers' involvement in the schools and schooling of their children is important and should be encouraged.

Reflection...

Given that many children are living in female-headed households and have little or no contact with their fathers, what can teachers and schools do for these children, or should they do anything? Are children "doomed" because their fathers are not involved in their lives? Or given current norms of gender equality and inclusion, is it appropriate to design interventions specifically for fathers only? Will this make children without fathers feel left out?

Benefits of Involving Fathers in Schools and Schooling

We believe there are several reasons for attempting to increase and support the involvement of fathers in schools and schooling and there are many means or strategies for doing so. Although direct involvement in the school is highly desirable, fathers can also be involved in the schooling of their children in other ways, such as encouraging academic achievement, engraining a strong work ethic, supervising homework, and offering intellectual and cultural activities and experiences. Included among the reasons and means are:

- *Fathers* deserve, and some need, involvement support and services. Many men are interested in and open to this type of involvement, and others can be. The new father image has created a cultural expectation for more involvement in parenting, schooling, and schools. This expectation requires buttressing with new strategies by schools and other institutions to invite and engage fathers (Darling, 2008; Epstein et al., 2009; Harvard Family Research Project, 2010; Shedlin, 2004). An example would be the security dads at Arlington High in Indianapolis. Fathers, instead of security guards, ride buses on field trips and to sporting events.
- There are many positive effects on *children* related to father involvement. Lamb (2010) and Stuchell and Barrett (n.d.), among others, reviewed the many strengths that fathers confer on children's development and how these differ from the important contributions of mothers. Fathers can assist in a variety of ways with their school-age children's intellectual and social development. Empathy development is one area. Children who have fathers spending time doing routine child care at least twice weekly are more likely to grow up to be compassionate. Fathers also play an important role in the development of prosocial behavior, especially for boys (Dudley & Stone, 2001). Other research indicates the important role fathers play in their children's academic success and how early involvement has long-lasting effects (Lu et al., 2010; Seitsinger et al., 2008; Tan & Goldberg, 2009). Examples include the development of a strong work ethic, the importance of money and its association with education and good jobs, intellectual skills, preparedness for school, mathematics readiness, engagement with books, early learning (especially in low-income families), literacy development, academic competency, and boys' mastery motivation.

  Fathers can send both subtle and more direct messages to their children about the value of literacy, schooling, and knowledge acquisition. Fathers are generally less engaged than mothers with their children's school, and fathers with less than a high school education are less likely to be involved than fathers with higher levels of education. Fathers from disadvantaged and minority backgrounds are less likely than others to be involved with their children's schooling. They might not want to be involved or have no experience or understanding of how they can help or be involved. Low-income fathers often have high hopes for their children and want help in ensuring that the children will become "someone" with high achievement. Even when fathers have low academic achievement, their involvement in the schools of their children is related to higher academic achievement for their children. Ethnic minority fathers might be less engaged with school in terms of visiting the school or belonging to the PTA, but they nonetheless can encourage and assist their children in other ways. Fagan and Palm (2004) found that some African American fathers who became engaged in Head Start programs developed a sense of responsibility for other children in addition to their own biological children. Nonresident fathers are less involved than fathers who reside with their children, but involvement by nonresident fathers is not trivial. Fathers of all types can encourage early literacy and phonemic awareness through reading to their children, telling stories and nursery rhymes, and singing songs and reciting poetry. A father can also explain what he is doing while performing home-related chores and ask his young children to predict what he is going to do next. These are just a few illustrations; fathers can encourage and support intellectual development and academic achievement in a multitude of ways. It can be concluded from a variety of research that children with a positive father influence benefit, being better able to deal with the many challenges presented by schools, peers, and other adults (Brotherson et al., 2005; Hennon, Olsen, & Palm, 2008).

- *Families* benefit by increased participation of fathers in their children's schooling. Such attention and interest can strengthen and reinforce family interactions and ties in many important areas, including marriage and transgenerational relationships. A greater involvement by fathers also reinforces the importance placed on education by the family (Brotherson et al., 2005; Doherty et al., 1998; Lamb, 2010; Marsiglio et al., 2000; Parke, 2004).

- *Schools* benefit from more father involvement. This involvement enriches the resources to draw on. That is, fathers' knowledge and skills can be tapped. Teachers' reports of children having few problems at school, such as poor attendance or failing a grade, are associated with children's reports of positive paternal behavior (Epstein et al., 2009).

- Increased involvement in schools by fathers would also have positive influences on *society*. The style of male parenting in U.S. society offers a number of important strengths that support school success. These include encouragement to be independent, fostering of competition that raises levels of achievement, and high expectations that fathers often hold for their children that fosters competence. Social life can be more stable, with less violence, addictions, crime, and other pathologies. A more informed and involved citizen strengthens society.

Strategies for Involving Fathers in Schools

Efforts to enhance and support father involvement in schools and schooling should be sensitive to three levels of intervention: the macro-, meso-, and microcultures of fathers. In some cases, efforts to involve fathers more can be considered primary in nature. That is, efforts to change culture and social systems that provide the framework guiding and shaping what men believe to be appropriate fathering. These primary interventions are attempts at negotiated social change that leads to new male socialization practices and values. They include expectations held by the military, religion, economy, education, or other institutions concerning appropriate male behavior toward children. These types of interventions invest in the future of society by encouraging fathers to be supportive in the human and social capital development of their children.

Other interventions are secondary in nature in the sense that they are intended to overcome preexisting conditions and patterns. Such efforts are likely aimed at individual employers, churches, families, or men. These include attempts to convince fathers that, contrary to what they have learned and believe, other ways of acting are better. That is, fathers are to be nurturing, caring, and involved, bringing the strengths and perspectives of men to parenting. Other interventions of this genre include those for fathers who are believers in more involvement but are looking for more resources, support, and services to further this involvement.

It can be argued that fathers can be typed as those who "won't, can't, and want to" change. Those who will not change are perhaps a "lost cause." However, some might be doing an acceptable job of raising their children and some with appropriate stimulation might change their parenting conduct. Those fathers who cannot change are "stuck" in perhaps older modes of fathering and might be motivated and searching for information and other resources and services such as family life education to help make the transition to a new mode of fathering. This new mode could be more responsible and generative. These fathers might need help in overcoming personal, family, and social barriers to be more involved with their children. Fathers in the "want to change" category are perhaps highly motivated and just need the support, skills, and other resources to change that can be provided by family members, educators, family life educators, and others.

Educators can design and/or support good interventions including appropriate resources, support, and services. Schools can assist in the provision of, or help in identifying, the resources available to fathers (such as family resource centers in schools that are father friendly, or parental leave policies and other employment benefits). Schools can also involve themselves in providing or assisting fathers in locating the support they deem necessary (such as a wife's words of encouragement or a network of other fathers in similar situations who can provide information and encouragement). Likewise, schools can offer empowering services (such as parenting classes for divorced fathers) that are useful tools for enhancing fathers' involvement with their children's schooling. However, this is not to discount the necessity of considering family- or relationship-level interventions.

Parenting is a relationship, and it is conducted under the influence of other relationships (Brotherson et al., 2005; Cook et al., 2005; Hennon & Wilson, 2008; Peterson et al., 2010). "Fatherizing" a program or practice does not necessarily mean reducing interventions to individual characteristics or psychological terms. The support necessary could include information about how to talk with one's wife or ex-wife about concerns the father has about parenting. Resources include skills training on how fathers can achieve more involvement without trespassing on the mothers' turf. The self-efficacy of fathers concerning their role as fathers influences their conduct; thus programs to help develop capacity for fathering are important (Junttila et al., 2007). Other relationship-oriented practices could include school lessons to children about fathers in diverse families, and working directly with fathers and children in ways that reinforce positive mutual interactions. Parenting or school involvement programs that authentically involve all parents may prove to be of more benefit than a program targeted only to fathers or mothers.

What efforts are needed to provide more resources, support, and services at the macro-, meso-, and microlevels for families and fathers so that men can be more involved with schools? Some ideas for such efforts to create and reinforce social change follow.

Reflection...

Why has there been an apparent sudden change in how fathers want to be involved in schools? Why didn't this change take place in the 1960s and 1970s? Are the changes that are taking place an overreaction to fathers' current and perhaps less involved roles? Do you think a discussion about fathers' lack of school involvement will be taking place 20 years from now?

Society-Level Interventions

People interested in negotiating social change that values father involvement in schooling should consider more primary interventions that are oriented to helping families and men develop values, themes, strategies, and rules that support and encourage father involvement with their children. These might include:

- Working for peace, social justice, equitable wealth distribution, safe neighborhoods, and sustainable development that considers the equitable distribution of the consequences of economic development.
- Advocating policies of full employment in meaningful work at a living wage.
- Supporting and encouraging the use of parental leaves, flex time, working at home, and other practices allowing fathers to be able to get time away from work to be engaged with their families.
- Ensuring equal opportunities for quality schooling that allows all people to achieve and maintain at least an adequate standard of living.
- Writing, preparing, or encouraging mass media portrayals of men in diverse positive family roles, including the strengths those fathers bring to parenting.
- Widely sharing the positive outcomes of efforts to have fathers be more involved, as well as sharing stories of how fathers are involved.

- Advocating for fathers' rights, fair child support and visitation guidelines (and strong enforcement of such), cooperative coparenting (perhaps with joint custody), and other measures to keep fathers in contact, involved, and supportive of their children after divorce (or if unwed).

Community and School-Level Interventions

Fathers often are challenged in their efforts at achieving a reasonable balance of home and work life. This challenge can create additional stress, influencing their parenting. However, success at achieving an acceptable balance can be a source of support. In addition, environmental factors, such as regular work hours; vacations; job security; the ability to attend school conferences in the early morning, late evening, or on weekends; the ability to communicate with school via e-mail, and so on, might be resources for helping fathers maintain a lower level of stress. Attitudes toward employment and specific work are also important. For instance, research notes an elevated incidence of child abuse among unemployed fathers who would rather be working, compared to working fathers (Anderson & Sabatelli, 2010). Absorption in work is related to fathers being more irritable and impatient with their children, whereas other employment or work conditions influence how available fathers are and their approach to parenting (Kalil & Ziol-Guest, 2007; Oren & Oren, 2009).

School systems can work to encourage community development and economic growth. Holistic paradigms, rather than education-centered ones, can encourage viewing schools, employers, and families as all part of the same mesoculture. Working for what is good for the community as a whole appears to be an important strategy.

Proactive steps must be taken if fathers are to be involved in more appropriate and active ways in schools and schooling. Waiting for fathers to "show up at the door" might not prove effective and other approaches are required. We present here some ideas for resources, supports, and services that may prove essential in enhancing father involvement. These tips are offered for teachers, administrators, and school support staff (social workers, family educators, school psychologists, etc.) as well as parents and others concerned about schools and families. Staff and administration must:

- Commit to the importance of involving fathers.
- Help create family-friendly communities.
- Structure schools that are accessible and family (especially father) friendly, including flexibility in scheduling meetings with parents.
- Guarantee that schools are accountable and responsive to families.
- Focus on the strengths of fathers and what they bring to parenting and in supporting children's education. Schools should make the most of fathers' encouragement of students to solve problems and to excel. Many fathers like taking on the role of teacher/mentor. This role reinforces feelings of competence, and

fathers feel they are doing something important. Inviting fathers to share skills or knowledge is a way of taking advantage of these feelings.

- Create environments that are father friendly and portray fathers positively. An obvious example would be male teachers. Other ways to enhance the school environment are posters in the school and classroom of men at work, play, or with families. Videos, music, and other multimedia material about men in their varied roles can be used. Invite men to visit the classroom, not only on Father's Day or Career Day, to share something about themselves (work, hobbies, or special interests).

- Provide opportunities geared toward fathers' interests. Building and setting up playground equipment, helping to coach a basketball team, or judging a science fair are some possibilities. These may be stereotypical opportunities, but they can help fathers feel welcome and comfortable. They also encourage male openness to less stereotypical activities. Be sure to not overgeneralize as to what fathers want or are willing to do. Talking to fathers to determine their desired level of involvement and the activities they wish to participate in is important. Some fathers might want to build something, some might want to move boxes, and some might want to read a story, direct a play, teach a lesson, offer computer advice, tutor, or organize playground activities.

- Sponsor more naturally occurring positive fathering activities involving fathers in clubs, Scouts, outings, projects (including building and repairing), games, camping, fishing, and the like. More fun and active events can be opportunities for fathers to observe parenting and share information, as well as for "experts" to provide parenting information and model behavior.

- Include fathers in invitations. A generic invitation to "parents" can still be a code name for mothers. Fathers might need explicit invitations to know that they are both expected and welcome.

- Offer father-only or father–child events. Be inclusive in invitations so that male father figures (e.g., uncles, grandfathers, and mother's boyfriend) feel welcome.

- Sensitize to male communication styles. Fathers may want to get right to business and have relationship building as a secondary priority.

- Establish family resource centers in schools that are father friendly and help individuals and couples build capacity for better quality parenting. Such centers can help families in meeting the totality of their needs (such as health, financial management, stress management, and leisure).

- Include fathers or other significant males in early intervention services for children with special needs. Many fathers, including those who are divorced or otherwise not residing with the child, want and need involvement in decisions affecting the well-being of their children.

- Encourage fathers to become involved in PTA/PTO.

- Ask parents to imagine the life path of their child, what they hope the child to achieve, and what resources and skills parents and others need to provide for this dream to become reality. Determine what resource shortfalls parents have in this regard (lack of skills, knowledge, etc.) and work to have the school and other organizations fill the resource gap.

- Realize that there are diverse ways for fathers to be involved. Fathers may already be involved in their children's education, but searching for creative approaches to exploit their involvement.

Achieving more school involvement by fathers goes beyond the important stride of making schools more father friendly. Perhaps more primary interventions or comprehensive programs are necessary (Seitsinger et al., 2008; Shedlin, 2004; Souto-Manning & Swick, 2006). These more comprehensive interventions can assist fathers in enhancing their capacity for engaging with children and the other parent. Consequently, the importance of school involvement can be more readily understood, appreciated, and desired.

Parent Education

Peterson, Hennon, and Knox (2010), Lamb (2010), Stuchell and Barrett (n.d.), and others have identified some specific gender differences that are pertinent to effective parent education. These differences include the following:

- Goals of mothers and fathers can differ in parent education. Mothers appear more interested in getting support from other parents, whereas fathers seem most interested in building a close relationship with their children and learning about discipline techniques.
- Acknowledging the difference between mothers and fathers in relation to a knowledge and experience base is essential. Girls play more at being parents as part of their childhood experience, whereas boys more often practice other roles. Girls and young women take classes on child development and family relations more frequently than boys. These differences suggest that educational opportunities for boys and men are critical if fathers are to be more competent in skills and knowledge related to child rearing.
- Differences in interaction style are another area identified. In studies based on research concerning infants, fathers' interactions are described as being more physical, tactile, and arousing, whereas mothers are more verbal, soothing, and calming. Androgynous fathers appear to engage in the typical male styles of interactions (i.e., rough-and-tumble play), but are able to express affection.
- Discipline is another area of perceived differences. Being strict and harsh is more characteristic of fathers. Fathers seem able to be firmer, uphold limits, and be authoritative because of hierarchical views. Perhaps fathers focus more on the immediate outcomes (obedience and compliance) and less on longer-term implications of relationships. This style difference may be changing as more men try to avoid the role epitomized by the phrase "wait till your father gets home."
- Solving parenting problems also differs by gender. Mothers appear more effective at solving infants' crying problems, for example. The differences are explained by mothers' greater exposure to and experience with this type of problem.

Fathers' Involvement with Schools

"The idea that parent involvement in children's lives is an exclusively female domain is a misperception that hurts thousands of American children and haunts educational and social efforts to help them" (National Head Start Association, n.d., p. 1).

Fathers are getting more involved in schools for a variety of reasons:

- Fathers are being specifically asked to be involved. This involvement includes attending PTO meetings, riding buses in place of security guards, giving presentations to students, and being included in home–school communication and conferences.
- Fathers are creating work schedules or their companies have family-friendly policies allowing personal time off to engage in school activities. Some fathers are working at or from their homes (including in their own or family businesses), which can allow more flexibility for involving themselves in their children's schools. Some men would like more flexibility in employment responsibilities but face resistance from employers. Some men refuse promotions, some change jobs, but some do not have this luxury or determination.
- Fathers are finding that schools are creating more father-friendly environments, including the curriculum. These environments result in more fathers participating in schools as speakers, volunteer aides, or PTO/PTA board members. Some school districts in Minnesota have young dad programs. These programs include young fathers talking to elementary children about the responsibilities and problems associated with being a teen father. Some school districts, in conjunction with other organizations, identify teen dads who want older fathers for a mentor. Some schools have tried breakfast gatherings. Positive ways of portraying fathers and other men in the curriculum is another idea. The U.S. Department of Education (2000), U.S. Department of Health and Human Services (n.d.), National Head Start Association (n.d.), SEDL National Center for Family and Community Connections with Schools (n.d.), Lee (n.d.), Hutchins et al. (2009), Epstein et al. (2009), and Shedlin (2004), among others, offer many suggestions for creating a father-friendly environment.

There may be some negative reactions to these activities. Educators must listen to the needs of single mothers and others who could feel excluded when schools attempt to reach out to fathers. Providing opportunities for all parents, especially single or lesbian parents who could be left out when fathers are specifically invited, is encouraged.

Reflection...

Schools want to involve parents more, but if fathers don't get involved, how can schools reach out to fathers? Is this a gender equity issue? Would you anticipate a backlash, and if so, what would it be?

Barriers to Fathers' Involvement in Schools

Fathers can offer various accounts and disclaimers for why they do, or do not, engage in certain behaviors (LaRossa, 1988). These vocabularies of motive help in presenting to themselves and others the images of "father" they wish to offer. Self-image can be thought of as a retelling of a narrative: "This is my story; this is who I am." Perhaps the telling of the fathering story is more often to self than to others. Fathers need to know who they are and give it justification so that they can be comfortable and secure. Father inclusion programs based primarily or exclusively on outsider expert knowledge and delivered in a prescription mode are likely to be ineffective.

The real needs, desires, and wishes of men must be considered in order to overcome barriers to father involvement in schools. Likewise, those wishing to negotiate social change must understand the lived realities of the men they are targeting, as perceived by those men. This does not mean accepting at face value the excuses, justifications, and disclaimers offered by men. Fathers should be held accountable for their actions. But realizing that these actions and justifications are part of the parenting-self as constructed by each father is important. These narratives are aspects of the fathers' stock of knowledge and form part of the material that must be used for enhancing father involvement.

One study found that only 24% of fathers of children aged 3 to 5 years and only 33% of fathers of school-aged children were highly involved in school activities (Hennon, Olsen, & Palm, 2008). Other research indicates that parental involvement declines as children advance in their school grade with little involvement by high school (National Network of Partnership Schools, 2010; U.S. Department of Education, 2000). What keeps fathers away from schools?

- A main barrier appears to be time and schedule conflicts. Most fathers work full-time, and many work during typical business and school hours. In comparison, mothers are involved more often in part-time employment.
- A unique barrier is fathers' perceptions that the school involvement tasks are not part of their role. For example, one of the authors was meeting with a group of Even Start fathers and talking about the importance of reading to young children. The response from the men was that their wives did the reading; it was not their job.
- Another barrier is fathers' not feeling invited to a program. If a father walks into a program and looks around and sees adult females and children, he gets the message that this place is for women and children.
- Mothers can also play a gatekeeper role and either decide to push for fathers going to an event or class, or discourage them from going. Often fathers do not know about opportunities for involvement because they are not in the direct line of communication. If the children come home to mother, they are likely to pass on information from the school directly to mother who then takes responsibility for requests from school. Fathers often do not get involved in schools until there is a problem identified with the child.
- Barriers can also include programs being hesitant to make specific efforts to reach out to fathers. With a large portion of children not living with their dads on a regular basis, events and outreach targeted toward dads may seem offensive and

disrespectful of family diversity. The fear of offending parents, especially single-female parents, makes it uncomfortable to make specific overtures toward fathers.

- Head Start reported research indicating four factors that impede Head Start and state-funded prekindergarten programs from achieving father involvement: fathers' fears of exposing inadequacies, ambivalence of program staff members about father involvement, gatekeeping by mothers, and inappropriate program design and delivery (Levine, 1993).

The barriers listed suggest that special efforts need to be made to capitalize on the benefits of father involvement. Understanding subtle barriers that can be addressed by schools is an important advance in involving more fathers. Suggestions for overcoming barriers to fathers' involvement and best practices can be located in many publications and on the Internet *A Call to Commitments: Father's Involvement in Children's Learning* (www2.ed.gov/pubs/parents/calltocommit/index.html) is a good place to start.

Family-Level Interventions

Marital stress influences the quality of parenting (Peterson et al., 2010). In some cases, parents attempt to compensate for a poor marriage by using their children as a source of support and gratification. This might translate into more involvement with school activities. In other cases, parents blame children for the marital strife or scapegoat the children to focus the problem elsewhere. Children will also keep the marital and family systems balanced by acting out or being compliant. Doing well or poorly in school can be a child's device to divert attention away from marital strife and toward the child and his or her needs. The outcome, as seen by school personnel, may be less or more father involvement in schools. In any situation, fathers will likely be less attentive to their children in appropriate ways when there are marital problems or in adjustment to divorce.

Earlier in this chapter we documented some of the gender dynamics and turf issues involved with parents. The mothers (especially divorced ones or others estranged from their children's fathers) can be nonsupportive and resistant to changes in father involvement. Even in good marriages there can be resistance to change. A way for counteracting this tendency is for mothers to learn to expect such territorial feelings and to talk about them with the fathers. Fathers should not be "junior mothers" playing secondary roles, or be "competing mothers" for their children's attention and love. Children benefit from having parents who cooperate together as the parenting team, supporting each other while playing complementary roles (Biblarz & Stacey, 2010; Pleck, 2010). Fathers should not try so hard to connect with their children to be superfathers that their wives are neglected. Keeping marriages strong is one of the best ways to facilitate being a better father (Anderson & Sabatelli, 2010; Peterson et al., 2010). Here are some ways in which schools can facilitate family-level intervention:

- Schools can include in their curricula value-based parent and family life education from the primary school years through adulthood (Hennon et al., 2007; Hennon et al., in press; Peterson et al., 2010; Radina et al., 2008). Evidence-based or best-practices programs include Parenting Wisely (http://familyworksinc.com); the California Evidence-Based Clearinghouse (www.cebc4cw.org); the Incredible Years Program (www.incredibleyears.com); the Nurturing Parent Program (www.nurturingparenting.com); and Triple P: Positive Parenting Program (www.triplep-america.com). U.S. Department of Health and Human Services (2009a, 2009b) is also a good source.

- School systems and individual school personnel, such as social workers or trained lay leaders, can encourage, support, advertise, and offer marital enrichment programs as well as interventions of a more therapeutic nature. Program possibilities include stress management, positive discipline techniques, parenting after divorce, couples' communication techniques, conflict management strategies, co-parenting, and exercises to help parents become more self-aware, self-reflexive, and self-effective about their behavior. Such resources can help parents realize how they respond to others' behavior and their influence on how others respond to them. Reflexivity is a critical process of increasing self-awareness and sensitivity to the experiences of both self and others. Reflexivity is a crucial component of any efforts directed toward enhancing in the fathering role. Enrichment and education can be offered in conjunction with businesses, social service agencies, or religious institutions.
- Educators can help people in understanding that family interaction, interpersonal competency, and love for family, as well as spending quality time with family, are as important as occupational or other achievements.
- School personnel can establish their own quality marriages and interpersonal relationships.

Familial behavior is context sensitive, conditioned by where it occurs. Men tend to experience what is termed *organizational embeddedness*; that is, the social systems men are involved in are not discrete, but rather men carry the meanings of one into others. Whereas analytically one can separate family from work, fathering from truck driving, in the wholeness of life as known to fathers, may not be meaningful. To do so can create differences without distinction. But scholars and laypersons alike do discuss how one role affects another. A case in point is how driving a long-haul truck interferes with or shapes fathering, due to time, energy, stress, and so on. Interventionists need to take this embeddedness and wholeness into account. In this way, they can become more empathetic with fathers in how they concurrently perceive themselves as situated in family, employment, and community. Simple, one-factor or single-sector (such as education) interventions will miss the richness and interdependency of a father's total life. More family-centric (or if necessary, father-centric) paradigms and practices might prove more effective.[5] In all, more holistic "fatherized" strategies for negotiated change in parenting and involvement in schools and schooling are necessary.

Case Study

Julio Valdez is the father of two children. The youngest is in Mrs. Olson's kindergarten class. His name is Alex and he and his parents moved from Texas to a small town (population 8,000) in southwestern Minnesota right before school started. They moved because jobs were hard to come by in Texas, they had relatives in Minnesota, and there were several industries looking for employees. Julio, his wife, Teresa, kindergartner Alex, and 9-year-old Maria are Hispanic. Although Spanish is their first language, all are fluent in English.

When Julio first brought Alex to kindergarten, he asked Mrs. Olson if he could come into the class to help her. Mrs. Olson hesitated, but said yes. She did not know the father yet, and the mother had not been in to see her or to even bring Alex to school. Julio was also a bit intimidating with long hair, biker boots, and tattoos on his arms, neck, and shoulders. However, Julio had been there for the parent orientation to kindergarten and had dropped Alex off every day, not at the school door, but at Mrs. Olson's kindergarten door.

Alex appears to be a very nice, well-mannered boy who just turned 6. During the first few weeks he did a lot of watching and not much participating. He tended to play alone, even when other children asked him to play. He did seem excited when other children were given Albert the Bear to take home on weekends. While at a child's house, the child and his/her family was responsible for keeping a journal about Albert and what he did over the weekend. Mrs. Olson noticed Alex perk up when Albert was mentioned and spoke with Alex about it.

By conference time Alex had started to come out of his shell. His fine motor skills were good although his writing was not clear at times. In addition he was having trouble with prereading and writing activities. Mrs. Olson wanted to recommend him for Title I because he did not qualify for any special education assistance. However, Mrs. Olson also knew that she needed a parent's signature. She was not sure how the parents would receive this idea, although since she had only spoken to or seen Alex's father, she believed that he probably would be the one that she would speak to about Title I.

At conference time, Julio showed up and at the end of the 15 minutes, she approached him about the Title I idea. He became upset and told her his son was not stupid. Mrs. Olson said it was not because he was stupid, but rather just to offer him help so he could continue to make gains in those areas. She said it was just a suggestion. Julio also said he did not want Alex to bring Albert home in 3 weeks. Mrs. Olson felt the conference had turned out badly. What should she do about Albert and Alex?

The next week Alex came into class and was very quiet. He told Mrs. Olson that his dad did not want him to take Albert home. Mrs. Olson told Alex just to wait and see what happens. Mrs. Olson decided to do a home visit and talk with both parents about how Alex was doing and revisit bringing Albert home. She called and arranged the visit. When she arrived at Alex's home, she was cordially invited in and she discussed Alex with both parents. While there, Alex again asked to bring Albert home and finally begged to bring Albert home. Later that week Dad called and said Alex could bring the bear home. Mrs. Olson told Alex the next day that she was glad he was bringing the bear home.

The Monday after Alex had the bear at home Julio showed up in her kindergarten classroom. He said he came to tell her that the care and responsibility that Alex had shown for Albert had demonstrated to him another side of his son and he appreciated what she had done with his son. He apologized for the direction the conference had taken and thanked her for all she had done for Alex. He told Mrs. Olson that he would like to volunteer in her classroom one morning a week.

Questions and Considerations

1. How could the conference have turned out differently?

2. Should Mrs. Olson have invited the mother in to visit, or were there gender and/or cultural differences present?

3. Although the parents were fluent in Spanish and English, they never spoke Spanish in the classroom or around their own children if non-Hispanics were present. Is there any significance to this?

4. What do you think went through Mrs. Olson's mind when Alex's father asked to volunteer in the classroom one morning a week? If she says yes, how will she utilize his talents or willingness to help? What happens if she says no?

Summary

In this chapter, we present background information and conceptualizations helpful to educators in understanding fathering as a socially constructed role having different norms and role-performance expectations in different historical eras, subcultures, and situations. We highlight that even within a more general cultural expectation for how to be a good father, there will be diversity in terms of how the conduct of fathering is actually experienced. Areas where we believe higher standards for fathers should be created and sustained are engagement (direct play, leisure, and caregiving), accessibility (availability to the child), and responsibility (knowing the child's needs and making responsive decisions). Although promoting the value of having more responsible, generative fathering, we recognize that there is no one way to be such a father and that not everyone has the abilities or desires to be such a father. We emphasize that fathers do not necessarily separate fathering from other important roles, and the quality of fathering is affected by the context in which fathers live. Conditions at work, the quality of the marriage, if the father is married to the mother of his children, and being gay or heterosexual, for example, influence fathering. Other factors such as the number of hours the wife/mother is employed, the number and age of children, children's abilities and language skills, occupational status, religious values, ethnicity, culture, personal expectations about being involved, and the father's and mother's gender role ideology also help determine the extent and quality of fathering. Motivation, skills, social support, and institutional practices are factors conditioning fathers' involvement with their children. Fathers can appropriate or thrust aside cultural and media messages about how to father. Each father formulates a fathering identity and develops skills, works out feelings about their own fathers to a better or worse extent, and deals more or less collaboratively with their children's mother. Fathers consequently engage in the social construction of fatherhood as an evolving creation. Each father lives in his own ethnoculture or lifeworld and has a self-narrative about his engagement, accessibility, and responsibility as a father.

We underscore that father involvement in families, schooling, and schools is valuable and should be further encouraged by educators. Men bring diverse strengths and capabilities to fathering, and no single model or mode is necessarily the best, although we do argue for a more responsible or generative style of fathering. Fathers are important; and although attempts to encourage more quality involvement with children are beneficial for families, schools, communities, and society, attempts to create androgynous fathers or to feminize the role might not be appropriate. Educators who appreciate the benefit of father involvement while respecting gendered and individual differences are more likely to enjoy successful efforts at increasing father involvement. Negotiating social change is difficult; trying to do so without engaging and being empathetic with those most affected (fathers especially, but also wives, lovers, ex-wives, and children) is extremely problematic. Understanding flesh-and-blood fathers in one's own community, rather than generalities gained from the mass media and popular culture of disengaged or modern fathers, appears more profitable in creating the types of communities, schools, and families conducive to best educating and serving all children. The educator should thus focus on "real" culture and norms for parenting as known to "real men."

We offer a multitude of examples and general strategic ideas for making fathers more appreciated and respected for their strengths and abilities. These can be capitalized on to make schools more father friendly and to have fathers involved in meaningful ways with their families, schooling, and schools. Although we believe that these ideas are solid, they only scratch the surface of the fertile soil of ideas. We are confident that the reader will generate and utilize other, equally good if not better, strategies. We hope that these ideas will also be shared.

What can we say in closing? Examine all ideas for parent involvement to check for gender bias. Provide for the needs of both mothers and fathers. Measure success of father involvement not by the number, but by the quality of experiences for men and children. Schools often must build programs slowly and expect some trial and error in learning what the men in their communities will respond to. For some communities it may mean bringing out a sports figure to draw men to an event, for others special invitations from the children to their fathers may work. There are many barriers in men themselves, their families, communities, and schools that make father involvement a challenge.

Just inviting fathers into schools, or engaging in a discourse conducted in academic texts, magazines, and on PBS could not be enough. Reaching beyond the white, suburban middle class is necessary if widespread change in fathering culture and conduct is desired. There are many ways of getting men involved. As a set of starter ideas, consider the following: (1) expect men to be involved; (2) talk to, survey, and/or hold focus groups with fathers and others functioning as fathers (stepdads, granddads, etc.) to learn what they want in terms of involvement and their perceived barriers to a more quality engagement with the school and the schooling of their children; (3) make the school father friendly, ask fathers to engage with the school, and put out the welcome mat; (4) work to have schools, civic organizations, businesses, adult education organizations, religious groups, and community groups and agencies offer the resources, services, and support that allow men to become more motivated and skilled for authentic, responsible, and generative fathering; (5) recognize and advocate for father involvement in schooling that does not need to take place in the school building; supervision of homework, discussion of career possibilities, encouragement, rewarding achievements and the like are important.

Engaging fathers to learn their strengths, hearing their stories, taking advantage of their stocks of knowledge, participating in their lives, and appreciating their parenting strategies are important. This allows educators better recognition of rationalizations versus role conflicts, desires to change without knowing how versus not wanting to change, technically present fathers as well as functionally present fathers, and perhaps new ways to appreciate traditional fathering for what it offers to children and society, as well as the promise of "new" fathering.

One aspect of promoting quality fathering and school involvement consists of efforts to support, strengthen, and enrich marriages. School personnel demonstrate interest in promoting quality marriages because children are observed to have negative developmental outcomes when raised within family systems that include marital conflict and parenting styles characterized by lack of supervision, hostility, rejection, coercion, inconsistency, indulgence, or neglect. These outcomes include academic failure, substance abuse, aggressiveness, delinquency, poor health, psychological disorders, and psychopathology (Anderson & Sabatelli, 2010; Bronte-Tinkew, Moore, & Carrano, 2006; Conway & Hutson, 2008; DeBell, 2008; Dwairy, 2008; Featherstone, 2009; Garasky & Stewart, 2007; Gordon & Conger, 2007; Menning, 2006b; Menning & Stewart, 2008; Pong et al., 2005; Steinberg, Blatt-Eisengart, & Cauffman, 2006). Divorced and other fatherless homes appear especially problematic.

Educators concern themselves with community and society change. Making communities more family friendly and working to create a culture respectful and supportive of fathers' myriad roles in the nurturing of children can be useful efforts. In some cases, educators can work to change culture in primary ways; in other cases, the efforts are secondary in that they are directed to changing preexisting conditions. Thinking holistically, acting assertively, listening to and respecting real fathers, and being committed to father involvement can allow educators to provide resources, services, and supports that men deserve and need. Ultimately, it is children and society that benefit.

Recommended Activities

1. Interview fathers from different generations, from the 1950s on. Discuss with the fathers their roles in the family regarding child care, work, nurturing children, activities with children, amount of time spent with children, responsibility for discipline, and gender issues relating to their children.

2. Interview fathers who had their first children when they were teenagers, in their twenties, in their thirties, and in their forties. Ask them to address the following issues: their age in respect to raising children, responsibility of child rearing, types of interaction with their children, and their ability to father.

3. Observe a parent education class predominantly made up of males. What types of interaction do you observe between the fathers and their children? What types of interaction do you observe between the fathers and the parent educator?

4. Invite a panel of fathers into the class to describe parenting from their perspective. How is it different from mothering? How has the role of fathers changed over the years?

5. Locate an electronic mailing list that is designed to be a fathers' discussion group. Monitor or speak through this medium to identify issues that fathers may be discussing.

6. Describe the role your father played or did not play in your life. If this is too difficult, describe the role any significant male played in your life prior to age 18.

Notes

1. LaRossa (1988) noted that middle-class men have authored most books and other texts about the "new" fatherhood.

2. Additionally, researchers such as LaRossa (1988) showed how couples socially construct gender relationships by offering accounts, justifications, and excuses for why fathers are not more involved in parenting.

3. In some studies, housework includes aspects of child care. Also, some families' strategies allocated the division of labor such that men do some housework tasks as a tradeoff, in terms of egalitarianism, as women do some child-care tasks.

4. Due to the research designs, the direction causality or whether there is mutual influencing (school achievement influences in family life, and vice versa) cannot be determined. From a systems viewpoint, the argument appears to be that they are mutually influencing and reinforcing one another.

5. That is, social policy and program from the inside out; practices that put families (rather than schools or other systems) center stage with their needs and strengths as the foundation for policy and practice agendas that are accountable to the end-users, that is, accountable to families.

Children's Books

The following children's books are suggested as a way of helping your students consider issues in this chapter.

For Younger Children (Ages 2–4)

Baby Dance (1999) by Ann Taylor
A board book in which an African American father croons to his baby daughter and dances while holding her.

Because Your Daddy Loves You (2005) by Andrew Clements
When things go wrong during a day at the beach, a father could do a lot of things but always picks the loving one.

The Daddy Mountain (2004) by Jules Feiffer
A little girl's step-by-step account of climbing all the way up on top of her daddy's head.

Night Shift Daddy (2000) by Eileen Spinelli
A father who works the night shift has a special bond with his daughter.

Octopus Hug (1993) by Laurence Pringle
A burly father entertains his children with active games and imaginative play while mom goes out for the evening.

On a Wintry Morning (2000) by Dori Chaconas
A graceful poem of a father and baby bundling up for an early morning outing.

Papa, Do You Love Me? (2005) by Barbara
   M. Joosse
When a Masai father in Africa answers his son's
   questions, the boy learns that his father's love
   for him is unconditional.

Pete's A Pizza (1998) by William Steig
A dad brightens up a rainy day with a fun game
   of making his son into a pizza.

The Very Best Daddy of All (2004) by Marion
   Dane Bauer
Pictures and rhyming text show how animal,
   bird, and human fathers take care of
   their children.

Vroomaloom Zoom (2000) by John Coy
A father takes his daughter on an imaginary
   car ride, lulling her to sleep with various
   sounds.

For Older Children (Ages 4–8)

Carlos and the Cornfield/Carlos y la milpa de maiz
   (1995) by Jan Romero Stevens
In this English/Spanish bilingual story, a boy
   learns the meaning of his father's statement,
   "You reap what you sow."

Dad and Me in the Morning (1994) by Patricia
   Lakin
A young deaf boy spends a glorious morning
   sharing the beauty of a sunrise with his dad.

Dad, Jackie, and Me (2005) by Myron
   Uhlberg
A boy learns the connection between his deaf
   father and the first black baseball player in the
   Major Leagues.

Just the Two of Us (2001) by Will Smith
A popular song adds to the story of a father's
   love as his child grows from a boy into a man.

Loon Summer (2001) by Barbara Santucci
A girl and her father spend their first summer at
   the lake without the girl's mother.

My Father's Boat (1998) by Sherry Garland
A Vietnamese immigrant tells his son how he
   learned to fish from his father.

Night Driving (1996) by John Coy
A father and son drive into the night and watch
   for night animals, swap baseball stories, play
   games, and sing songs on their trip to the
   mountains.

Owl Moon (1987) by Jane Yolen
On a winter's night under a full moon, a father
   and daughter trek into the woods to go
   owling and see other animals along
   the way.

Papa's Latkes (2004) by Michelle Edwards
A father and his two daughters try to make
   latkes and celebrate on the first Hanukkah
   after the girls' mother died.

Tell Me What We Did Today (2003) by
   Rick Kupchella
A father and daughter share special time
   reviewing the real and made-up things that
   happened during their day.

Two Old Potatoes and Me (2003) by
   John Coy
After a girl finds two old potatoes at her
   father's house, they plant and tend
   them and harvest them to make mashed
   potatoes.

Visiting Day (2002) by Jacqueline Woodson
A young girl and her grandmother visit the girl's
   father in prison.

When Dad's at Sea (2004) by Mindy
   L. Pelton
A soldier's daughter worries about her dad on
   military duty far away from home.

Adapted from the Reading with Dads
   Booklist from the Minnesota Humanities
   Center. For the complete list, see
   http://minnesotahumanities.org/programs/
   ReadingwithDad

Additional Resources

Websites

Center for Successful Fathering
www.fathering.org

The Center for Family Policy and Practice
www.cffpp.org

Father Involvement Research Alliance
www.fira.ca

Fatherhood Institute (UK fatherhood
think-tank)
www.fatherhoodinstitute.org

National Center for Fathering
www.fathers.com

National Center on Fathers and Families
www.ncoff.gse.upenn.edu

National Latino Fatherhood Family Institute
www.nlffi.org

National Responsible Fatherhood Clearinghouse (U.S. government website on fathers)
www.fatherhood.gov

Minnesota Fathers and Families Network
www.mnfathers.org

Shared Parenting Organization
www.acfc.org

References

Adamsons, K. L. (2006). *The effect of congruence of mothers' and fathers' beliefs regarding fathering roles on father involvement.* Unpublished doctoral dissertation, University of North Carolina at Greensboro.

Adamsons, K., O'Brien, M., & Pasley, K. (2007). An ecological approach to father involvement in biological and stepfather families. *Fathering, 5,* 129–147.

Amato, P. R., & Booth, A. (1997). *A generation at risk: Growing up in an era of family upheaval.* Cambridge, MA: Harvard University Press.

Anderson, S. A., & Sabatelli, R. M. (2010). *Family interaction: A multigenerational development perspective* (5th ed.). Boston: Allyn & Bacon.

Ashbourne, L. M. (2009). Reconceptualizing parent–adolescent relationships: A dialogic model. *Journal of Family Theory and Review, 1,* 211–222.

Aulette, J. R. (2010). *Changing American families* (3rd ed.). Boston: Allyn & Bacon.

Avenilla, F., Rosenthal, E., & Tice, P. (2006, July). *Fathers of U.S. children born in 2001: Findings from the Early Childhood Longitudinal Study, Birth Cohort (ECLS-B).* (NCES 2006-002). U.S. Department of Education, National Center for Education Statistics, Washington, DC: U.S. Government Printing Office.

Beckert, T. E., Strom, R. D., Strom, P. S., & Yang, C-T. (2006). The success of Taiwanese fathers in guiding adolescents. *Adolescence, 41,* 493–509.

Bernard van Leer Foundation. (2003). *Supporting fathers: Contributions from the International Fatherhood Summit.* Report from conference held at Oxford University, England, available from www.bernardvanleer.orp/page.asp?pid=25#. Supporting and a summary from www.fathersdirect.com/index.php?id=14&cID=256

Biblarz, T. L., & Stacey, J. (2010). How does the gender of parents matter? *Journal of Marriage and Family, 72,* 3–22.

Braithewaite, D., & Baxter, L. (2006). "You're my parent but you're not"; Dialectical tensions in stepchildren's perceptions about communicating with the nonresidential parent. *Journal of Applied Communication Research, 34,* 30–48.

Bronte-Tinkew, J., Moore, K. A., & Carrano, J. (2006). The father–child relationship, parenting styles, and adolescent risk behaviors in intact families. *Journal of Family Issues, 27,* 850–881.

Brotherson, S. E., Dollahite, D. C., & Hawkins, A. J. (2005). Generative fathering and the dynamics of connection between fathers and their children. *Fathering, 3,* 1–28.

Brown, R., Copeland, W. E., Costello, E. J., Erkanli, A., & Worthman, C. M. (2009). Family and community influences on educational outcomes among Appalachian youth. *Journal of Community Psychology, 37,* 795–808.

Canary, D. J., Emmers-Sommer, T. M., & Faulkner, S. (1997). *Sex and gender differences in personal relationships.* New York: Guilford.

Coakley, J. (2006). The good father: Parental expectations and youth sports. *Leisure Studies, 25,* 153–163.

Coltrane, S. (2000). Research on household labor: Modeling and measuring the social embeddedness of routine family work. *Journal of Marriage and the Family, 62,* 1208–1233.

Conway, T., & Hutson, R. Q. (2008, May). *Healthy marriage and the legacy of child maltreatment: A child welfare perspective.* (Couples and Marriage Series, Brief no. 12). Washington, DC: Center for Law and Social Policy.

Cook, J. L., Jones, R. M., Dick, A. J., & Singh, A. (2005). Revisiting men's role in father involvement. *Fathering, 3,* 165–178.

Cooper, M., Sabol, W. J., & West, H. C. (2009). *Prisoners in 2008.* Washington, DC: Bureau of Justice Statistics. Retrieved July 19, 2010, from http://bjs.ojp.usdoj.gov/index.cfm?ty=pbdetail&iid=1763

Crowl, A. L., Ahn, S., & Baker, J. (2008). A meta-analysis of developmental outcomes for children of same-sex and heterosexual parents. *Journal of GLBT Family Studies, 4,* 105–114.

Culbertson, P. (2010). Review of Chen Z. Oren and Dora Chase Oren (Eds.), *Counseling fathers* (New York: Routledge, 2009). *Journal of Men, Masculinities and Spirituality, 4,* 43–46.

Darling, S. (2008, August). Family must be part of the solution in closing the achievement gap. *The Clearing House,* 245–246.

Davis-Kean, P. E. (2005). The influence of parent education and family income on child achievement: The indirect role of parental expectations and the home environment. *Journal of Family Psychology, 19,* 294–304.

DeBell, M. (2008). Children living without their fathers: Population estimates and indicators of educational well-being. *Social Indicators Research, 87,* 427–443.

Doherty, W. J., Kouneski, E. E., & Erickson, M. F. (1998). Responsible fathering: An overview and conceptual framework. *Journal of Marriage and the Family, 60,* 277–292.

Domina, T. (2005). Leveling the home advantage: Assessing the effectiveness of parental involvement in elementary school. *Sociology of Education, 78,* 233–249.

Duchesne, S., & Larose, S. (2007). Adolescent parental attachment and academic motivation and performance in early adolescence. *Journal of Applied Social Psychology, 37,* 1501–1521.

Dudley, J. R., & Stone, G. (2001). *Fathering at risk: Helping nonresidential fathers.* New York: Springer.

Dwairy, M. (2008). Parental inconsistency versus parental authoritarianism: Association with symptoms of psychological disorders. *Journal of Youth and Adolescence 37,* 616–626.

Epstein, J. L., Sanders, M. G., Sheldon, S. B., Simon, B. S., Salinas, K. C., Jansorn, N. R., et al. (2009). *School, family, and community partnerships: Your handbook for action* (3rd ed.). Thousand Oaks, CA: Corwin.

Fagan, J., & Palm, G. (2004). *Fathers and early childhood programs.* Albany, NY: Delmar.

Featherstone, B. (2009). *Contemporary fathering: Theory, policy, and practice.* Bristol, UK: Policy Press.

Ferguson, C. (2008). *The school–family connection: Looking at the larger picture* (A review of current literature). Austin, TX: National Center for Family and Community Connections with Schools.

Garasky, S., & Stewart, S. D. (2007). Evidence of the effectiveness of child support and visitation: Examining food insecurity among children with nonresident fathers. *Journal of Family and Economic Issues, 28,* 105–121.

Gilbert, L. A. (1993). *Two careers/One family: The promise of gender equality.* Beverly Hills, CA: Sage.

Goldberg, W. A., Tan, E. T., & Thorsen, K. L. (2009). Trends in academic attention to fathers, 1930–2006. *Fathering, 7,* 159–179.

Gordon, L., & Conger, R. D. (2007). Linking mother–father differences in parenting to a typology of parenting styles and adolescent outcomes. *Journal of Family Issues, 28,* 212–241.

Harvard Family Research Project. (2010). *FINE: Family involvement network of educators.*

Retrieved July 15, 2010, from www.hfrp.org/family-involvement/fine-family-involvement-network-of-educators

Hawkins, D., Amato, P. R., & King, V. (2006). Parent–adolescent involvement: The relative influence of parent gender and residence. *Journal of Marriage and Family, 68,* 125–136.

Hawkins, D. N., Amato, P. R., & King, V. (2007). Nonresident father involvement and adolescent well-being: Father effects or child effects? *American Sociological Review, 72,* 990–1010.

Henderson, A. T., & Mapp, K. L. (2002). *A new wave of evidence: The impact of school, family, and community connections on student achievement.* Austin, TX: National Center for Family & Community Connections with Schools, Southwest Educational Development Laboratory.

Henley, K., & Pasley, K. (2005). Conditions affecting the association between father identity and father involvement. *Fathering, 3,* 59–80.

Hennon, C. B., Hildenbrand, B., & Schedle, A. (2008). Stepfamilies and children. In T. P. Gullotta & G. M. Blau (Eds.), *Family influences on childhood behavior and development: Evidence-based prevention and treatment approaches* (pp. 167–192). New York: Routledge.

Hennon, C. B., Olsen, G. W., & Palm, G. (2008). Fathers, schools, and schooling. In G. Olsen & M. L. Fuller (Eds.), *Home–school relations: Working successfully with parents and families* (3rd ed., pp. 286–324). Boston: Pearson Allyn & Bacon.

Hennon, C. B., Peterson, G. W., Hildenbrand, B., & Wilson, S. M. (2008). Parental stress amongst migrant and immigrant populations: The MRM and CRSRP models for interventions [Stress Parental em Populações Migrantes e Imigrantes: Os Modelos de Intervenção MRM e CRSRP]. *Pesquisas e Práticas Psicossociais, 2,* 242–257.

Hennon, C. B., Peterson, G. W., Polzin, L., & Radina, M. E. (2007). Familias de ascendencia mexicana residentes en Estados Unidos: recursos para el manejo del estrés parental [Resident families of Mexican ancestry in United States: Resources for the handling of parental stress]. In R. Esteinou (Ed.), *Fortalezas y desafíos de las familias en dos contextos: Estados Unidos de América y México* (pp. 225–282) [Strengths and challenges of families in two contexts: The United States of America and Mexico]. México, DF: Centro de Investigaciones y Estudios Superiores en Antropología Social (CIESAS) y Sistema Nacional para el Desarrollo Integral de la Familia.

Hennon, C. B., & Wilson, S. M. (Eds.). (2008). *Families in a global context.* New York: Routledge.

Hennon, C. B., Wilson, S. M., & Radina, M. E. (in press). Family life education. In G. W. Peterson & K. R. Bush (Eds.), *Handbook of marriage and the family* (3rd ed.). New York: Springer.

Hill, N. E., & Tyson, D. F. (2009). Parental involvement in middle school: A meta-analytic assessment of the strategies that promote achievement. *Developmental Psychology, 45,* 740–763.

Hutchins, D. J., Maushard, M., Colosino, J., Greenfeld, M. D., & Thomas, B. G. (Eds.). (2009). *Promising partnership practices 2009.* Baltimore, MD: Johns Hopkins University, National Network of Partnership Schools.

Kuhmann, R. C. (2004). *Father involvement in the lives of their children.* Retrieved July 18, 2010, from www.kuhmann.com/dads/Involvement.htm

Junttila, N., Vauras, M., & Laakkonen, E. (2007). The role of parenting self-efficacy in children's social and academic behavior. *European Journal of Psychology of Education, 23,* 41–61.

Kalil, A., & Ziol-Guest, K. M. (2007). Parental employment circumstances and children's academic progress. *Social Science Research, 37,* 500–515.

Kim, E., Cain, K., & McCubbin, M. (2006). Maternal and paternal parenting, acculturation, and young adolescents' psychological adjustment in Korean American families. *Journal of Child and Adolescent Psychiatric Nursing, 19,* 112–129.

Lamb, M. E. (Ed.). (2010). *The role of the father in child development* (5th ed.). Hoboken, NJ: Wiley.

LaRossa, R. (1988). Fatherhood and social change. *Family Relations, 37,* 451–457.

Lee, D. (n.d.). *Father's matter! Involving fathers in children's learning: A kit for educators and other professionals.* Retrieved July 18, 2010, from www2.ed.gov/pubs/parents/fathers/presentation/index.html

Levine, J. (1993). Involving fathers in Head Start: A framework for public policy and program development. *Families in Society, 74*(1), 4–19.

Lu, M. C., Jones, L., Bond, M. J., Wright, K., Pumpuang, M., Maidenberg, M., et al. (2010). Where is the F in MCH? Father involvement in African American families. *Ethnicity and Disease, 20*, S2-49–S2-61.

Marsiglio, W., Amato, P., Day, R. D., & Lamb, M. E. (2000). Scholarship on fatherhood in the 1990s and beyond. *Journal of Marriage and the Family, 62*, 1173–1191.

Marsiglio, W., Roy, K., & Fox, G. L. (Eds.). (2005). *Situated fathering: A focus on physical and social space.* Lanham, MD: Rowman & Littlefield Publishers.

Martin, A., Ryan, R. M., & Brooks-Gunn, J. (2010). When fathers' supportiveness matters most: Maternal and paternal parenting and children's school readiness. *Journals of Family Psychology, 24*, 145–155.

McBride, B. A., Schoppe-Sullivan, S. J., & Ho, M-H. (2005). The mediating role of fathers' school involvement on student achievement. *Applied Developmental Psychology, 26*, 201–216.

Meek, R. (2007). The parenting possible selves of young fathers in prison. *Psychology, Crime, and Law, 13*, 371–382.

Menning, C. L. (2006a). Nonresident fathering and school failure. *Journal of Family Issues, 27*, 1356–1382.

Menning, C. L. (2006b). Nonresident fathers' involvement and adolescents' smoking. *Journal of Health and Social Behavior, 47*, 32–46.

Menning, C. L., & Stewart, S. D. (2008). Nonresident father involvement, social class, and adolescent weight. *Journal of Family Issues, 29*, 1673–1700.

Michigan Department of Education. (n.d.). *What research says about parent involvement in children's education in relation to academic achievement.* Retrieved July 18, 2010, from Final_Parental_Involvement_Fact_Sheet_14732_7.pdf

Miller, S. R., Murry, V. M., & Brody, G. H. (2005). Parents' problem solving with preadolescents and its association with social withdrawal at school: Considering parents' stress and child gender. *Fathering, 3*, 147–163.

Morman, M. T., & Floyd, K. (2006). Good fathering: Father and son perceptions of what it means to be a good father. *Fathering, 4*, 113–136.

National Center on Fathers and Families. (n.d.a.). *Fathers figure facts: Research on father involvement proves that fathers matter in the lives of children and families.* Retrieved July 4, 2010, from www.ncoff.gse.upenn.edu/resources/fathers-figure-facts

National Head Start Association. (n.d.). *Introduction to the male and father-involvement initiative: Responding to the need for male involvement in children's and families' lives.* Retrieved July 7, 2010, from www.nhsa.org/services/general_services/fatherson_resources

National Institute of Child Health and Human Development Early Child Care Research Network. (2008). Mothers' and fathers' support for child autonomy and early school achievement. *Developmental Psychology, 44*, 895–907.

National Network of Partnership Schools. (2010). Type 2: Increase father involvement: Four elements for success. Retrieved January 14, 2010, from www.csos.jhu.edu/p2000/type2/issue29/type2-issue29-4.htm

Newsome, W. S., Bush, K., Hennon, C. B., Peterson, G. W., & Wilson, S. M. (2008). Appalachian families and poverty: Historical issues and contemporary economic trends. In D. R. Crane & T. B. Heaton (Eds.), *Handbook of families and poverty* (pp. 104–118). Newbury Park, CA: Sage.

Oates, J. (2010). *Supporting parenting.* Milton Keyes, UK: The Open University.

Oren, C. Z., & Oren, D. C. (Eds.). (2009). *Counseling fathers.* New York: Routledge.

Paquette, D. (2004). Theorizing the father-child relationship mechanisms and developmental outcomes. *Human Development, 47*, 193–219.

Parcel T. L., Dufur, M. J., & Cornell, Z. R. (2010). Capital at home and at school: A review and synthesis. *Journal of Marriage and Family, 72*, 828–846.

Parke, R. D. (2004). Fathers, families, and the future: A plethora of plausible predictions. *Merrill-Palmer Quarterly, 50*, 456–470.

Parsons, T. (1955). Family structure and socialization of the child. In T. Parsons & R. F. Bales (Eds.), *Family socialization and interaction processes* (pp. 35–131). Glencoe, IL: Free Press.

Pehlke, T. A., Hennon, C. B., Radina, E., & Kuvalanka, K. K. (2009). Does father still know best? An inductive thematic analysis of popular TV sitcoms. *Fathering, 7,* 114–139.

Peterson, G. W., & Hennon, C. B. (2007). Influencias parentales en la competencia social de los adolescentes en dos culturas: una comparación conceptual entre los Estados Unidos y México [Parental influences on the social competence of adolescent in two cultures: A conceptual comparison between the United States and Mexico]. In R. Esteinou (Ed.), *Fortalezas y desafíos de las familias en dos contextos: Estados Unidos de América y México* (pp. 111–166). México, DF: Centro de Investigaciones y Estudios Superiores en Antropología Social (CIESAS) y Sistema Nacional para el Desarrollo Integral de la Familia (DIF).

Peterson, G. W., Hennon, C. B., & Knox, T. R. (2010). Conceptualizing parental stress with family stress theory. In S. J. Price, C. A. Price, & P. C. McKenry (Eds.), *Families and change: Coping with stressful events and transitions* (4th ed., pp. 25–49). Thousand Oaks, CA: Sage.

Pew Research Center. (2007). *Being dad may be tougher these days, but working moms are among their biggest fans.* Retrieved July 5, 2010, from http://pewsocialtrends.org/pubs/510/father-day

Pleck, J. H. (2010). Fatherhood and masculinity. In M. E. Lamb (Ed.), *The role of the father in child development* (5th ed., pp. 27–57). Hoboken, NJ: John Wiley & Sons.

Pong, S-l., Hao, L., & Gardner, E. (2005). The roles of parenting styles and social capital in the school performance of immigrant Asian and Hispanic adolescents. *Social Science Quarterly, 86,* 928–950.

Potter, D. (2010). Psychosocial well-being and the relationship between divorce and children's academic achievement. *Journal of Marriage and Family, 72,* 933–946.

Radina, M. E., Wilson, S. M., & Hennon, C. B. (2008). Parental stress among U.S. Mexican heritage parents: Implications for culturally relevant family life education. In R. L. Dalla, J. Defrain, J. Johnson, & D. Abbott (Eds.), *Strengths and challenges of new immigrant families: Implications for research, policy, education, and service* (pp. 369–391). Lanham, MD: Lexington Books.

Raikes, H. H., Summers, J. A., & Roggman, L. A. (2005). Father involvement in Early Head Start programs. *Fathering, 3,* 29–58.

SEDL National Center for Family and Community Connections with Schools. (n.d.). Connection collection. Retrieved July 18, 2010, from www.sedl.org/connections

Seitsinger, A. M., Felner, R. D., Brand, S., & Burns, A. (2008). A large-scale examination of the nature and efficacy of teachers' practices to engage parents: Assessment, parental contact, and student-level impact. *Journal of School Psychology, 46,* 477–505.

Shedlin, A., Jr. (2004). Is your school father-friendly? *Principal, 83*(3), 22–25.

Souto-Manning, M., & Swick, K. J. (2006). Teachers' beliefs about parent and family involvement: Rethinking our family involvement paradigm. *Early Childhood Education Journal, 34,* 187–193.

Steinberg, L. (2007). *Adolescence* (8th ed.). Boston: McGraw Hill.

Steinberg, L., Blatt-Eisengart, I., & Cauffman, E. (2006). Patterns of competence and adjustment among adolescents from authoritative, authoritarian, indulgent, and neglectful homes: A replication in a sample of serious juvenile offenders. *Journal of Research on Adolescence, 16,* 47–58.

Stuchell, S., & Barrett, R. H. (n.d.). *Did you know: Fatherhood is being redefined?* Retrieved July 15, 2010, from Fatherhood.Pdf

Sweeney, M. M. (2010). Remarriage and stepfamilies: Strategic sites for family scholarship in the 21st century. *Journal of Marriage and Family, 72,* 667–684.

Tan, E. T., & Goldberg, W. A. (2009). Parental school involvement in relation to children's grades and adaptation to school. *Journal of Applied Developmental Psychology, 30,* 442–453.

Tasker, F. (2010). Same-sex parenting and child development: Reviewing the contribution of parental gender. *Journal of Marriage and Family, 72,* 35–40.

Taylor, B. A., & Behnke, A. (2005). Fathering across the border: Latino fathers in Mexico and the U.S. *Fathering, 3,* 99–120.

Terrel, B. P. (2005). The impact of ethnic socialization and ethnic identity on the self-esteem
and parenting attitudes of African American
fathers. *Best Practices in Mental Health, 1,*
86–104.

U.S. Department of Education. (2000). *A call to
commitment: Fathers' involvement in children's
learning.* Retrieved July 4, 2010, from http://npin
.org/library/2000/n00490/n00490.html1

U.S. Department of Health and Human Services.
(n.d.). *Father involvement in Head Start and
Early Head Start.* Retrieved July 18, 2010, from
fatherhood.hhs.gov/Parenting/hs.shtml

U.S. Department of Health and Human Services.
(2009a). *National registry of effective prevention
programs.* Retrieved January 9, 2010, from
www.nrepp.samhsa.gov

U.S. Department of Health and Human Services.
(2009b). *Parent training programs: Insight for
practitioners.* Centers for Disease Control and
Prevention. Atlanta, GA: Author.

White, J. M., & Kline, D. M. (2008). *Family
theories: An introduction* (3rd ed.). Thousand
Oaks, CA: Sage.

Wical, K. A., & Doherty, W. J. (2005). How reliable
are fathers' reports of involvement with their
children?: A methodological report. *Fathering,
3,* 81–93.

Williams, S. K., & Kelly, F. D. (2005). Relationships
among involvement, attachment, and behavioral problems in adolescence: Examining
father's influence. *Journal of Early Adolescence,
25,* 168–196.

Wood, J. J., & Repetti, R. L. (2004). What gets
dad involved? A longitudinal study of change in
parental child caregiving involvement. *Journal
of Family Psychology, 18,* 237–249.

Chapter Fourteen

The Implications of Home–School Partnerships for School Violence and Bullying

John H. Hoover
St. Cloud State University

Kathryn E. Johnson
St. Cloud State University

Glenn Olsen
The University of North Dakota

In the past 10 years there has been an outbreak of school violence that is unprecedented in public and private school education. These severely violent episodes have resulted in deaths of teachers and students and have received considerable attention. However, educators must remember that school is still a safe place–perhaps students' safest milieu. We need to address issues affecting school climate including both face-to-face aggression and cyberbullying. Any type of bullying, including verbal harassment, is unacceptable. This chapter looks at how parents and schools, working together, can create a positive school social climate.

This chapter helps you explore the:

▶ Impact of violence on the school climate.

▶ Impact of bullying on perpetrators, victims, and bystanders.

▶ Role of the school and families in preventing, ending, and ameliorating bullying.

▶ Common language used by researchers and educators in studying bullying.

▶ Curriculum and other resources available to help with issues of bullying and school violence.

School Violence

Students enjoy more physical safety *inside* the doors of their schools than they do elsewhere (DeVoe et al., 2002; National Center for Educational Statistics [NCES], 1998). Students may well be up to 10 times safer in school than anywhere else in our otherwise violent society (Goldstein & Conoley, 1997). After roughly two decades of steady increase, violent crime among youth dropped during the 1990s; this reduction in school violence maintained itself throughout the first decade of the 21st century (Dinkes, Kemp, Baum, & Snyder, 2009). This reduction in youth violence occurred both inside and outside of school. Despite these data and years of progress in violence prevention, schools are not as safe as practitioners would like them to be (Braaten, 2004; Dinkes et al., 2009). The following factors provided by Stephens (1997) remain an excellent summary of the factors predicting rates of school violence:

- *Dropping out, literally and symbolically.* Students experiencing difficulty conforming to the social and behavioral demands of institutions are at much greater risk for committing violent acts such as bullying and fighting (Patterson, DeBaryshe, & Ramsey, 1989).
- *Discipline problems, bullying and harassment.* Levels of mild violence and bullying probably predict the overall level of risk for more serious violence in a school. Certainly this issue came to the fore with the seminal and oft-cited Secret Service report suggesting that many targeted school shootings can be traced to bullying (Vossekuil, Reddy, Fein, Borum, & Modzeleski, 2000).
- *Drug and alcohol abuse.* A clear association between substance abuse and violence has been noted. More recently, it has been observed that students who pick on their peers are more likely than other students to abuse mind-altering chemicals, including alcohol. Bullying was found to be a primary predictor of substance abuse (Simanton, Burthwick, & Hoover, 2000).
- *Gang membership.* The violence of "within-gang" rituals and the aggression perpetrated by gang members on others add to the potential risk within the walls of schools.
- *The ready availability of weapons.* Easy access to weapons in American society all too often escalates simple fights and minor disputes into bloody ordeals attended by increased potential for serious injury and death (pp. 75–78).

It is our contention that to address school violence, future teachers must first understand milder forms of aggression—forms that are too often perceived by some educators as falling within the normal range of child behavior (Pervin & Turner, 1994). Recently, investigators have undertaken many studies of bullying and teasing. These are addressed below.

Bullying and Violence

Many lines of evidence suggest that bullying in school, especially when adults do not intervene, produces risk for more serious forms of violence. For example, a strong correlation exists between minor interpersonal incidents, perhaps eliciting a trip to the principal's office, and more serious offenses in schools (NCES, 1998; Wilson & Petersilia, 1995). As Goldstein and Conoley (1997) put it, "Parallel to (and in many instances also underlying) the very substantial levels of student assault, weaponry, theft, intimidation, and other serious violence is lower-level aggressive behavior" (p. 8). It is highly likely, therefore, that failure of school personnel to intervene in low-level interpersonal violence increases risk for serious disturbances. There is a correlation between bullying and criminality. Vossekuil and colleagues (2000) carefully organized information from 37 targeted school shootings by 41 attackers. By far, the most common characteristics shared by school shooters was either having been bullied or believing that they had been (71%). In addition, Vossekuil and colleagues (2000) argued that an appreciable percentage of perpetrators had publicly stated or written that they were thinking of perpetrating an attack.

Although it is not clear that bullying has increased either in frequency or intensity over the past 30 years as some educators assert, no doubt exists that it is a significant problem in North American schools (Simanton et al., 2000). It has been conservatively estimated that approximately 10% of students in rural, Midwest schools suffer bullying-related psychological trauma; rates of bullying nationally are explored in more depth in the following section.

Parent–School Partnerships: Important in Violence Reduction

Partnerships between families and schools lie at the core of nearly every successful program aimed at reducing risk behavior. Certainly this is true of programs dealing with bullying reduction, violence deterrence, and substance abuse prevention (Duncan, 2004; Ryan, Martin, & Brooks-Gunn, 2006; Sheridan, Warnes, & Dowd, 2004). As students confront school bullies, educators and parents pick up the pieces and work to avoid future peer harassment. It is essential that family members and educators form strong, healthy working partnerships. In summarizing research on familial issues in bullying, Duncan (1999) noted that families often set the stage for school aggression by tolerating or encouraging domestic violence, by parenting in a cold or overly hostile manner, or through permissiveness for sibling attacks. Examples of successful partnerships from around the world and the parameters of such partnerships are explored in this chapter.

In fashioning a model for successful parent–school partnerships in bullying reduction, several issues are addressed. In an initial section, a brief overview of bullying research is undertaken followed by information specifically related to the link between family life and bullying or violence. We dedicate a third section to exploring school–parent partnerships for bullying and violence reduction.

In reviewing models for school–parent partnerships, parents and educators must come to know and understand the make-up of the school population. Because diversity factors influence school–parent partnerships, having cross-cultural knowledge and understanding of families in the school community will greatly assist in promoting a more inclusive school–parent partnership. All families should have a role and a voice in schoolwide campaigns and programs, in adopting classroom curriculum that is culturally sensitive, and in working with individual families that may have children who are either bullies or victims in the school setting (see Hoover & Oliver, 2008, Chapter 12, for a lengthy review of essential connections between bullying prevention and multiculturalism). Davis, Hoover, and Oliver (2008) addressed the importance of considering racial and ethnic factors when dealing with cyberbullying, arguing that African American students frequently encounter hate sites online—a society-wide form of bias.

Reflection...

If you were being bullied or harassed in junior high or high school, where would you go for help? Are there places outside of school that you would go to for help? Did young people in your school system have places to go for help, both inside and outside the school system? Was this help effective?

Can you picture a role for self-advocacy in bullying? For example, would it be helpful for a group of middle school students who have experienced bullying to form an anti-bullying advocacy group?

What resources are available in your community to assist you in your cross-cultural understanding of the families in your school?

Basic Bullying Information

Definition

Bullying is the purposeful infliction of psychological or physical pain on one individual by another or by a group. In bullying, the perpetrators are physically or psychologically more potent than victims. The analysis of bullying episodes can be made more complex in that the defenselessness of injured parties may be more a matter of subjective perception than objective reality.

Frequency and Severity of Bullying

The most carefully constructed large-scale study of bullying remains the investigation conducted and reported by Nansel and colleagues (2001). They surveyed nearly 16,000 intermediate (grade 6) through high school (grade 10) students regarding bullying. Just over 1 in 10 (13%) of U.S. students self-identified as aggressive bullies (bullied others, seldom bullied), with 11% listing themselves as passive victims (victimized only, rarely bullied others) and another 6% as bully-victims (participated in bullying and experienced victimization). These data are similar to those reported among just over 1,000 students in the rural Midwest (Simanton et al., 2000; DeVoe, Kaffenberger, & Chandler, 2005).

Estimates of the prevalence of bullying depend a great deal on both the definitions and research methods employed by investigators (questionnaires vs. observations, for example; Bovaird, 2010; Swearer, Siebecker, Johnson-Frereichs, & Cixin, 2010). When researchers adjust for the severity of bullying, reported incidence levels are lower than when questions are put to students on a "yes-no" basis (Hoover, Oliver, & Hazler, 1992). To date, no agreement has been reached in the field as to standardized methods for measuring bullying; this is particularly true for the case of cyberbullying, a field still truly in its infancy (Hoover & Oliver, 2008; Swearer et al., 2010).

Age affects prevalence estimates, with the proportion of students experiencing bullying (and those experiencing significant levels of trauma from it) peaking during the middle-school years, with slightly lower numbers during the intermediate and secondary grades (Hoover et al., 1992).

Estimates of the prevalence of bullying tend to be time-based, momentary snapshots. Most researchers have adopted the convention of classifying bullying participants into roughly three groups: aggressive bullies (bully only), passive victims (victims only), and bully-victims or provocative victims, students who (over a relatively short time period) report both experiencing peer harassment and picking on others (Schwartz, Proctor, & Chien, 2001; Olweus, 2007). In this perspective, the status of students is treated as nearly static—that is, as if bullying status is parallel to a psychiatric disorder or a personality type that the individual "carries around." Although some data exist to support the notion of aggression being a relatively stable trait (Olweus, 1978), many experts question the permanence of bullying and victimization status. Ma (2001, 2002) demonstrated that bully and victim status may change over longer periods of times based on year in school and other administrative characteristics of the institution (e.g., middle school vs. junior high). The characteristics of bullying-related subgroups in the school population and, indeed, questions about the longitudinal stability of bullying patterns remain unsettled.

Bullying affects students' perceptions of safety at school, with up to 10% of all students and most of those chronically bullied either typically afraid or expressing the wish to stay home at least once per semester (Simonton, Burthwick, & Hoover, 2000). Berthold and Hoover (2000) concluded that three times as many bully victims felt unsafe at school (25%) as students not suffering peer harassment (8%).

Bullying Behaviors

When young people describe either personally experiencing bullying (Hoover et al., 1992) or observing the harassment of others (Hazler, Hoover, & Oliver, 1991), they describe it as largely verbal. Indirect and subtle bullying, such as social ostracism or friendship interference, is the second most common form of bullying experienced by females, whereas mild physical attacks are the second most common form of bullying reported by boys (Hoover & Oliver, 1996).

No statistical relationship is typically observed between the bullying behaviors that students are subjected to and the degree of trauma they experience. In other words, long-term verbal harassment is just as devastating to victims as periodic, mild physical attacks. Some writers have even concluded that dealing with verbal harassment and teasing are central to anti-bullying campaigns (Hoover & Olsen, 2001). Childhood verbal bullying also appears to be the "testing ground" for later sexual harassment, with the result that school officials not dealing with mild sexualized teasing and verbal gay bashing set themselves up for greater levels of overtly illegal and life-threatening forms of sexual harassment (Kosciw & Diaz, 2005; Stein, 1995). Of course, the verbal climate at school often reflects the linguistic patterns emerging from the home (Duncan, 2004).

Cyberbullying

In recent years, a new phenomenon related to bullying has been identified, so-called cyberbullying. The term, coined by Canadian psychologist Bill Belsey (Belsey, n.d.), is defined as the repeated harassment of individuals utilizing indirect or electronic means. The objective prevalence and severity of cyberbullying can be debated (Hoover & Oliver, 2008); however, even passing references to the popular media and the Internet will reveal anecdotal evidence of its severity via gut-wrenching stories of suicides, solicitations, and homicide (NBC4i.com, 2010).

To date, the best studies that include cyberbullying estimates are the Youth Internet Safety Studies. According to these data, a credible estimate is that about 3% to 5% of American youth aged 9 to 17 receive online harassment that they perceived as intrusive (Ybarra, Mitchell, Wolak, & Finkelhor, 2006). Although several other research teams have shown higher estimates, they have employed less defensible samples (Li, 2007; Patchin & Hinduja, 2006).

Several points need to be raised about cyberbullying issues for home–school relations. First, the distinctive psychological features of cyber attacks need to be dealt with—primarily those relating to the principle of depersonalization. Second, information about familial interactions around electronic media needs addressing. Third, we want to argue that, although Internet-based behavior remains legally well protected, the courts have provided parents and educators significant rights to deal with cyberbullying affecting behavior at school. Finally, a central issue for parents and parent educators is to attend to the degree to which manufacturers of computer hardware and software currently target young children—in ways that may be invidious to the well-being of families.

Depersonalization and Cyberbullying.   In something of an irony, although researchers lack objective evidence for considerable levels of harm from cyberbullying, the potential exists for particularly nasty electronic exchanges. Bandura's (e.g., 1999) seminal work on depersonalization reveals that persons will behave more brutally in situations where social distance is greatest. This very well might be the case with cyber attacks, where perpetrators often cannot track victims' misery.

In the case of an online hate campaign, students, not experiencing a target's distress, may proceed with an attack that they might discontinue in a face-to-face episode. Put in Bandura's terminology, the depersonalization of electronic media contributes to the lack of inhibition for aggression that might be afforded via a face-to-face bullying episode.

Two identity factors related to depersonalization increase the risk for harm online: *masquerading* and *faking* (Smith, Mahdavi, Carvalho, & Tippett, 2005). In the former, students pretend to be someone other than who they are; in the latter, a student might lie about his or her age in such venues as chat rooms. Masquerading lends itself to considerable mischief at school: Bob pirates Sam's e-mail account and sends a nasty message to Jim (ostensibly from Sam). The point of the exercise is to motivate Jim to attack Sam. Faking is considered a safety issue, where young people can get in over their heads in chat rooms by pretending to be older than they are. In either case, parent educators should work with parents to understand the risk attending identity issues.

Risk Factors. The following list of risk factors for either experiencing cyberbullying or feeling harmed by online incidents was developed by Hoover and Oliver (2008, Chapter 7), based on an extensive literature review:

- The more time spent online the more likely that a youngster will encounter safety issues through the new electronic media.
- Lack of parental supervision proved to be a predictor of experiencing safety issues and harm from cyberbullying in the Youth Internet Safety Surveys.
- As mentioned previously, manipulating identities can exacerbate harm associated with the Internet.
- Sending personal information, particularly a photograph, generates hazards for risky electronic exchanges.
- More harm is associated with cyber attacks when they combine with face-to-face conflicts.
- Some indication exists that females, on average, experience more cyberbullying incidents and report slightly greater levels of harm from these episodes.

Researchers addressing the new media note that bullying occurs most commonly in text [instant] messaging, followed by chat rooms, electronic mail, and various forms of websites (e.g., weblogs) (Patchin & Hinduja, 2006; Ybarra & Mitchell, 2004). A particularly insidious form of cyber attack is making private electronic messages or images public—the latter form of cyberbullying appears to generate significant harm (e.g., naked pictures from locker rooms broadcast over the Internet; see Lenhart, 2008 and the Pew Internet and American Life Study, 2006).

School–Family Interactions Around the New Media. A dilemma facing educators and parents is that the etiquette of online interactions has not been firmly coded into societal behavioral norms. This means that parents and educators must work extremely closely on at least two fronts. First, caregivers must communicate clearly and directly with children about school and family expectations for online behavior and safety. Several excellent media sites exist for the development of cyber etiquette (Kaboose Family Network [n.d.] offers an impressive site). Second, educators and parents need to codify developing expectations into behavioral contracts that specify expectations about familial use of electronic communication media. Hoover and Oliver (2008) have developed contract formats for parents to employ with their offspring (available in that resource for reproduction). Several other useful forms can be attained via online sources:

- www.wiredsafety.org
- http://us.mcafee.com/virusinfo/vil/parents/article_pcinternet.pdf
- www.wiredkids.org

Online use, safety, and behavioral expectations, in the form of social contracts, should be reviewed at least twice per year, more often with younger children. Parents and educators must familiarize themselves with the Internet and its uses—perhaps not to the point of starting social networking sites—but certainly parents must familiarize themselves with the nomenclature employed by their offspring as they explore the cyber universe (Hoover & Oliver, 2008).

The Rights of Parents and Schools to Address Online Aggression.   In the effort to protect freedom of Internet users, legal protections of the new media remain quite stringent (McGrath, 2006; Shariff, 2004; Willard, 2007). It is quite difficult to sue Internet hosts and related organizations over harm done to young people. Thus, legally, the Internet remains something of a wild west—keeping with the theme of an underdeveloped civilization "out there." However, the courts have recognized the rights of schools, parents, and law enforcement agencies to intervene behaviorally when online situations either cause harm at school or could reasonably be expected to do so. Several recent volumes have explored in depth the legal principles involved, and these make top-notch resources for the libraries of both parents and educators (McGrath, 2006; Willard, 2007).

Marketing of Electronic Media to Young Children and Their Parents.   An aspect of cyberbullying is the very ubiquity of the new electronic media. We have come to a place and time in society where participation in online media seems a normal part of a young person's cultural vocabulary. Note, for example, how readily we recognize and accept terms such as *dot-com* and *cyberspace*. Tellingly, young people fail to distinguish between online and face-to-face interactions—rather seeing them as part of the same phenomenon (Slater, 2002).

Widespread acceptance of the new media is not a natural event, but rather socially constructed. It is largely created via the media—particularly the advertising industry. Parents and parent educators should recognize that even very young children are targeted for admission to the cyber world via such marketing ploys as enlarged keyboards. Although we see and value the exciting possibilities reflected by the Internet, we encourage parents to at least think critically about how their offspring are socialized into thinking of the new media as a natural ecology, to exert skepticism about the process, and to realize when they and their children are being targeted as consumers in ways that are not healthy for them (Calvert, 2008).

A Final Concern: Sexting.   Cyberbullying among teenage girls has become an international concern, with severe cases ending in tragedy around the globe. An example of this is with young teens (or even tweeners) victimized via a phenomenon dubbed "sexting," where peers distribute photos or videos of young girls participating in sexual acts (*What Is Sexting*, 2010). The distribution of video and texts on cell phones has become all too easy. Via social networks, peers may send images and videos meant for one or two individuals to the majority of the students in a school and beyond. Once the "send" button is hit, no ability exists to recall the damaging content (Inbar, 2009; Marshall, 2009). Educators and parents need to monitor and instruct their young children about Internet safety (Claussen, 2010). Some incidences of sexting may fall into the category of relational aggression, which we discuss next.

Relational Aggression Among Girls

In the past decade a sea change has occurred in the understanding of bullying and other aggressive behaviors among females. The seminal work of Crick and colleagues (e.g., Crick et al., 2001; Cullerton-Sen & Crick, 2005; Ostrov & Crick, 2007) has been picked up by the popular media (e.g., Simmons, 2003). Nearly eight times as many girls as boys participate in what has been termed *relational aggression*. Relational aggression is defined as manipulating relationships (e.g., friendships, flirting with another's love interest) in a manner purposely designed to hurt others. These behaviors are perceived as very damaging over the short and long haul (Crick et al., 2001).

If relational and other purely verbal forms of aggression are included in the mix, the long assumed proportional difference between males and females in aggression estimates actually disappears (Crick & Bigbee, 1998). Educators have found such behaviors as rumor mongering and aggressive flirting to be difficult to manage, perhaps because of the subtlety of these aggressive forms. As of this writing (2010), no clearly effective method for dealing with relational aggression has been validated.

Reflection...

When is teasing okay, or is it ever okay? How (and how often) do we give bullies the power to bully? If your best friend was being bullied or severely teased, what would you do? Do you know adult bullies? Have you ever heard someone being teased and thought that the teasing had gone beyond appropriate limits (whatever you feel those are)? Why are some episodes of cyberbullying so particularly vicious? What are some ways that you have seen young children bully by manipulating relationships? Do you accept Crick's findings that girls perpetrate relational aggression more frequently than their male counterparts? Think about some of the reasons that girls might perpetrate aggression via manipulating relationships and why boys might not? What are the implications of relational aggression for working with families?

Adjustment Problems Associated with Bullying

Experts currently recognize roughly three categories of students involved with bullying: bullies, passive victims, and provocative victims (Olweus, 2007). Bullies tend to act out—to direct their behavioral problems outward. Passive victims tend to match the personality style that some experts call *overcontrolled*. Specifically, these youngsters tend to be sad, shy, and anxious. Chronic victims tend to become even more anxiety-ridden as they suffer peer harassment. Finally, a small group of youngsters tends to pick on others at times and to suffer bullying at others. These individuals demonstrate the rare combination of being alternatively sad and angry (Olweus, 2007; Swearer, Grills, Haye, & Cary, 2004).

The childhood experience of bullying produces a slew of negative long-term adjustment effects. For example, being the target of bullies during their formative years is the most common complaint registered by adults seeking psychiatric care for depression and anxiety (Egan & Perry, 1998).

Recently, the long-term consequences of bullying have been directly addressed. For example, Rigby (2001, 2003, 2004) has demonstrated that bullying affects both mental and physical health:

> Research findings support the view that peer victimization is reliably associated with seriously impaired mental and physical health among both boys and girls. . . . it has recently become clear that they [victims] are more likely than others to experience particularly distressing mental and physical states, being more anxious, more depressed, more socially dysfunctional, less physically well, and more prone to suicidal ideation than other children. (Rigby, 2001, p. 322)

Jantzer, Hoover, and Narloch (2006) found that bullying in childhood produced small, but detectable, reductions in the ability of college-age students to experience trust in and satisfaction with friendships. Bullying, in other words, is a serious problem that transcends physical and mental health as well as quality of life.

Not just victims, but also bullies, manifest significant relational problems as they age. Basing relationships exclusively on the exercise of power may well be habit-forming, setting the stage for a lifetime of maladjustment. Bullies evidence significantly greater risk for dropping out of school as well as for encountering drug and alcohol abuse problems (Simanton et al., 2000). Childhood bullies are four to five times as likely as nonbullies to experience mental health, legal, and job-related difficulties as they age into adulthood (Olweus, 2007). The negative effects of bullying are so strong that, despite the real and significant sequelae experienced by chronic victims, a world-renowned expert in the field concluded that childhood bullies suffer *worse* adulthood adjustment problems than do victims (Olweus, 2007).

Bullying pejoratively affects the lives of students—both bullies and victims. It extends beyond the lives of bullies and victims, worsening the learning climate for everyone at school. It is difficult for students to tackle learning tasks through the clouds of fear produced by bullying. As bad as peer harassment's effects on individuals are, bullying also reigns as a social problem, contributing to the climate of violence that troubles U.S. society (Hoover & Olsen, 2001).

To a significant degree, bullying can be addressed by an understanding of family dynamics, including child-rearing practices. In other words, elements of family life may either contribute to or reduce risks that an individual child will become a bully or a victim. This, of course, means that partnerships between educators and parental caregivers are essential in reducing the problems associated with bullying and, by extension, reducing school violence. Finally, partnerships between helping professionals and school personnel play a central role in reducing bullying and victimization among school-aged youngsters (Committee for Children, 2010). We explore family issues in bullying in the remainder of this chapter.

Reflection...

Consider a situation in which a physically robust fifth-grade boy picks on a shy third-grade girl. What do you see as the motivations, experiences, and emotions of members of the following three groups: the bully, the victim, and the bystanders?

Family Interaction Patterns Affecting Bullying and Victimization in Children

Three patterns or styles of parenting associated with the development of bullying have been identified: intrusive-overprotective parenting, parental psychological overcontrol, and parental coercion (Perry et al., 2001). Young people with healthy social and emotional adjustment, bullies, passive victims, and provocative victims can all emerge from any of these styles. Other factors, such as individual temperament, results of first experiments with violence, and resilience also affect a child's role in bullying. However, the intrusive-overprotective style and the overcontrolled style are generally associated with victimization status, whereas coercion appears to foreshadow bullying behavior (Duncan, 2004; Perry et al., 2001).

In conclusions drawn from a review, Duncan (2004) concluded that subtle gender interactions between parents and children affect the advent of victimization status. Male victims tend to have overprotective and controlling yet warm mothers. The fathers of male victims tended to be critical and either distant or absent. The mothers of female victims tended to be overtly hostile—at least in a verbal and psychological manner.

The Overprotective Parent or Caregiver

Hoover and Oliver (2008) referred to the "hothouse" family as an analogy to the intrusive-overprotective parenting style. A hothouse can be set up to tightly control all factors leading to health in plants. Yet when flowers from closely controlled hothouses are transplanted into natural surroundings, they often wither because they cannot tolerate less-than-perfect conditions.

Likewise, young people, primarily boys (Duncan, 2004), frequently receive so much protection at home that they grow to be poor at tolerating other children's rough-and-tumble ways. Such youngsters become accustomed to adults' predictability and find the playground's confusion distressing. Overprotective parents may not afford their children the opportunity to enter into the roughhewn negotiations that facilitate acquisition of conflict-resolution skills. Children frequently learn the often-indelicate art of conflict resolution through arguments about the rules of neighborhood games. These negotiation and related social skills learned informally among peers are often missing in children raised in an overprotective style. This may be particularly problematic if the youngster is born with a tendency toward social anxiety.

Boys recognize the importance of roughhousing during informal play. When Gamliel, Hoover, Daughtry, and Imbra (2003) asked intermediate students about aggression, they replied that they participated in a lot of "horsing around" and did not define this behavior as bullying. When these same individuals were asked about bullying, they noted that some boys did not like rough play and that horsing around with such individuals may have been perceived as bullying. This in turn places a great deal of pressure on young boys who do not wish to play out what Kimmel and Mahler (2003) called masculine scripts.

Parental Overcontrol

Parents may exert more than a healthy degree of psychological control over their offspring. Overcontrol refers to invalidation of children's feelings by frequently interrupting and remonstrating with children regarding the invalidity of their feelings (Perry et al., 2001, p. 84). Youngsters often, as a result, lose confidence in the validity of their own emotions. Such individuals manifest internalizing (shy and anxious) symptoms.

Coercive Parenting

In summarizing over a decade of research, Olweus (1993, 2007) characterized the family lives of bullies as a cold emotional environment punctuated by episodes of "heated" physical and verbal violence. Perry and colleagues (2001) described the coercive parenting style in the following terms:

> Coercion encompasses direct verbal attacks, bossiness, sarcasm, and power-assertive discipline and surely undermines the child's feelings of being loved and respected. (p. 84)

Young people with the physical and psychological resources to be aggressive with their peers frequently learn their belligerent response patterns from hostile parents and caregivers. It stands to reason that youngsters approach relationships aggressively if the preponderance of interpersonal episodes they encounter reflect physical or psychological control of the weak by the strong. Generally, students learn to be aggressive via coercive parenting styles, but occasionally a youngster will react to parental hostility by becoming shy and anxious and thus become prone to victimization (Duncan, 2007; Perry et al., 2001). The most toxic mix for the advent of aggression and bullying in youngsters of both sexes is permissiveness for violence directed toward siblings and other young people combined with a physically harsh discipline style (Duncan, 2004).

Perry and colleagues (2001) pointed out that boys tend to become bullies if parenting styles are hostile and aggressive. Girls in hostile environments, on the other hand, tend to manifest the set of behaviors associated with victimization. Boys with oversolicitous, overprotective parents are most at risk for becoming bully victims.

Reflection...

List three specific mannerisms related to dealing with others that you can trace to the parenting you received. Discuss how each mannerism was passed along to you. Now describe the way that child–caregiver interactions form structures of thought about social situations and styles of interacting in social situations.

Home–School Relations and Bullying: What Educators and Future Educators Should Know

Next we present two brief discussions of solutions to bullying. Initially, the high points of a well-documented systemwide campaign for dealing with bullying is offered. This discussion of prevention is largely based on a model tested first by the Norwegian Ministry of Education but shown also to be effective in North America. Readers interested in this model can find out more by looking at Olweus's (2007) English-language version of the model. A second section deals with the specific implications of the social schema model for understanding parents' role in bullying.

A Systemwide Approach for Reducing Violence and Bullying

Under the leadership of Daniel Olweus (1993, 2007) an anti-bullying program was developed and tested in Norway. The same model has been evaluated in the United States, where it has been determined that the frequency and intensity of bullying can be reduced by up to 50% during the first program year (e.g., California Department of Education [CDE], 2003; Olweus Bullying Prevention Program, 2010). These gains are sustained over time as long as the program is kept in place. Olweus concluded that activities at three levels of involvement were required to reduce bullying and school violence. Measures are proposed at the whole school level, the class level, and the individual level.

School Level.   To reduce bullying and school violence, data regarding the school climate must be collected. Data can include surveys (Olweus, 2007; Hoover & Oliver, 2008), observations, and interviews. Sprague, Sugai, Horner, and Walker (1999) argued that incident reports were the most sensitive data that could be collected to identify dangerous spots in the school and with which to track interpersonal climate in the building.

Other core features of a successful program at the school level included school conference days and improved supervision during lunch, hallway time, and recess. School conferences refer to large-scale assemblies scheduled to encourage student and parent enthusiasm for anti-bullying efforts. In addition, school mediation programs have been used successfully in some schools as an alternative way to break the chain of bullying. However, the mediator must make certain that those involved in mediation are perceived to be equals. If the victim does not have power, or is perceived to not have the power of an equal, the mediation is doomed to failure. Many good mediation programs exist (Olsen & Hoover, 1997), including a couple of promising peer-involvement programs directed specifically toward bullying reduction. One is called Operation Respect (www.dontlaugh.org), and the other is called Safe School Ambassadors (Phillips, Linney, & Pack, 2008).

Classroom Level.   Classroom rules against bullying must be spelled out in the clearest possible terms. Educators must clearly communicate them to students and their parents. In addition, it is best if teachers instruct students about the meaning of classroom regulations, just as they would any other material. Olweus's data suggest that mild consequences for violations of rules must be applied if any of the other methods are to work. It is essential that teachers enforce rules calmly, gently, and with a minimum of emotional overlay.

Educators (and parents) are placed in something of a bind as they apply consequences for bullying. Failure to gently punish bullying may communicate the subtle message that it is appropriate to pick on fellow students. However, if sanctions are too severe or students' dignity is damaged, bullying relationships are actually modeled. This is something to be avoided. A middle ground between overly permissive and overly authoritarian styles is desirable. This is referred to as an authoritative discipline style.

Social skills instruction including role plays, regular classroom meetings, and instructive readings are other classroom methods. Primary teachers will recognize Anderson's *The Ugly Duckling* as a wonderful story about bullying and redemption.

We have held the Olweus program up as an excellent template for schoolwide interventions that require a change in an institution's social climate—or, in other words, alterations in a school's culture. Educators, however, must go into such a project with their eyes open to the difficulty of such an effort. For example, in many schools the peer climate may actually support the institution of bullying as a way for students to gather prestige (Espelage, Holt, & Henkel, 2003); in such an institution, prestigious students may actively resist anti-bullying programming. Educators who ask students to refrain from ridiculing peers who do not match highly prized sexualized behaviors might be fighting a losing battle if the surrounding culture strongly supports traditional views of, for example, masculinity and femininity (Kimmel & Mahler, 2003).

Research support has been derived for at least two other systemwide interventions: Project Second Step (Committee for Children, 2010; Holsen, Iversen, & Smith, 2009) and Bully Busters (Horne et al., 2003). Both of these programs are worth exploration as schoolwide models.

Individual Level. The systemic model includes counseling and intensive social skills instruction for students who bully others and for some students at high risk for peer harassment. For the former group, anger management is recommended; for the latter, friendship-making and assertive skills training are recommended. Olweus recommends involving the parents of bullies in intensive discussions of the long-term problems associated with bullying.

Implications for Understanding Parents' Role in Bullying

The information about bullying related to child-rearing styles can be captured and organized most clearly by means of a social learning or cognitive–social schema model. But unless this organizational rubric leads educators to solutions, it is not particularly worthwhile. Several implications are explored below for maximizing the utility of interactions between educators and the parents of bullies, passive victims, and provocative victims.

Knowledge and Skills. Future teachers must explore the relationship between students' worldviews (schemes) and their behavior. In addition, educators must recognize that students' angry or timid outlooks are often related to the modal or overall tone of parent–child interactions. For example, students who have been able to avoid conflict by means of passivity tend to experience a great deal of difficulty learning to demonstrate the recommended use of assertiveness in the face of mild aggression (Hoover & Oliver, 2008). Furthermore, this student's difficulty with assertiveness may help the school social worker or counselor see why parents, for example, react strongly to mild conflict situations at school and why the same elders may insist that their child be protected from the rough-and-tumble of school life.

The relationship between a bully's aggressive behavior and the hostility visited upon the well-meaning educator makes more sense if the teacher understands the relationship between the student's behaviors, as well as his or her understanding of relationships, and the child-rearing patterns practiced by the student's caregivers. School officials may also legitimately worry about whether a parental referral for bullying may result in abuse at home—not because the caregiver is opposed to the use of force in relationships—but because of the humiliation associated with a call from the school.

Working with Parents.   An educator armed with information about the relationship between parental attitudes and student behavior is much better prepared to work with parents on a strengths-based basis (Duncan, 2004; Sheridan, Warnes, & Dowd, 2004). An essential starting point is *reframing* the problems seen by educators that are seen by the family as strengths. The assets of the family are acknowledged as a solution is sought, a practice that may be particularly useful in situations where the educator and the parent experience differing cultural or linguistic backgrounds. For each of the family patterns mentioned previously, some strengths-based statements are suggested:

1. Educators could reframe what they see as an overinvolved, overcontrolling family as tight-knit and close. The strength and vitality of that child's relationships with adults, especially parents, should be acknowledged and supported as a solution is sought to the child's passivity.
2. Families seen by educators as violent and coercive could be recast as preparing the child for independence in a tough, no-nonsense world (Hoover & Oliver, 2008).

Without some acknowledgment of familial strengths, family members are unlikely to work with educators on problems related to bullying and peer victimization. It is important that educators admit the strengths inherent in certain modes of interactions prior to initiating interventions.

Reflection...

Relate how you would rephrase the following behaviors as strengths, as you might in discussing a behavior situation with parents:

▸ A child often verbally threatens others
▸ A child is extremely shy with other children, but likes to talk one-on-one with adults
▸ A student frequently fights with others during unsupervised periods, and when asked about the scuffles, replies that the other child was behaving unfairly

Avoiding Blame and Secondary Victimization.   It is all too easy to see pathology in struggling families or in situations where the perspectives of family members differ significantly from educators' experiences. A parent advocacy group might be helpful in interceding in instances in which an impasse is reached between educators, who feel that the students' troubled or troubling behavior is pathological, and parents, who view the responses as essentially normal.

The Federation of Families for Children's Mental Health is a wonderful resource and advocacy organization operated by and for parents. They are dedicated to putting forth a strengths-based model and to working cooperatively with school personnel. The organization publishes an excellent magazine entitled *Reclaiming Children* (www.ffcmh.org).

Educators must listen to and believe parents when they share that their son or daughter is being bullied. Too often parents are not provided the support they need when it is their child who is the victim. When action is not taken, it may result in a tragedy. Marr and Field (2000) coined the termed *bullycide*, which refers to children who commit suicide after being bullied. All too often, we hear stories of parents who contacted the schools with concerns, only to not be heard, with the result of their child committing "bullycide." Parents' concerns need to be taken seriously and action must occur quickly. It is the responsibility of the educator to be an advocate for parents and their child, regardless of whether the bullying is happening within the confines of the school, the school bus, or in cyberspace.

Parent Training and Support Models.   A useful mindset for educators is to rethink what they perceive as parenting weaknesses as a lack of knowledge and skill. We see this as the most important piece in the anti-bullying puzzle. Once parents and the educators establish a relationship based on mutual respect and built around problem solving for the child in question, a referral to a parent support and education center could be made.

Parent resource centers should include child care and all the other types of supports that would allow parents to effectively access the program. If such programs do not exist, educators can become part of a team that advocates for such an approach and develops grant projects to start and support parent education and advocacy centers.

Monitoring Television, Internet, and Media Use.   As Garbarino (2000) and Pipher (1994) argued so persuasively, one manifestation of our culture's toxicity to youth is the huge menu of violence offered to children not yet developmentally prepared to manage these images and ideas. Evidence demonstrating that the media exacerbates violence is so strong that it is no longer arguable that they do not contribute to social conflict (Garbarino, 2000).

Reflection...

What can be done by working with parents and children to help them understand the violence that is in the media (television, music, the Internet, and video games)? How do we protect our children? Are there organizations that are working in the area of violence in the media and its effects on children?

Educators and parents could work together on discussing media violence and the subliminal messages of revenge and violent problem solving that are being subtly (and sometimes quite obviously) sold to youth. Educators could foster such partnerships by the use of well-designed media analysis lessons imbedded in social studies and language arts curriculums (Adbusters, 2001; Media Awareness Network, 2001). Educators could send letters to parents that include methods for either avoiding or at least discussing media violence with their offspring. This is one domain where parents could really use educators' support. Frequent meetings within the structure of the PTA or PTO may be useful, but it is also possible for teachers and parents to forge partnerships to work specifically on the issue of violence and media's role in fostering conflict. For example, together they could plan and hold informational communitywide meetings and lobby advertisers and local affiliates of television networks.

Programs.   All the programs that we have inspected that effectively deal with violence and bullying in schools contain a parent-cooperation component. Three programs deserve particular mention, though many more excellent packages are available for educators. Second Step and Bullying Prevention (Committee for Children, 2010) are excellent packages that include parent partnership and involvement components. Likewise, the Johnston Institute's Respect and Protect will serve the needs of educators. Finally, a program based on many years of testing by the Norwegian Ministry of Education has found its way to the United States (Olweus, 2007).

Case Study

Tasha, a 13-year-old, African American seventh-grader, attends a junior high school in the upper Midwest. Students of color represent a distinct minority in Tasha's school (15%).

Tasha resides with her married biological parents, as well as two older brothers and an older sister. Her mother, after a recent cancer diagnosis, does not work and stays home with the children. Tasha's father has a substantial criminal record and is unable to attain steady employment. With neither parent employed, the family lives below the poverty level.

During the first 2 months of seventh grade, Tasha became greatly admired by the other female students as a natural leader. She "bossed" a clique of about five girls, and many young girls of color, desirous of establishing a sense of belonging, longed to join Tasha's group.

Tasha willingly exercised the power to decide who belonged and who did not. She walked the hallways with assertive confidence, perhaps as a result of having so many friends and associates. However, the majority of girls in Tasha's set confided to teachers that they were afraid of her. Tasha controlled the dynamics of the "out" list through instigating rumors of boyfriend interference or publicly teasing and humiliating girls regarding purported sexual encounters. The "in" list, as might be imagined, constantly fluctuated, with Tasha exercising control through rumor-mongering and teasing.

Tasha's seventh-grade academic skills showed a lack of progress, though ironically teachers did not view her as a problem in school. She appeared in class on time, participated, and displayed respectful behavior toward teachers. Nonetheless, she regularly failed to complete required work. When school officials arranged meetings to address her schoolwork, Tasha's mother, attending on her own, verbally and publicly (in front of students and staffers) humiliated Tasha for her lack of academic progress. The mother's level of sarcasm and blame appeared to shame Tasha in front of the staff. During these times, Tasha remained silent—to all appearances cold and emotionless.

After three parent meetings had resulted in no academic improvement, Tasha's bullying began to escalate from teasing and public humiliation of "friends" to hallway fights. The fisticuffs were, in each case, with girls who ended up on the out list presumably trying to defend their right to remain in Tasha's set. Tasha or one of the out girls initiated the battles with verbal abuse and insults, quickly leading to hitting, hair pulling, and body slams. Even with staff members responding as quickly as possible, blood was often shed during these brawls. Generally, one or two bystanders, members of Tasha's set, joined the fighting. The first three fights occurred during transition time in school when the hallways were full of students.

The fights affected more than the immediate participants and hangers-on. One bystander noted, in her daily journal for a language arts class, "I am afraid to come to school. I saw a fight today, and even saw blood on one girl's face . . . it makes it scary to be in school." The tension resulting from Tasha's altercations filtered through the junior high's halls and classrooms.

By the beginning of the third trimester, Tasha's band had shrunk to just a few hangers-on, as the girls began to weary of Tasha's efforts to exert control, her incessant fighting, and her increasingly negative attitude toward school.

The consequences reaped by Tasha from her first three fights exerted no effect on her behavior. Each time, school officials administered out-of-school detention, with more days out for each disturbance. The follow up upon her return to school was minimal; Tasha returned to classes after assuring the principal that she would refrain from further fights. A few teachers expressed mild dissatisfaction with these arrangements because they seemed to have no say in Tasha's situation.

The fourth fight in school for Tasha centered around a rumor that she spread regarding a peer engaging in sex with someone else's boyfriend. This time, the young man involved in the rumor confronted Tasha in the hallway. Tasha, having two older brothers, held her ground in the fight. A staff emergency all-call rang through the building, with teachers trained in crisis management arriving on the scene in minutes. By the time that staff members arrived, Tasha had lost all control and was pounding on the young man, simultaneously holding him to the floor. Three teachers attempted to remove her from the situation; the assistant principal finally calmed Tasha, convincing her to halt the attack.

Once more, the young lady was removed from school, this time for a full week. During an all-school faculty meeting dealing with Tasha's physical aggression, staff members addressed safety concerns for all members of the school community. When she returned from her out-of-school suspension, Tasha was placed in an all-day, one-on-one supervised situation in school. A staff member escorted Tasha during all hallway transitions. Although Tasha's behavior proved to be under control in these circumstances, no improvement was seen in her academic standing.

Questions and Considerations

1. What do you see as the central problem in Tasha's situation?
2. How did Tasha attain power and maintain control in her peer group?
3. What contributing factors led to Tasha's behavior?
4. What interventions would you implement?
5. Who else could be involved in the intervention process?
6. Why might a student put up with Tasha's relational aggression—at least at first?

Summary

In this chapter we have established that although schools are relatively safe places within the larger context of violence in U.S. society, they are not as safe as educators would like them to be. In addition, we spelled out the relationship between bullying and violence, noting that low-level violence sets the stage for and increases risk for more dangerous sorts of behaviors.

Because primary caregivers are so intimately involved in socializing children's problem-solving styles, they also lie at the core of effective intervention programs. A well-documented intervention model at the school or district level was spelled out, as were specific suggestions for involving parents in solving problems with school violence.

Recommended Activities

1. Working with one classmate, describe a bullying episode each has observed or where one of you suffered bullying. The event could involve either children or adults. Pick one of the stories and attempt to analyze it in terms of (a) what motivated the bullying, (b) what you as an educator would do to deal with or say to the bully, and (c) what you as an educator would do to deal with the victim. Be as specific as you can about the dynamics of the incident and how you would deal with it. Be prepared to report to the larger group.

2. Consider both teasing and cyberbullying. When might a teasing episode be seen as bullying by the recipient? Can you think of some reasons that misunderstandings would likely occur in e-mail or e-text exchanges?

3. With at least two other discussants, complete the following task: Outline a parent meeting that includes a 2-hour education session on cyberbullying. In your outline, organize information around the following topics: (1) bullying and cyberbullying definitions, (2) the relationship between cyberbullying and bullying, (3) risk factors for experiencing harm from cyberbullying, (4) online dangers and their prevention, (5) factors designed to improve parent–child communication around the use of media. Be specific about the materials and resources that you will use.

4. Debate the following proposition: Verbal teasing should not be allowed in classrooms because it leads to bullying and raises the risk for school violence. Use material in the chapter

and your experience to either support or dispute the proposition. Present your arguments in a formal debate.

5. Meet in groups of three to four and propose a model or theory explaining how child-rearing practices affect children's behavioral styles. As you develop your model, you might want to consider the components listed below. Your theory should be as specific as possible and should make exact predictions regarding the relationship(s) between parental and child behavior.

   a. Sense of humor and the absurd: How is this passed down through the generations?
   b. Anger and its expression: Why are some children quick to anger and why do children differ in their ability to cope with anger-arousing situations?
   c. Verbal interaction style: What is the relationship, if any, between parental and child language style?
   d. Beliefs about the world and unstated assumptions: How and why, if at all, do children acquire parents' unstated assumptions?

6. Develop a role play related to holding a parent conference for a student who consistently bullies others (and/or for a student who is frequently the victim of peer harassment). Role plays can be based on one or more of the following assumptions:

   a. The parents become hostile and angrily state that the child's behavior is the school's fault.
   b. The parents become angry with one another, blaming the child's misbehavior on one another.
   c. The parents calmly but assertively state that fighting and bullying are just part of life and they do not see it as a problem. They argue that the problem is with the "wimpy kids who tattle."
   d. The parents passively listen to the educator's issues but resist or don't respond when solutions are suggested.

Request feedback from the rest of the class regarding the group's role play and try it again, instituting worthwhile improvements.

7. Conduct library research and write a report on the relationship between media and violence. Summarize your report by suggesting specific ways for educators, school administrators, and parents to work together on dealing with violence in the media.

8. Devise a survey regarding school safety and school–parent issues with the help of your instructor. Administer the survey to at least 20 parents. Summarize the information and write a report about your findings. End your report with specific suggestions for working with parents and guardians to reduce violence in schools.

Children's Books

The following children's books are suggested as a way of helping your students consider issues in this chapter.

Primary Level (Ages 4–6)

We Both Read—Stop Teasing Taylor!
Jana Carson and Meryl Treatner
Treasure Bay, Inc. (2005)

Toestomper and the Caterpillars
Sharleen Collicott
Houghton Mifflin (2002)

Stop Picking on Me: A First Look at Bullying
Pat Thomas and Lesley Harker
Barron's Educational Series (2000)

Video

Boulden, J. (2003). *Buddy learns about bullying video kit.* Weaverville, CA: Boulden Publishing, Inc.

Juvenile Level (Ages 7–12)

Long Walk to School: Safety Outdoors
Cindy Leaney
Rourke Publishing (2003)

Dog House Blues
Jacqueline Pearce
Orca Book Publishers (2005)

Don't Pick on Pepper!
Pamela Ruben
Peppery Press (2005)

Bullying: Deal with It before Push Comes to Shove
Elaine Slavens and Brooke Kerrigan
James Lorimer & Company (2003)

Dimples Delight
Frieda Wishinsky and Louise-Andree Laliberte
Orca Book Publishers (2005)

Video

The big deal about bullying: And what you can do about it. (2005). Jacksonville Beach, FL: Linx Educational Publishing, Inc.

Additional Resources

Books

Beane, A. (1999). *Bully free classroom.* Minneapolis: Free Spirit.

Conoley, J. C., & Goldstein, A. P. (Eds.). (2004). *School violence intervention: A practical handbook* (2nd ed.). New York: Guilford Press.

Dorn, M. (2005). *Weakfish—Bullying through the eyes of a child.* Macon, GA: Safe Havens International.

Espelage, D. L., & Swearer, S. M. (Eds.). (2004). *Bullying in American schools: A social-ecological perspective on prevention and intervention.* Mahwah, NJ: Lawrence Erlbaum.

Garbarino, J. (2000). *Lost boys: Why our sons turn violent and how we can save them.* New York: Anchor Books.

Henkin, R. (2005). *Confronting bullying: Literacy as a tool for character education.* Portsmouth, NH: Heinemann.

Hoover, J. H., & Oliver, R. O. (1996). *The bullying prevention handbook.* Bloomington, IN: National Educational Service.

Hoover, J. H., & Olsen, G. W. (2001). *Teasing and harassment: The frames and scripts approach for teachers and parents.* Bloomington, IN: National Educational Service.

Juvonen, J., & Graham, S. (Eds.). (2001). *Peer harassment in school: The plight of the vulnerable and victimized.* New York: Guilford Press.

Olweus, D. (1993). *Bullying at school: What we know and what we can do.* Cambridge, MA: Blackwell.

Sprung, B., Froschl, M., & Hinitz, B. (2005). *The anti-bullying and teasing book: A preschool guide.* Beltsville, MD: Gryphon House.

Curriculum Guides

Committee for Children. (1997). *Second step: A violence-prevention curriculum.* Seattle, WA: Author.

Committee for Children. (2001). *Steps to respect: A bullying prevention program.* Seattle, WA: Author.

Eggert, L. L., Nicholas, L. J., & Owen, L. M. (1995). *Reconnecting youth: A peer group approach to building life skills.* Bloomington, IN: National Educational Service.

Garrity, C., Jens, K., Porter, W., Sager, N., & Short-Camilli, C. (1995). *Bully proofing your school: A comprehensive approach for elementary schools.* Longmont, CO: Sopris West.

Videos

Let's Get Real. (2003). Women's Educational Media. www.bapd.org/gwoaia-1.html

Preventing sexual harassment. (With leader's guide, 2000). (1999). Virginia Beach, VA: Coastal Training Technologies (800–695–0756).

School violence: Draw the line. (With leader's guide, 1999). (1999). Virginia Beach, VA: Coastal Training Technologies (800–695–0756).

Set straight on bullies. (with Leader's Guide by J. H. Hoover). Bloomington, IN: National Educational Service.

Weakfish—Bullying through the eyes of a child. (2005). Macon, GA: Safe Havens International.

Websites

Anti-Bullying network
www.antibullying.net

Illinois Office of Education Online Safety
Assessment
www.schoolsafetyonline.org

National Association of Elementary School
Principals
www.naesp.org/whatsnew.html

The New Jersey Commission on Holocaust
Education/Getting Along Curriculum
www.state.nj.us/holocaust/curriculum

Operation Respect
www.dontlaugh.org

The Safe and Drug Free Schools Program
www.ed.gov/legislation/ESEA/sec4011.html

Safe School Ambassadors
www.safeschoolambassadors.org

Stop Bullying Now
www.stopbullyingnow.net

What Parents and Teachers Should Know
About Bullying
www.accesseric.org:81/resources/parents/
bullying.html

Workplace Violence
www.bullybusters.org

References

Affordable Care Act. (2010). *Understanding the Affordable Care Act.* Retrieved at January 14, 2011 at www.healthcare.gov/law/introduction/index.html

Bandura, A. (1999). Moral disengagement in the perpetration of inhumanities. *Personality and Social Psychology Review, 3*, 193–209.

Belsey, B. (n.d.). Cyberbullying Canada: Home page. Retrieved July 5, 2010, from http://cyberbullying.ca/

Berthold, K., & Hoover, J. (2000). Correlates of bullying and victimization among intermediate students in the Midwestern USA. *School Psychology International, 21*(1), 65–78.

Bovaird, J. A. (2010). Scales and surveys: Some problems with measuring bullying behavior. In S. R. Jimeson, S. M. Swearer, & D. L. Espelage (Eds.), *Handbook of bullying in schools: An international perspective* (pp. 277–292). New York: Routledge.

Braaten, S. (2004). Creating safe schools: A principal's perspective. In J. C. Conoley & A. P. Goldstein (Eds.), *School violence intervention: A practical handbook* (2nd ed., pp. 54–67). New York: Guilford Press.

California Department of Education. (2003). *Preventing bullying: A manual for schools and communities (a U.S. Department of Education document).* Retrieved April 2, 2003, from www.cde.ca.gov/spbranch/ssp/bullymanual.htm

Calvert, S. L. (2008). Children as consumers: Advertising and marketing. *Children and Electronic Media, 18*, 205–234. A special issue of the journal is available online at http://ccf.tc.columbia.edu/pdf/Children%20and%20Electronic%20Media_Spring%2008.pdf

Claussen, L. (2010). Stay connected: Teaching children about cell phone safety. *Family Safety & Health, 69*(2), 20–21.

Crick, N., & Bigbee, M. (1998). Relational and overt forms of peer victimization: A multi-informant approach. *Journal of Consulting and Clinical Psychology, 66*, 337–347.

Crick, N. R., Nelson, D. A., Morales, J. R., Cullerton-Sen, C., Casas, J. F., & Hickman, S. E. (2001). Relational victimization in childhood and adolescence: I hurt you through the grapevine. In J. Juvonen & S. Graham (Eds.), *Peer harassment in school: The plight of the vulnerable and victimized* (pp. 196–214). New York: Guilford Press.

Cullerton-Sen, C., & Crick, N. R. (2005). Understanding the effects of physical and relational victimization: The utility of multiple perspectives in predicting social-emotional adjustment. *School Psychology Review, 34*, 147–160.

Davis, M., Hoover, J. H., & Oliver, R. (2008). Cyberbullying and equal access. *The California School Counselor, 5*, 8–10, 20.

DeVoe, J. F., Kaffenberger, S., & Chandler, K. (2005). *Student reports of bullying: Results from the 2001 school crime supplement to the National Crime Victimization Survey* (NCES 2005–310). U.S. Department of Education, National Center for Education Statistics. Washington, DC: U.S. Government Printing Office.

DeVoe, J. F., Ruddy, S. A., Miller, A. K., Planty, M., Snyder, T. D., Duhart, D. T., & Rand, M. R. (2002). *Indicators of school crime and safety: 2002 (*NCES 2003-009/NCj196753). Washington, DC: U.S. Departments of Education and Justice.

Dinkes, R., Kemp, J., Baum, K., & Snyder, T. D. (2009). *Indicators of school crime and safety 2009.* Washington: National Center for Educational Statistics. Also available online at http://bjs.ojp.usdoj.gov/content/pub/pdf/iscs09.pdf

Duncan, R. D. (1999). Peer and sibling aggression: An investigation of intra- and extra-familial bullying. *Journal of Interpersonal Violence, 14*, 871–886.

Duncan, R. D. (2004). The impact of family relationships on school bullies and victims. In D. L. Espelage & S. M. Swearer (Eds.), *Bullying in American schools: A social-ecological perspective on prevention and intervention* (pp. 227–244). Mahwah, NJ: Lawrence Erlbaum.

Duncan, N. (2007). Bullying in school, or bullying schools. In G. Richards and F. Armstrong (Eds.), *Key issues for classroom assistants working in diverse and inclusive classrooms.* London: Routledge Press.

Egan, S., & Perry, D. (1998). Does low self-regard invite victimization? *Developmental Psychology, 34*(2), 299–309.

Espelage, D., Holt, M., & Hinkel, E. (2003). Examination of peer group contextual effects on aggression during early adolescence. *Child Development, 74*(1), 205–220.

Gamliel, T., Hoover, J. H., Daughtry, D. W., & Imbra, C. (2003). A qualitative investigation of bullying: The perspectives of fifth, sixth, and seventh graders in a USA parochial school. *School Psychology International, 24*, 405–420.

Garbarino, J. (2000). *Lost boys: Why our sons turn violent and how we can save them.* New York: Random House.

Goldstein, A. P., & Conoley, J. C. (1997). Student aggression: Current status. In A. P. Goldstein & J. C. Conoley (Eds.), *School violence: A practical handbook* (pp. 3–19). New York: Guilford Press.

Hazler, R., Hoover, J., & Oliver, R. (1991). Student perceptions of victimization by bullies in school. *Journal of Humanistic Education and Development, 29*, 143–150.

Holsen, I., Iversen, A. C., & Smith, B. (2009). Universal social competence programme in school: Does it work for children with low socioeconomic background? *Advances in School Mental Health Promotion 2*(2), 51–60.

Hoover, J. H., & Oliver, R. (2008). *The bullying prevention handbook.* Bloomington, IN: Solution Tree.

Hoover, J. H., Oliver, R., & Hazler, R. J. (1992). Bullying: Perceptions of adolescent victims in the Midwestern USA. *School Psychology International, 13*, 5–16.

Hoover, J., & Olsen, G. (2001). *Teasing and harassment: The frames and scripts approach for teacher and parents.* Bloomington, IN: Solution Tree.

Horne, A., Bartolomucci, C., & Newman-Carlson, D. (2003). *Bully Busters: A teacher's manual for helping bullies, victims, and bystanders (Grades K–5).* Champion, IL: Research Press.

Inbar, M. (2009, December 2). *Sexting bullying noted in teens suicide.* Retrieved July 31, 2010, from http://today.msnbc.msn.com/id/34236377

Jantzer, A., Hoover, J. H., & Narloch, R. (2006). The relationship between school-aged bullying and trust, shyness, and quality of friendships: A preliminary research note. *School Psychology International, 27*, 639–640.

Kaboose Family Network. (n.d.). *A kid's guide to etiquette on the Net.* Retrieved July 31, 2010, from www.kidsdomain.com/brain/computer/surfing/netiquette_kids.html

Kimmel, M. S., & Mahler, M. (2003). Adolescent masculinity, homophobia, and violence: Random school shootings, 1982–2001. *American Behavioral Scientist, 46*, 1439–1458.

Kosciw, J. G., & Diaz, E. M. (2005). The 2005 national school climate survey: The experiences of lesbian, gay, bisexual and transgender youth in our nation's schools. Gay, Lesbian and Straight Education Network. Retrieved July 15, 2010, from www.glsen.org/cgi-bin/iowa/all/library/record/1927.html

Lenhart, A. (2008). *Data memo of the Pew Internet & American Life Project.* Retrieved August 1, 2010, from www.pewinternet.org/~/media/Files/Reports/2008/PIP_Adult_gaming_memo.pdf.pdf

Li, Q. (2007). New bottle but old wine: A research of cyberbullying in schools. *Computers in Human Behavior, 23*(4), 1777–1791. Retrieved October 23, 2007, from http://dx.doi.org/10.1016/j.chb.2005.10.005

Ma, X. (2001). Bullying and being bullied: To what extent are bullies also victims? *American Educational Research Journal, 38,* 351–370.

Ma, X. (2002). Bullying in middle school: Individual and school characteristics of victims and offenders. *School Effectiveness and School Improvement, 13,* 63–89.

Marr, N., & Field, T. (2000). *Bullycide: Death at playtime, An exposé of child suicide caused by bullying.* Oxfordshire, UK: Success Unlimited.

Marshall, P. (2009, March 18). Generation sexting: What teenage girls really get up to on the Internet should chill every parent. Retrieved July 31, 2010, from www.dailymail.co.uk/femail/article-1162777/Generation-sexting-What-teenage-girls-really-internet-chill-parent.html

McGrath, M. J. (2006). *School bullying: Tools for avoiding harm and liability.* Thousand Oaks, CA: Corwin PressMedia Awareness Network. 2001. www.media-awareness.ca

Nansel, T. R., Overpeck, M., Pilla, R. S., Ruan, W. J., Simon-Morton, B., & Scheidt, P. (2001). Bullying behaviors among U.S. youth: Prevalence and association with psychosocial adjustment. *Journal of the American medical Association, 285,* 2094–2100.

National Center for Educational Statistics. (1998). *Violence and discipline problems in U.S. public schools, 1996–1997: Executive summary.* Retrieved from http://nces.ed.gov/pubs98/violence/98030001.html

NBC4i.com. (2010). Retrieved January 14, 2011 from www2.nbc4i.com/news/2010/oct/11/ohio-district-where-4-died-says-it-fights-bullies-ar-256695/

Olsen, G., & Hoover, J. (1997). Conflict resolution in schools: A review. *North Dakota Journal of Human Service, 1*(2), 28–37

Olweus, D. (1978). *Aggression in the schools: Bullies and whipping boys.* New York: Wiley.

Olweus, D. (1993). Victimization by peers: Antecedents and long-term outcomes. In K. H. Rubin & J. B. Asendorf (Eds.), *Social withdrawal, inhibition, and shyness in childhood* (pp. 315–26). Hillsdale, NJ: Lawrence Erlbaum.

Olweus, D. (2007). *Olweus bullying prevention program: Teacher Guide.* Circle Pines, MN: Hazelden Foundation.

Olweus Bully Prevention Program. (2010). Hazelden Institute and Clemson University (Homepage). Retrieved July 1, 2010, from: www.olweus.org/public/news.page

Ostrov, J. M., & Crick, N. R. (2007). Forms and functions of aggression during early childhood: A short-term longitudinal study. *School Psychology Review, 36,* 22–43.

Patchin, J. W., & Hinduja, S. (2006). Bullies move beyond the schoolyard: A preliminary look at cyberbullying. *Youth Violence and Juvenile Justice, 4*(2), 148–169.

Patterson, G., DeBaryshe, B., & Ramsey, E. (1989). A developmental perspective on antisocial behavior. *American Psychologist, 44*(2), 329–335.

Perry, D., Hodges, E., & Egan, S. (2001). Determinants of chronic victimization by peers: A review and new model of family influence. In J. Juvonen & S. Graham (Eds.), *Peer harassment in schools: The plight of the vulnerable and victimized.* New York: Guilford Press.

Pervin, K., & Turner, A. (1994). An investigation into staff and pupil knowledge, attitudes, and beliefs about bullying in an inner city school. *Pastoral Care in Education, 12,* 16–22.

Pew Internet and American Life Project. (2006). *Generations online.* Retrieved August 1, 2010, from www.pewinternet.org/PPF/r/170/report_display.asp

Phillips, R., Linney, J., & Pack, C. (2008). *Safe school ambassadors: Harnessing student power to stop bullying and violence.* San Francisco: Jossey-Bass.

Pipher, M. (1994). *Reviving Ophelia: Saving the selves of adolescent girls.* New York: Ballantine.

Rigby K. (2001). Health consequences of bullying and its prevention in schools. In J. Juvonen & S. Graham (Eds.), *Peer harassment in school: The plight of the vulnerable and victimized* (pp. 310–331). New York: Guilford Press.

Rigby, K. (2003). Consequences of bullying in schools. *Canadian Journal of Psychiatry, 48,* 583–590.

Rigby, K. (2004). *Bullying in schools: How successful can interventions be?* London: Cambridge University Press.

Rivers, I., Duncan, N., & Besag, V. (2007). *Bullying: A handbook for educators and parents.* Lanham, MD: Rowan & Littlefield Education.

Ryan, R., Martin, M., & Brooks-Gunn, J. (2006). Is one good parent good enough? Patterns of father and mother parenting and their combined associations with concurrent child outcomes at 24 and 36 months. *Parenting, Science, & Practice, 6*(2), 211–228.

Schwartz, D., Proctor, L. J., & Chien, D. H. (2001). The aggressive victim of bullying: Emotional and behavioral dysregulation as a pathway to victimization by peers. In J. Juvonen & S. Graham (Eds.), *Peer harassment in school: The plight of the vulnerable and victimized* (pp. 147–174). New York: Guilford Press.

Shariff, S. (2004). Keeping schools out of court: Legally defensible models of leadership. *The Educational Forum, 68*(3), 222–233.

Sheridan, S., Warnes, E., & Dowd, S. (2004). Home-school collaboration and bullying: An ecological approach to increase social competence in children and youth. In D. Espelage & S. Swearer (Eds.), *Bullying in American schools: A social-ecological perspective on prevention and intervention* (pp. 245–268). Mahwah, NJ: Lawrence Erlbaum Associates.

Simanton, E., Burthwick, P., & Hoover, J. H. (2000). Small-town bullying and student-on-student aggression: An initial investigation of risk. *The Journal of At-Risk Issues, 6,* 4–9.

Simmons, R. (2003). *Odd girl out.* Orlando, FL: Harcourt.

Slater, D. (2002). Social relationships and identity online and offline. In L. Lievrouw & S. Livingstone (Eds.), *The handbook of new media* (pp. 534–547). London: Sage.

Smith, P., Mahdavi, J., Carvalho M., & Tippett, N. (2005). An investigation into cyberbullying, its forms, awareness and impact, and the relationship between age and gender in cyberbullying. Retrieved July 10, 2008, from www.antibullyingalliance.org.uk/downloads/pdf/cyberbullyingreportfinal230106_000.pdf

Sprague, J. R., Sugai, G., Horner, R. H., & Walker, H. M. (1999). *Using office referral data to evaluate schoolwide discipline and violence prevention intervention.* Oregon School Study Council, 42(2).

Stein, N. (1995). Sexual harassment in school: The public performance of gendered violence. *Harvard Education Review, 65,* 145–162.

Stephens, R. D. (1997). National trends in school violence: Statistics and prevention methods. In A. P. Goldstein & J. C. Conoley (Eds.), *School violence: A practical handbook* (pp. 72–90). New York: Guilford Press.

Swearer, S. M., Grills, A. E., Haye, K. M., & Cary, P. T. (2004). Internalizing problems in students involved in bullying and victimization: Implications for intervention. In D. L Espelage & S. M. Swearer (Eds.), *Bullying in American schools: A social-ecological perspective on prevention and intervention* (pp. 63–84). Mahwah, NJ: Lawrence Erlbaum.

Swearer, S. M., Siebecker, A. B., Johnson-Frerichs, L. A., & Cixin, W. (2010). Assessment of bullying/victimization: The problem of comparability across studies and across methodologies. In S. R Jimeson, S. M. Swearer, & D. L. Espelage (Eds.), *Handbook of bullying in schools: An international perspective* (pp. 305–327). New York: Routledge.

Vossekuil, B., Reddy, M., Fein, R., Borum, R., & Modzeleski, W. (2000). *U.S.S.S. safe school initiative: An interim report on the prevention of targeted violence in schools.* Washington, DC: U.S. Secret Service, National Threat Assessment Center.

What is sexting? (2010). Retrieved July 31, 2010, from www.crisisinterventioncenter.org/index.php? option=com_content&view=article&

id=147:what-is-sexting&catid=39:teens&
Itemid=79

Willard, N. E. (2007). *Cyberbullying and
cyberthreats*. Champaign, IL: Research Press.

Wilson, J. Q., & Petersilia, J. (1995). *Crime*. San
Francisco, CA: Institute for Contemporary
Studies Press.

Ybarra, M., & Mitchell, K. (2004). Online
aggressors, victims, and aggressor/victim: A
comparison of associated youth characteristics. *Journal of Child Psychology and Child
Psychology, 45*(7), 1308–1310.

Ybarra, M. L., Mitchell, K. J., Wolak, J., &
Finkelhor, D. (2006). Examining characteristics and associated distress related to Internet
harassment: Findings from the second Youth
Internet Safety Survey. *Pediatrics, 118*, e1169–
e1177.

Chapter Fifteen

Finding a Voice for Children and Families: Public Policy, Social Services, and Advocacy in Action

Barbara Arnold-Tengesdal
University of Mary

Educational reform and cultural shifts often lead to public policy changes that deeply affect the fabric of our society. It is often the role of professionals and parents to advocate for changes that will make a lasting impact on how we educate and care for children. Advocacy takes place on many levels, personal and professional. We use the latest research and the newest theories on child development to guide our decisions about what is best for children. This chapter helps you to:

▶ Identify landmark public policy initiatives that have changed the course of our work with children and families.

▶ Examine current issues and trends leading a public policy agenda for future changes in the education of children, including the care and education of young children.

▶ Define the role of advocacy and its role in personal career development.

▶ Outline major advocacy efforts that created cultural shifts in how we educate children.

▶ Identify ways to serve as a resource for families.

Everyone agreed on one crucial thing; that no one in America should harm children and that everyone can do more to ensure that you grow up safe, healthy, and educated, in nurturing families and in caring communities. You are *entitled* to your childhood, safety and hope. (Edelman & Yorinks, 1998)

In her speech, Marian Wright Edelman inspired over 300,000 people in 1996 at the first Stand for Children rally in Washington, DC. She called for adults everywhere to make a commitment, joining each year on June 1 to participate in Stand for Children events throughout the nation. In her monumental speech, she referred to children being *entitled* to feeling safe and filled with hope. It leads to the question—Do children have a right to safe living environments, basic education, food, and transportation? Many advocates maintain not enough is being done to ensure that children's basic human rights are being met, and yet vast amounts of federal dollars and resources have been moved into entitlement programs created to provide education, food, and medical care for children living in poverty. It leads one to ask, Does public policy drive reform—such as the federal education initiative in 2001 called No Child Left Behind—or does the need for reform, as was the case with the American Disabilities Act of 1990, drive the creation of public policy? In this chapter, we will outline major advocacy efforts that have made possible cultural shifts in how we look at children's rights, identify landmark public policy initiatives, examine current issues and trends that already have advocacy efforts underway, and look at the role individuals can take to advocate for the rights of children.

Rights of Children

In the National Association for the Education of Young Children's *Code of Ethical Conduct* (NAEYC, 2005), a statement of commitment maintains that early childhood practitioners should keep the rights of children in the forefront of their professional obligations. The *Convention on the Rights of the Child* ratified in 1989 by the United Nations identifies that all children throughout the world should be given the opportunity for survival and optimal development. Many believe that over the past few decades, we have seen a growing global, political, and social commitment to giving children rights previously afforded only to adults (Ruck & Horn, 2008). Some examples of what many groups see as the fundamental rights of children often begin as legal battles that examine the role of children in decision making such as what parent to live with in a divorce, whereas others uphold personal safety or civil freedoms in educational, health, or criminal systems. Whatever the venue, the discussion of children's rights provides a compass that gives direction and a call to action to those who have personal and professional commitments to children, families, and communities to advocate on their behalf.

Treading lightly on issues considered parental prerogatives and determining the government's responsibility can become murky when working with families in a culturally sensitive manner. Values about discipline and when legal intervention should take place are sometimes opposed to a parent's right to decide how best to raise a child. Laws have been created to identify what is excessive and abusive behavior toward a child. Decisions made regarding how to discipline are ultimately parental choices. We have laws dictating that children must go to school, but it is the parent's choice how that will happen. Home schooling serves as an example of rules governing this type of education. Public policy is the creation of laws and rules that determine how certain practices or public monies are used. It is often public policy that initiates rules and laws that are then put in place to govern or distribute resources.

Reflection...

Can you think of instances when your professional viewpoint might contradict a parent's perspective on an issue—for example, TV watching, discipline, age for children to be home alone or use of a computer?

One might believe that a child's right to grow up is threatened by a changing world in which violence and crimes against children cast fear in communities and schools. An unstable economy can lead to poverty, leaving families homeless or without necessary medical care, food, shelter, and transportation in the wake of such disasters as hurricanes, earthquakes, and oil spills. Educational reform has shifted public opinion about highly qualified teachers and poor-performing schools as they relate to creating a literate society. As society changes, the laws and regulations that govern and provide funding have policy implications that are often at the center of reform. Thus, health, education, and safety are driven by what lawmakers decide regarding the rights of children.

Creating Change in Public Policy

Does the need for reform drive change or does public policy push reform? Depending on whom you talk to, the passage of the Affordable Care Act in 2010 providing health care options for families, or the landmark piece of legislation No Child Left Behind, which passed in 2001, are examples of this quandary. No Child Left Behind changed the face of education throughout the nation. Teacher unions and state departments of education were not in favor of this federal law that created unfunded mandates, excessive testing, and arbitrary standards identifying what constituted a highly qualified teacher. Legislators, citing public concerns about poor student performance, low graduation rates, and students passing to higher-grade levels without the ability to read, pushed reform on a somewhat resistant educational system. This clearly is a case in which legislation was the impetus for change.

Examples of public policy that created systems change include:

- Family Support Act (1988). This act affects child support and parental access, and safeguards the relationship between child and parents.
- Women, Infants and Children (1974). WIC provides supplemental foods, health care referrals, and nutrition education for low-income pregnant, breastfeeding, and nonbreastfeeding postpartum women, and to infants and children up to age 5 who are found to be at nutritional risk.
- Temporary Assistance to Needy Families (1996). Welfare reform added work and training requirements for eligibility to receive cash assistance.
- No Child Left Behind (2001). This act introduced kindergarten through grade 12 educational reform.
- American Recovery and Reinvestment Act (ARRA) (2009). This act provides a broad range of economic support to states with heavy emphasis on job recovery and school investments.
- Affordable Care Act (2010). This law puts into place comprehensive health insurance reforms for all Americans.

When cultural shifts and the need for system change come from the affected group and not from within the government system, we see the use of grassroots activism to force reform of existing policies. The act of speaking out or taking a stand on an issue and working to improve the conditions that are in need of change is called *advocacy*. Advocacy can be personal or professional. It can take many forms and usually evokes strong emotion. Years of grassroots advocacy by many individuals culminated in the passage of the Americans with Disabilities Act (ADA) in 1990. Throughout the debate, legislators were torn between costs that employers, schools, and states said would be substantial and the need to create accessible environments in all public places, as later enacted in the ADA law. Reform did not come easy or quickly. Years of advocacy work by individuals and organizations pushing for reform eventually forced significant changes in accessibility to all public buildings, now standard practice in all architectural designs.

Reflection...

Address the ramifications of a hypothetical national policy that required all 4-year-olds to attend preschool. Who would be affected by this change in policy? What might be the economic consequences?

Advocacy movements that forced system reform include:

- Civil rights movement (1968). Campaign of civil disobedience to force recognition of human and constitutional rights.

- Head Start (1965). Early childhood preschool for 3- to 5-year-olds living in poverty.
- The Act for Better Child Care (1988). Child-care licensing and funding.
- Americans with Disabilities Act (1990). Law to provide accessibility to all public places.
- AMBER Alert System (1996). America's Missing: Broadcast Emergency Response was created as a legacy to 9-year-old Amber Hagerman, kidnapped while riding her bicycle in Arlington, Texas, and then brutally murdered.

When strong advocacy efforts prevail and public policy is created, important landmark pieces of legislation are created that respond to shifting social systems and force reform and change on many levels. These shifts can change public ideology and force resources and funding to be reallocated to implement reforms that have been created by the legislation.

Landmark Public Policy Initiatives

Many public policy efforts have created a cornerstone of support for children and families changing the face of educational and social services for decades. Examples are:

- 1942 Lanham Act, federal legislation funding child care at the time when WPA nursery schools were closing
- 1965 Creation of Head Start, antipoverty initiative
- 1966 The Child Nutrition Act, the School Lunch Act
- 1975 IDEA, the Individuals with Disabilities Education Act
- 1981 SSBG, the Social Services Block Grant
- 1988 The Family Support Act
- 1988 ABC, the Act for Better Child Care, comprehensive child-care legislation
- 1989 United Nations adopts the Convention on the Rights of the Child
- 1990 ADA, Americans with Disabilities Act
- 1991 CCDBG, Child Care and Development Block Grant
- 1996 Personal Responsibility and Work Opportunity Reconciliation Act, welfare reform
- 2001 NCLB, No Child Left Behind Act, K–12 educational reform legislation
- 2010 Affordable Care Act, health care reform

There have been many legislative initiatives passed throughout the years affecting children and families. Some addressed in other chapters in this book are outlined in detail, such as Head Start and Individuals with Disabilities Education Act. Families are directly affected by legislation that has created entitlement programs. The past several decades have seen growth in the number of government entitlement programs. Laws created to meet the needs of a specific population such as the disabled, elderly, children in poverty, and others who without this assistance would not be able to survive are provided for by federal entitlement programs. Entitlement programs such as the Social Services Block Grant (SSBG), which mandates housing assistance, Temporary Assistance to Needy Families (TANF), which provides cash assistance to the poorest families, and Medicaid, which provides medical assistance, provide minimal safety nets for individuals who would not otherwise have food, shelter, or health care. These federally funded programs are managed by each state, which in turn set policies and regulations based on how that individual state chooses to work within the federal mandates. This is why programs such as child-care assistance or housing assistance have different requirements or guidelines. It depends on the state in which one lives. These important family support programs have seen many changes.

Child Care and Development Block Grant

The Child Care and Development Block Grant (CCDBG) was created in 1991 in the midst of welfare reform brought on with the passage of the Personal Responsibility and Work Opportunity Reconciliation Act in 1996 that required individuals to move from welfare to work. Parents with young children were required to pursue employment or job training, and this required states to provide assistance with finding and paying for child care. This block grant provides state money to help subsidize child care for low-income working parents and sets reimbursement levels for providers. The flexibility of these funds has been an important resource to states that use these funds to provide child-care resource and referral services, licensing, training, and education to providers, as well as assistance to parents paying for child care.

Temporary Assistance to Needy Families

Many low-income families who are working still find moving out of poverty difficult for many reasons. The Temporary Assistance to Needy Families program (TANF) is an entitlement program run by states to assist families to meet basic needs. This is a block grant much like CCDBG and is often blended with other forms of noncash assistance such as Medicaid and food stamps to provide basic help for low-income families.

Whereas some legislative initiatives have created programs to support families moving out of poverty, some initiatives have focused on educational goals to better prepare citizens for careers in an ever-changing world. Although educating all people would seem to be a nonpartisan issue, the focus of public policy often depends on the politics of legislators and government officials. This is why the pendulum seems to swing in educational reform throughout the decades. The inclusion of drama, music, and fine arts might be seen as valuable curriculum needed in preparing young people, yet a decade later politicians with different political leanings can easily erase funding for these programs and promote an agenda that pushes for more assessment in reading and math curriculum. This is why educational reform is usually a platform issue for politicians. It gets at the heart of a voting constituency and can elicit strong feelings from many people and advocacy groups. Several recent educational initiatives, such as No Child Left Behind have seen heavy debate in recent years.

No Child Left Behind

As stated earlier, the No Child Left Behind Act (NCLB) was passed in 2001 as an effort to meet the needs of the Goals 2000: Educate America Act (1994). One goal was to ensure that 90% of high school students would graduate. This seemingly simple and straightforward goal has caused heated debate over educational reform. Schools are implementing grade-level testing, states are developing curriculum standards, and teachers must now be "highly qualified" as designated by the federal government. Schools are penalized for not raising the test scores of underperforming students. Teachers' unions are at odds about what constitutes a qualified teacher under this new act. States are pushing schools to perform in an effort to meet federal mandates, and children find themselves spending days preparing for and taking tests that many teachers say do not measure the child's ability to learn. Questions abound regarding the effectiveness of this new educational reform initiative. These federal funds are received by each state and passed on to local school districts.

Universal Health Care for Families

On March 23, 2010, President Obama signed into law the Affordable Care Act. The law puts into place comprehensive health insurance reforms that guarantee more health-care choices for families, setting in motion that all children will be afforded medical care. This initiative provides federal funds that pass through to states to enhance Medicaid for low-income families and sets up a federal buy-in program for employers who do not currently provide health care. This will provide many child-care providers affordable health care not previously available for these low-paying jobs.

Reflection...

How can a teacher address the topic of health care with a parent or suggest finding a medical home for their children that would include preventive care such as dental and vision?

Current Trends and Issues

As we have seen, public policy can drive the issues that create a cultural climate looking for change. Several issues that are finding platforms for discussion among politicians, teachers, and communities could provoke changes in the next few years. The trends we currently see in family support services are:

- States adopting a variety of tax credits for working families, giving them help with child care and in-home care expenses (Hirschhorn Donahue, 2002)
- Family-leave policies, allowing both parents opportunities to spend time with newborn babies

- Flexible work schedules and job-sharing opportunities for parents who want to continue on their career path
- Internet and media control legislation to assure parents that children will not view or find inappropriate materials while using these media for learning
- Improvement in the quality and availability of infant and toddler care

Educational trends and research that we will see in the coming years include:

- Standards-based education, focusing on outcomes for student learning (Schumacher, Irish, & Lombardi, 2003) including common state standards for early childhood programs (NAEYC, 2010)
- Full-day kindergarten providing more time for in-class experiential learning (Walston & West, 2004)
- Research on the economic impact of the child-care industry and its effect on the local community; employment needs are identified to maintain a workforce (Rolnick & Grunewald, 2003)
- Prekindergarten opportunities for 4-year-olds in the United States (Pre-K Now, 2010)
- National School Readiness Indicators Initiative, creating a set of measurable indicators defining school readiness (Getting Ready, 2005)
- Quality Rating Systems, a system of rating the quality of child-care programs that is tied to incentives and reimbursement rates provided through ARRA (NAEYC, August 2010)
- T.E.A.C.H., professional development for early-care and early-education teachers tied to education and training incentives (T.E.A.C.H., 2004)
- Early childhood professional development, looking at degrees, credentials, and the development of highly qualified early childhood teachers (NAEYC, 2010)
- Gubernatorial Leadership for Early Care and Education (Lovejoy, 2003)
- Environmental rating scales used in measuring the quality of early childhood environments (Harms, Clifford, & Cryer, 1998)
- Classroom Assessment Scoring System, measuring teacher–child interactions (Pianta, LaParo, & Hamre, 2008)

Reflection...

Examining the trends identified in this section, which issue has the most achievable outcomes in the next 10 years?

To move any trend or issue forward it takes many years of hard work and passion by a committed group of professionals. This work takes concentrated focus and calculated grassroots advocacy to make new and creative ideas become reality. It is by the impassioned work and advocacy of many organizations and groups that we have seen the changes in past years.

Advocacy

A small boy lived by the ocean. He loved the creatures of the sea, especially the starfish and spent much of his time exploring the seashore. One day he learned there would be a minus tide that would leave the starfish stranded on the sand. The day of the tide he went down to the beach and began picking up stranded starfish and tossing them back into the sea. An elderly man who lived next door came down to the beach to see what he was doing. "I'm saving the starfish," the boy proudly declared. When the neighbor saw all of the stranded starfish, he shook his head and said, "I'm sorry to disappoint you young man, but if you look down the beach one way, there are stranded starfish as far as the eye can see. If you look down the beach the other way, it is the same. One little boy like you isn't going to make much of a difference." The boy thought about this for a moment. Then he reached his small hand down to the sand, picked up a starfish, tossed it out into the ocean, and said, "I sure made a difference for that one." (paraphrased from Eiseley, 1978)

Advocacy means standing up and speaking out for something you believe in. As professionals working with children and families, we find ourselves advocating for others at many points in our career. It might be in a parent–teacher conference, participating in a community Stand for Children event, or sending a letter to a member of Congress asking for support to expand Head Start programs. There will be times on both a personal and professional level that you must make your voice heard. As professionals, we utilize our knowledge and expertise to ensure public policy and laws reflect what is good and right for children. Personally, there will be some issues that affect you and evoke strong emotions. In your church, family, school, or workplace there could be a reason to make a stand regarding a specific issue. When you gather with others to create a collective voice, the power becomes stronger. You can make change happen. According to Adele Robinson, the vice president of public policy for the National Association for the Education of Young Children, there are three types of advocacy—personal, public policy, and private sector advocacy—that can bring about change.

Personal advocacy means sharing our personal views and philosophies with others (Robinson & Stark, 2002). This can happen informally in conversations with friends, at church, or another place you find outside of your work environment. It is important to realize when you are giving a personal opinion as opposed to your professional viewpoint. Teachers are seen as experts by parents and children and thus have the power to persuade; however, it can be confusing for parents. It is in this role that the NAEYC *Code of Ethical Conduct,* mentioned earlier in the chapter, serves as a compass for our actions and communications with parents, colleagues, and the community. Your personal advocacy must be outside of your work environment and clearly delineated from your professional role. As an example, you might take an active role in a political party and run for a position on your local school board on your out-of-work time. It would be important to excuse yourself from decision making and voting if a clear conflict of interest is apparent on a particular issue.

Public policy advocacy is working toward influencing policy and laws that affect a large number of children (Robinson & Stark, 2002). At the end of this chapter is a list of national organizations that have created strong advocacy networks you may wish to join. These groups and others speak out on many issues affecting children and families. Research is often the impetus for seeing future trends and eventually creating a vision for policy that supports new ways of doing things. The AMBER Alert missing persons broadcast system began as an individual effort to effect change

Case Study

Krista was 18 years old and excited to head off to college 3 hours away from her home. She was staying in the dormitory and living on campus. Excited about being out on her own and partying with new friends from school, she soon found her grade-point average slipping; adjusting to college life the first semester was becoming difficult. One weekend, she met a friend from high school at a party. Things got out of control and Krista had sex for the first time. It was not until the middle of spring semester that she found out she was 5 months pregnant. How would she tell her parents? What would happen to her academic scholarship? How would she support a baby? She felt hopeless, not sure where to turn for answers and help.

Krista and her beautiful 2-year-old daughter, Carmen, have finally moved into their own apartment with the help of a housing assistance program for low-income families. Krista has continued her education as a full-time student, making good grades while working evenings and weekends at the local coffee shop. Her mom watches Carmen when she works on the weekends. Carmen loves her family child-care provider. It has been a struggle, but working with a county social services case manager, she receives TANF, WIC, and Child Care Assistance Payments, helping to make ends meet. Next spring she will student teach and graduate. She wants to make a better life

for her daughter and knows a college degree will give her career options.

The letter arrives. As of July 1, she will no longer be eligible for child-care assistance. The state has changed the eligibility requirements, and students working toward a 4-year baccalaureate degree are no longer eligible for the program. Her caseworker tells her that if she would attend the local community college and enroll in a certificate program, she would still receive the funding. On top of this bad news, she reads in the paper that funding for student financial aid programs is being reduced. She was counting on that money so she could cut down her hours at the coffee shop while student teaching. Decisions affect her over which she feels she has no control. Her caseworker seems sympathetic and knows that Krista will be a wonderful success story if they can just get her through this last year of school. Krista is frustrated and knows two other single parents who got the same letter regarding child-care eligibility.

Questions and Considerations

1. What could Krista do to advocate for the reinstatement of her child-care assistance?
2. Are there any alternatives available to her if she cannot be reinstated?
3. Why does a 2-year degree seem to be more important to some government agencies than a 4-year degree?

in 1996 after Amber Hagerman, a 9-year-old from Texas, was abducted and later found murdered. By 2006, the AMBER Alert system is in all 50 states with a national coordinator running the program from within the Department of Justice. Public policy advocacy is the collective voice of many for making change. It typically takes many years to effect large-scale national policies.

Private sector advocacy is working toward changing private sector policies and practices that affect families (Robinson & Stark, 2002). This can happen in your local community or on a national level. The research done in many states on the economic impact of the child-care industry is astounding. Business and community leaders are taking note of what is required to create and sustain a workforce. Around the nation, the buzzword "economic development and job recovery" is on most political agendas. Private sector advocacy can take the form of asking for workplace reform, starting a community recycling program, or mandating equipment such as car seats. Laws regarding seat-belt usage, child abuse, or movie ratings are examples of private sector advocacy.

Finding Your Voice and Speaking Out

There are many ways to take action on an issue affecting children and families. The first step is to do something. Like the little boy in the story trying to save the starfish, you must make an effort to make a difference, even for one child. Several ways to get started are:

- Vote in your local, state, and national elections
- Communicate by phone calls, media, letters, in-person visits, e-mail
- Involve others—neighbors, friends, coworkers, and family
- Find out what social service agencies and programs are available locally
- Research the issue and examine the facts of a situation
- Join a service or professional organization
- Sign up for an advocacy e-mail network to receive updates on legislative activities
- Attend community forums or town hall meetings
- Start a parent group to discuss issues and call for action
- Learn about the legislative process
- Model advocacy to your children and others

Children cannot vote. They do not have a say in many of the policies that will affect their future. They will only live with what is created now. Find your voice and speak out for children.

Summary

As professionals working with families, we are ethically called to act and speak out on behalf of the rights of all children. We do this as advocates. This can take place both personally and professionally. Historically, we have seen major advocacy efforts create cultural shifts and change public policy. Social causes such as the civil rights movement and the inclusion of people with disabilities in schools have forced changes in federal laws. In some instances, it has been the laws that forced changes on a system.

In education, the trends will be a push for universal preschool opportunities for 4-year-olds and more research on developmentally appropriate assessments used in early childhood programs. These will require concentrated effort and the gathering of collective voices for success. As a professional, you can participate in a variety of advocacy activities: personal, public policy, or private sector actions. You must be careful to delineate when you are acting in your professional role and when you are acting because of your personal beliefs.

Recommended Activities

1. Interview a Head Start program director. Find out what types of information and surveys of community needs must be included when submitting an application for continued funding or applying for new program funds.
2. Write a letter to the editor in a local or national newspaper or online news service that advocates for more flexible family-leave policies from businesses within your community.
3. Research your state reimbursement rates for parents and providers who receive child-care assistance funds.
4. Interview a principal of an elementary school or middle school. Ask about the main issues affecting his or her school. Are the issues ones that parents and/or teachers can advocate for now or in the future?
5. Join a public policy electronic mailing list from a national organization that advocates for parents or teachers, such as NAEYC's Children's Champions.
6. Write a position paper either in support of or against universal preschool for all 4-year-olds.
7. Do we value children in our society? In what ways do we show it?

Additional Resources

Federal Government

U.S. Department of Education
Phone: 800-USA-LEARN
(800-872-5327)
www.ed.gov

U.S. Department of Health and Human Services
Administration for Children and Families
Child Care Bureau
Phone: 202-690-6782
www.acf.dhhs.gov/programs/ccb

U.S. Department of Health and Human Services
Head Start Bureau
Administration for Children and Families
Phone: 202-205-8572
www2.acf.dhhs.gov/programs/hsb

State Government

National Conference of State Legislatures
www.ncsl.org

National Governors' Association
Phone: 202-624-5300
www.nga.org

Organizations and Web Resources

Afterschool Alliance
Phone: 202-347-1002
www.afterschoolalliance.org

Alliance for Justice
Phone: 202-822-6070
www.allianceforjustice.org

American Academy of Pediatrics
Phone: 847-434-4000
www.aap.org

American Association of University
Women
Phone: 800-326-AAUW
www.aauw.org

Center for Community Change
Phone: 877-777-1536
www.communitychange.org

The Center for the Child Care Workforce
Phone: 202-662-8005
www.ccw.org

Child Care Services
Association
Phone: 919-967-3272
www.childcareservices.org

Child Trends
Phone: 202-572-6000
www.childtrends.org

Child Welfare League of America
Phone: 202-638-2952
www.cwla.org

Children's Defense Fund
Phone: 202-628-8787
www.childrensdefense.org

Council for Exceptional Children
Phone: 888-CEC-SPED
TYY: 866-915-5000 (Text only)
www.cec.sped.org

Education Commission of the States
Phone: 303-299-3600
www.ecs.org

Families and Work Institute
Phone: 212-465-2044
www.familiesandwork.org

Future of Children
www.futureofchildren.org

High/Scope Educational Research
Foundation
Phone: 734-485-2000
www.highscope.org

Kids Count
The Annie E. Casey
Foundation
Phone: 410-547-6600
Fax: 410-547-6624
www.kidscount.org

National Association for Family
Child Care
Phone: 800-359-3817
www.nafcc.org

National Association for the Education
of Young Children
Phone: 202-232-8777
www.naeyc.org

National Association of Child Care Resource
and Referral Agencies
Phone: 703-341-4100
www.naccrra.org

National Black Child Development
Institute
Phone: 202-833-2220
www.nbcdi.org

National Child Care Information Center
(NCCIC)
Phone: 800-716-2242
TYY: 800-516-2242
www.nccic.org

National Education Association
Phone: 202-833-4000
www.nea.org

National Head Start Association
Phone: 703-739-0875
www.nhsa.org

National Institute for Early Education
Research
www.nieer.org

National Women's Law Center
Phone: 202-588-5180
www.nwlc.org

Parents Action for Children
(formerly known as I Am Your Child)
Phone: 202-238-4878

Fax: 202-986-2539
www.parentsaction.org

T.E.A.C.H. Early Childhood
800-4-FED-AID

USA Child Care
Phone: 703-875-8100
www.usachildcare.org

Voices for America's Children
Phone: 202-289-0777
www.voices.org

Zero to Three: National Center for
    Infants, Toddlers and Families
Phone: 202-638-1144
www.zerotothree.org

References

AMBER Alert. (2006). *Amber Alert: America's Missing: Broadcast Emergency Response.* Retrieved February 11, 2006, from www.amberalert.gov/faqs.html

American Recovery and Reinvestment Act of 2009. Retrieved December 21, 2010 from www.recovery.gov

Americans with Disabilities Act, Public Law 336 of the 101st Congress, enacted July 26, 1990. Retrieved January 30, 2006, from www.usdoj.gov/crt/ada/adahom1.htm

Convention on the Rights of the Child. (1989). *Ratification and accession by General Assembly resolution 44/25, November 20, 1989.* United Nations. Retrieved from www.unhchr.ch/html/menu3/b/k2crc.htm

Edelman, M. W., & Yorinks, A. (1998). *Stand for children.* New York: Hyperion Books.

Eiseley, L. (1978). *The star thrower.* New York: Random House.

Family Support Act. (1988). Public Law 100–485, 13 October 1998.

Getting Ready. (2005, February). *National school readiness indicators initiative.* Retrieved from www.GettingReady.org

Goals 2000: Educate America Act. (1994). H.R. 1804, enacted by the 103rd Congress on January 25, 1994. Retrieved February 10, 2006, from www.ed.gov/legislation/GOALS2000/TheAct/ index.html

Harms, T., Clifford, R. M., & Cryer, D. (1998). *Early childhood environment rating scale-revised* (Rev. ed.). New York: Teachers College Press.

Hirschhorn Donahue, E., & Duff Campbell, N. (2002). *Making care less taxing: Improving state child and dependent care tax provisions* (Rev. ed.) [Electronic version]. Washington DC: National Women's Law Center.

Lovejoy, A. (2003). Delivery and governance of quality preschool. Paper presented at the National Governor's Association Forum on Quality Preschool.

National Association for the Education of Young Children. (2005). *NAEYC code of ethical conduct* (rev. ed.). Washington, DC: Author.

National Association for the Education of Young Children. (2010). *Introduction to standards and criteria.* Washington, DC: Author.

No Child Left Behind Act of 2001. Public Law 107 of the 110th Congress, enacted January 8, 2002. Retrieved from www.ed.gov.nclb.landing.jhtml?src=pb

Pianta, R., LaParo, K., & Hamre, B. (2008). *Classroom Assessment Scoring System Manual Pre-K.* Baltimore, MD: Paul H. Brookes.

Pre-K Now. (2010, April). *Measuring pre-K pressure in the States.* Retrieved from www.preknow.org

Robinson, A., & Stark, D. R. (2002). *Advocates in action.* Washington, DC: National Association for the Education of Young Children.

Rolnick, A., & Grunewald, R. (2003, March). *Early childhood development: Economic development with a high public return.* Retrieved from http://minneapolisfed.org/research/studies/earlychild/earlychild.pdf

Ruck, M., & Horn, S. (2008, December). Charting the landscape of children's rights. *Journal of Social Issues, 64*(4), 685–699.

Schumacher, R., Irish, K., & Lombardi, J. (2003). *Meeting great expectations: Integrating early education program standards.* Retrieved from www.clasp.org

T.E.A.C.H. (2004). *T.E.A.C.H. Early childhood project*. Retrieved February 10, 2006 from www.childcareservices.org/ps/teach.html

Temporary Assistance for Needy Families. (2010). U.S. Department of Health and Human Services. Retrieved December 21, 2010 from www.acf.hhs.gov/programs/ofa/tanf/about.html

Walston, J., & West, J. (2004, June). *Full-day and half-day kindergarten in the United States: Findings from the Early Childhood Longitudinal Study, Kindergarten Class of 1998–99* (NCES 2004-078). U.S. Department of Education Institute of Education Sciences.

Women, Infants and Children. (1974). Retrieved December 21, 2010 from www.fns.usda.gov/wic/

Index